Russel Forbes

**Rambles in Rome**

An archæological and historical guide to the museums, galleries, villas, churches,

and antiquities of Rome and the Campagna. Sixth Edition

Russel Forbes

**Rambles in Rome**
An archæological and historical guide to the museums, galleries, villas, churches, and antiquities of Rome and the Campagna. Sixth Edition

ISBN/EAN: 9783337262082

Printed in Europe, USA, Canada, Australia, Japan

Cover: Foto ©Andreas Hilbeck / pixelio.de

More available books at **www.hansebooks.com**

# RAMBLES IN ROME.

# RAMBLES IN ROME

An Archæological and Historical Guide

TO THE

MUSEUMS, GALLERIES, VILLAS, CHURCHES,
AND ANTIQUITIES OF ROME AND
THE CAMPAGNA.

*By*

*S. RUSSELL FORBES, PH.D.,*

*Archæological and Historical Lecturer on Roman Antiquities.*

## Sixth Edition,

Revised and Enlarged ; embracing all the Recent
Excavations and Discoveries.

**WITH MAPS. PLANS, AND ILLUSTRATIONS.**

LONDON: THOMAS NELSON AND SONS.
EDINBURGH: AND NEW YORK.

ROME: S. RUSSELL FORBES, 93 VIA BABUINO.
1892.

# Preface.

—————+—————

THE object of our work is to describe in a practical manner the points of interest in and around the Eternal City. One half of our life has been spent in studying Rome on the spot. For our guides we have had the classic authorities and recent excavations; and it has been with us a labour of love to work out from our authors the meaning of the ruins uncovered, and impart the information thus obtained to others.

The excavations of the last few years have thrown an entirely new flood of light upon the existing remains and Roman history, and have proved beyond doubt that there is a great deal more truth in the early history of Rome than has generally been supposed. It has been our privilege to watch the excavations year after year, and elucidate the remains found; and our labours have been rewarded with some not unimportant discoveries. We state nothing without citing classic authority to bear us witness, and the authority so cited agrees in a marvellous way with the ruins discovered. We feel that our efforts have been appreciated by the many hundreds whom we have guided to these classic spots, and we hope our book may be likewise valued by those who cannot come to Rome.

These Rambles will enable the visitor who is making a brief stay in Rome to see the principal objects of interest in a short time.

By following the instructions given much time will be saved, and the Rambler will not have to go over the same ground unnecessarily.

Visitors whose stay is limited to a few days should select the subjects they are most interested in ; whilst others, who have "plenty of time," are advised to divide the Rambles according to the time at their disposal.

Since our last edition, immense changes have taken place: new streets have been opened up, old ones destroyed, new quarters have been added to the city, and there have been grand improvements. Three new and interesting museums have been opened to the public, and several galleries have been rearranged. Further light and knowledge have been reflected on the past by recent discoveries and earnest study.

It is in this Sixth Edition our pleasant duty to record all these changes, and to chronicle them in such a way that visitors and students may derive pleasure and profit thereby.

S. R. F.

ROME, *January 1892.*

*N.B.*—A large map will be found in the pocket of the right-hand cover of the work.

# Contents.

# List of Illustrations.

# FIRST IMPRESSIONS.

To get a good idea of Rome and its topographical situation, take a carriage and drive for three hours through the principal streets; more can be learned in this way than in any other.

*Start from the* Piazza di Spagna; drive down the Via Babuino to the Piazza del Popolo, up to the Pincio, for a view of Rome, looking west; then along the Via Sistina, up the Quattro Fontane, to the right, down the Via Quirinale; stop in the square for the view. Proceeding to the Via Nazionale, turn up it to the left as far as the Via Agostino Depretis; then turn to the right past S. Maria Maggiore direct to the Lateran, from the front of which see the view eastwards; then follow the Via S. Giovanni down to the Colosseum, passing by the most perfect part. By the Via del Colosseo, Tor di Conti, Via Croce Bianca, Arco dei Pantani, Forum of Augustus, and Via Bonella, you reach the Forum, under the Capitoline Hill. Continuing by the Via Consolazione and Piazza Campitelli, follow the line of streets to the Ponte Sisto; crossing this, proceed up the Via Garibaldi to S. Peter in Montorio. Grand view of Rome and the Campagna, looking north, east, and south.

Hence, by the new Villa Corsini, drive to the left down the Lungara to S. Peter's; drive round the square; then down the Borgo Nuovo to the Castle of S. Angelo. Crossing the bridge, take the Via Coronari to the Circo Agonale; then on to the Pantheon, and by the Minerva to the Piazza di Venezia; thence up the Corso as far as the Via Condotti, up which street you return to the Piazza di Spagna, after having thus made the most interesting drive in the world.

# THE TOPOGRAPHY OF ROME.

Rome commences at a point—Piazza del Popolo—and spreads out southwards like a fan, the western extremity being occupied by the Vatican, and the eastern by the Lateran ; both these head-quarters of the Papacy are isolated from the rest of the city.   Modern Rome occupies the valley of the Campus Martius, which was outside ancient Rome, and the hills that abut it.   Rome is divided into two unequal parts by the river Tiber, which enters the line of the walls, with the Popolo on its left.   For a short distance it flows southwards; then it makes a great bend to the west; then again takes a southerly direction ; and at the island again turns westerly.   One mile south of the Popolo Gate is the Capitoline Hill, the Arx of ancient Rome, dividing, as it were, Old from New Rome.   It rises two hundred yards east of the Tiber, and from it in an eastern direction lie the other six hills, curving in a horse-shoe form round the Palatine till the Aventine abuts the river.   Of the hills, the Palatine, Capitoline, Cœlian, and Aventine were only isolated mounts, the Quirinal, Viminal, and Esquiline being three spurs jutting out from the high tableland on the east side of Rome.   These hills can easily be distinguished from the Tower of the Capitol ; but the best way to understand them is to walk round them.   Then it will be seen that they are hills indeed ; and if we take into consideration that the valleys have been filled in from thirty to forty feet, and that the tops of the hills have been cut down, we may get some idea of their original height.   Rome still occupies four of them ; but the Aventine, Cœlian, and Palatine are left to ruins, gardens, and monks.

The original Rome was on the Palatine, and as the other hills were added they were fortified ; but it was not till the time of Servius Tullius that the seven were united by one system of fortifications into one city.   The plan was simple.   From the Tiber a wall went to the Capitoline, and from that to the Quirinal ; across the necks of the three tongues the great agger was built, then across the valleys from hill to hill till the wall again reached the river under the Aventine. The aggers across the valleys were built right up towards the city, so that the hills on either side protected the walls and gates commanding the approach.   Of all the maps of Rome that have been published, the new one accompanying this work is the only one which correctly shows the line of the Servian fortifications.

## THE PLAN OF OUR RAMBLES.

From the Piazza del Popolo four great lines of thoroughfare inter-
sect the city, and passing up one of these for a few hundred yards we
may count five lines.  First we take the centre thoroughfare; then
the two lines on its right; then the two upon its left: in this way,
by dividing Rome up into five Rambles, pointing out as we go along
every place of interest to the right and left, we mark out for a day's
work no more than can be thoroughly done.  Having thus seen the
city, we take the environs outside each gate, commencing at the
Porta del Popolo and working round by the east, with the exception of the Porta Appia, which leads out on to the Appian Way.
As this Way presents so many points of interest, and as no visitor
should think of leaving Rome without "doing it," we have made
it a special Ramble for their benefit.

## HEALTH AND CLIMATE.

Perhaps the health of no city in the world is so much talked
about by people who know nothing whatever of the subject, as
Rome.  We meet with many visitors entertaining all sorts of curious
ideas of the health of Rome—what they may and may not do; and
when we ask them their authority they cannot give any, but "they
have heard so."  There seem to be mysterious ideas and impressions
floating about that get lodged in some minds no one knows how.
People get ill in Rome, of course, just as in any other place; but
more than half the sickness is caused through their own imprudence,
such as getting hot and going into cold places, and going "from
early morn till dewy eve" without rest and refreshment.  In all hot
climates certain precautions should be observed, and then there is
no fear.

We ourselves have lived many years in this much-abused climate,
never knowing any illness, and enjoying far better health than when
residing in London.  O ye rain, mud, and fog !

The well-known Roman physician, Dr. C. Liberali, M.D., in his
"Hygienic Medical Hand-book for Travellers in Italy," says :—
"The climate of Rome is in the highest degree salubrious and favourable to all, but especially to delicate persons; but they should follow
the advice of a skilful physician of the country."

People rush through Europe at express rate, eat all sorts of things
that they are unused to at unusual hours, over-exert themselves,

change the whole course of the living to which they have been accustomed, get ill, and then say, "It's the climate of Rome."

There is no doubt that malaria fever does exist in the neighbourhood of Rome, but only during the three hot months; and as there are no visitors at Rome then, they are not likely to get it. It does not walk about the streets seeking whom it may devour, as some people suppose.

The fever visitors get is ague fever, like that known in the Fen districts, and this is invariably taken through imprudence.

## USEFUL HINTS.

Avoid bad odours.

Do not ride in an open carriage at night.

Take lunch in the middle of the day. This is essential. It is better to take a light breakfast and lunch, than a heavy breakfast and no lunch.

No city in the world is so well supplied with good drinking water as Rome. The best is the Trevi water. Do *not* drink Aqua Marcia; it is too cold.

If out about sunset, throw an extra wrap or coat on, to avoid the sudden change in the atmosphere. There is no danger beyond being apt to take a cold. Colds are the root of all evil at Rome.

Do not sit about the ruins at night. It may be very romantic, but it is very unwise. There is no harm in walking.

Close your windows at night.

If you get into a heat, do not go into the shade or into a building till you have cooled down.

Do not over-fatigue yourself.

Follow these hints, and you will avoid that great bugbear, Roman fever.

"A hint on the spot is worth a cart-load of recollections."—GRAY.

## THE TIBER.

The work of clearing the bed of the Tiber is in active progress. It is proposed to clear away the accumulation of the mud at different parts, remove some of the old masonry that stands in the bed of the river, and widen it at certain points. We very much doubt if this will have any effect upon the floods, as during the republic and empire, when there was not all this accumulation, Rome was flooded several times. The valley of the Tiber, in which Rome stands, is very low, forming, as it were, a basin which is easily overflowed.

It would be advisable if the authorities were to clean out the old drains, and put swing trap-doors over their mouths, so that the drainage might flow out, and the river prevented from flowing in. Every winter some part of the city is under water, which is caused by the river rushing up the drains into the city, and not by the overflow of the Tiber. This inpouring might easily be stopped.

Some people think that treasures will be found in the bed of the Tiber, but this is a delusion. Nothing of any value has ever been found in the river, and it is not likely that anything of value was thrown there. Small objects only have been found in the recent dredging. The story of the seven-branched candlestick being thrown into the river is a delusion, for we have direct evidence to the contrary. (See p. 91.)

The piers of the bridges show that the actual bed of the river has not been much raised; indeed the stream flows so fast that everything is carried down to the sea.

*Punch* says anticipations may be entertained of finding the footstool of Tullia, the jewels of Cornelia, the ivory-headed sceptre of the senator Papirius, and the golden manger of the horse of Caligula.

The length of the Tiber is 250 miles. It rises due east of Florence, in the same hills as the Arno. Its bed at the Ripetta in Rome is 5.20 metres above the sea, and it discharges at the rate of 280 cubic metres a second. The fall from Rome to the sea is 4.20 metres, or about thirteen feet, and it flows about five miles an hour.

> "'Behold the Tiber!' the vain Roman cried.
> Viewing the ample Tay from Baiglie's side;
> But where's the Scot that would the vaunt repay,
> And hail the puny Tiber for the Tay?"
> SIR WALTER SCOTT.

The river was originally called the Albula, from its colour, and it was named Tiberis, from King Tiberinus of Alba Longa, who was drowned in it, and became the river-god (Dionysius, i. 71).

The ancient Romans looked upon their river with veneration; their poets sang its praises, its banks were lined with the villas of the wealthy, and its waters brought the produce of the world to Rome.

## HOW ROME BECAME RUINS.

> "The Goth, the Christian, time, war, flood, and fire,
> Have dealt upon the seven-hilled city's pride."

Rome was founded in the year 753 B.C., and it gradually increased, as we all know, till it became the capital of the world. By a sum-mary of dates we will endeavour to give an idea of the manner in which Rome became ruins.

In July 390 B.C. it was devastated by fire. Up to 120 B.C. it was subject to numerous raids by the Northerners, who, with the help of civil war, and a devouring fire in 53 B.C., caused the destruction of several of its most splendid buildings. In 64 A.D., during the reign of Nero, a terrible fire ravaged the city for six days ; and again in 80 A.D. another fire took place, lasting three days. In the reign of Commodus a third fire occurred, which consumed a large portion of the city. In 330 A.D. Constantine took from Rome a number of monuments and works of art to embellish Constantinople. From 408 to 410 A.D. Rome was three times besieged by the Goths, under Alaric, who plundered and fired the city ; and in 455 A.D. the Vandals took possession of Rome and plundered it. On June the 11th, 472 A.D., the city was captured by the Germans, under Ricimer, and in 476 A.D. the Roman Empire was broken up.

About 590 A.D. continual wars with the Lombardians devastated the Campagna. In 607 A.D. the Bishop of Rome was made Pope. In 755 A.D. the Lombards again desolated Rome ; and up to 950 A.D. it was held successively by the Emperor Louis II., Lambert Duke of Spoleto, the Saracens, the German king Armilph, and the Hungarians. In 1083 it was taken by Henry IV. of Germany ; and in 1084 it was burned, from the Lateran to the Capitol, by Robert Guiscard. From the eleventh to the sixteenth century many of its buildings were turned into fortresses by the nobles, who made continual war upon each other ; and during the "dark ages" the Romans themselves destroyed many monuments, in order to make lime for building their new palaces and houses.

Thus we see that when, in 55 B.C., Julius Cæsar, with his "Veni, vidi, vici," conquered the little island now called Great Britain, Rome contained in ruins many evidences of past splendour, and whilst the Romans were overrunning the rest of Europe, their empire was hastening to decay. We, the savages of those days, have ever since been growing in strength and wisdom, laying the foundations of future empires, overturning others, but not with the idea of "universal conquest," but simply for a "balance of power." Ancient Rome, by the help of invaders, flood, fire, the Popes, and its inhabitants, was reduced to ruins, which have been in considerable part preserved by an immense accumulation of soil, which, again, caused them to be forgotten till recent explorations once more brought them to light.

Modern Rome stands thirty feet above the level of Ancient Rome, and is a strange mixture of narrow streets, open squares, churches, fountains, ruins, new palaces, and dirt. Built during the seventeenth century, the city is situated in a valley which formed part of the ancient city, and lies to the north of it, being divided from it by the Capitoline Hill, and offering to the visitor attractions which no other city can boast. The germ of the old Roman race which civilized the world is still alive, and is quickly rising to a new life—lifting itself, after twenty centuries of burial, from the tomb of ignorance and oppression. Here is the centre of art and of the world's past recollections; here is spoken in its purity the most beautiful of languages; here are a fine climate and a fine country; and here are being strengthened the power and the splendour of united Italy.

## THE WALLS OF ROME.

### FIRST WALL—ROMA QUADRATA.

The city of Romulus, upon the Palatine Hill, was called from its shape Roma Quadrata. It occupied the half of what we know as the Palatine, and was surrounded by a wall built up from the base of the hill, and on the top of the scarped cliff: this wall can be still traced in part. It was formed of large blocks of tufa, hard stone, and must not be confounded with the remains of the Arcadian period, on the Palatine, composed of soft tufa.

"Romulus called the people to a place appointed, and described a quadrangular figure about the hill, tracing with a plough, drawn by a bull and a cow yoked together, one continued furrow" (Dionysius, i. 88).

"He began to mark out the limits of his city from the Forum Boarium, so as to comprise within its limits the Great Altar of Hercules. The wall was built with Etruscan rites, being marked out by a furrow, made by a plough drawn by a cow and a bull, the clods being carefully thrown inwards, the plough being lifted over the profane places necessary for the gates" (Tacitus, xii. 24).

When the Sabines were approaching to attack the Romans, in revenge for carrying off their women, Romulus strengthened the wall of Roma Quadrata, and the Capitoline Hill was occupied as an outpost.

"He raised the wall of the Palatine Hill by building higher works upon it, as a farther security to the inhabitants, and surrounded the adjacent hills—the Aventine, and that now called the Capitoline Hill—with ditches and strong palisades" (Dionysius, ii. 37).

"The city was difficult of access, having a strong garrison on the hill where the Capitol now stands" (Plutarch, "Romulus," 18). This hill was taken by treachery, and was not previously occupied by the Sabines. It was called the Hill of Saturn, but after its capture the Tarpeian Hill. Tarquin the Great changed its name to Mons Capitolinus.

"While the Sabines were passing at the foot of the Capitoline Hill, to view the place, and see whether any part of the hill could be taken by surprise or force, they were observed from the eminence by a virgin"—"Tarpeia, in execution of her promise, opened the gate agreed upon to the enemy, and calling up the garrison, desired they would save themselves"—"After the retreat of the garrison, the Sabines, finding the gates open and the place deserted, possessed themselves of it" (Dionysius, ii. 38, 39).

After peace was agreed upon, the two kings, Romulus and Titus Tatius, reigned jointly, and surrounded the Palatine and Capitoline Hills with a wall. The other hills, at this period, were not walled.

## SECOND WALL—THE WALL OF THE KINGS.

We give it this title because it was built by the two kings jointly; considerable portions still remain on the Palatine, under S. Anastasia, and near the Forum of Augustus. The walls of Romulus and Tatius would naturally be of similar construction to the original wall of Romulus; there was but little difference in this short time.

"Romulus and Tatius immediately enlarged the city......Romulus chose the Palatine and Cœlian Hills, and Tatius the Capitoline, which he had at first possessed himself of, and the Quirinal Hills" (Dionysius, ii. 50).

Numa erected the Temple of Vesta "between the Capitoline and Palatine Hills; for both these hills had already been encompassed with one wall; the Forum, in which this temple was built, lying between them" (Dionysius, ii. 66).

The other hills were inhabited, and surrounded at different times with walls, forming fortresses outside the city for the defence of the city proper.

Numa "enlarged the circuit of the city by the addition of the Quirinal Hill, for till that time it was not enclosed with a wall" (Dionysius, ii. 62).

Ancus Martius "made no small addition to the city by enclosing Mount Aventine within its walls, and encompassing it with a wall and a ditch. He also surrounded Mount Janiculum with a wall" (Dionysius, iii. 44).

Florus says : "He [Ancus Martius] encompassed the city with a wall." Again : "What kind of a king was the architect Ancus ! how fitted to extend the city by means of a colony [Ostia], to unite it by a bridge [the Sublicius], and secure it by a wall ?"

"The Quiritian trench also—no inconsiderable defence to those parts, which from their situation are of easy access—is a work of King Ancus" (Livy, i. 33).

## THIRD WALL AGGERS OF SERVIUS TULLIUS.

These seem to have been commenced by Tarquinius Priscus, and completed by Servius Tullius, and so called by his name.

"He [Tarquinius Priscus] was the first who built the walls of the city [of which the structure was extemporary and mean] with stones, regularly squared, each being a ton weight" (Dionysius, iii. 68).

Tarquinius (616 B.C.) "intended also to have surrounded the city with a stone wall, but a war with the Sabines interrupted his designs" (Livy, i. 36).

"He set about surrounding with a wall of stone those parts of the city which he had not already fortified, which work had been interrupted at the beginning by a war with the Sabines" (Livy, i. 38).

"He [Servius] surrounded the city with a rampart, trenches, and a wall, and thus extended the Pomerium," 578 B.C. (Livy, i. 44).

"As the Esquiline and Viminal Hills were both of easy access from without, a deep trench was dug outside them, and the earth thrown up on the inside, thus forming a terrace of six stadia in length along the inner side of the trench. This terrace Servius faced with a wall, flanked with towers, extending from the Colline to the Esquiline gate. Midway along the terrace is a third gate, named after the Viminal Hill" (Strabo, v. 3).

"Tullius had surrounded the seven hills with one wall" (Dionysius, iv. 14).

The seven hills were not surrounded, strictly speaking. Each hill formed a bastion, and aggers, or curtains of earth faced with stone, were built across the valleys, uniting these bastions. The Esquiline, Viminal, and Quirinal, being ridges jutting out of the table-land and not isolated hills, had one long agger built across their necks.

"Some parts of these walls, standing on hills, and being fortified by nature itself with steep rocks, required but few men to defend them, and others were defended by the Tiber......The weakest part of the city is from the gate called Esquilina to that named Collina, which interval is rendered strong by art ; for there is a ditch sunk before it, one hundred feet in breadth where it is narrowest, and thirty in depth. On the edge of this ditch stands a wall, supported on the inside with so high and broad a rampart that it can neither be shaken by battering-rams nor thrown down by undermining the foundations. This rampart is about seven stadia in length and fifty feet in breadth" (Dionysius, ix. 68).

This grand agger can be traced almost in its entire extent, as also the smaller aggers. There seems to have been no wall—that is, stone or earth fortification—between the Aventine and Capitoline, the Tiber being considered a sufficient defence.

"The city, having no walls in that part next the river, was very near being taken by storm" (Dionysius, v. 23) when Lars Porsena advanced to attack the city, after having taken the Janiculum, intending to cross the river by the only bridge, which, as we know, was defended by Horatius Cocles, and broken down by the Romans in his rear.

The walls of Servius Tullius were strengthened at the time of the war with Gabii.

"Tarquinius Superbus was particularly active in taking these precautions, and employed a great number of workmen in strengthening those parts of the city walls that lay next to the town of Gabii, by widening the ditch, raising the walls, and increasing the number of the towers" (Dionysius, iv. 54).

"On the eastern side it is bounded by the Agger of Tarquinius Superbus, a work of surpassing grandeur ; for he raised it so high as to be on a level with the walls on the side on which the city lay most exposed to attack from the neighbouring plains. On all the other sides it has been fortified either with lofty walls or steep or precipitous hills ; but so it is that its buildings, increasing and extending beyond all bounds, have now united many other cities to it" (Pliny, iii. 9).

"After Camillus had driven out the Gauls, both the walls of the city and the streets were rebuilt within a year" (Plutarch, "Cam." 32).

"The legions being brought to Rome, the remainder of the year was spent in repairing the walls and the towers," 350 B.C. (Livy, vii. 20).

"They received a charge from the senate to strengthen the walls and towers of the city," 217 B.C. (Livy, xxii. 8).

After the republic was firmly established, and the boundaries of the state enlarged, the walls of the city became obsolete, and it was to all intents and purposes an open city until the time of Aurelian.

" All the inhabited parts around it [the city], which are many and large, are open, and without walls, and very much exposed to the invasion of an enemy. And whoever considers these buildings, and desires to examine the extent of Rome, will necessarily be misled, for want of a certain boundary that might distinguish the spot to which the city extends, and where it ends. So connected are the buildings within the walls to those without, that they appear to a spectator like a city of an immense extent " (Dionysius, iv. 13).

## FOURTH WALL—THE WALL OF AURELIAN.

From the time of Servius to Aurelian the city, though much enlarged, had no new wall, though the boundaries had been extended. To continue our last quotation from Dionysius, who died 7 B.C., this is evident.

"But if any one is desirous to measure the circumference of it by the wall—which, though hard to be discovered, by reason of the buildings that surround it in many places, yet preserves in several parts of it some traces of the ancient structure—and to compare it with the circumference of the city of Athens, the circuit of Rome will not appear much greater than that of the other" (Dionysius, iv. 13).

The Pomœrium, or city bounds, was enlarged, as we know, by several emperors, some of their *cippi*, or boundary-stones, being still *in situ ;* but there was no wall. Where the roads crossed the line of the Pomœrium, gates were built, between which there were no walls. The Romans considered the rivers Tigris, Euphrates, and Danube, the desert and the ocean, as the walls of Rome.

" When he [Aurelian] saw that it might happen what had occurred under Gallienus, having obtained the concurrence of the senate, he extended the walls of the city of Rome" (Vopiscus, in " Aur.," 21).

"Thus also Rome was surrounded by walls which it *had not before*, and the wall begun by Aurelian was finished by Probus" (Zosimus, i. 49).

Other quotations might be given to show that Aurelian surrounded the Rome of the empire with walls which it had not before his time. He incorporated with his wall everything that stood in his way,— tombs, aqueducts, palaces, camps, and amphitheatre. It was commenced and finished in nine years, and had twenty-two gates, nineteen of which still remain.

These present walls have been in part rebuilt, repaired, and strengthened at different intervals, as occasion might require, from the time of Honorius, who improved and added to the existing gates, to that of Totila, who "resolved to raze Rome to the ground. So, of the circuit of the walls he threw down as much in different places as would amount to about a third part of the whole" (Procopius, "Bello Gothico," iii. 22).

Belisarius "made hasty repairs," after which the Popes stepped in and took up the tale, and put up inscriptions, so that there should be no mistake about it. Leo IV. built the walls of the Leonine city, to protect it from the Saracens, besides repairing the Aurelian walls. The Leonine walls can still be traced, the ruins standing boldly out in the landscape at the back of the Vatican.

The present wall on the Trastevere side was built by Innocent X. and Urban VIII. The complete circuit of the present walls is between twelve and thirteen miles; they contain twenty gates, ancient and modern, nine of which are closed.

Whilst the Romans considered the defences of the city to be the Tigris, Euphrates, Danube, desert, and ocean, their power was at its zenith; but when for the defence of their capital it was necessary to surround it with a wall, "the decline and fall of the Roman empire" had already begun.

## THE GATES.

In the third wall of Rome we learn from different authorities that there were in all eighteen gates, commencing from the northern point at the river bank,—Flumentana, Carmentalis or Scelerata, Ratumena, Fontinalis, Sangualis, Salularis or Salutaris, Collina or Agonalis or Quirinalis, Viminalis, Esquilina, Mæcia or Metia, Querquetulana, Cœlimontana, Firentina, Capena, Nævia, Randuscula, Lavernalis, Trigeminia. The sites of all of these have been identified. These names are culled from various authors, no one author having given us a list of them.

Pliny gives us an account of the number of the gates in his time— thirty-seven in all—which has puzzled a great many writers; but, studying them on the spot, the description of Pliny is very plain and easily to be understood. He says (iii. 9) :—

"When the Vespasians were emperors and censors, in the year from its building 827, the circumference of the Mœnia 'boundary' reckoned thirteen miles and two fifths. Surrounding as it does the seven hills, the city is divided into fourteen districts, with two hundred and sixty-five cross-roads, under the guardianship of the Lares. The space is such that if a line is drawn from the mile column placed

FIRST IMPRESSIONS. xxiii

at the head of the Forum to each of the gates, which are at present
thirty-seven in number, so that by that way enumerating only once
twelve gates, and to omit the seven old ones, which no longer exist,
the result will be a straight line of twenty miles and seven hundred
and sixty-five paces. But if we draw a straight line from the same
mile column to the very last of the houses, including therein the
Prætorian encampment, and follow throughout the line of all the
streets, the result will then be something more than seventy miles."

The gates may thus be analyzed :—

3 in Roma Quadrata ⎫ the 7 old ones to be omitted.
4 in City of Two Hills ⎭
18 in the Agger of Servius Tullius.
12 double—that is, 12 in the outer boundary built over the roads where they crossed
    the Pomœrium, corresponding with twelve in the line of Servius, thus making
    in all,—

37, as mentioned by Pliny.

Of the twelve gates in the outer boundary, eight still remaining are
composed of work of an earlier date than the Wall of Aurelian. The
twelve may thus be named : the four gates of the Prætorian camp
(two of these partially remain, showing brick-work of Tiberius),
Porta Chiusa or Viminalis, Tiburtina, Esquilina now Maggiore,
Lateranensis, Latina, Appia, Ardeatina, Ostiensis.

Pliny (iii. 9) tells us that Tarquinius Superbus raised an outer
agger on the eastern side of Rome. Traces of this still remain, and
the tufa stones have been reused in Aurelian's work, whilst the
Porta Chiusa is partly formed on the inside of these blocks, and was
probably the work of the last of the Tarquins. The Porta S.
Lorenzo, or Tiburtina, bears inscriptions of Augustus and Vespasian ;
Porta Maggiore, of Claudius, Vespasian, and Titus ; whilst Porta
Lateranensis and Porta Ardeatina were undoubtedly built, as the
construction shows, by Nero ; and the inner arch of the Porta S. Paolo,
or Ostiensis, is of the time of Claudius.

Tacitus (xii. 23) says : "The limits of the city were enlarged by
Claudius. The right of directing that business was, by ancient
usage, vested in all such as extended the boundaries of the empire.
The right, however, had not been exercised by any of the Roman
commanders (Sylla and Augustus excepted), though remote and
powerful nations had been subdued by their victorious arms."

"With regard to the enlargement made by Claudius, the curious
may be easily satisfied, as the public records contain an exact
description" (xii. 24).

# ROMAN CONSTRUCTION.

When we speak of construction, we mean the material used in building and the way it is put together. The different historical periods of building are now classed into distinct dates, which have been arrived at by observing the material used, and the way it is used, in buildings of which there is no doubt as to the date of erection, and comparing it with others. The early Greek Period in Italy is marked by massive walls of masonry—walls built from the stone of the vicinity, the blocks being rough as hewn out of the quarry,—polygonal. The later Greek Period and the Etruscan are identical, being formed of square blocks of stone, headers, and stretchers. In the time of the kings of Rome the stones were squared, and were of tufa, lapis ruber, tophus. In the earliest walls they are close jointed; in the second period the edges are bevelled.

During the Republic the stones were also squared, but the material was of peperino. Lapis Albanus and other forms of working up the material were introduced. Pieces of stone, fixed together with cement, gave a new kind of wall called *opus insertum*. This was improved upon by facing the outside of the small pieces of stone and making them of one uniform size—small polygonal. Then the stones were cut into wedge shapes : the point being inwards, and being laid in regular rows it has the appearance of network, and is called *opus reticulatum*. This work, introduced in the last years of the Republic, went out of fashion after the time of Tiberius, but was revived by Hadrian, who always set his reticulated work in bands of brick like a picture frame, thus distinguishing his from the earlier work, the inside of the walls in those cases being rubble. The earliest brick building which we have is the Pantheon. Thus it was under Augustus that brick was first used by the Romans. It was his boast that he found Rome of brick, and left it marble ; which is only true in a certain sense, for he did not build of solid marble, but cased veneering marble on to the brickwork.

One period of Roman brickwork can easily be distinguished from the others by measuring the number of bricks in a foot, and noticing their uniformity of size. This, of course, does not refer to ornamental brickwork. The brickwork of Nero is the best in the world —thin narrow bricks, tiles, with very little mortar between them. Before his time it was not quite so good; but after, it gradually declined till the cement is as thick as the bricks.

The stone used during the Empire was travertine, *lapis Tiburtinus*, but brick was the material generally used then. They are of two colours, red and yellow, according to the clay from which they were made. The walls were not of solid brick all through; but the interior was made of pieces—rubble-work—the outside course being entire brick, whilst at every four or five feet all through the construction were laid the great tie-bricks to keep the rubble-work from shifting. The brickwork was called *opus lateritium*. The great tie-bricks are usually stamped with the names of the consul or emperor and the maker, and these date the walls by measuring the number of bricks there are in a foot. In the fourth century another system —*opera decadence*—came into vogue, and walls were built with layers of brick and pieces of tufa-stone a little larger than our English bricks. This work continued down to the thirteenth century, when *opera Saracenesca*—tufa-stones without the bricks between— came into use. In the stone walls no cement was used; one stone was simply placed upon another, its weight keeping it in its place, and clamps were inserted to keep it from shifting. In the walls of Roma Quadrata we know of no clamps having been found; but in the wall of the two kings wooden clamps were found. In the walls of Servius Tullius iron clamps were found; and in the Colosseum clamps can still be seen in several places where pieces of the facing of the stone have been split off.

Tufa is found all over the Campagna, and is of volcanic origin. When the Alban Hills were active volcanoes, the ashes and scoriæ thrown up fell into the sea, now the Campagna. The pressure of water on it formed it into stone : where there has been a great pressure, it is very hard ; where little pressure, it is softer; and where there was no pressure, it still remains a sort of sand—this mixed with live lime is the celebrated Roman cement. The softer tufa was used by the Greek colonists, and the hard stone by the kings of Rome. Some tufa from the neighbourhood of Gabii is dark gray, the other is brown and reddish. Peperino is also volcanic. It was ejected in the shape of hot mud from the volcano, and on cooling formed a good stone: this comes from the Alban hills, and was used in the time of the Republic.

Travertine comes from Tivoli, and is a petrifaction formed by the action of lime and sulphur on vegetable decay. This was not used as a building material to any great extent before the time of Cæsar. It is white, and becomes yellow on exposure. Silex is another volcanic stone very little used for building, but entirely for paving the roads both ancient and modern. This came out of the volcano as a red-hot stream of lava, and on cooling down became a capital paving material. The bed of the road was first properly prepared, and then it was paved with polygonal blocks of blue basalt called silex. The stones fitted close to one another. Many of the roads are in a good condition to this day; the best specimen is opposite the Temple of Saturn in the Forum, B.C. 175. This stone is used for *opus reticulatum* in some of the tombs on the Appian Way and at the Temple of Hercules; also for concrete.

## TABLE OF CONSTRUCTION.

### TUFA OF THE KINGS.

| STYLE. | SPECIMEN. | DATE. |
|---|---|---|
| Polygonal | Tusculum | |
| Opus quadratum. First period, squared edges | Veii | |
| | Gabii | |
| | Palatine Hill | 753 B.C. |
| Second period, bevelled edges | Second Wall of Rome | 746 B.C. |
| | Aventine Hill | 600 B.C. |
| | Ostia | 600 B.C. |

### PEPERINO OF THE REPUBLIC.

| | | |
|---|---|---|
| Opus quadratum | Tomb of Scipio | 298 B.C. |
| | Temple of Hope | 240 B.C. |
| Opus insertum | Temple of Cybele | 191 B.C. |
| Opus insertum, polygonal | Emporium | 190 B.C. |
| Opus quadratum | Tabularium | 78 B.C. |

### TRAVERTINE AND BRICK OF THE EMPIRE.

| | | |
|---|---|---|
| Opus quadratum | Tomb of Cecilia Metella | 78 B.C. |
| | Theatre of Marcellus | 13 B.C. |
| | Arch of Dolabella | 10 A.D. |
| | Colosseum | 80 A.D. |
| Opus reticulatum | Muro Morto | 80 B.C. |
| | Tomb of Augustus | 10 B.C. |
| | Palatine Tiberius' House | |
| | Palatine Germanicus' House | |
| | Hadrian's Villa | |
| | Hadrian's Ostia | |

| STYLE. | SPECIMEN. | DATE. |
|---|---|---|
| Opus lateritium — | | |
| Bricks, 6 to foot | Pantheon | Augustus. |
| | Prætorian Camp | Tiberius. |
| | Palace | Caligula. |
| Bricks, 8 to foot | Aqueduct | Nero. |
| Bricks, 7 to foot | Palace | Domitian. |
| Bricks, 6 to foot | Temple of Venus and Rome | Hadrian. |
| Bricks, 7 to foot | Nymphæum, on Palatine | M. Aurelius. |
| Bricks, 5 to foot | Baths | Caracalla. |
| | Nymphæum | Alexander Severus. |
| | Walls of Rome | Aurelian. |
| | Thermæ | Diocletian. |
| | Basilica | Constantine. |
| Bricks and tufa | Circus of Maxentius | 300 A.D. |
| | House of Gregory | 590 A.D. |
| Opera Saracenesca | S. Sisto Vecchio | 1200 A.D. |
| Opus Spicatum | Herring-bone pavement. | |
| Opus Signinum | Cement for reservoirs, etc. | |

PLAN OF
ANCIENT ROME

AUGUSTAN
REGIONS of the CITY:

I. Porta Capena.
II. Cælimontana.
III. Isis et Serapis.
IV. Via Sacra.
V. Esquilina.
VI. Alta Semita.
VII. Via Lata.
VIII. Forum Romanum.
IX. Circus Flaminius.
X. Palatium.
XI. Circus Maximus.
XII. Piscina Publica.
XIII. Aventinus.
XIV. Transtiberina.

REGION I
REGION II
REGION III
REGION IV
REGION V
REGION VI
REGION VII
REGION VIII
REGION IX
REGION X
REGION XI
REGION XII
REGION XIII
REGION XIV

WALL OF SERVIUS TULLIUS

Porta Nomentana or Porta Viminalis Sinistra
Porta Principalis Dextra
Porta Principalis Sinistra
Praetorian Camp
Porta Viminalis
Porta Tiburtina
Porta Chiusa
Porta Nævia
Baths of Diocletian
Viminal Mount
Quirinal Mount
Gardens of Sallust
Baths of Gallienus
Porta Esquilina or Galienaria
Porta Labicana and Prænestina
Amphitheatrum Castrense
Porta Asinaria
Porta Latina
Porta Metronia
Porta Latina
Tomb of the Scipios
Cælian Mount Temple of Claudius
Esquiline Mount
Coliseum
Arch of Constantine
Baths of Titus
Baths of Caracalla
Arch of Drusus Porta Appia
Porta Ardeatina
REGION I
Palatine
Capitoline Mount
Forum of Nerva
Forum of Augustus
Forum Trajani
Forum Romanum
Forum of Cæsar
Circus Maximus
Aventine Mount Testaceus
Porta Ostiensis
Porta Trigemina
Porta Carmentalis
Trajan Mount
Tomb of Augustus
Via Flaminia
Mausoleum of Augustus
Column of M. Aurelius
Pantheon
Baths of Agrippa
Circus of Flaminius
Theatre of Pompey
Theatre of Marcellus
Campus Martius
Via Flaminia
Forum of Trajan
Hadrian's Mausoleum
Porta Flaminia
Porta Septimiana
Sublician Bridge
Porta Aurelia
Porta Portuensis

* To those going out.   † To those coming in, according to which hill they were going to.

# RAMBLES IN ROME.

## RAMBLE I.

## THE CENTRE OF ROME.

### THE PIAZZA DEL POPOLO

is a circular open space, adorned with fountains, and surrounded with foliage. From this circle Rome spreads itself out like a fan southwards. The four principal lines of thoroughfare diverge from this spot—the Pincio, the Via Sistina, and the Via Quattro Fontane, leading to the Esquiline, on the extreme left, along the hills; the Via Babuino, leading into the Piazza di Spagna, on the left; the Corso, leading into the Forum, in the centre; and the Via Ripetta, leading into the oldest part of the present city, on the right: at the corners of the three latter are the twin churches S. MARIA IN MONTE

Santo, and S. Maria dei Miracoli, with domes and vestibules designed by Rinaldi, and completed by Bernini and Fontana. In the
centre of the Piazza is an Egyptian obelisk, supported by a fountain
with four lionesses at the corners spouting water. *On the right*, under
the Terraces of the Pincio, are the statue of Rome by Ceccarini,
of Neptune between two Tritons, and statues of Spring and Summer,
by Laboureur. *On the left* are the statues of Autumn, by Stocchi,
and Winter, by Baini.

## THE EGYPTIAN OBELISK

of the Piazza del Popolo was brought to Rome by Augustus, and
erected in the Circus Maximus. It is 78 feet 6 inches high, and
was erected on its present site by Pope Sixtus V. in 1589. This was
the first obelisk erected in Rome, having been brought by Augustus
after the death of Antony and Cleopatra. Pliny (xxxvi. 16) says :—

"But the most difficult enterprise of all was the carriage of these
obelisks by sea to Rome, in vessels which excited the greatest admiration. Indeed, the late Emperor Augustus consecrated the one which
brought over the first obelisk, as a lasting memorial of this marvellous undertaking, in the docks at Puteoli ; but it was destroyed by
fire.

"And then, besides, there was the necessity of constructing other
vessels to carry these obelisks up the Tiber ; by which it became
practically ascertained that the depth of water in that river is not
less than that of the river Nile.

"The one that he erected in the Campus Martius is nine feet less
in height, and was originally made by order of Sesothis. They are
both of them covered with inscriptions which interpret the opera-
tions of Nature according to the philosophy of the Egyptians."

This has the name of two kings upon it : Seti, who went blind,
and his son Rameses, who succeeded him. It stood before the
Temple of the Sun at Heliopolis, and was placed by Augustus on the
Spina of the Circus Maximus, and re-dedicated, 10 B.C., to the Sun, as
the inscription informs us: IMP. CAES. DIVI. F.—AUGUSTUS—PONTIFEX
MAXIMUS—IMP. XII. COS. XI. TRIB. POT.—POPULI ROMANI REDACTA.—
SOLI DONUM DEDIT.

Ammianus Marcellinus (xvii. 4) supplies us with the following
information relative to obelisks :—

"In this city of Thebes, among many works of art and different
structures recording the tales relating to the Egyptian deities, we
saw several obelisks in their places, and others which had been

PIAZZA DEL POPOLO.

thrown down and broken, which the ancient kings, when elated at
some victory or at the general prosperity of their affairs, had caused to
be hewn out of mountains in distant parts of the world, and erected in
honour of the gods, to whom they solemnly consecrated them.

" Now, an obelisk is a rough stone, rising to a great height, shaped
like a pillar in the stadium ; and it tapers upwards in imitation of a
sunbeam, keeping its quadrilateral shape, till it rises almost to a
point, being made smooth by the hand of a sculptor.

" On these obelisks the ancient authority of elementary wisdom
has caused innumerable marks of strange forms all over them, which
are called hieroglyphics.

" For the workmen, carving many kinds of birds and beasts, some
even such as must belong to another world, in order that the recollec-
tion of the exploits which the obelisk was designed to commemorate
might reach to subsequent ages, showed by them the accomplishment
of vows which the kings had made.

" For it was not the case then, as it is now, that the established
number of letters can distinctly express whatever the human mind
conceives ; nor did the ancient Egyptians write in such a manner,
but each separate character served for a separate noun or verb, and
sometimes even for an entire sentence.

" Of which fact the two following may for the present be sufficient
instances :—By the figure of a vulture they indicate the name of
nature ; because naturalists declare that no males are found in this
class of bird. And by the figure of a bee making honey they indicate a king ; showing by such a sign that stings as well as sweetness
are the characteristics of a ruler. And there are many similar
emblems."

*To the right of the Porta del Popolo is the*

## CHURCH OF S. MARIA DEL POPOLO,

founded by Paschal II. in 1099. Its interior consists of nave, aisles,
transept, and octagonal dome lavishly decorated by Bernini.

In the first chapel, to the right, the picture over the altar, the
Nativity of Jesus Christ, and the frescoes of the lunettes are by Pinturicchio. The second chapel is that of the Cibo family—rich in
marbles, and adorned with forty-six columns of Sicilian jasper. The
picture of the Conception is by Maratta. The third chapel is painted
by Pinturicchio. In the fourth chapel is an interesting bas-relief of
the fifteenth century. The painting of the Virgin, on the high altar,
is one of those attributed to S. Luke ; the paintings of the vault in the

choir are by Pinturicchio. The two monuments in marble ornamented by statues are by Contucci da S. Savino. The last chapel but
one, in the small nave, is that of the Chigi family, and is one of the
most celebrated in Rome. Raphael gave the design for the dome, for
the paintings of the frieze, and for the picture of the altar, which
was commenced by Sebastiano del Piombo, and terminated by Francesco Salviati. The statues of Daniel and Habakkuk were executed by
Bernini. The front of the altar and the statues of Elias and Jonah
are by Lorenzetti; but the design of the last is by Raphael.

### THE CORSO (Il Corso).

Starting on our first ramble, we will take the line of the principal
street, the Corso, which takes its name from the races held during
the Carnival. It is on the line of the old Via Flaminia, the great
highroad which ran through the Campus Martius to the north. Many
handsome churches and palaces face the street, which is rather narrow
compared with our modern requirements. The Corso is the principal
promenade of the Romans, and possesses many points of interest.
At No. 18, *on the left*, lived Goethe; just beyond, *on the right*, in the
short Via S. Giacomo, was Canova's studio. *On the right*, further
down, is the Church of S. Carlo; passing by which, crossing the line
of the Via Condotti, *on our right* opens out the small square of
Lucina, in which is the

### CHURCH OF S. LORENZO IN LUCINA,

containing the grand work of Guido Reni, "The Crucifixion." It
is said that, being absorbed in his subject, he crucified his model.
The church contains a monument to Poussin, the relief being a copy
of his landscape of the tomb of Sappho in Arcadia. Opposite this
church is the English Baptist Chapel, under the Rev. James Wall,
founded for Romans.

*Turning to the right, down the Corso, on the left, the Via Con-
vertite leads to*

### THE GENERAL POST OFFICE (La Posta),

in the Piazza S. Silvestro. *on the left*. It is a new building, recently
opened, and is fitted up with every modern appliance. The garden
in the centre, and the surrounding arcade with its frescoes, present
a refreshing appearance, and give a good idea of what the court
of a palace should be. *In front* is the statue of Metastasio.

*Opposite*, in the right corner of the square, is

1

## THE ENGLISH CHURCH OF THE HOLY TRINITY,

being the first Protestant church erected in Rome. It is in the form of a basilica without aisles, and was designed by the late architect Cipolla.

*Regaining the Corso,* we soon arrive at the Piazza Colonna, in which is

## THE COLUMN OF MARCUS AURELIUS.

On the spot where the Palazzo Chigi now stands (*on our right*) a temple was erected to M. Aurelius, in front of which was placed a splendid pillar, with a spiral frieze winding up the shaft, and representing the chief incidents of the war against the Marcomanni (A.D. 174).

The shaft of this pillar is of precisely the same height as that of the Pillar of Trajan. The pedestal, on the other hand, is much higher, and rises considerably above the level of the modern pavement. The present marble facing of this pedestal has been employed to strengthen the foundations of the monument, which had been much injured. The pillar, after having been frequently struck and much damaged by lightning, was restored, at the command of Sixtus V., by Fontana and his nephew Carlo Maderno. Looking up, we perceive the iron cramps used to keep together the blocks of marble, which had slipped out of their original position. But for this support, this fine monument would long since have sunk beneath the pressure of its own weight.

The sculptures are very interesting, but can no more be enjoyed on the spot than those on the Pillar of Trajan. They represent scenes from the battles fought in Germany. The column is formed of 28 blocks of white marble, is 137 feet high, and is crowned with a statue of S. Paul. Sixtus V., in restoring the Column of Marcus Aurelius, in error inscribed it to Antoninus Pius.

*Facing* the Piazza Colonna is a large palace. The columns which form the portico were found in the ruins of Veii. *Our attention is next attracted by*

## THE PARLIAMENT HOUSE,

*situated in the Piazza Monte Citorio, behind* the Palace. Orders for admission to special seats may be obtained from any deputy, but there is a compartment in the gallery open to the public.

*Opposite the Parliament House is an*

COLUMN OF MARCUS AURELIUS.

### EGYPTIAN OBELISK.

It was erected originally at Heliopolis to Psammeticus I., of the twenty-fourth dynasty, more than six centuries B.C. It is 72 feet high. Its first site in Rome was in the Campus Martius, where is now the Piazza dell'Impresa, where it was found and taken to its present site. The Roman pedestal with inscription is in the Church of S. Lorenzo in Lucina. The obelisk was repaired, and its present pedestal formed of fragments of the Antonine Column, which stood near by. The obelisk was brought to Rome by Augustus at the same time as the one in the Piazza del Popolo, and was put up, according to Pliny (xxxvi. 15), as a sun-dial :—

"The one that has been erected in the Campus Martius has been applied to a singular purpose by the late Emperor Augustus—that of marking the shadows projected by the sun, and so measuring the length of the days and nights. With this object, a stone pavement was laid, the extreme length of which corresponded exactly with the length of the shadow thrown by the obelisk at the sixth hour on the day of the winter solstice. After this period the shadow would go on day by day gradually decreasing, and then again would as gradually increase, correspondingly with certain lines of brass that were inserted in the stone—a device well deserving to be known, and due to the ingenuity of Facundus Novus, the mathematician. Upon the apex of the obelisk he placed a gilded ball, in order that the shadow of the summit might be condensed and agglomerated, and so prevent the shadow of the apex itself from running to a fine point of enormous extent, the plan being first suggested to him, it is said, by the shadow that is projected by the human head. For nearly the last thirty years, however, the observations derived from this dial have been found not to agree,—whether it is that the sun itself has changed its course, in consequence of some derangement of the heavenly system ; or whether that the whole earth has been in some degree displaced from its centre—a thing that, I have heard say, has been remarked in other places as well; or whether that some earthquake, confined to this city only, has wrenched the dial from its original position; or whether it is that, in consequence of the inundations of the Tiber, the foundations of the mass have subsided, in spite of the general assertion that they are sunk as deep into the earth as the obelisk erected upon them is high."

*Regaining the Corso, the first turning on the right, Via Pietra, leads into the* PIAZZA DI PIETRA, *in which are the ruins of*

## THE TEMPLE OF NEPTUNE.

Eleven Corinthian columns, which formed a part of one side of the temple, still stand, forming the entrance into a building once used as a custom-house. They are 42½ feet high and 4½ feet in diameter, supporting an architrave of marble which has been recently restored. In the interior are some immense blocks of marble which formed part of the vaulting. The temple, with the Portico of the Nations which surrounded it, was erected by Agrippa. It is now used as a chamber of commerce.

*Continuing our ramble along the Corso, on the right* is the Palazzo SIMONETTI, *on the left* the PALAZZO SCIARRA. The pictures here have not been shown to the public for some years.

## THE KIRCHERIAN MUSEUM.

*Open from 9 to 2.30 daily. Fee, 1 lire; Sundays free.*

*The door facing down the short street on the right gives access* to the Library Vittorio Emanuele and Reading-room, open to the public daily. It is located in the Collegio Romano palace, formerly the headquarters of the Jesuits. On the top floor of the palace is the museum founded by Father Kircher, to which the Government have added a valuable ethnographical collection.

ENTRY CORRIDOR.—The mosaic pavement is ancient. Terra-cotta fragments are inserted into the walls. The most interesting objects are placed in cases. *1st, on left.* Terra-cottas. *2nd.* Silver cups, on which are engraved the itineraries, from Cadiz to Rome, of the time of Augustus, Vespasian, and Nerva. Found in a mineral spring, whose waters are supposed to have cured the travellers, near Bracciano. *3rd.* Early bronze money, the æs and its parts. *4th.* Small bronze objects, glass, and dice. *5th.* Bronze money, gems. *6th.* Case of lamps. A hemicircle at the end contains busts and statuettes. *Returning: 7th case.* Terra-cotta lamps. *8th.* Coins. *9th.* Lead pipes with inscriptions, and bullets, 90 and 40 B.C. *10th.* Case of æs. *11th.* Inscriptions in bronze; one is a ring with a label: "I have run away; take and restore me to my master, who will reward you with a solidus." *12th.* Case of lamps. *13th.* Etruscan pottery.

BRONZE ROOM.—*1st on left off Entry Corridor.* On the left, case containing Lares, reflectors, and sacrificial hooks (1 Sam. ii. 13). In the centre of the last compartment is a model of a plough, followed by two figures; that on the left is Minerva. It is the kind of plough used by Romulus in making the bounds of Roma Quadrata, and in use to this day on the Campagna. Case of domestic utensils. Cases of Egyptian objects. In front of window, *Bisellium* or chair of state. Case of pipes. Mithraic group. A *cista* or bronze cylindrical casket for holding articles for the toilet. The handle of the cover is formed by a group of three Bacchi, beneath which is the maker's name and that of the daughter who received it from her mother : NOVIOS . PLAVTIOS . MED . ROMAI . FECID . DINDIA . MACOLNIA . FILEAI . DEDIT. It was found at Præneste, and dates about 200 B.C. The cylinder is beautifully engraved with the story of Amicus being killed by Pollux. Case of bronze lamps.

CHRISTIAN ROOM.—*Case on right.* 126. Vase of bigio marble, having in relief Madonna and Child. 130. Lamb of bronze, with a cross on the head. 131. Crucifix, feet supported on a pedestal. 132. Byzantine figure of Christ. Lamps and other small objects. *In front of the* window is the piece of plaster from the Domus Gelotiana of the Palatine, on which is scratched the caricature of the Crucifixion—a man with an ass's head being crucified, with a figure of a man in adoration on the left ; beneath, in Greek, is written, "Alexamenos adores his God." The Romans believed the Jews worshipped a white donkey (Tacitus, "H." v. 3 ; Plutarch, "Sym." Ques. v. ; Tertullian, "Apol." i. 16). At first they did not distinguish between Christian and Jew ; and understanding the Christian's God was crucified, they drew these skits to chaff their Christian comrades (Tertullian, "Apol." i. 16). The Egyptian god Anubis had a jackal's head ; this is distinctly a donkey's (see altar, No. 33, Atrium, Capitol Museum), and is unlike the Gnostic Anubis or Typhon (Epiphanius, "Birth of Mary"). The wall on which it was found is of the time of Septimius Severus, 196, at which time Tertullian was in Rome, and so may have seen it.

THE ETHNOGRAPHICAL AND ANTHROPOLOGICAL Collection is entered from the right-hand end of Entry Corridor, and is of considerable interest, particularly the flint, bronze, and iron periods. At the end of these is the case of PALESTRINA TREASURE TROVE, found in 1876. The objects are Phœnician, and date about a thousand years before Christ, and were personal ornaments and domestic utensils. The most attractive is the gold plate with one hundred and thirty-one animals, probably part of a mitre or crown ; a gold brooch ; fringe ; gold cup ; blue glass vase ; silver vases and plates.

*Regaining the Corso, lower down, standing back on the left, is the* founded in the fourth century on the site where the Bishop Marcellinus was compelled by Maxentius to work as a stableman in the oratory of Lucina. In front of the church Rienzi's body was hung up by the feet for two days.

In the third chapel on the right is the tomb of the English Cardinal Weld, 1837. On the roof of the next chapel is the Creation of Eve, by Perino del Vaga, the finest conception of this subject, surpassing even that of Michael Angelo in the Sistine Chapel. On the left are S. Mark and S. John, the cherubs between whom are the most exquisite things ever done in fresco. We are sorry to say damp is affecting them. Opposite, S. Matthew and S. Luke are by Daniele da Volterra. The Angels bearing the Cross, over the altar, is by Garzi. The tomb on the left is that of Cardinal Consalvi, 1824. The fourth chapel, on the opposite side of the church, contains frescoes of the life of S. Paul, by F. Zucchero ; the altar-piece being his conversion, by F. Zucchero. A very fine work.

Over the door, and occupying the whole of the width of the church, is a very graphic and realistic representation of the Crucifixion, by Marco Ricci, 1730

*Below, on the opposite side of the Corso, is*

## THE CHURCH OF S. MARIA, IN VIA LATA,

which was founded in the eighth century, but was rebuilt in 1485, when the tradition arose that it was on the site of the hired house of S. Paul in Rome. Dodwell, the English explorer in Greece, was buried here. There are also tombs of several members of the Bonaparte family. *A door on the left* of the portico, built in 1662 from the designs of Pietro da Cortona, leads down into the subterranean chambers, where a well is shown said to have been used by S. Paul to baptize his converts. In an adjoining chamber S. Luke is said to have painted his Madonna. Here are some remains of the materials of the Arch of Claudius, which spanned the Via Flaminia at this point ; and an old piece of fresco, said to be by S. Luke. These remains below the church formed part of

## THE SEPTA.

Cicero (Ad Atticum, iv. 15) informs us that Julius Cæsar commenced a septa in the Campus Martius for the Comitia Centuriata and Tributa. It consisted of a beautiful building of marble, surrounded with a portico a mile square. It adjoined the Villa Publica. It was completed by Lepidus the triumvir, and dedicated by Agrippa (Dion Cassius, liii. 23). Frontinus (Aq. xxii.) says the arches of the Aqua Virgo ended in the Campus Martius, in front of the Septa.

The Comitia Centuriata, when the people assembled in their military order, to elect their highest magistrates, to pass their laws, and to vote upon peace or war, always met outside the walls in the Campus Martius.

Comitia Tributa, for less important magistrates, tribunes, and ædiles, met sometimes in the Campus Martius.

The Septa consisted of pens (hence the name), into which the tribes passed to record their votes, which were given by ballot. Every voter received a *tabella* (tablet), on which he wrote the name of the candidate for whom he voted. He then dropped it into an urn.

Near by, Agrippa built the Diribitorium, a large building used for distributing and counting the ballot tickets. It was dedicated by Augustus (Dion Cassius, lv. 8; Pliny, xvi. 40). During a fire Claudius passed two nights here (Suetonius, "Claudius," xviii.).

These ruins extend under the Doria Palace, and have nothing to do with any house. There were no houses on the Campus Martius in Paul's time. (See page 195.)

*Just beyond, on the same side of the way, is*

## THE DORIA PALACE GALLERY (Palazzo Doria),

*open on Tuesday and Friday from 10 till 2. Catalogues in each room. Fee, half-franc.*

GRANDE SALLE.—*Left.* 6. The Deluge, by Scarsellino, above sarcophagus of the Meleager Hunt. *Opposite.* Landscape, by Poussin, above sarcophagus of Diana and the Sleeping Endymion. No. 33 is a good representation of the Nymphæum of Alexander Severus in the Piazza Vittorio Emanuele, by Salvator Rosa.

IL BRACCIO.—First Gallery, *right of entry.* 3. Holy Family, by Bellini. *Left.* Christ Bearing the Cross, by Bronzino. 12. S. Francis, by A. Caracci. 14. Portrait, by Titian. 17. Money-Changers, by Quentin Matsys. 24. Holy Family, by Bellini. 26. Abraham and Isaac, by Lieven. 27, 28. Landscapes, by Domenichino. Portrait of Andrea Doria, by Sebastiano del Piombo. 40. Daughter of Herodias, by Pordenone. 49. A Monk, by Rubens. 53. La Jaconda, Joanna II. of Naples, after Raphael. 55. Magdalen, by Titian, copy of original in Pitti Palace, a very fine work. 61. Birth of Christ, by

Benvenuto da Ortolano. 69. Glory Crowning Valour, a sketch, by Correggio. 71. Portrait, by Rubens. 77. Titian and his Wife, by Titian.

SECOND GALLERY.—3. Assumption, by A. Caracci. 5. Mercury Stealing the Herd of Apollo, by Claude Lorraine. 8. Flight into Egypt, by A. Caracci. 42, 43. Holbein and his Wife. 13. The Mill, by Claude. 17. A Crucifixion, said to be by M. Angelo. 19. Pietà, by Caracci. 21. S. Catherine, by Garofalo. 24. Sacrifice to Apollo, by Claude. A Village Feast, by Teniers. 28. A fine portrait, by Paul Veronese, called Lucrezia Borgia. 34. Hunt of Diana, by Claude. 32. A woman with a helmet, called La Venozza (mother of the children of the Borgia, Pope Alexander VI.), by Dosso Dossi. 5. Marriage of S. Catherine, by Sassoferrato.

CABINET, *to the left.* Bust of Pope Innocent X., Pamfili, 1655. Portrait of the same, by Velasquez. Baldo and Bartolo, two Venetians, by Raphael.

GALLERY OF STATUES AND MIRRORS, containing ancient statuary.

IX. SALA.—7. Greek Charity, by Valentin. 6. Slaughter of the Innocents, by Andrea Vekiceven.

VIII. SALA.—Jesus and the Angels, by Both.

VII. SALA.—17. Sebastian, by Ludovico Caracci. 2. The Supper at Emmaus (Luke xxv. 30), by Bassano.

VI. SALA.—19. Slaughter of the Innocents, by Mazzolini. 8. Belisarius, by Salvator Rosa.

FOURTH GALLERY. — 4. Galatea, by Vaga. 29. Crucifixion, by Scipio da Gaeta. 31. Portrait of Giannetto Doria, by Angelo Bronzino. 19. Jesus Bearing the Cross, by P. Brill. 20. Flight into Egypt, by Claude. 25. Repose on the Way, by Claude. 26. Visitation of S. Elizabeth, by Garofalo. 31. Last Supper, by D. Ryckant. 37. Copy, by Poussin, of the ancient fresco in the Vatican Library of the Marriage of Peleus and Thetis, found near the Arch of Gallienus in 1606. Pius VII. gave £2,000 for the original. 38. Madonna, by Andrea del Sarto. 1. Venus and Paris, by Bordone. 49. Angel Playing the Tambourine, by Paul Veronese. 46. Adoration of the Virgin, by Guido Reni. 50. Holy Family, by Raphael, copy by Giulio Romano. 51. Christ Expelling the Venders, by Dosso Dossi.

*Proceeding down the Corso, we reach the Piazza di Venezia. On the left* is the Torlonia Palace,* and *on the right* the Venetian Palace (now the Austrian Embassy), a building of the Middle Ages. *On the right-hand side of the narrow street, in a line with the Corso, Via Marforio, is the*

* Gallery open Tuesday and Friday from 11 till 2.

## TOMB OF ATTIA CLAUDIA,

recently isolated by the public works being carried out here. By descending into the vault, it will be seen that it is hewn out of the natural rock. The Claudii family " received, from the state, lands beyond the Anio for their followers, and a burying-place for themselves near the Capitol" (Suetonius, "Claudius," i. 1).

## THE MONUMENT TO VICTOR EMMANUEL.

Upon the north-east end of the Capitoline Hill, the national monument to the first king of united Italy is being erected from the designs of Cav. Sacconi. It will consist of a series of steps and terraces, ornamented with statues, leading up to a piazza, in the centre of which will be the equestrian statue of the king, and in the background a colonnade with reliefs of scenes in the story of the unity. It will form a very handsome termination to the Corso, and will be the grandest monument in existence.

*A few steps beyond, on the left-hand side of the same street, is the*

## TOMB OF BIBULUS.

The inscription records the virtue and public honour of a Roman magistrate of the time of the republic. It is supposed to be two thousand years old.

C. PUBLICO . L. Q. F. BIBULO . AED . PL. HONORIS
VIRTUTISQUE . CAUSSA . SENATUS
CONSULTO . POPULIQUE . IUSSU . LOCUS.
MONUMENTO . QUO . IPSE . POSTEREIQUE
EIUS . INFERRENTUR . PUBLICE . DATUS . EST

It is of travertine stone and plain Doric architecture. There is some talk of pulling the house down, so that this interesting monument may be better seen.

*Continuing our ramble down the street, we arrive, on the right, at the Church of S. Giuseppe dei Falegnami. It is built over part of*

## THE MAMERTINE PRISON,

erected, according to Livy (i. 33), by Ancus Martius. "In order to suppress the terror, the boldness which the vicious assumed from hence (A.U.C. 121),* and which gained ground continually, a prison

---

* *Ab urbe condita*, From the foundation of the city (B.C. 753).

was built in the middle of the city, adjoining the Forum." Servius Tullius added a lower cell, called the TULLIANUM, 6½ feet high and 19 feet by 9. Prisoners who were condemned to be strangled or to die of hunger were thrust down the aperture; hence the phrase, "to cast into prison." Sallust ("Catiline," lv.) thus describes it :—

"There is a place in the prison which is called the Tullianum Dungeon. It is about 12 feet deep in the ground when you have ascended a little to the left.* It is secured round the sides by walls, and over it is a vaulted roof, connected with stone arches; but its appearance is disgusting and horrible, by reason of the filth, the obscurity, and the stench. When Lentulus had been let down into this place, certain men, to whom orders had been given, strangled him with a cord."

The upper part of the Mamertine Prison was partly rebuilt in the time of Tiberius, as we know from an inscription remaining in the cornice over the flight of steps under the church.

C. VIBIUS . C. F. RUFINUS . M. COCCEIUS . NERVA . COS . EX . S. C.
Consuls A. D. 23.

It seems to have been used exclusively for state prisoners. We have records of the following, amongst others, who were confined here :—

Manlius, who had defended the Capitol against the Gauls.— B.C. 382.

Quintus Pleminius, a prisoner for sedition.—B.C. 194.

Jugurtha, King of Numidia, who was starved to death B.C. 104. He exclaimed, when cast in, "By Hercules! how cold is this bath of yours!" (Plutarch, in "Caius Marius"), evidently speaking of the spring as existing in those days.

Catiline conspirators, strangled by order of the Consul Cicero.— B.C. 55.

Vercingetorix, King of the Gauls, by order of Julius Cæsar.

Sejanus, the minister of Tiberius.—A.D. 31.

Simon, the son of Giora, the defender of Jerusalem against Vespasian.—A.D. 69.

In the centre of the upper chamber is the round aperture, covered by a grate, down which the prisoners were cast.

Juvenal says : "Happy ages of the just, happy centuries, it may be said, those which saw, formerly under the kings, as under the tribunes, Rome content with one prison."

* From the Forum.

One prison may have been enough in those times when it was against the law to confine a Roman citizen before he was tried. We have records of other prisons. Appius Claudius constructed a prison for common offenders near the Forum Olitorium, the scene of "Roman Charity." (See page 191.) Pliny mentions "*Stationes Municipiorum*" —barracks of the municipal soldiers—near the Forum of Julius Cæsar. These may likewise have been prisons. In addition to these, there was the *Lautumiæ*.

*Below* the church, the Chapel of the Crucifixion occupies part of the buildings of the prison, and from the sacristy a flight of modern steps leads down into a lower cell, the Chapel of SS. Peter and Paul. The entrance and steps from the street are also modern. In this chamber, to the right of the altar, is a closed-up passage; it evidently communicated with other chambers. On the tufa, carefully guarded by iron bars, an indentation is shown which, they say, was caused by the jailers beating Peter's face against the rock. (He must have had rather a hard head !)

Another flight of modern stairs leads down into the Tullianum : the opening down which the prisoners were cast can still be seen. The iron door is the opening of a sewer leading into the Cloaca Maxima, by which means the dead bodies, &c., were taken away. This drain is of the same construction as the Cloaca Maxima, and comes from beyond the other chambers, mentioned below, with which it also communicates.

The Roman Catholic tradition is, that SS. Peter and Paul were confined here, and they show the pillar to which they are said to have been chained, though there are no marks of a staple having been fixed in the stone, as represented in the bronze bas-relief ; and a fountain which miraculously sprang up when they had converted their keepers, and they wished to be baptized : this was evidently alluded to by Jugurtha.

The name Mamertine Prison is medieval. By the ancients it was called *the Prison*, or the Tullian Prison.\* The two chambers are only a small part of the ancient prison, which extended up the left side of the Clivus Argentarius, the modern Via Marforio, and evidences of its extent can be seen in the cellars of the houses. It evidently extended up as far as No. 68, for under that wine shop we found two chambers corresponding with the two under the church. The prison was approached from the Forum by a flight of stairs called

---

\* Diodorus Siculus, lib. xxxi , calls it the jail Albinus.

## THE SCALÆ GEMONIÆ,

or Stairs of Wailing. Criminals were often put to death on them, and others were exposed there after death. "Those who were put to death were exposed on the Scalæ Gemoniæ, and then dragged into the Tiber" (Suetonius, "Tiberius," lxi.).

*At a short distance from the church in the little lane opposite, Via Marmorelle, 29,* are some more remains of the Prison, which eventually became the

## "STATIONES MUNICIPIORUM" AND FORUM OF JULIUS CÆSAR.

"Julius Cæsar, with money raised from the spoils of war, began to construct a new Forum" (Suetonius, "Cæsar," xxvi.)—the site costing about £807,291. This new Forum was necessary, on account of the old Forum becoming too small for the public business. Pliny (xvi. 86) mentions the barracks of the municipal guards as being between the Vulcanal and the Forum of Julius Cæsar. These remains consist of a series of five large chambers; one is forty feet long and fourteen wide, divided by modern walls and partitions in various ways, and not easy of access. The walls are of tufa. The vaults are of brick, with openings for letting down prisoners. These are of later date than the tufa walls, and one of them is supported by a fine arch of travertine.

## THE ROMAN FORUM (Il Foro).

*The new excavations are open to the public every day without fee.*

To understand the Roman Forum and its surroundings, visitors should attend the lectures given on the spot by the author of these Rambles, descend with him to its level, and examine each remaining object in detail; thus they may learn something of the buildings and the history that crowded on its space. For particulars, apply at 93 Via Babuino, Rome.

Mutilated fragments still speak of the former grandeur of the spot, dead men of its fame, and living authors of its past and present history.

In these Rambles we shall only treat of the most important and present remains, which are classed in the order in which they should be visited, and not chronologically.

The real foundation of the ancient city had long been covered over by the heaping up, during ages, of earth, stones, rubbish, &c., to the depth of thirty feet. The thick crust had lain untouched by shovel during the long series of popes; especially was this, until recently, the condition of the Roman Forum. With the exception of the north side, between the Senate House (S. Adriano) and the Temple of Antoninus and Faustina, the whole of the Forum has been excavated. The property on this north side has been acquired by the Government, and the excavations are expected to commence shortly.

In shape the Forum is a parallelogram, and consisted of a series of buildings round an open space called the Comitium, the white travertine pavement of which still exists, but much of it is occupied with erections of the empire. From the building of the Cloaca Maxima to the erection of the Column of Phocas, we here read the sermons in stones of 1,200 years.

*We will follow the modern road, which crosses the Forum, and turning to the left, proceed along the side of the Basilica Julia to the Temple of Castor and Pollux, where a flight of steps gives access to the Forum.*

Standing upon the platform of the temple, we propose to explain the various buildings that surrounded the Forum, and then to descend to its ancient level to examine the chief points of interest.

The word *forum*, in its simple signification, means market-place ; and the Roman Forum was the market-place when Rome consisted of but two hills, the Palatine and Capitoline. It soon lost its primitive use, and became the centre of the religious, civil, and political life of the Romans. Then other market-places were formed, and called after the principal commodity sold therein. In the time of Cæsar the Forum was found too small, and then was commenced the first of the Imperial Fora. The Forum, from the time of Constantine, gradually fell into decay, and was finally ruined in the year 1084, when Robert Guiscard, the Norman chief, burned all Rome from the Lateran to the Capitol.

### HOW THE SOIL ACCUMULATED.

We may learn from the erection of the Column of Phocas, in A.D. 608, that the Forum was then unencumbered with soil. Rome having been at that time deserted for a long period by its emperors, its principal monuments began to fall into decay, the Romans themselves hastening on the work for the sake of the marble ; the steady hand of time, allied with the luxuriant vegetation, working slowly but surely, added to the *débris;* whilst deposits from the Tiber floods, the wind, and the wash of the rain-shed, helped still more to fill in the valleys. During a long course of years Rome was almost abandoned ; the streets remained unswept, and the rubbish of the city collected upon them. At length a new life sprang up, and to the

# PLAN OF THE ROMAN FORUM

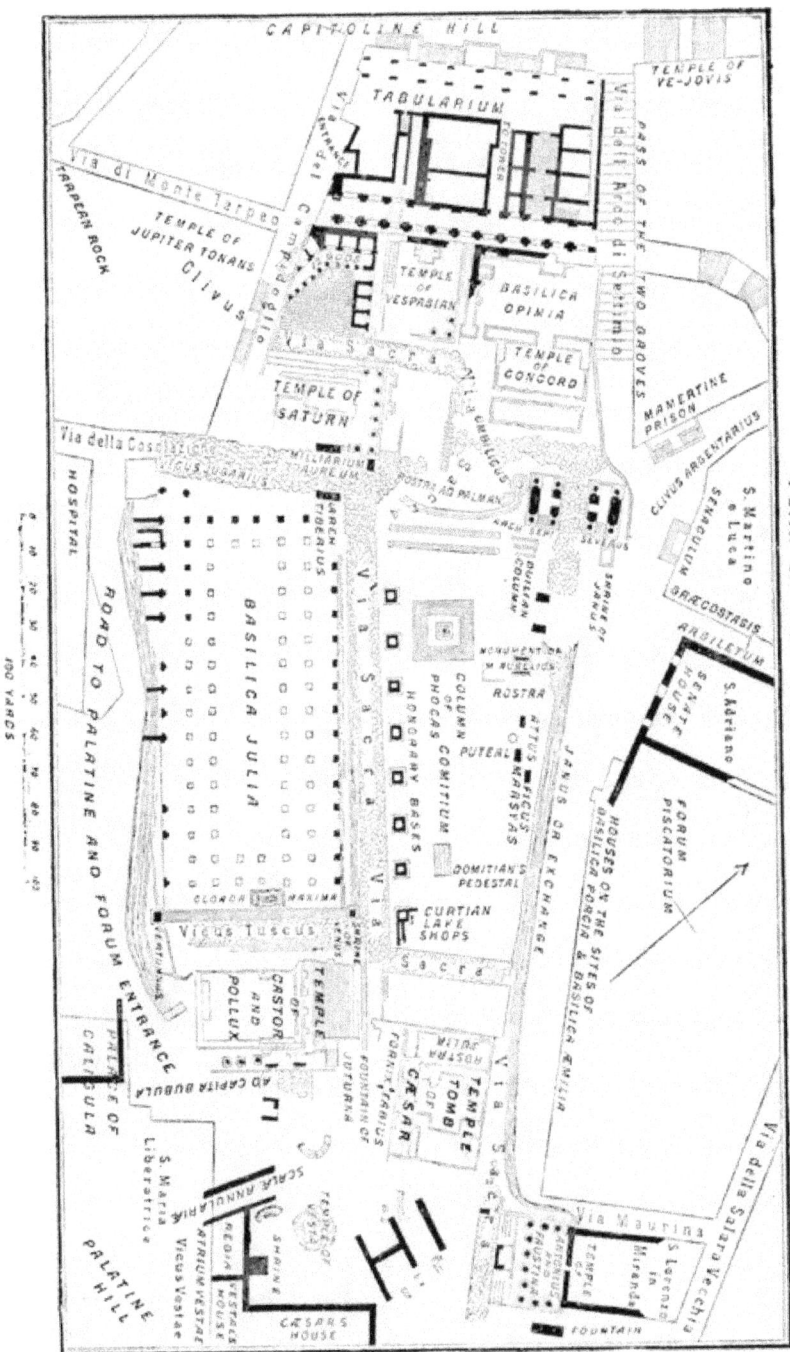

CAPITOLINE HILL

TEMPLE OF VE-JOVIS

TABULARIUM

Via delle Tre Pile

Via di Monte Tarpeo

TARPEAN ROCK

TEMPLE OF JUPITER TONANS

Clivus Capitolinus

PASS OF THE TWO GROVES

TEMPLE OF VESPASIAN

BASILICA OPIMIA

MAMERTINE PRISON

Via Sacra

TEMPLE OF CONCORD

TEMPLE OF SATURN

VIA UMBILICUS

Via della Consolazione

CLIVUS JUGARIUS

MILLIARIUM AUREUM

ROSTRA AD PALMAM

ARCH SEPT. SEVERUS

CLIVUS ARGENTARIUS

S. Martino e Luca

SENACULUM

GRÆCOSTASIS

ARCH OF SEPT. SEVERUS

SHRINE OF JANUS

HOSPITAL

ARCH OF TIBERIUS

BASILICA JULIA

DUILIAN COLUMN

MONUMENT OF M. AURELIUS

SHRINE OF JANUS

ARGILETUM

S. Adriano SENATE HOUSE

ROAD TO PALATINE AND FORUM ENTRANCE

Via Sacra

COLUMN OF PHOCAS

COMITIUM

HONORARY BASES

ROSTRA

PUTEAL

ATTIUS NÆVIUS

FICUS RUMINALIS

JANUS OR EXCHANGE

FORUM PISCATORIUM

DOMITIAN'S PEDESTAL

CURTIAN LAKE

SHOPS

HOUSES ON THE SITES OF BASILICA PORCIA & BASILICA EMILIA

CLOACA MAXIMA

Vicus Tuscus

TEMPLE OF CASTOR AND POLLUX

FOUNTAIN OF JUTURNA

ROSTRA JULIA

TEMPLE OF CÆSAR

TOMB OF CÆSAR

Via Sacra

Via Maurina

S. Lorenzo in Miranda

TEMPLE OF

S. Lorenzo

AD CAPITA BUBULA

FORUM JULII

Via della Salara Vecchia

SCALÆ ANNULARIA

S. Maria Liberatrice

ATRIUM VESTAE

REGIA NUMÆ HOUSE

VESTALS HOUSE

FOUNTAIN

PALACE OF CALIGULA

TEMPLE OF VESTA

SHRINE

CÆSAR'S HOUSE

PALATINE HILL

Vicus Vestae

S. Maria

ATRIUM VESTAE

100 YARDS

dust of ages was added the refuse of building materials for the new
city, till in the year 1650 we have the Forum presented to us on a
level with the modern streets, under the name of the Campo Vaccino
(the Cow-field); and thus was the Forum filled up. Such are the
fluctuations of worldly splendour!

EXTENT OF THE FORUM.

The Forum was not, as many have supposed, a building, but an
open space surrounded with buildings, the whole forming the Forum.
It was 260 yards long, and 55 yards wide at the bottom. The top, under the Capitol, was 140 yards wide. The temples were built on lofty
platforms (*podia*), to give them a more commanding appearance.

## TEMPLE OF CASTOR AND POLLUX.

Founded by Aulus Posthumius, A.U.C. 268-74, in commemoration
of the battle of Lake Regillus. It was afterwards rebuilt by Lucius
Metellus. "Tiberius dedicated the Temple of Castor and Pollux,
which had been rebuilt out of the spoils of the German war, in his
own and his brother's name" (Suetonius, "Tiberius," xx.). "Caligula
converted it into a kind of vestibule to his house" (*Ibid*, "Caligula,"
xxii.).

The three magnificent pillars still standing belonged to the side
facing the Palatine. They indicate approximately the south-east
boundary of the Forum. The narrower front looked down from a
terrace of considerable elevation upon the Forum, and was connected
with it by means of a double flight of stairs, the remains of which
were discovered during excavations made some time ago. These
pillars, as well as the fragments of the architrave and cornice supported by them, are among the most beautiful architectural remains
of ancient Rome. The ornaments of the capitals and of the entablature are as rich and splendid as they are pure and simple. It is
therefore probable that they belong to the time of Tiberius.

Pliny (x. 60) tells us of "a raven that was hatched upon the roof of
the Temple of Castor and Pollux, and flew into a bootmaker's shop
*opposite*. Every morning it used to fly to the Rostra which looked
towards the Forum (the Rostra Julia), where he would salute the
Emperor Tiberius, Germanicus, Drusus, and others, as they passed;
after which he returned to the shop. This the bird did for several
years, till the owner of an opposition shop, through jealousy, killed
him, for which the man was put to death; and such a favourite had
the bird become that he had a public funeral, and was buried in the

THE ROMAN FORUM, LOOKING TOWARDS THE CAPITOLINE HILL.

1. The Temple of Castor and Pollux.
2. The Basilica Julia.
3. Shrine of Venus.
4. Temple of Saturn.
5. Tabularium.
6. Arch of Severus.
7. Mamertine Prison.
8. Column of Phocas.
9. Temple of Vespasian.
10. Temple-tomb of Cæsar.
11. Senate House.
12. Shop.
13. Via Sacra.
14. Bases.
15. Pedestal of Domitian's Statue.
16. Puteal.
17. Marsyas.
18. Attus Navius.
19. Old Rostra.
20. Reliefs of M. Aurelius.
21. Site of Statue.
22. Portico of the 12 Gods.
23. Clivus Capitolinus.
24. Tarpeian Rock.
25. Tower of Capitol.
26. Vicus Tuscus.
27. Street of Ox Heads.
28. Curtian Lake.

field of Rediculus, on the right-hand side of the Via Appia, at the
second milestone. No such crowds had ever escorted the funeral of
any one out of the whole number of Rome's distinguished men."

*The Church of S. Maria Liberatrice, on our right, occupies the site of*

## THE REGIA NUMÆ.

"Numa erected a palace near the Temple of Vesta, called to this
day Regia" (Plutarch, "Numa"). Horace (O. i. 2) says : "We see
the tawny Tiber, its waves violently forced back from the Tuscan
shore, proceed to demolish the monumental Regia (Numæ) and the
Temple of Vesta." It was the residence of the Pontifex Maximus,
or chief priest, down to the time of Augustus. "Augustus presented
the Regia to the Vestal Virgins, because it adjoined their residence"
(Dion Cassius, liv. 27). In the sixteenth century twelve inscriptions
relative to the Virgins were found near the church.

*Opposite the church*, on the level of the Forum, is the round podium
of

## THE TEMPLE OF VESTA.

"Numa erected the Temple of Vesta (A.U.C. 37) between the Capitoline and Palatine Hills; the Forum in which this temple was built
lying between them" (Dionysius, ii. 66). "It was made round, as a
symbol of the earth" (Ovid, "Fasti," vi. 265). "The roof was covered
with bronze of Syracuse" (Pliny, xxxiv. 7). It was destroyed by fire
under Nero and Commodus, and rebuilt by Vespasian and Septimius
Severus. It was the conservatory of the Palladium and Holy fire.
The number of Virgins was originally four, afterwards increased to
six. They were bound to their ministry for thirty years. If they
broke their vow they were buried alive: they took their vows for
thirty years. "Ten years they were being instructed in their duties,
ten years they practised them, and ten years they passed in instructing others" (Plutarch).

*On the opposite corner of the Forum* ten columns and the side
walls remain of

## THE TEMPLE OF ANTONINUS AND FAUSTINA.

Erected by Antoninus Pius, A.D. 160; and dedicated by the Senate
on his death to himself and wife, who were deified, as we learn from
the inscription,—

DIVO. ANTONINO. ET. DIVAE. FAUSTINAE. EX. S. C.

The vestibule of this edifice, composed of ten Corinthian pillars
of variegated green marble (cipollino) supporting an architrave and

part of the cellæ, built of square blocks of peperino, still remain. The architrave is adorned at each side with arabesque candelabra guarded, as it were, by griffins.

The portico was excavated in 1876: the ascent to the Temple from the Via Sacra was found to be by a flight of twenty-one steps, fifteen feet in height. The portico now fulfils the same office to the Church of S. Lorenzo in Miranda, which we understand is to be pulled down.

*Between this temple and our vantage point* a mass of rubble work marks the site of

## THE TEMPLE-TOMB OF JULIUS CÆSAR.

Ovid ("Met." xv., "Let." ii. 2), describes it as "close to Castor and Pollux, having its aspect towards the Forum and the Capitol." "They [the Triumvirs] likewise built a tomb to Julius Cæsar in the middle of the Forum, with an asylum, that should be for ever inviolable" (Dion Cassius, "Aug."). Before the temple was built, "a column of Numidian marble, formed of one stone twenty feet high, was erected to Cæsar in the Forum, inscribed—TO THE FATHER OF HIS COUNTRY" (Suetonius, "Cæsar," lxxxv.). This gave place to the temple, which had four columns in front, as we learn from a relief and a coin. It was decorated with the statues of the Julian line. "About the time of the death of Nero, the Temple of Cæsar being struck with lightning, the heads of all the statues in it fell off at once; and Augustus's sceptre was dashed from his hand" (Suetonius, "Galba").

*We must now call attention to the buildings between the Temple of Antoninus and the Church of S. Adriano on the line of the houses shortly to be pulled down : but till the excavations are made, we cannot be certain of the details. Next to the temple stood*

## THE BASILICA ÆMILIA.

In B.C. 180, "Marcus Fulvius made contracts for a court of justice behind the new bankers' shops" (Livy, xl. 51). It was destroyed by fire, and rebuilt by Paullus Æmilius, B.C. 53.

Plutarch says that Paullus expended on it the large sum of money he had received from Cæsar as a bribe.

Pliny (xxxvi. 24) tells us it was celebrated for its columns of Phrygian marble.

*For explanation of the word Basilica, see page 84.*
*Between this and the Church of S. Adriano stood*

## THE BASILICA PORCIA.

In B.C. 185, "Cato purchased for the use of the people the two houses, Mænius and Titius, in the Lautumiæ, and four shops, erecting on that ground a court of justice, which was called the Porcian" (Livy, xxxix. 44). "The tribunes likewise opposed him very much in his building, at the public charge, a hall below the Senate House, by the Forum, which he finished notwithstanding, and called it the Porcian Basilica" (Plutarch, in "Cato").

This is where the tribunes of the people used to hold their courts. It was destroyed by fire at the same time as the Curia.

*Behind was*

## THE FORUM PISCATORIUM,

or Fish-Market. Plautus ("Capteivei," Act iv., Scene 2) says "that the stench of the fish frequently drove the frequenters of the Basilica Porcia into the Forum Romanum."

The Market was destroyed by fire B.C. 212 (Livy, xxvi. 27), and rebuilt B.C. 180 (Livy, xl. 51). "Marcus Fulvius contracted for the rebuilding of the Fish-Market."

*In this district was also*

## THE LAUTUMIÆ.

It was not only a district near the Forum, but a prison, as the name signifies, made out of stone quarries. It is first mentioned (B.C. 212) by Livy (xxvi. 27) in his account of the fire. Livy (xxxii. 26; xxxvii. 3) says it was a place for the custody of hostages and prisoners of war. When Q. M. Celer the consul was imprisoned there by the tribune L. Flavius, Celer attempted to assemble the Senate in it (Dion Cassius, xxxvii. 50); so we may infer that it was a large building. The *Lautumiæ* was *entirely distinct* from the Mamertine Prison.

*The church with the plain front, S. Adriano, and the house with the green shutters, occupy the site of*

## THE SENATE HOUSE,

originally built by Tullus Hostilius one hundred years after the foundation of Rome, and called the Curia Hostilia. "He built a Senate House, which retained the name Hostilia even within the memory of our fathers" (Livy, i. 30).

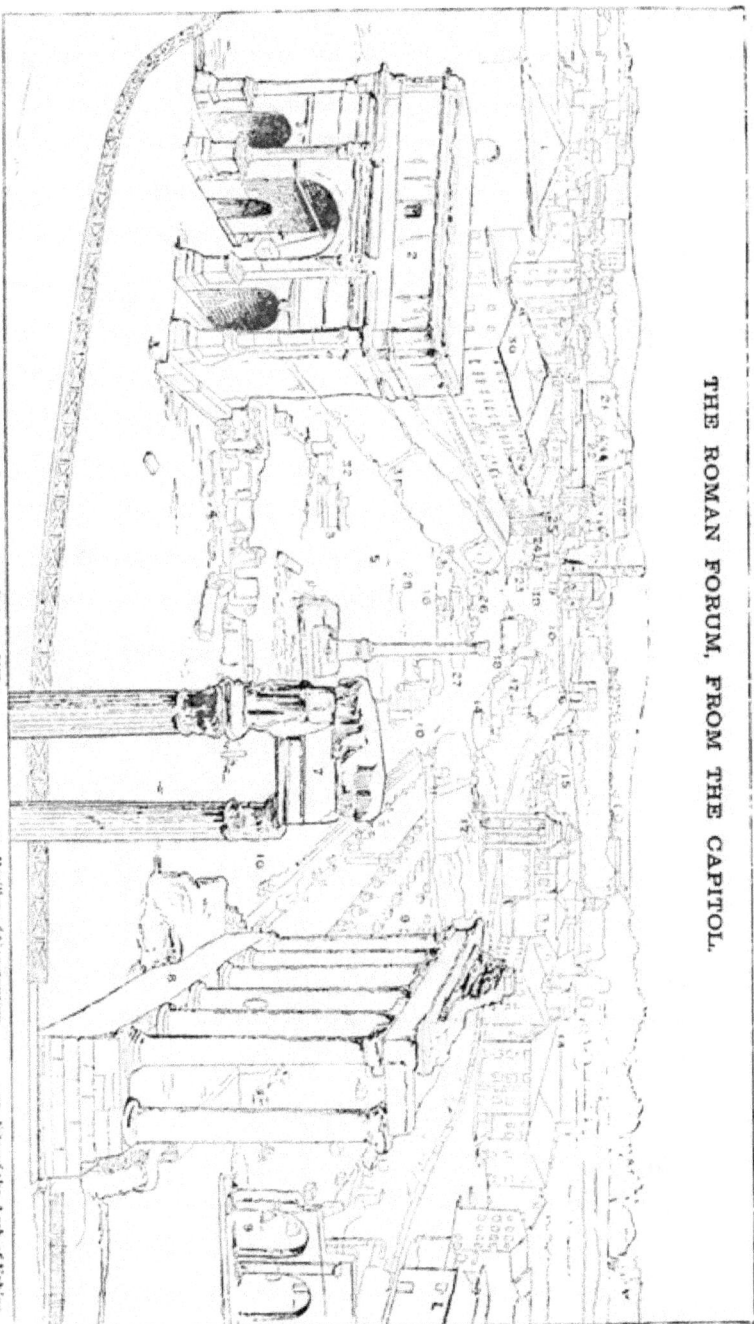

THE ROMAN FORUM, FROM THE CAPITOL.

1. Senate House.
2. Arch of Septimius Severus.
3. Monument of Marcus Aurelius.
4. Rostra ad Palisnan, S. Cosnitium.
5. Column of Phocas.
6. Column of Phocas.
7. Temple of Vespasian.

8. Temple of Saturn.
9. Basilica Julia.
10. Vicus Tuscus.
11. Vicus Tuscus.
12. Temple of Castor and Pollux.
13. Palace of Caligula.
14. Temple of Vesta.

15. Palatine Hill.
16. Arch of Titus.
17. House of Cæsar.
18. Arcade of the Pearl-Dealers.
19. S. Francesca, Forum of Cupid.
20. Colosseum.

21. Basilica of Constantine.
22. Temple of Venus and Roma.
23. Temple of the Penates.
24. Temple of Romulus.
25. Temple of Antoninus Pius.
26. Temple-Tomb of Cæsar.

27. Site of the Arch of Fabius.
28. Curtian Lake.
29. Site of Basilica Æmilia.
30. Site of Basilica Porcia.
31. The Janus or Exchange.
32. Site of Original Rostra.

It was destroyed by fire when the body of the tribune Clodius was burned, A.U.C. 702. Rebuilt by Faustus, the son of Sylla. Destroyed a second time, to do away with the name of Sylla, on pretence of erecting the Temple of Felicity ; rebuilt by Julius Cæsar, A.U.C. 711, completed by the Triumvirs, and consecrated by Augustus, who named it the Curia Julia. Again destroyed by fire under Titus, and rebuilt by Domitian, and called Senatus.

It was approached by a flight of steps; for "Tarquin carried old Servius out of the Curia, and threw him down the steps to the bottom " (Livy, i. 48).

This was the proper Senate House ; and when we read of the senators meeting in other places, there was always some special reason for their so doing. The tradition of the church, S. Adriano, is, that it was erected out of the remains of the Senate House, the bronze doors of which were carried off to the Lateran by Alexander VII., where they still remain.

An anonymous writer, quoted by Eckhard, states that in A.D. 283, under Carinus, a fire destroyed the Curia Julia, the Græcostasis, the Basilica Julia, and the Forum of Cæsar, all of which were restored by Diocletian, 290. The Senate House seems to have been again destroyed, and rebuilt by Flavianus, prefect of the city, in 399, under the title of "Secretarium Senatus;" another prefect, Eucharius, restored it in 407.

*The Church of S. Martina occupies the site of*

## THE GRÆCOSTASIS AND SENACULUM.

Varro ("Ling. Lat.," v. 155) says : " The Græcostasis was on the right of the Curia, and projected in front of it; and here the Senate received the foreign ambassadors in audience. The Senaculum lay above the Græcostasis, and towards the Temple of Concord, and the senators deliberated in this building with the magistrates who were not entitled to enter the Senate House."

Between S. Martino and S. Adriano the Via Bonella runs out of the Forum on the line of

## THE ARGILETUM,

which passed through the Fora of Cæsar and Augustus to the Suburra. It was the Paternoster Row of ancient Rome. " Thou preferrest, little book, to dwell in the shops in the Argiletum" (Martial, i. 3).

*At its entrance stood*

## THE BRONZE SHRINE OF JANUS.

In A.U.C. 39, "Numa built a shrine to Janus, near the foot of the hill Argiletum, which was to notify a state either of war or peace" (Livy, i. 19). Ovid ("Fasti," i. 259) says, "Thou hast a shrine adjoining two Fora" (the Forum of Cæsar and the Roman Forum). "There was a Janus in the Forum before the Curia. This temple was made entirely of bronze, and of a square form; it was hardly large enough to hold the figure of Janus. The bronze image was four cubits high; in other respects like a man, except that it had two faces, one look-ing towards the east and the other towards the west. There were bronze doors in each front" (Procopius, "Bel. Got." i. 20). A brick podium under the right end column of the Arch of Severus marks its site.

*Somewhat in the foreground is*

## THE ARCH OF SEPTIMIUS SEVERUS,

erected, A.D. 205, in honour of the emperor and his two sons, Cara-calla and Geta, by the senate and people of Rome.* The sculptures

adorning it are interesting, and re-present his victories over the Par-thians, Arabians, and Adiabenes.

A chariot, containing the statues of the emperor and his sons, drawn by six horses (now in S. Mark's, Venice), stood on the summit. The sculptures represent details of the Roman mili-tary harangues, sieges, camps, assaults with battering-rams, and the submis-sion of prisoners. The front towards the Forum represents the emperor addressing his troops, the taking of Carrha, the siege of Nisibis. The front facing the Capitol represents another harangue, the siege of Atra, and the passage of the Euphrates and Tigris.

*In front of the arch are the bases of*

## THE DUILIAN COLUMN,

erected A.U.C. 493. "Caius Duilius was the first to gain a naval triumph

DUILIAN COLUMN.

* S. P. Q. R., Senatus Populusque Romanus.

over the Carthaginians: his column still remains in the Forum"
(Pliny, xxxiv. 11). It was of bronze, made out of the rostra
of the captured ships. Being struck by lightning, it was restored by Germanicus, under Tiberius, and part of his inscription
is still to be seen in the column made to receive it by Michael
Angelo in the Palazzo dei Conservatori, on the Capitol.

### THE MÆNIA COLUMN

"was erected in honour of C. Mænius, who conquered the ancient
Latins, A.U.C. 416, and to whom the Romans gave a third of the
spoil" (Pliny, xxxiv. 11).

*Immediately behind the Arch of Severus are the remains of*

### OPIMIUS'S TEMPLE OF CONCORD.

Here was originally a shrine erected by Flavius. Livy (ix. 46) says,
"In A.U.C. 449, to the great displeasure of the nobles, Caius Flavius performed the dedication of the Temple of Concord, in the area of Vulcan."

Pliny (xxxiii. 6) gives us further particulars, and points out the exact
site :—" Flavius made a vow that he would consecrate a temple to
Concord, if he should succeed in reconciling the privileged orders
with the plebeians ; and as no part of the public funds could be voted
for the purpose, he accordingly built a small shrine of bronze near
the Græcostasis, then situated above the Comitium, with the fines
which had been exacted for usury.

" Here, too, he had an inscription engraved upon a tablet of brass,
to the effect that the shrine was dedicated 203 years after the consecration of the Capitoline Jupiter."

The third temple, Livy (xxii. 33) says, " was erected in the Citadel,
A.U.C. 538, the Temple of Concord vowed by the Prætor Lucius Manlius, on occasion of the mutiny of some soldiers in Gaul, A.U.C. 536."

The fourth temple was dedicated to Concord by the Consul Lucius
Opimius, after the death of Gracchus, A.U.C. 632. Appianus (i. 26) says "it
was in the Forum." Varro ("L.L." v.) says, "The Senaculum was above
the Græcostasis, towards the Temple of Concord and Basilica Opimia."
Festus says it was " between the Capitoline Hill and the Forum."

The Senaculum was distinct from the Curia. Thus Livy (li. 27)
says, "The censors constructed a portico from the Temple of Saturn
on the Capitol to the Senaculum, which was above the Curia." The
inscription has been preserved to us :—

S. P. Q. R. AEDEM CONCORDIAE VETVSTATE COLLAPSAM IN MELIOREM
FACEM OPERE ET CVLTV SPLENDIDIORE RESTITVERVNT.

## THE BASILICA OPIMIA.

At the back of the ruins of the temple are the remains of the Basilica Opimia. Part of the ground-plan is shown on a fragment of the marble map of Rome, with a fragment of a basilica behind. On examination of the ruins, the two buildings can be distinctly made out.

In front are the ruins of the steps and portico, with the cella behind. There seems to have been at the back of the cella an entrance into the basilica, both being closed with independent doors. The marble threshold of the temple is *in situ*, and upon it is cut a *caduceus*, the emblem of Concord, which was once filled in with bronze ; parallel to this, but distinct, is the marble threshold of the basilica, with the holes where the pivots of the doors turned. Under the podium of the basilica is a long narrow vault of *opus incertum*, but it does *not* lead into the Tabularium, that being built long afterwards, A.U.C. 675, as the old inscription records, B.C.78. It was probably the place where the utensils for the temple were deposited. Some of the marble decorations of the basilica still remain ; and this was no doubt the hall used when the Senate are spoken of as having sat in the Temple of Concord. "The Senate assembled in the building near the Temple of Concord" (Dion Cassius, lviii. 2). "In this temple, in which, whilst I was advising the Senate, you placed around it armed men" (Cicero, "2 Phil." vii. and viii.). "Here, in this Cella of Concord, on the slope of the Capitol."

It may be that this is the basilica spoken of in later times as the Basilica Argentaria, probably taking that name from being frequented by the silversmiths. It was restored, after a fire, by Septimius Severus, and the inscription quoted is probably of his date. In A.D. 731–741, Pope Gregory III. turned the remains into a Christian church, which exists no longer. In 1817, three inscriptions were found here, referring to the temple and basilica. Cicero ("Per Sest." lxvii.) tell us "that the monuments of L. Opimius in the Forum were very much frequented."

A Temple of Concord seems to have been decorated with many statues, but there is nothing to show whether it was that of Camillus on the Capitol, or Opimius's.

"Piston also made the statues of Mars and Mercury, which are in the Temple of Concord at Rome." "Sthenius made the statues of Ceres, Jupiter, and Minerva, which are now in the Temple of Concord." "Augustus consecrated in the Temple of Concord, as something marvellous, four figures of elephants made of obsidian stone." "Also, a picture of Marsyas bound by Leuxis" (Pliny, xxxiv. 19, xxxv. 36, xxxvi. 67).

"Vitellius left the palace to lay down the ensigns of sovereignty in the Temple of Concord" (Tacitus, "II." iii. 68).

*To the left is*

## THE TEMPLE OF VESPASIAN.

Vespasian having rendered such services by restoring the Capitol, and collecting the records in the Tabularium, no more suitable site could be found for the erection of a temple to the deified emperor than in front of an old entrance to this latter building. The three pillars, which are all that remain of the building, stand upon a lofty terrace; and the skill of the architect in concealing the limited depth of the space allotted to the temple is shown in his having placed the columns of the flank nearer to each other than those of the front.

The beauty of this ruin excites universal admiration. It approaches that of the Temple of Castor and Pollux in the Forum. The inscription on the architrave, copied, whilst still entire, by a monk of the monastery of Einsiedeln, in the eighth century, refers to the restoration of the building by Septimius Severus and Caracalla, who appear to have also restored other sanctuaries in the same neighbourhood.

DIVO. VESPASIANO. S. P. Q. R. IMP. CAES. SERVUS.

ET. ANTONINUS. PII. FELIC. AUG. RESTITUER.

*Looking across the front of this temple is*

## THE TEMPLE OF SATURN.

"The temple was consecrated to Saturn, upon the ascent leading from the Forum to the Capitol. Before this, the altar erected by the followers of Hercules stood there" (Dionysius, vi. 1. See *ibid.*, i. 34).

Only eight Ionic columns, with their capitals and architraves, remain. It was on the steps of this temple that the generals took the oath that they had given a correct account of their spoil and prisoners. It contained the public treasury, and, according to Solinus, was called the Treasury of Saturn. Livy (ii. 21) says, "In the consulate of Aulus Sempronius and Marcus Minucius, A.U.C. 257, the Temple of Saturn was dedicated." Plutarch says, "Publicola appointed the Temple of Saturn to be the treasury, which they still make use of for that purpose, and empowered the people to choose two young men as quæstors or treasurers." The inscription is still *in situ*.

SENATUS. POPULUSQUE. ROMANUS. INCENDIO.

CONSUMPTUM. RESTITUIT.

TEMPLE OF VESPASIAN, TABULARIUM, AND
PORTICO OF THE TWELVE GODS.

## THE MILLIARIUM AUREUM,

or Golden Milestone, set up by Augustus (Dion Cassius, liv. 5), the
site of which is at the angle of the temple on the side of the old
Clivus Capitolinus, the ancient road leading up from the Forum.  It
was a gilded stone, on which the distance of all the principal towns
was recorded, the distance being always measured from the city
gates.  Suetonius ("Otho," vi.) tells that "Otho gave his accomplices
notice to wait for him in the Forum near the Temple of Saturn, at
the Golden Milestone."  Tacitus ("II." i. 27) relates the same ; and
Plutarch (in "Galba") agrees with them both, adding, "There ter-
minate all the great roads in Italy."

*Behind the Temple of Saturn, in the corner, is*

## THE PORTICO OF THE TWELVE GODS,

the Schola Xantha, and the portico of the Dii Consentes, restored
by Visconti in 1858, marked by eight Corinthian columns, partly
modern, but with antique capitals and architraves; and the cellæ
arranged in compact masonry behind them.  It was called the Schola
Xantha, from Fabius Xanthus, a curator of the monuments, who
placed here the images of the household gods of Rome—Dii Consentes,
because admitted to the council of Jove—Juno, Vesta, Minerva,
Ceres, Diana, Venus, Mars, Mercurius, Jovi', Neptunus, Vulcanus,
Apollo (Ennius).  The inscription tells us they were reinstated under
Vettius Pretextatus, A.D. 367.

*Facing towards the Forum, at the back of the line of buildings at its
top, is*

## THE TABULARIUM.

(See page 169.)

*In front of the Senate House, S. Adriano, is*

## THE COLUMN OF PHOCAS,

which formerly supported the statue of that emperor.  It faced the
Senate House; and is placed upon a pedestal rising from a pyramidal
basement of steps, the whole evidently the plunder of other edifices.

It was erected by Smaragdus, the Exarch of Italy, in A.D. 608, and
was excavated by the Countess of Devonshire in 1816.

It is thus mentioned by Byron,—

> "Tully was not so eloquent as thou,
> Thou nameless column with the buried base!"
>
> *Childe Harold,* iv. 90.

*Between the Temples of Saturn and Castor are the remains of*

## THE BASILICA JULIA,

on the site of the Basilica Sempronia, erected by Sempronius Grac chus, B.C. 169 (Livy, xliv. 16). This was burned down, and rebuilt by Julius Cæsar, and called Julia, after his daughter. It was destroyed by fire, and rebuilt by Augustus (Dion Cassius, "Augustus"). It was again destroyed by fire, and rebuilt A.D. 283. Suetonius tells us that Caligula, "during three days successively, scattered money to a prodigious amount among the people, from the top of the Julian Basilica" ("Caligula," xxxvii.). It is shown on two pieces of the marble plan.

In the "Mon. Ancyr.," Augustus says, "He rebuilt the Basilica Julia between the Temples of Castor and Saturn." Thus we see that the Will of Augustus, the marble plan, and the ruins, all three exactly agree. The portico was dedicated to his grandsons, Lucius and Caius (Suetonius, "Augustus," xxix.). It was the great court of appeal. (See Pliny, Jr., "Letters," v. 21, vi. 33.)

The old pavement has been well exposed, and put in proper condi-tion for preservation ; the remnants of frieze, and cornices, and columns found in the diggings have been set up on brick pedestals,— an innovation of Signor Rossa's. The old bits of pavement have been very smoothly linked together by the laying of Venetian mosaic cement, and the contrast between the modern and the antique is very apparent.

The principal streets that ran into the Forum were :—

## THE VIA SACRA.

It commenced on the Palatine Hill at the Ædem Larum. Passing by the Arch of Titus, it turned to the left : thus far it was called the Clivus Palatinus and Summa Sacra Via ; the slope down to the Forum was called the Clivus Sacer. It entered the Forum at the Temple of Antoninus, past which it turned again to the left, passing in front of the Temple of Cæsar ; then turning to the right, passed through the centre of the Forum to the foot of the Capitol. The ascent here was called the Clivus Capitolinus. It was paved B.C. 174 (Livy, xli. 27).

Its windings are easily accounted for when we remember that it had to come from the top of the Palatine to the top of the Capitoline, passing through a narrow valley. It was called the Sacred Way from the sacred processions that passed along it, and from the sacred buildings that lined it.

*Between the Basilica Julia and the Temple of Castor*

## THE VICUS TUSCUS

ran to the forum of the cattle-dealers and Circus Maximus. "They had ground allotted to them for building houses, which was afterwards called the Vicus Tuscus" (Livy, ii. 14). "Verres had caused it to be paved so badly, that he made a point of never going along the street that he had taken the contract for paving" (Cicero, "Ver." i. 59). It was the route for the festal processions to the Circus and Aventine. Where it entered the Forum was a statue of the Tuscan god Vertumnus, the base of which statue was found near where the street first touched the Basilica Julia. This street was sometimes called the Vicus Thurarius, from the perfumers' shops.

## THE VICUS JUGARIUS

went out of the Via Sacra between the Temple of Saturn and the Basilica Julia, running under the Capitol to the Porta Carmentalis, the gate in the wall from the Capitol to the river that led into the forum of the vegetable-dealers. Where it left the Via Sacra it was spanned by the Arch of Tiberius, erected A.D. 16 in commemoration of the lost eagles of Varus being recovered by Germanicus (Tacitus, "Annals," ii. 41). In this street was the Lacus Servilius.

Under our (right) side of the Temple of Castor are some remains of

## THE STREET OF THE OX-HEADS.

From the Porta Romana on the Palatine, a short street went to the right out of the Via Nova into the Forum, ending between the Temples of Castor and Vesta. "It chanced that I was returning from the festival of Vesta by that way by which the Nova Via is *now* joined to the Roman Forum" (Ovid, " Fasti," vi. 395.) We wish Mr. Naso had been a little more explicit, and had given us the name of this short street; but we will endeavour to demonstrate what the name of this street was. We know from Suetonius that under the Palatine was the temple to the deified Augustus, and over it Caligula built his bridge, connecting the Palatine with the Capitol. Now, at the corner of the Palatine we have the ascent to this bridge remaining, so that it will not be difficult to find the probable site of the Temple of Augustus (Suetonius, " Caligula," xxii.). Dedicated in 37 A.D. by Caligula (Dion. lix. 7), the temple, Servius says, was near the Tuscan colony. Suetonius tells us it was on the site of the house in which he was born, and gives us the name of the street: "In the quarter of the Palatine Hill, and the street called the Ox-heads, where *now*

stands a temple dedicated to him, and built a little after his death"
("Aug." v.). We conclude from the above that the probable name of
this short street was AD CAPITA BUBULA, and in confirmation of this,
ox-heads may still be seen sculptured on the fragments found at the
end of this street, between the Temples of Castor and Vesta.

## MINOR STREETS.

We must call attention to a cross street that ran from the Clivus
Capitolinus to the Prison and the Clivus Argentarius, the name of
which we cannot determine, unless it was reckoned part of the
Argentarius. When the triumphal processions arrived at this point,
the general and prisoners separated. He went up the Capitol to
sacrifice, they to the Prison to death.

The road passing under the Arch of Severus is of very late date,
and artificially formed. It ran from the cross street down the north
side of the Forum for a short distance, when it turns to the left,
apparently passing out of the Forum between the Curia and the
Basilica Porcia. The roads, as a rule, did not pass under the triumphal arches, as they are represented on reliefs and coins, with the
archways occupied with statues.

*The open paved space, which was very much larger in the time of the
Republic, was called*

## THE COMITIUM.

Varro says it was so called "from *coïre*, to meet,—the place of the
ratification of the treaty between the Romans and Sabines." Livy
tells us "it was an open space marked out in the Forum, where the
assemblies called Comitia Curiata took place for the purpose of
electing ministers of religious rites, making laws of a certain description, and deciding some suits, and inflicting punishment on criminals."

Domitian ordered the gallants of Cornelius, the president of the
Vestal Virgins, to be whipped to death with rods in the Comitium.

A line of seven brick bases for honorary statues occupies one side :
the edge of the paved area marks the top ; the remains of a row of
shops, destroyed by Signor Rossa in 1872, the bottom. The line of
the modern road on the right was called

## THE JANUS.

This was the Roman Exchange, where the money-changers trans-
acted their business, and must not be confounded with the Temple
of Janus already mentioned ; nor must it be thought that there were
a series of arches here, as some authors have supposed. Horace says

(Sat. ii. 3), "Since all my fortunes were dissipated at the middle exchange" (Janus).    Again (Ep. i. 1), "O citizens, money is to be sought first; virtue after riches.   This is inculcated from the top to the bottom of 'change."   He here distinguishes the *summus, medius,* and *imus,* or the top, middle, and bottom of the exchange.

## SHRINE OF VENUS.

Having thus pointed out the principal buildings of the Forum, we will descend to its level, and identify some of its historical sites.

*At the left-hand corner* of the Vicus Tuscus and the Via Sacra, a

DEATH OF VIRGINIA.

brick pedestal marks the site of the Shrine of Venus Cloacina, erected in commemoration of Tarquin making the Cloaca Maxima.  *Cloacina* comes from *cluere = purgare,* to purge.

## THE DEATH OF VIRGINIA.

*Opposite* this shrine, facing up the Vicus Tuscus, is some brick-work—remains of a line of shops that faced towards the Temple of Cæsar, and which were destroyed by Signor Rossa in making the excavations. The end shop only was saved. This was the site of the butcher's stall from which Virginius snatched the knife that saved his daughter's honour.

"Virginius demanded to speak with Virginia; and permission being granted, he drew the maiden and her nurse aside to the shops near the shrine of Cloacina, now called the new shops, and there, snatching a knife from a butcher's stall, plunged it into his daughter's breast" (Livy, iii. 48).

## THE FOUNTAIN OF JUTURNA.

*At the left-hand corner*, facing the Temple of Castor, the oval basin of this fountain has been cleared, and the spring which supplied it is covered with an iron grating, and has been turned into the Cloaca. It is no doubt the same at which the twin-gods, Castor and Pollux, washed their horses after fighting for Rome in the battle of Lake Regillus, when they announced to the people that the battle was won. Similar stories are told by Florus. When the Romans conquered Perses, king of Macedonia, the twin-gods washed themselves at the Lake of Juturna; and when they defeated the Tigurini, the gods were seen to deliver a letter to the prætor in front of their temple.

Juturna was the sister of Turnus, immortalized by Jupiter, and turned into a fountain, whose waters were used in Vesta's sacrifices, and had curative powers.

## THE FORNIX FABIUS

stood between the Temples of Cæsar and Castor; some slight remains can still be seen. It was erected to Fabius Maximus, the conqueror of the Allobroges, now Savoy. It was erected B.C. 121, being the first triumphal arch in the Forum. The Romans originally called their triumphal arch *fornix*, not *arcus*.

The pseudo-Ascon says it stood before the Temple of Castor. The inscription was found in the sixteenth century, and is given by Gruter, ccccvi. 5— Q . FABIO . ALLOBROGICINO
MAXIMO.

Another fragment is given in the Vatican Codex, 3368, 4—

Q . FABIUS . Q . F . MAXIMUS . AED . CVR . REST.

Cicero is the first author who speaks of this arch, and he alludes to it several times. In "Verres" (i. 7) he says : " He (Caius Curio) sees Verres in the crowd by the Fornix Fabius. He speaks to the man, and with a loud voice congratulates him on his victory." Asconius, commenting on this passage, says: " Fornix Fabius arcus est juxta Regiam in Sacra Via a Fabio censore constructus, qui a devictis Allobrogibus Allobrox cognominatus est, ibique statua ejus posita propterea est."

3

In "Pro Plancio" (vii.) Cicero says: "When I am hustled in a crowd, and pushed against the Arch of Fabius, I do not complain to the man who is at the top of the Sacra Via, but to him who pushes me." Again ("De Orat." ii. 66) he says: "Crassus said in a speech to the people that Memmius, though himself so great a man, as he came into the Forum, stooped his head at the Arch of Fabius."

Seneca ("De Constantia Sapientis," i.) says: "Cato was dragged from the (old) Rostra to the Arch of Fabius"—that is, nearly the whole length of the Forum. Trebellius Pollio ("Saloninus Gallienus," i. 10) says: "There was at this time at the foot of the hill Romulus (Palatine) a statue, that is before the Sacred Way, between the Temples of Faustina and Vesta, near to the Arch of Fabius." This exactly describes the site.

We have two views of this arch preserved to us on ancient reliefs. The first, from the Arch of Marcus Aurelius, now on the stairway of the Palazzo dei Conservatori on the Capitol, represents the arch on the left of the Temple-Tomb of the deified Cæsar. The second, a relief on the monument of Marcus Aurelius on the Comitium, nearest the Arch of Septimius Severus, depicts the Arch of Fabius to the right of the Temple of Castor and Pollux.

*Under the bank of earth to the right of Cæsar's Temple-Tomb stood*

### THE ARCH OF AUGUSTUS.

Dion Cassius records (liv. 8) that Augustus built an arch in commemoration of the Parthian treaty near the Temple-Tomb of Cæsar. This is borne out by Maii, an interpreter of Virgil ("Æn." viii. 606), who says the Arch of Augustus was near to the temple of the deified Julius. The "Mirabilia" mentions it, and gives the same site: "Templum Minervæ cum arcu conjunctum est ei, nunc autem vocatur Sanctus Laurentius de Mirandi;" that is, the Temple of Antoninus Pius and Faustina, now the Church of San Lorenzo in Miranda. Accordingly, it was on the right of the Temple of Cæsar. Between it and the Temple of Antoninus the following inscription on marble was found in 1540-46:—

SENATVS . POPVLVSQVE . ROMANVS
IMP . CAESARI . DIVI . IVLI . F . COS . QVINCT
COS . DESIGN . SEX . IMP . SEPT
REPVBLICA CONSERVATA.
(Gruter, ccxxvi. 5.)

It is doubtful whether this refers to the Arch of Augustus or to the Temple of Cæsar, both having been built by Augustus. A coin of

Augustus represents this arch, with the legend, CIVIB . ET . SIGN . MILIT . A . PART . RECVP. In the early part of 1884, on the Via Sacra,

near the Temple of Antoninus, some thirty travertine *voussoirs*—which formed part of an arch, the diameter of which was 12 feet 17 inches—were brought to light. So far, the excavations do not show where this arch stood; but when the road between the Temples of Cæsar and Antoninus is cut away, we may hope to find the site.

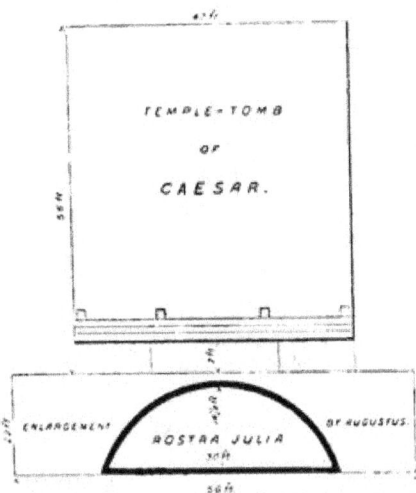

PLAN OF THE ROSTRA, AND TEMPLE-TOMB OF C.ESAR.

## THE ROSTRA JULIA.

We know from Dion Cassius that Cæsar encouraged the popular business to be carried on at the lower end of the Forum, and that he turned the steps of the Temple of Castor into a temporary rostra. On this becoming popular he built a new rostra, which was called the plebeian rostra or Rostra Julia.

HADRIAN ADDRESSING THE PEOPLE FROM THE ROSTRA JULIA.

We learn from Suetonius that it was before the Temple of Cæsar. Cicero, speaking from it against Mark Antony, bids his audience look to the (*their*) left at the gilt equestrian statue of Antony which stood before the Temple of Castor.

This is one of the most interesting spots in the Forum. Cæsar built the second rostra with its rear towards the Forum, represented by the darker lines in the above plan. In front, towards the curved edge, Antony spoke, Cæsar's body being on the level below. The body was burnt and buried " in the Forum in that place visible from the old monumental Regia of the Romans. On the spot was placed an altar *where now* is the Temple of Cæsar" (Appian, ii. 42). "The same men were erecting a tomb in the Forum who had performed that irregular funeral" (Cicero, "First Phil." ii.).

It was decorated with the rams of the captured ships of Antony and Cleopatra. It was the custom to speak from the circular edge; but when the Temple of Cæsar was built, it was erected close up to his rostra, on the site where the people had previously stood, and so they had to turn about and address the people from the flat edge. "As he was seated on the rostra at the festival of Pan, Mark Antony placed upon his brow a royal diadem" (Velleius Paterculus, ii. 56).

### MARK ANTONY'S SPEECH.

When Cæsar was killed, it was not in the Capitol, as Shakespeare makes it, nor in the Senate House upon the Forum, but in Pompey's Senate House (see page 156). From there the body was carried to his house, and next day into the Forum, on its way to the Campus Martius, and was placed in front of the Rostra Julia for some friend to make the funeral oration over it. Mark Antony mounted the rostra, and there made his famous speech, "which moved the people to that degree that they immediately burned the body in that very place, and afterwards interred his ashes" (Dion Cassius, "Cæsar").

Livy ("Epit." xcvi.) says that "Cæsar's body was burned before the plebeian rostra." Dion Cassius says his temple-tomb was built on the very spot where his body was burned.

Unfortunately Antony's address has not come down to us, so we must accept Shakespeare's immortal version.

### THE CURTIAN LAKE.

Crossing the Sacred Way, which passes along the front of Cæsar's Tomb, we arrive at the space occupied by the shops destroyed in excavating. The construction remaining shows that they were rebuilt at a late date. It will be noticed that the soil is damp and sandy. This spot was once marshy, and took its name from Mettius Curtius, a leader of the Sabines, getting mired here in the battle which took place about the carrying off of the women. Plutarch, Livy, Dionysius, and Ovid agree in this; and not from the fable related by Livy (vii. 16) of the Forum opening, and Marcus Curtius jumping in, horse, armour, and all. The former event is commemorated in a relief in stone now in the Capitol; whilst the latter fable is depicted in the marble relief now in the Borghese Museum.

### THE PEDESTAL OF THE STATUE OF DOMITIAN.

The Statue was destroyed by the people after his death, and the base of the pedestal is all we have left, standing upon the travertine pavement of the Forum. It is interesting to archæologists as putting to rest the arguments in reference to the names and positions of the different buildings in the Forum. The poet Statius ("Silvæ," i. 1, 22) describes the relative position of the different buildings and this statue. He tells us that the statue was situated in the middle of the Forum, near the Curtian Lake. In front of it was the temple of the deified Julius; behind it were the Temples of Vespasian and Concord; on one side the Basilica Julia, and on the other the Basilica Æmilia;

MARCUS CURTIUS LEAPING INTO THE GULF.
(Relief in the Villa Borghese.)

whilst the rider looked towards the Temple of Vesta and the Imperial Palace.

Suetonius tells us that the tablet inscribed upon the base of Domitian's triumphal statue was carried away by the violence of a storm, and fell upon a neighbouring monument.

*A little beyond this pedestal, to the right,* are the remains of another pedestal, a deep round hole recently closed, and beyond it a third pedestal.

*Upon the first we will place*

## THE STATUE OF MARSYAS.

Servius informs us that this statue was put up in the principal forum of every city as an emblem of civic liberty and even-handed justice. It stood in front of the old rostra. Horace and Martial both refer to it as being near the judge's seat. It had a pig-skin of wine on one shoulder, denoting the plentiful supply to the city, and had the other arm extended with the hand open, showing that every one should have equal justice.

*Over the round hole stood*

### THE PUTEAL SCRIBONIUS LIBO,

or well altar. This is shown on a coin as being round.

" At a small distance from the statue of Attus, both the hone and the razor are said to be buried under a certain altar ; the place is called *Puteus* by the Romans" (Dionysius, iii. 72). Cicero ("De Div. " i. 17) says, "It was on the Comitium, and was erected over the spot where the hone and razor were buried." (See also Horace, Ep. i. 19.)

*Upon the other base we will place*

### THE STATUE OF ATTUS NAVIUS.

" Tarquin erected a brazen statue of him in the Forum to eternalize his memory with posterity. This statue is still remaining, and stands before the Senate House, near to the holy fig-tree. It is less than a middle-sized man, and has a veil over the head" (Dionysius, iii. 72). " The statue of Attus Navius was erected before the Senate House, the pedestal of which was consumed when the Senate House itself was burned at the funeral of Publius Clodius" (Pliny, xxxiv. 11). "There was a statue of Attus, with a fillet on his head, in the place where Tarquin had the whetstone cut in two with a razor, on the Comitium, or place of assembly, just by the steps, at the left-hand side of the Senate House " (Livy, i. 36).

### THE FICUS NAVIA

was a fig-tree that, according to Festus, was planted by Tarquin in commemoration of his having had the whetstone cut in two with a razor, according to the augury of Attus Navius. It should not be confounded with the Ruminal fig-tree which grew upon the Palatine, as has been done by some writers. It is rather a curious incident that since the excavations were made, a fig-tree sprang up near the pedestal of Marsyas. This is the tree shown on the reliefs of the monument of Marcus Aurelius.

*Just beyond these three objects,* a semicircular mark on the pavement points to the site of

## THE ROSTRA.

The original Rostra was first called the Suggestum or Pulpit, but in A.U.C. 416 the name was changed into Rostra (beaks).

"The prows from the six ships captured from the Antiates were ordered to be placed as decorations on the Suggestum in the Forum, which was hence called Rostra " (Livy, viii. 14 ; Florus, i. 11 ; Pliny, xxiv. 11).

"The Rostra stood on the Comitium in front of the Curia " (Varro), from which the orators harangued the people assembled in the open air ; and it was evidently only a temporary structure, probably of wood, and not a building like the other two Rostra. It stood upon a circular basement, but the top was square : on the outside were fixed the brazen beaks which belonged to the captive vessels of the Antiates. About the Rostra were placed the statues of the ambassadors put to death by Lar Tolumnius, king of Veii, and others who suffered on similar occasions ; the three Fates, Horatius Cocles, Camillus, Hercules, the father of Vitellius, and others who deserved well of their country.

"When Caius Gracchus brought in his bill to regulate the courts of judicature, there was one thing very remarkable: whereas the orators before him, in all addresses to the people, stood with their faces towards the Senate House and the Comitium, he then, for the first time, turned the other way,—that is to say, towards the Forum,—and continued to speak in that position ever after. By this he intimated that the people ought to be addressed, and not the senate " (Plutarch).

Suetonius tells us that on the death of Augustus "two funeral orations were pronounced in his praise, one before the Temple of Julius by Tiberius, and the other before the Rostra, under the old shops, by Drusus." Some read this passage, "from the old Rostra ; " but our rendering is more correct, though in either case he is referring to the Rostra that stood in front of the Curia.

The first time Cicero spoke from the Rostra was when he delivered his oration for the Manilian Law, A.U.C. 687, when in his forty-first year. After his assassination, the head and hands of Cicero were placed upon this Rostra, from where he had so often addressed the Romans—"that very Rostra, which he had made his own ; nor was there a less concourse to see him there than had formerly been to hear him " (Florus, iv. 6). "That everybody might see them in the very place where he had formerly harangued with so much vehemence " (Dion Cassius, " Augustus ").

The form of this Rostra is preserved to us, being represented on a coin.

There is an important passage in Pliny which shows the exact site of the Rostra, as it was used to mark the hour of noon. When the summoner caught sight of the sun passing the edge of the Rostra, he declared the hour of noon. A man standing on this site will roughly represent the Rostra, and as the gun fires at mid-day the edge of the sun can be seen coming past him by a person standing by the pedestal at the bank in front of S. Adriano, who will roughly represent the summoner. We have tried this numerous times with our audience, and it is the only spot on the Forum where it answers.

THE ROSTRA.

"The *accensus* of the consuls proclaiming mid-day aloud, as soon as, from the Senate House, he caught sight of the sun between the Rostra and the Græcostasis: he also proclaimed the last hour, when the sun had gone off the Mænian Column to the Prison" (Pliny, vii. 60).

### THE MONUMENT OF MARCUS AURELIUS.*

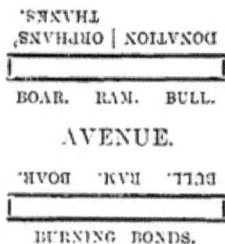

In excavating the open space of the Comitium upon the Forum in the summer of 1872, an interesting discovery was made of two marble screens or balustrades sculptured on each side, the one

* For a full detailed account of this important discovery see our photograph, a panoramic view of the Forum from ancient reliefs, with descriptive letterpress.

being some historic scene, the other representing animals. At the time, and since their discovery, many suggestions have been offered as to their signification and use, but none seemed satisfactory, at least to us. After considerable thought, examination of the ground, and putting this and that together, we have arrived at an estimate of their use and meaning entirely different from the hitherto received opinion ; in which we are supported by their construction and the classic passages relating to them. They are *in situ* as found, but a new piece of marble has been put under them.

From this it will be seen that we have made an important discovery bearing upon the topography of the Forum, which will be of interest not only to classical students, but to every one interested in the word Rome.

We have discovered that the reliefs on the screens upon the Comitium in the Forum portray scenes from the life of Marcus Aurelius, showing in their backgrounds the buildings occupying two sides of the Forum—from the Temple of Concord to the Arch of Fabius—and that these marble balustrades led up to the statue of that emperor. The space where it stood can be plainly traced upon the pavement ; and that is why these pictures refer to epochs of his life. The statue is still existing, and now stands in the square of the Capitol, where it was erected by Michael Angelo, who brought it from the Lateran in 1538, where it had been placed about 1187, when it was removed from the Forum, near the Column of Phocas, where it had long been looked upon as a statue of Constantine, and is so called in the Regiona Catalogue; hence its preservation.

The whole group was evidently erected in honour of Marcus Aurelius, and in commemoration of the important events in his life depicted on the screens, as recorded by Dion Cassius.

The first relief represents a scene upon the Forum between the old Rostra Marsyas and the fig-tree—burning the forty-six years' arrears of debts which Marcus Aurelius had forgiven the people.

" After that he remitted all that had been due to the Public and Imperial Treasuries for the course of forty-six years, without including therein Hadrian's reign, and ordered all the papers of claims to be burned in the Forum " (Dion Cassius, " Marcus Aurelius ").

This was on the marriage of his son Commodus with Crispina.

It will be noticed that the relief is to the right of the fig-tree and Marsyas. Now, if we go round to the other relief, we have the same tree and Marsyas in the same relative positions ; but the relief is to the left, and the scenes are taking place between the Rostra Julia, the fig-tree, and Marsyas :—

Giving the donation of eight pieces of gold.

Roma, or perhaps Faustina, thanking him for the Puellæ Faustinianæ.

"After he had come back to Rome, as he was one day haranguing the people, and speaking of the number of years he had spent abroad in his expeditions, the citizens with a loud voice cried out, 'Eight,' at the same time extending their hands to receive as many pieces of gold. The emperor, smiling, repeated, 'Eight,' and ordered every Roman eight pieces, which was so considerable a sum, that so great a one was never given before by any emperor" (Dion Cassius, "Marcus Aurelius").

It will be noticed that two men are holding up their hands with fingers extended, one five, the other three—eight.

The other scene on this relief represents a female figure advancing to the seated figure of the Emperor Marcus Aurelius, leading a child and carrying another, to thank him for the orphan schools he founded in Rome in memory of his wife after her death, and which he named after her. "New Faustinian schools he instituted in honour of his dead wife" (Julius Capitolinus, "M. Antoninus," xxvi.).

## THE SUOVETAURILIA.

Upon the inner sides of the Avenue are represented on each balustrade a boar, a ram, and a bull—the animals offered at the triple sacrifice, or *suovetaurilia* (from *sus, ovis, taurus*), which was performed once every five years, or *lustrum*, for the purification of the city.

It was an institution of Servius Tullius, the ceremony consisting in leading the boar, ram, and bull thrice round the assembly of the people, and then offering them to Mars. There is a similar representation upon a relief of Trajan on the Arch of Constantine, and upon a pedestal found near the Arch of Septimius Severus.

*To our left of the Arch of Severus is*

## THE ROSTRA AD PALMAM.

Neither the position nor the construction of this Rostra answers to that of the original Suggestum, which took the name of Rostra from having fixed on it the *six* bronze beaks of the Antiates' ships. The original Rostra, shown on a coin of Palikanus, the orator mentioned by Cicero ("Brutus," lxii.)—see page 44—was a wooden pulpit. Its exact site we have already identified. The last historical notice that we have of it is in Spartianus's "Life of Didius Julianus" (iv.), A.D. 193. After saying that the emperor addressed the Senate, he adds, "but the people expressly in the Rostra before the Curia."

Under the Empire the Rostra had lost its use, and only served occasionally for the emperor to address the people from, or for reading out edicts and proclamations. The western end of the Forum saw many changes after the fire under Commodus, and was rearranged under Septimius Severus, who restored the old edifices, retaining the names of the founders, and erected others (Spartianus, "Severus,"

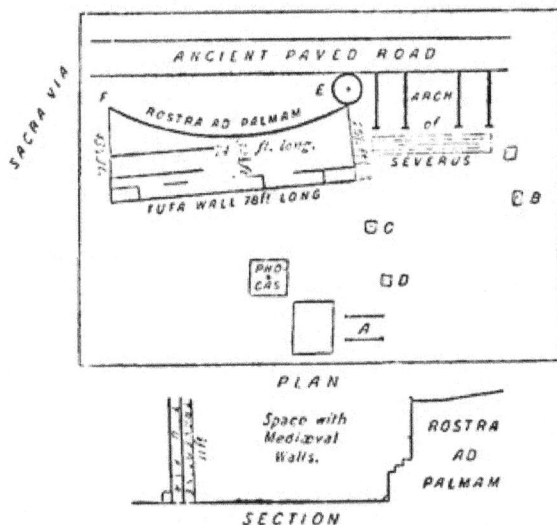

PLAN

SECTION

xxiii.). In 203 an arch was erected to Severus and his two sons, and a new Rostra was made on the south side of this arch. By cutting away a piece of the slope of the Capitoline Hill, he formed an escarpment 11 feet high, which was faced with a curved brick wall, and cased with Porta Santa marble, in panels 3 feet 1 inch wide. Between each pair of panels there is a space $6\frac{1}{2}$ inches wide, from which a piece of marble jutted out $3\frac{1}{2}$ inches. Only one of these exists. On it there was fixed a bronze beak, probably made in imitation of the old ones, for in that day they had no naval foes from whom to capture ships. If there was one row only, there were eighteen in all ; if two rows, thirty-six. This in itself is sufficient to show the ridiculousness of calling this the original Rostra, which had six beaks only. The peculiar marble casing also shows late work. At the north end of this platform was erected the Umbilicus (E), and on the south end was placed the Milliarium Aureum (F). From the level space on the top of this escarpment the orator would speak ; whilst at a short distance in his rear was the street Clivus Argentarius, leading from the Via Sacra to the Porta Rutuminia. This Rostra was popularly known as the People's Rostra, because from it they were addressed— "Deinde ad Rostra Populum convocarunt" (Capitolinus, "Maximus et Balbinus," iii.). The narrowness of the level space on the top of this Rostra caused great inconvenience ; and as room could not be gained in the rear, it had to be taken in front, encroaching on the Comitium. Forty-three and a half feet in front of the curved wall of Porta Santa a straight wall was built of travertine and tufa, 78 feet long, with side walls from it back to the extreme ends of the Rostra, and this was cased with Carrara white marble, the space between the two walls being filled with earth, thus making a large platform with a square instead of a curved front. The blocks of tufa and marble were tied together by iron clamps, of which fragments remain, of a shape not used in the earlier days, but used now.  ⊏⊐  That the curved wall and the straight wall are not contemporary is shown by the construction, as well as by the fact that the curved wall is faced with coloured marble, which would not have been the case if it had not at one time been open to the Forum. The curved wall is on a line with the Arch of Severus ; but the tufa wall comes out $25\frac{1}{2}$ feet beyond the arch, and is not parallel with the curved wall behind it. The tufa and travertine wall is erected on the travertine pavement of the Comitium.

We believe these changes on this Rostra were made in the time of Aurelian (270), after the death of Claudius II., whose statue was erected on this Rostra. "Illi totius orbis judicio in rostris posita est columna palmata statua superfixa" (Pollio, "Claudius," iii.). Upon this Rostra also Aurelian erected a statue of the Genius of the Roman People. Aurelianus—"Genium Populi Romani in rostra posuit" ("E. Chronicis antiquis excerpta Aurelianus"). The fourth century guides, "Curiosum Urbis" and "De Regionibus" (in Regio viii.), mention the Genium Populi Romani, the latter adding "aureum." They both mention three Rostra in the Forum. The statue of Claudius was not represented as wearing the Roman toga, but the Greek pallium, from which this Rostra became known as the Rostra ad Palmam ; and this part of the Forum in later times was called ad Palmam.

Theodoric—"Deinde veniens ingressus urbem venit ad Senatum, et ad Palmam populo adlocutus" ("Excerpta Valesiana," lxvi.).

" Ligaverunt ei manus a tergo et decol-
laverunt extra Capitolium et extrahentes
jactaverunt eum juxta arcum triumphi ad
Palmam " (" Acta SS., Mai." vii.).

Ammianus Marcellinus (xvi. x. 13) describes Constantius's visit in 356 to this
Rostra : " When he arrived at the Rostra,
he gazed with amazed awe on the Forum,
the most renowned monument of ancient
power ; and being bewildered with the
number of wonders on every side to which
he turned his eyes, having addressed the
nobles in the Senate House and harangued
the populace from the Rostra, he retired."
This expresses the feelings of many visitors in our day. The site commands a good
view of the Forum.

The remains of this Rostra are best illustrated by the representation of it in the
relief on the Arch of Constantine ; and by
no possible imagination can it be made to
agree with the coin of Palikanus.

In the centre is a platform with a straight
front, having a lattice balustrade ; on the
right is a statue of Claudius II., and on the
left the statue of the Genius of Rome. A
group of people stand behind the railing
and surround Constantine, who is addressing the people. Behind are five Corinthian
columns surmounted with statues. The
balustrade stood on the top of the tufa
wall, and some of the fallen gray granite
columns still exist. To our right, clear of
the Rostra, is the Arch of Severus, a group
of people being in front, looking up to the
Rostra. On the left, in the background, are
the Arch of Tiberius, spanning the Vicus
Jugarius, and four of the arches of the
Basilica Julia—the foreground being occupied by a crowd of people facing towards
the Rostra.

RELIEF FROM THE ARCH OF CONSTANTINE, REPRESENTING THE ROSTRA AD PALMAM, ETC.

The scene here depicted was no doubt that which took place on the entry of Constantine into Rome : "And with a loud voice and by inscriptions he made known to all men the salutary standard" (Eusebius, "Life of Constantine," xl.).

In the relief the head of Constantine is unfortunately missing; but it seems very appropriate that he should be represented addressing the Roman people from that Rostra, which was decorated with the statue of his ancestor Claudius II.

There are no beaks shown on the relief ; but along the tufa wall, at regular intervals of 3 feet 4 inches, are cut grooves $6\frac{1}{2}$ inches wide and $1\frac{1}{2}$ inch deep : in these grooves are holes which, if they were to sustain beaks, would give thirty-six for a single row, and seventy-two for a double row.

We doubt if these grooves and holes were for beaks. They were more probably for the supports of the marble casing ; they do not go completely through the wall.

Some authorities call these remains on the Clivus the Rostra Vetera, or the original Rostra. But it does not answer classic description, and the construction shows it to be of late date. It does not stand *on* the Comitium, or *before* the Curia, nor *under* the old shops. Besides, it looks down the Forum ; so from here how could Gracchus have *turned* from the Senate House and Comitium towards the Forum ?

### THE UMBILICUS

was a monument marking the centre of the Roman world. The ruin of the Umbilicus is at the side of the Arch of Septimius Severus, at the end of the Rostra ad Palmam. Its pyramidal shape upon a round base can easily be distinguished.

### THE ASYLUM OF ROMULUS.

This was between the Clivus Capitolinus and the Pass of the Two Groves (Via Arco di Septimo Severo), under the Capitoline Hill, and served afterwards as an advanced fort to the citadel. "He opened a sanctuary, in the place where the enclosure now is, on the road down from the Capitoline [Temple], called the Pass of the Two Groves" (Livy, i. 8). "He surrounded it with a high stone wall" (Ovid, "Fasti," iii. 231). The gate leading into it was called the Porta Pandana— "ever-open gate" (Solinus, i. 13. See Plutarch, in "Romulus ;" Diony- sius, ii. 15 ; Florus, i. 1 ; Varro and Festus). The remains of the tufa wall exist on the left of the Clivus, in front of the Temple of Saturn.

## THE CLOACA MAXIMA,

or great drain, begun by Tarquin the Great, containing a large stream of water rushing along, as it did over two thousand years ago, is exposed to view at the east end of the Basilica Julia.

It was finished by Tarquin the Proud, B.C. 556 (Livy, i. 38, 55).

" Men spoke in admiration of the public sewers, too, a work more stupendous than any, as mountains had to be pierced for their construction, and navigation might be carried on beneath Rome ; an event which happened in the ædileship of M. Agrippa, after he had filled the office of consul." (See Dion Cassius, " Augustus," A.U.C. 721.)

" For this purpose there are seven streams turned into the artificial channels, and flowing beneath the city. Rushing onward, like so many impetuous torrents, they are compelled to carry off and sweep away all the sewerage " (Pliny, xxxvi. 24).

## FRAGMENTS

of different buildings lie scattered about ; to what edifices they belonged " pronounce who can." More than two hundred columns, and fifty capitals of exquisite workmanship, have been discovered in the excavations of the Forum. Near the reliefs on the Comitium is a pedestal with an inscription to Arcadius Augustus. Between the Arch of Severus and the reliefs of Marcus Aurelius (a)* is the base of the equestrian statue of Constantinus II. (b), erected by Orfitus in 357 (Marcellinus, xvi. 10, 4), and a base with reliefs, and the inscription (c)—CÆSARUM . DECENNALI . FELICITER ; erected, with ten years' good wishes, to Constantine the Great (Eusebius, " Life of Constantine," c. 48, 40 ; and " E. II.," ix. 9). Beyond is a large base (d), with an inscription to Arcadius, Honorius, and Theodosius. This was evidently once the base of an equestrian statue, and was re-used by setting it on end and mounting it on another block of travertine.

*Having now made the circuit of the Forum, we will proceed to*

## THE SCALÆ ANNULARIÆ.

Beyond the Temple of Castor, to the right of the Temple of Vesta, are remains of these stairs. " Augustus lived at first near the Roman Forum, above the Ring-maker's Stairs, in a house which had once been occupied by Calvus the orator" (Suetonius, " Augustus," lxxii.). Calvus the orator, a friend of Cicero, lived on the Palatine ; and the Scalæ Annulariæ was a flight of stairs that led from the east end of the Forum up the north side of the Palatine to the Clivus Victoriæ.

* See Plan, page 47.

On the 12th of April 1882, a piece of the marble plan was found here which, curiously enough, represents this part of the Forum, showing the side of the Temple of Castor and the Ringmaker's Stairs.

### HOUSE OF THE VIRGINS.

Between the Temple of Vesta and the Sacra Via was the original dwelling-place of the Vestals, of which little remains beyond tufa walls beneath the more recent level. These walls were again exposed to view in some excavations made in the spring of 1886. They are marked in black on our Plan (page 63), being now again covered up.

Martial (i. 70), in addressing his book which he sends to Proculus, says, "You will pass by the Temple of Castor, near that of ancient Vesta, and that goddess's virgin home."

Dionysius (ii. 67) says: "They live near by the temple of the goddess."

### VESTA'S DUST-BIN.

By the side of the temple is a pit four feet square, where the ashes and sweepings of the temple were deposited; which were cleared out on the 15th of June, and thrown down the Porta Stercoraria, on the Clivus Capitolinus, into the Cloaca. (Ovid, " F." vi. 237, 712 ; Varro, " L. L." v.; Festus.)

### THE SHRINE OF MERCURY.

Beyond the Temple of Vesta, on the right, is a small brick shrine. The base of the statue of this shrine was fortunately found telling us the name.

DIO

MERCVRIO

On the flank of the base is another inscription, giving us the date of its erection, April 26, 275 A.D.

The brick podium of the shrine was cased with marble, one piece, one foot four inches high, being *in situ* on the side towards the steps. It supported an entablature of Carrara marble formed by two half-columns at the rear and two columns in front, of the fluted composite order.　On the frieze is the inscription, in beautifully cut letters five inches high, recording its erection by the Roman senate and people—

SENATVS . POPVLVSQVE . ROMANVS

PECVNIA . PVBLICA . FACIENDAM . CVRAVIT.

The podium is 4 feet 7 inches high, 9 feet 9 inches wide, 8 feet 2 inches deep. The fragments found are to be built up in their original sites, and so the shrine will be preserved. It was originally erected by Antoninus Pius, and is represented on a bronze coin of his—the pediment being supported by four Hermes (the Greek name for Mercury) busts. In the tympanum are the tortoise, cock, ram, winged cap, caduceus, and the magic purse. When it was restored in the consulship of Aurelian and Marcellino, columns and composite capitals took the place of the Hermes busts.

*The travertine steps by the side of the Shrine of Mercury led into*

## THE ATRIUM VESTÆ.

After the destructive fire of 192, the Forum and edifices on the Sacra Clivus were rebuilt by Septimius Severus and Julia Domna (Spartianus, Dion Cassius, Eutropius), the empress taking upon herself the special work of rebuilding the temple and residence of the Vestal Virgins; and although the original podium of the temple was used, it was considerably raised by rubble being placed on the top of the ancient tufa platform. This was necessary owing to the raising of the level from *débris*.

For the Atrium Vestæ a different site was selected, more to the south under the Palatine; in fact the whole disposition of the edifices about here was changed, as proved by comparing the earlier with the later classical notices, and the excavations of 1883-4.

To commemorate this rebuilding a silver coin was struck by the empress, bearing her head on the obverse; and on the reverse is the Temple of Vesta in the background, in front of which stands an altar, and on either side are three virgins, two of whom are pouring an oblation over the altar.

This new arrangement of the buildings is thus exactly described by Servius (in "Æn." vii. 153): "By the Temple of Vesta was the Regia of Numa Pompilius, but near to the Atrium of Vesta, which was DEDICATION OF THE TEMPLE. distinct from the temple."

Standing just inside, at the top of the steps, we have the whole Atrium Vestæ, as their residence was named, uncovered before us— a large peristylium paved with black and white mosaic, 222 feet long by 76 feet wide. Standing out thirteen feet from the boundary wall of the Atrium, and extending all round the court, were forty-

4

four columns of various marbles, whilst under the colonnade were the
pedestals bearing honorary inscriptions and statues of High Vestals:
sixteen on each side, six at the top, and six at the bottom. Of these,
thirteen honorary inscriptions have been found dedicated to six different High Vestal Virgins, the Lady Superiors of the nunnery.
Four slight fragments of other inscriptions were also found, making
seventeen in all. Twelve of the statues, more or less perfect, have
also been found: likewise an honorary pedestal to Caracalla; and a
statue to Vettius Agorius Prætextatus, erected to this champion of
paganism, 367 A.D., by Cœlia Concordia, the last of the High Vestal
Virgins.

At the east end of the Atrium is the fountain, beyond which is a
step up on to a tesselated pavement, and from that four steps lead
into the tabularium, or reception-room, having on each side three
chambers, in which most probably the Vestals deposited those objects
intrusted to their sacred keeping.

On each side of the Atrium were the residential chambers of the
High Vestals, the simple Virgins, and their domestics, two stories
high. Those on the south side are best preserved.

From the tesselated pavement a door gives access into a corridor,
once paved with white and black mosaic; at the end, on the left, is
a bath-chamber; and opening out from the corridor are several
chambers showing traces of marble pavements, frescoed and marble-
cased walls. In the second chamber are the remains of the mill for
grinding the salt used in sacrifice. (See Virgil, "Buc." viii. 82;
Horace, "O." iii. 23; Festus.) Pliny (xxxi. 41) says, "It is in our
sacred rites more particularly that the high importance of salt is to
be recognized, no offering ever being made unaccompanied by crushed
salt."

This corridor does not run the whole length of the Atrium, but
turns off to a flight of stairs leading to the upper chambers. The
remainder of the chambers on this side were reached direct from the
Atrium by steps. The first one contains a hexagonal pedestal to
Flavia Publicia. From the marble and fresco decorations found here,
these rooms were most probably the apartment of the High Vestal
Virgin.

The inscriptions to the High Vestals found, date between 180 and
364 A.D., and were erected in return for some advantage derived
from the patronage of the High Vestal. Historically they are of no
great importance, giving us only names of Vestals that were already
known. The most important inscriptions are those found here which

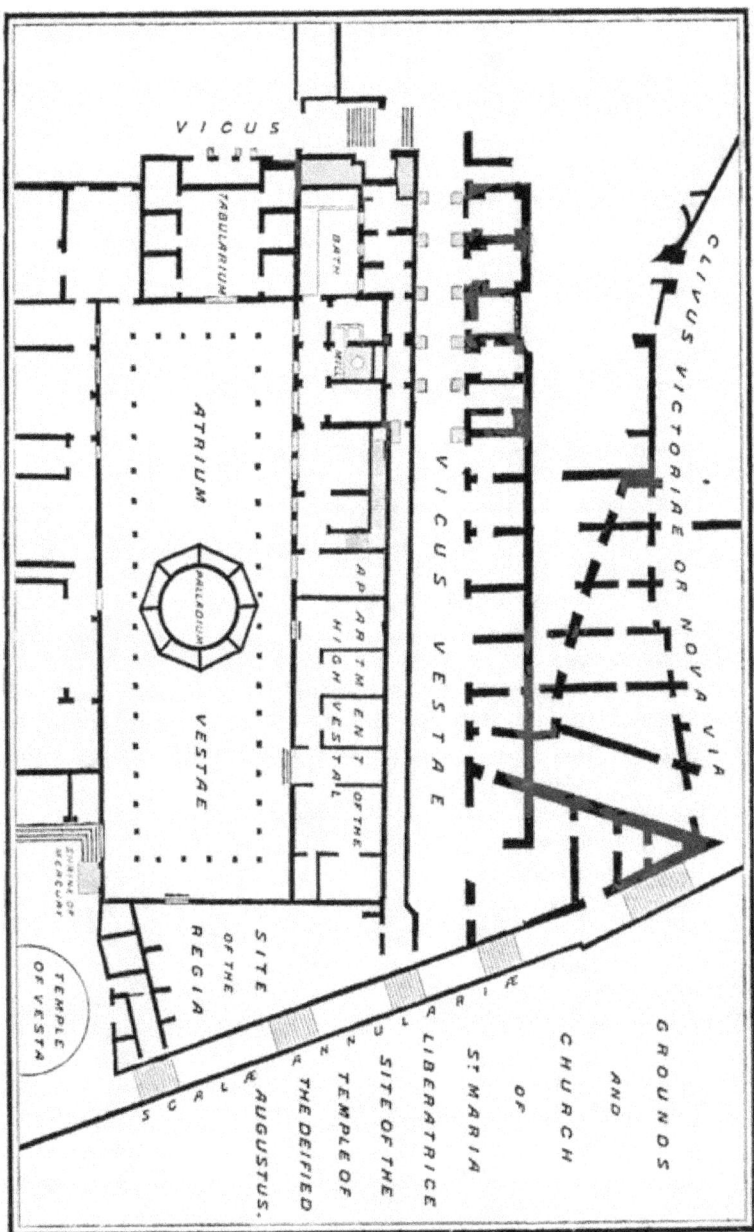

VICUS

CLIVUS VICTORIAE OR NOVA VIA

TABULARIUM

BATH

ATRIUM

PALLADIUM

VESTAE

APARTMENT OF THE HIGH VESTAL

VICUS VESTAE

SHRINE OF MERCURY

REGIA

SITE OF THE

SCALAE AUGUSTUS.

SITE OF THE DEIFIED

TEMPLE OF

SITE OF THE

LIBERATRICE

Sta MARIA

OF

RIÆ

GROUNDS

AND

CHURCH

OF

TEMPLE OF VESTA

do not refer to the Virgins. Commencing with the first pedestal at the top of the entry steps, they read as follows :—

Flavia Publicia. Erected July 9, 283 A.D.

Concordiæ. Dedicated June 9, 364. She was the last High Vestal, and her name was erased because she became a Christian.

Cœlia Claudiana. 253-7 A.D.

Caracalla pedestal. July 2, 114 A.D.

Prætextate Crassi. 180-200 A.D. The statue was removed in 1890.

Flavia Publicia. 257-284. ·

Numisia Maximilla. 201-216.

Statue of an unknown Vestal; no head.

Flavia Publicia. 257-84.

Another pedestal to her, with statue adjoining.

Pedestal to Trentia Flavola. About 350.

Blank pedestal, with statue of Ceres adjoining.

Pedestal to Flavia Publicia. September 30, 257.

Statue of Vettius Agorius Prætextatus. 380.

Fragment of a seated statue of Vesta herself.

Statue unknown.

Statue and pedestal to Flavia Publicia.

This part of the city was finally destroyed by the great fire, when Robert Guiscard burned Rome from the Lateran to the Capitol, in 1084. During this long period of nearly seven hundred years the Atrium Vestæ underwent many changes and received other tenants, for the new excavations show that it had been inhabited after the Vestals were abolished.

At the rear of the first pedestal a terra-cotta jar was discovered, containing a brooch bearing the name of Pope Martin III., 943-46; a gold coin of the Eastern Emperor Theophilus (827-42); and eight hundred and thirty Anglo-Saxon silver coins of Alfred the Great (871-900), Edward (900-24), Edgar Athelstan (925-41), and Edmund I. (941-48)—four kings of Northumbria—and of Plegmund, Archbishop of Canterbury (889-923). We may presume that this money was brought to Rome by some English tourist, who left his all and fled when the building was finally destroyed by fire; or that it formed part of a donation of "Peter's Pence." Ethelwulf, the English king during the time of Leo IV. (845-57), was the first English prince who gave tribute to the See of Rome; and as such his portrait is to be seen in *chiaro-oscuro*, by Caravaggio, in the Stanze of the Incendio del Borgo in the Vatican.

After running a course of one thousand and eighty years, Gratian in 367 "refused the office of Pontifex Maximus, and abolished the functions of the Vestal Virgins" (Zosimus, iv.), which were finally suppressed by Theodosius in 392. "Theodosius directed his attention towards the suppression of idolatry, and issued a law commanding the demolition of idolatrous temples." "The faithful emperor Theodosius interdicted these rites and consigned them to disuse" (Theodoret, v. 21).

The Bishop of Rome and his clergy came by right, as heads of the established religion, into the possessions of the defunct faiths, and inhabited the quarters of the Vestals, assuming the title of head of the ancient religion, Pontifex Maximus, a title held to the present day—a dignity two thousand five hundred and thirty-one years old, the oldest in the world.

## THE PALLADIUM.

In the centre of the peristylium, just coming to the surface and occupying the whole of the width of the open court, are the foundations of an octagonal edifice in brick, with ribs running from the angles to a central circle. Here, doubtless, was the shrine in which was kept the Sacred Palladium, or fatal token of the empire of the Romans. "Fatale pignus imperii Romani" (Livy, xxvi. 27). "Kept under the safeguard of Vesta's temple" (*ibid.* v. 52). This was a statuette of "Minerva, by no male beheld" (Lucan, ix. 994). "The Vestals alone were permitted to behold the Trojan Minerva" (*ibid.* i. 598). "That fell from heaven" (Dionysius, ii. 67). It seems it was originally kept in the Temple of Vesta itself (Pliny, vii. 45; Ovid, "T." iii. 1, 39).

"The sacred image of Minerva, to which the Romans pay uncommon veneration, and which, as they say, was brought from Troy, was exposed to public view (during the fire of 192), so that the men of our age beheld the Palladium, never seen by any before since the time it came from Ilium into Italy. For the Vestal Virgins laid hold on it in the hurry and confusion, and carried it openly through the Sacred Way into the Imperial Palace" (Herodian, in "Commodus").

"Elagabalus, wanting a wife for his sun-god, sent for the sacred image of Pallas, which the Romans worship in secret from human eyes, and had it brought into his own bed-room. Thus he dared to displace the Palladium, that had never been moved since the time it came from Ilium, except when the temple was destroyed by fire, and they conveyed the goddess into the Imperial Palace" (*ibid.* in "Antoninus;" Lampridius, in "Elagabalus," iii.).

Fragments of a statuette of Minerva were found in the excavations.

## THE VICUS VESTÆ.

From the Via Sacra, above the Arch of Titus, a street, passing
along a ledge on the northern side of the Palatine, runs into
the Vicus Tuscus at the back of the Temple of Castor. This was
the street of the Vestals, separating their house from the Imperial
Palace. Asconius ("ad Ciceronem pro Scauro,") speaks of it.

We now cross over to the Sacred Way.

*The first object that attracts our attention is the*

## ˙CHURCH OF SS. COSMO AND DAMIANO,

*on the left*, occupying the site and built out of the remains of two
temples by Felix IV., 527 A.D. The subterranean church contains a
spring said to have been called forth by S. Felix. Upon the apse of
the upper church is a mosaic of the time of Felix. *Entrance Via
Maranda.*

## THE TEMPLE OF ROMULUS,

son of Maxentius, formed the vestibule of the present church. It was
a circular building, and fronted towards the Via Sacra. The second
temple Felix made into the nave of the church; it was quadrangular,
and built of brick, but the eastern wall was of blocks of Gabii stone,
forming part of the second wall of Rome, which was here utilized for
the temple. It is thirty feet in diameter, and was erected in 302
A.D. Ligorio ("Vatican Codex," 3439) has preserved the inscription :—

IMP . CAES . AUGUSTUS . MAXIMUS . TRIUMPH

PIUS . FELIX . AUGUSTUS.

The two porphyry columns and the cornice belong to the temple ; but
the bronze doors are Etruscan, having been sent from Perugia by
Urban VIII. in 1630. The wings on either side of the doorway
were added in 772-95 by Hadrian I.; the niches, which still show
traces of frescoing, being for relics of the saints. In the year 1503,
the present flooring of the church was inserted some feet above the
ancient level. The church is now entered from the Via Maranda.

*On the left are slight remains of*

## THE TEMPLE OF VICAPORTA, VICTORY.

Remains of this temple have been discovered in the recent excavations on the Sacra Via, between the Temple of Antoninus Pius and the Temple of Romulus. From the slight remains found, it seems that three of its sides were formed by deep apses, the fourth side fronting towards the Via Sacra, and entered by a portico.

Dionysius (v. 19), Plutarch in "Publicola," and Livy (ii. 7) record that Publius Valerius, surnamed Publicola, built a house on the Velia overlooking the Forum ; but owing to the invidious remarks made he pulled the house down, and re-erected it at the foot of the Velia. Plutarch adds, "upon the spot where the Temple of Victory now stands." Livy also says, "The house was built at the foot of the hill where the Temple of Victory now stands." Dionysius (v. 48) says, after speaking of the poverty of Publicola, "The senate decreed that he should be buried at the expense of the public, and appointed a place in the city, under the hill called Velia, near the Forum, where his body was burnt and buried."

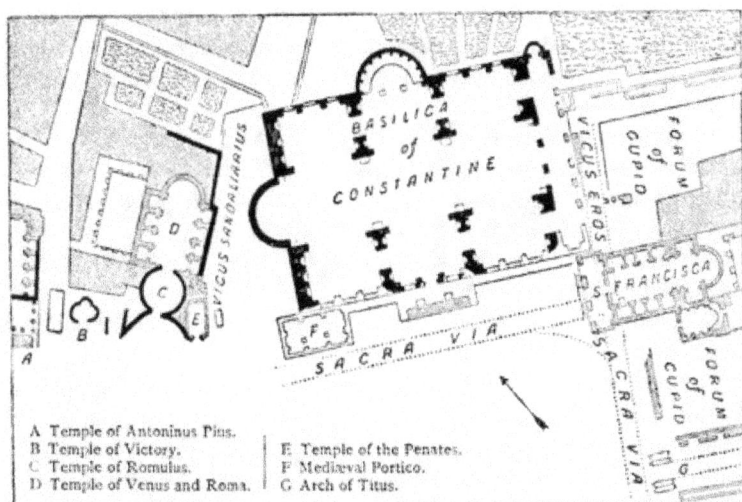

A Temple of Antoninus Pius.
B Temple of Victory.
C Temple of Romulus.
D Temple of Venus and Roma.
E Temple of the Penates.
F Mediæval Portico.
G Arch of Titus.

PLAN OF THE NORTH SIDE OF THE SACRA VIA.

This Temple of Victory was dedicated, B.C. 295, by the consul Lucius Postumus. "He dedicated the Temple of Victory, for the building of which he had provided, when curule ædile, out of the money arising from fines" (Livy, x. 33).

This temple is represented on a coin of Gordianus III., 240 A.D., who restored it after his Persian victories.

## TEMPLE OF VENUS AND ROMA,

erected by Hadrian in 134 A.D.    It was the largest and most
sumptuous in Rome.    It was designed by Hadrian himself, who
sent the drawings to the celebrated architect Apollodorus, whom
he had banished, to ask his opinion.    He replied, "That Hadrian ought to have made it more lofty, and with subterrane-
ous accommodation for receiving, as occasion might require, the
machinery of the theatre, and for giving it a more imposing
aspect towards the Via Sacra.    That as to the statues, they were
so disproportionate, that if the goddesses desired to get up and
walk out, they would not be able" (Dion Cassius; Xiphilinus,
"Hadrian").

For this criticism Apollodorus lost his head; and we learn that the
temple was *not* on a lofty platform, that there were *no* subterranean
chambers, and that it was *not* imposing towards the Via Sacra.

The portico, towards the Via Salaria Vecchia, was destroyed in
1632, and the travertine stone used in building the Church of
S. Ignazio.    It is mentioned by Prudentius as being in the vicinity
of the Via Sacra.

"The Sacred Way resounded (*they say*) with lowings before the
shrine of Rome; for she also herself is worshipped with blood after
the fashion of a goddess, and the name of the place (*Rome*) is
regarded as a divinity.    The temples also of the city and of Venus
rise with a like roof; and at one and the same time frankincense is
consumed to the twin-gods."

It could not have faced the Via Sacra, or Maxentius would not
have built the temple of his son against it, 311 A.D.

The bronze doors of the Round Temple were found at Perugia by
Urban VIII.    The two columns of porphyry, with the cornice, are
supposed to have been found amongst the ruins when it was turned
into a church.    On the right side of the present church is a piece
of wall of Gabii tufa stone of *opus quadratum*.    At the back of
the church is the brick front wall of the temple, on which the celebrated *Pianta Capitolina* was originally attached (see page 185)
by means of cement and cramps, and which was found below
the soil under the wall, having been thrown down by an earthquake.    This was excavated in 1891.

Suetonius tells us that Nero's colossus stood in the vestibule of his
palace ("Nero," 31).

Martial says, "It was removed by Vespasian, when he built

the Temple of Peace, to where the atrium (a more inward part) was" ("Dec. Spec.," 1, 2).

It was a second time removed, for Spartianus informs us that "Hadrian removed it with twenty-four elephants *from* the place where now stands the Temple of the City" ("Hadrian," 19).

Thus we learn that the spot where the Temple of Rome is, was formerly the atrium of Nero's Golden House, and that the Temple of Peace occupied the vestibule.

"Maxentius restored the Temple of Venus and Rome, which had been damaged by fire" (Aur. Victor, "Cæs." xl.).

The Emperor Heraclius gave permission to Pope Honorius I. to remove the bronze tiles of this temple in order to use them for the roof of S. Peter's; whence they were stolen by the Saracens in 846.

Dion Cassius (lxxi. 31) tells us that "Cleopatra's statue in gold is to be seen in the Temple of Venus to this day." Also that "the senate ordered two statues of silver to be erected in the Temple of Venus; one in honour of Faustina, and the other in honour of the Emperor Marcus Aurelius. They likewise ordered an altar to be set up before it, on which every contracted couple were to sacrifice before marriage."

Mr. J. H. Parker, C.B., made some excavations under the wall of Gabii stone in 1868-9, and found that a street ran from the Sacred Way along the side of the wall, in which was a small doorway into the temple. This has now been re-excavated by the Government (1880), who have taken possession of the Round Temple.

The government have recently pulled down the chapel of the burial society adjoining the Temple of Romulus, and on the two thousand six hundred and thirty-third anniversary of the foundation of Rome, April 21st, 1880, the two cipollino columns were found to have belonged to the

## TEMPLE OF THE PENATES.

As the Lares were the departed spirits of the ancestors of each family who watched over their descendants, so the Penates were the gods selected by each family as its special protectors. And as there were the Lares of the city, so there were the Penates, whose chapel was termed Ædes Deum Penatium, and the gods were called Penates Populi Romani. These Penates were supposed to have been the gods brought from Troy by Æneas.

We learn from the "Monumentum Ancyranum," that Augustus

rebuilt the Ædem Deum Penatium in Velia; and Solinus (i.) tells us that Tullus Hostilius lived on the Velia, where afterwards was the Chapel of the Penates. Dionysius thus describes it:—"For the things which I myself know, by having seen them, and concerning which no scruple forbids me to write, are as follows. They show you a temple at Rome, not far from the Forum, in the street that leads the nearest way to the Carinæ, which is small, and darkened by the height of the adjacent buildings. This place is called by the Romans, in their own language, *Veliæ*; in this temple are the images of the Trojan gods exposed to public view, with this inscription, ΔΕΜΑΣ, which signifies Penates. For, in my opinion, the letter Θ not being yet found out, the ancients expressed its power by the letter Δ. These are two youths, in a sitting posture, each of them holding a spear; they are pieces of ancient workmanship" (Dionysius, i. 68).

### THE RECENT EXCAVATIONS.

In the new excavations upon the line of the Via Sacra a monumental cippus has been found, with the following inscription,—FABIUS. TITIANUS.—V. C. CONSUL.—PRAEF. URBI.—CURAVIT.

He was consul and prefect of the city, A.D. 339 to 341, under the Emperor Constans I. This was one of three bases recorded as having stood in front of the Temple of Romulus in the sixteenth century, one of which is in the Museum of the Villa Borghese, and the other is in the Naples Museum.

Another base was found, dedicated to the Emperor Constantius II. by Flavius Leontius, prefect of Rome in 356 A.D. This is similar to the one in the Capitoline Museum.

The inscription reads,—TOTO. ORBE. VICTORI.—DN. CONSTANTIO. MAX.—TRIUMFATORI.—SEMPER. AUG.—FL. LEONTIUS. V. C.—PRAEF. URBI. ITERUM.—VICE. SACRA. INDICANS.—D. N. M. Q. EIUS.

Remains of Roman and medieval buildings and a fountain have been uncovered in the course of excavating, also some architectural fragments. The whole length of the Via Sacra has been now uncovered as far as the steps leading up to the Ædem Larum.

### THE HOUSE OF JULIUS CÆSAR.

The recent excavations along the line of the Via Sacra brought to light some unimportant remains of shops and houses facing towards the street. These buildings are of the time of Constantine, and agree in their construction with his Basilica on the opposite side of

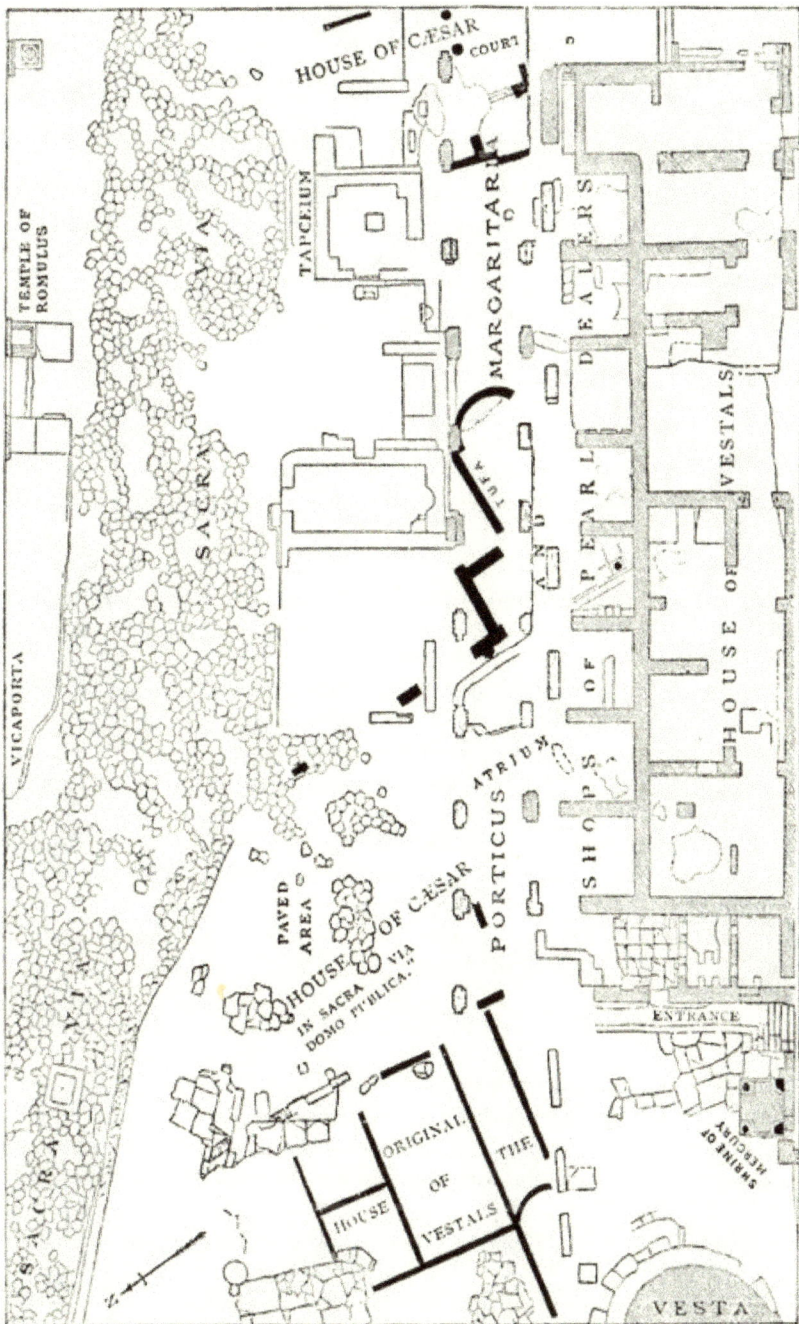

TEMPLE OF ROMULUS

VICAPORTA

VIA SACRA

SACRA VIA

SACRA VIA

HOUSE OF CÆSAR

COURT

TABCEIUM

MARGARITARII

TUFA AND

TUFA

SHOPS OF PEARL DEALERS

HOUSE OF VESTALS

VESTALS

PAVED AREA

HOUSE OF CÆSAR

IN SACRA VIA DOMO PUBLICA.

ATRIUM

PORTICUS

ENTRANCE

ORIGINAL OF THE HOUSE OF VESTALS

SHRINE OF MERCURY

N

VESTA

the street.  This part of Rome was destroyed by fire in the reign of
Commodus, and again under Maxentius (Dion Cassius, Herodian,
Galen, Capitolinus).  In this rebuilding they did not clear away
the remains of the older houses, but built on and over them—a not
unusual custom in Rome.  Let us carefully examine the older remains.
Our attention is first attracted by different fragments of beautiful
mosaic pavements of the best period of the art, and evidently the
flooring of no mean house.  The first piece that we come across is
composed of a pattern made up of several cubes in different colours;
in the rebuilding this was hid by a pavement of herring-bone brickwork.  Beyond is a beautiful black and white octangular and diamond
mosaic pavement, which also did duty to the rebuilt house.  In a
small room adjoining we notice a travertine base of a column, which
stands near a piece of black mosaic pavement, in which are inserted
small squares of white marble; in another chamber close by is a
white mosaic with a black border, and near this another, of white
and black sexangular and diamond shape.  Near the cube mosaic are
two more bases of columns of travertine, and a travertine well head:
travertine stone, from Tivoli, was not used in Rome as a building
material till about 50 B.C.  Amongst the constructions of the older
period we notice six distinct pieces of walls composed of tufa blocks,
perhaps old material re-used, some blocks of peperino, and a small
piece of *opus reticulatum*.  Tufa was used during the kingly period,
peperino during the republic, and *opus reticulatum*—net-work wedges
of tufa—by the late republic and early empire.  Amidst the later
construction, which is of brickwork, we notice terra-cotta hot-air
pipes, and one piece of a lead pipe, and remains of flights of stairs
leading to upper floors.  The brick stamps found were of the second,
third, and fourth centuries.  Amongst these remains was found a small
altar.  On the scroll at the top is a Roman eagle, and beneath,—

LARIBUS AUG. SACRUM.

From the line of the bases of the columns we see that the front of
the older house sloped back diagonally from the Via Sacra, the point
farthest from the Forum being nearest to the Via Sacra; whilst the
more recent construction was on a line parallel with, and abutting on
to, the Sacred Way.

This early house, appearing beneath the building of later date,
is in all probability the house in which Julius Cæsar lived.  The construction agrees with that of earlier and contemporary date.  It is

the first house on the Via Sacra, and the site coincides with the notices which we have of Cæsar's house :—

"He first inhabited a small house in the Suburra; but after his advancement to the pontificate, he occupied a palace belonging to the state in the Via Sacra. Many writers say that he liked his residence to be elegant......and that he carried about in his expeditions tesselated and marble slabs for the floor of his tent " (Suetonius, " Cæsar," xlvi.).

" As a mark of distinction he was allowed to have a pediment on his house " (Florus, iv. 3).

"Julius Cæsar once shaded the whole Forum and Via Sacra from his house, as far as the Clivus Capitolinus " (Pliny, xix. 6).

" The night before his murder, as he was in bed with his wife, the doors and windows of the room flew open at once......Calpurnia dreamed that the pediment was fallen, which, as Livy tells us (in the lost books), the senate had ordered to be erected upon Cæsar's house by way of ornament and distinction; and that it was the fall of it which she lamented and wept for" (Plutarch, in "Cæsar ").

" He lay for some little time after he expired, until three of his slaves laid the body on a litter and carried it home, with one arm hanging down over the side " (Suetonius, " Cæsar," lxxxii.).

The house of Cæsar was under the Palatine, on which, above Cæsar's, stood the house of Cicero. " He (Vettius) did not name me, but mentioned that a certain speaker, of consular rank (Cicero), and neighbour to the consul (Cæsar), had suggested to him that some Ahala Servilius, or Brutus, must be found " (Cicero, " Ad Att." ii. 24).

In Cæsar's fourth consulship, the year before he was killed, for some reason or other the defence of King Deiotarus by Cicero was heard by Cæsar in his own house. Cicero says to Cæsar: "I am affected also by the unusual circumstance of the trial in this place, because I am pleading so important a cause—one the fellow of which has never been brought under discussion—within the walls of a private house. I am pleading it out of the hearing of any court or body of auditors, which are a great support and encouragement to an orator. I rest on nothing but your eyes, your person, your countenance. I behold you alone; the whole of my speech is necessarily confined to you alone......But since the walls of a house narrow all these topics, and since the pleading of the cause is greatly crippled by the place, it behoves you, O Cæsar," &c. (" Pro Deiot." ii.).

It was in the year of his prætorship (62 B.C.) that the scandal of

Clodius being found in the house whilst they were about to celebrate the rites of the Bona Dea happened. "When the anniversary of the festival comes, the consul or prætor (for it is at the house of one of them that it is kept) goes out, and not a male is left in it" (Plutarch, "Cæsar"). The trial that such a scene gave rise to caused Cæsar's celebrated words on being asked why he had divorced his wife: "Because I would have the chastity of my wife clear even of suspicion" (Plutarch, "Cæsar").

Plutarch speaks of it as "a great house." Ovid says the house of Numa, the Regia, was "small," showing that the house of Cæsar and the Regia were two distinct edifices.

This old house of which we have been speaking fronted towards the Temple of Vesta, whilst the portico and shops, built at a late period over its ruins, ran parallel with the Via Sacra. The house side of the atrium is plainly marked by the fragments of columns, composed of travertine coated with stucco, and frescoed. There is the base of an isolated column near what must have been the middle of the house side; and to its right there is a half column of the same workmanship, and between these two bases runs a travertine gutter which drained the atrium. Amidst the shops built over the atrium are remains of beautiful black and white mosaic pavement, the fragments of the borders showing that they once belonged to the older edifice. On the right of the atrium, towards the Via Sacra, was an area-vestibulum, giving access to the house from the Via Sacra, and, like it, paved with polygonal blocks of silex.

There was another entrance to the house at the point where it nearly touched, at its north-eastern corner, the Via Sacra. The bases of two columns mark the ingress into a small vestibule which has a mosaic pavement, on the right of which was the entrance to the house, the threshold of travertine stone being *in situ*. There are the two holes at the ends where the doors turned on their pivots, and the bolt-hole in the middle.

## THE PORTICUS MARGARITARIA.

After the fire, the site of Cæsar's house was occupied by shops and dwellings, along the front of which was an arcade. As these shops were mostly kept by pearl-dealers, the arcade was known as the Porticus Margaritaria. It is mentioned in the "Curiosum" and the "Notitia" of the fourth century as in the eighth region, Forum Romanum Magnum.

In the recent excavations along the line of the Via Sacra, the remains of an arcade 201 feet long by 24 feet wide, and consisting of two rows of piers, have been found running parallel with the street, and having shops on either side. This no doubt is the Porticum Margaritarium of the catalogues. Beneath the arcade and the shops are the remains of Cæsar's house. Judging from the monumental stones, the pearl trade was an extensive one in Rome; and from the same authority we learn that the shops were on the Sacra Via. This is mentioned on the tomb of Ateilius Evhodus at the sixth mile on the Via Appia.

## THE SACRA CLIVUS.

Horace was wont to come down the Sacred Way ("S." i. 9), and talks of Britons descending it in chains ("Ep." vii.). Now we are free to ascend it. Where the Sacred Way ascends the Velia ridge it will be noticed that the road is extraordinarily wide (45 feet). This was no doubt made after the great fire under Commodus, for four feet below the pavement was found the original and narrower street, and beneath that the drain in the reticulated work of the republic.

The right-hand side of the ascent was bordered with honorary monuments and inscriptions to Trajan, Hadrian, Titus, Septimius Severus, Caracalla, and Constantine; but the most interesting, perhaps, was the monument with Greek inscription of Gordianus, erected to him by the citizens of Tarsus, St. Paul's city, and interesting as showing that the close friendship between Rome and Tarsus continued to this late period. Four columns of Porta Santa marble stood on a podium, 7 feet by 4 feet, and supported a canopy, under which was the emperor's statue. On the cornice was the inscription, ΤΑΡCΕωΝ, filled in with bronze.

## THE VICUS SANDALIARIUS.

This was the street mentioned by Dionysius as leading into the Carinæ.

In the "Curiosum" and "Notitia" is mentioned the Apollinem Sandaliarium. This was a statue of Apollo, which gave name to a street of the fourth region. Suetonius ("Aug." lvii.) says: "With which donations Augustus purchased some costly images of the gods, which he erected in several of the streets of the city, as that of Apollo Sandaliarius." It is mentioned by Aulus Gellius (xviii. 4): "In Sandaliario forte apud librarios fuimus." Also by Galen ("De Libris suis," iv. 361).

The marble plan of Rome shows this street by the letters DLARIVS. This was the street, recently excavated, between the Temple of the Penates and the Basilica Constantine, and which led into the Suburra.

At the entrance from the Via Sacra there still exists a brick pedestal on which the statue may have stood. For engraving of this, see Gruter, cvi. 7, and DCXXI. 3.

In this street the remains of the Temple of Venus and Rome can be distinctly seen. A short distance up it is tunnelled over to allow the Basilica of Constantine to square; but the tunnel is closed about half way through. From the level of the street the western tribunal of the Basilica has been built up. The tunnel, called Arco d'Ladroni, and the street itself, have been used as a burial-place by the monks of the church; and there is a ninth century fresco of the dead body of the Saviour over a shrine on the left.

*Beyond is the*

## BASILICA OF CONSTANTINE,

the colossal arches of which have served as models to architects for building all the larger churches in Rome. This splendid ruin usually bears the name of the Temple of Peace, erected by Vespasian in this neighbourhood and partly on this site, and which was destroyed by fire as early as the time of Commodus, A.D. 192. Herodianus, who saw the fire, says: "By the slight earthquake and the thunderbolt which followed it, the whole of the sacred enclosure was consumed." Claudius Galenus, the celebrated physician, says that the whole edifice was consumed, as also most of his writings, which were in his shop in the Via Sacra.

This is one of the most imposing ruins in Rome; the three noble arches which formed the northern side being almost perfect, rising to the height of 95 feet, and having a span of 80 feet. The southern side was similar; whilst a noble vaulted roof, supported from the side piers and arches, covered the centre. Thus, entering from the Vicus Eros, on the east, the spectator saw a magnificent hall 333 feet long by 84 feet wide, with aisles 60 feet in width. To the central hall the tribunal at the west end was added in the rebuilding of Constantine, when he made the main entry from the Sacra Via, the ruins of which exist in the porphyry columns. By this entry the nave is 227 feet long, the tribunal being 24 feet deep, and the aisles 80 feet wide.

Nibby has the merit of having been the first to prove that these ruins are the last remains of the Basilica erected by Maxentius, and completed and partially rebuilt by Constantine the Great. In 1828 a medal of Maxentius was found amongst the ruins of a piece of the vault which fell down. The principal entrance was originally intended to have been on the side facing the Colosseum, towards a street that ran out from the left of the Via Sacra, which, turning to the right, reached the Colosseum.

At a later period Constantine thought it more suitable to add a splendid portal on the side facing the Via Sacra; opposite to which, in the central side arch, a tribune was erected. So whichever way you enter it, it is a nave with two aisles. Of the vast vaulted arches spanning the middle space, only the supports from which the arches sprang still exist. These, however, suffice to indicate what they must have been. The Basilica contained many works of art, and the roof was supported by eight columns. The Via Sacra here passed along the front of the present Church of S. Francis of the Romans, and the Arch of Titus, to the Palatine.

*By applying at No. 61 Via del Colosseo, at the back of the Basilica, permission will be given to ascend to the top, from which a magnificent view is obtained.*

*On our right is the*

## CHURCH OF S. FRANCISCA ROMANA.

Built in the ninth century, and called S. Maria Nuova. The mosaic on the apse dates from 862. There is a monument to Gregory XI., and a relief representing the return of the Papal court to Rome from Avignon. In the transept are the two stones marked with depressions, said to have been where Peter knelt when he prayed that Simon Magus might fall. (See picture in S. Peter's, page 117.) The church contains a beautiful marble *ciborium*, and monuments to Cardinal Vulcani, 1322, and General Rido, 1475.

*In the Via S. Teodoro is the entrance to*

## THE PALATINE HILL AND THE PALACE OF THE CÆSARS.

*Open every day. Admission, one lira. Sunday, free. In order to fully understand these ruins, it is advisable to attend the lectures given on the spot by the author of these Rambles, Dr. S. Russell Forbes, who conducts visitors over, describing fully the remains of the Arcadian, Kingly, Republican, and Imperial Periods. Particulars to be had at 93 Via Babuino.*

The foundations of most magnificent buildings of the imperial times lie buried in the gardens. The paintings on the walls are in themselves sufficient to give us an idea of the splendour of the

5

PLAN OF THE
PALATINE HILL
AND
PALACE OF THE CÆSARS

# Itinerary for Visiting the Palatine.

*Turn to the left when through Entrance Gate.*

internal decorations of the Roman palaces. The streets, temples, palaces, &c., are full of interest. Some beautiful views may be had from various parts of the gardens, from the height near the entrance, as well as looking over the site of the CIRCUS MAXIMUS, which occupied the valley between the Palatine and Aventine Hills.

*In our description of the Palatine we have classed the remains in chronological order. In the accompanying plan they are numbered in the order in which they are best visited. The numbers correspond with those placed by the title of the different ruins in the Guide; so that the visitor can follow the numbers consecutively in his ramble, and turn to the corresponding number for the description. We only treat of the actual remains.*

### THE TOPOGRAPHY OF THE PALATINE.

In studying the Palatine Hill, the topography presents the first difficulty. It must be borne in mind that the form of the hill has undergone many important changes since the days of Romulus, and, as seen by us, is very different from what it was when Romulus built his city. Now it presents a lozenge-shaped form; then it was oblong and smaller. Our theory is, that if a line be drawn from about the Arch of Titus across the hill, that part to the right or west was the extent of the hill in the time of Romulus; and that to the left or east, formerly " the pastures round the old town " (Varro), now presenting the form of a hill, was no hill then. From a careful survey of the part to the left of our line, we find it to be artificially formed of imperial ruins upon the top of ruins, rubbish, and accumulation of soil, and not of rock or solid earth. This new light does away with innumerable difficulties in studying the form of Roma Quadrata, and presents to us instead a very simple story.

If the hill had been of the same form then as now, Romulus would have occupied the whole of it: this he certainly did not do, as his walls are to the right of our line; and it is not likely that he would have left part of the hill outside his boundary to command his city or to be occupied by foes.

Our view agrees with classic authority. Tacitus (xii. 24) describing the pomœrium or boundary of Roma Quadrata, which went round the base of the hill on the level below, thus showing its shape, says: " The first outline began at the Ox-Market, where still is to be seen the brazen statue of a bull, that animal being commonly employed at the plough. From that place a furrow was carried on of sufficient dimensions to include the great Altar of Hercules. By boundary stones, fixed at proper distances, the circuit was continued along the foot of Mount Palatine to the Altar of Consus, extending thence to the Old Curiæ; next, to the Chapel of the Lares." These buildings were built after Roma Quadrata, with the exception of the Altar of Hercules, and are mentioned by Tacitus to mark the line; they existed when he wrote. Ovid ("Fasti," iv. 825) says: "Pressing the tail of the plough, he traces out the walls with a furrow; a white cow with a snow-white bull bears the yoke." Dionysius (i. 88) says: "Romulus called the people to a place appointed, and described a quadrangular figure about the hill, tracing with a plough, drawn by a bull and a cow yoked together, one *continued* furrow." Taking these authors for our guides, we can easily trace the line of the pomœrium. Commencing at the Forum Boarium, which site is well known, it went down to the Altar of Hercules, which must have also been in the Forum Boarium, "in the spot where a part of the city has its name derived from an ox" (Ovid, "Fasti," i. 581). Taking in this altar, it passed under the Palatine's southern side to the Ara Consi, which Tertullian ("De Spec." v.) tells us was buried in the circus at the first meta. It here turned to the east, passing along the valley which then existed, along our imaginary line; for it is ridiculous to suppose that it would have passed right across the Palatine had the hill been then what it is now. From the Altar of Consus it extended past the Old Curiæ, which we think may be seen in the tufa walls under the south end of the Palace of Domitian (19), then to the Chapel of the Lares, which stands at the head of the Sacra Via below the Palace of Domitian (15).

"Ædem Larum in Summa Sacra Via" ("Mon. Ancyr."). "Ancus Martius (habitavit) in Summa Sacra Via, ubi ædes Larum est" (Solinus, i. 24). "Romulus built a temple to Jupiter, near the gate called Mugonia, which leads to the Palatine Hill from the Sacra Via" (Dionysius, ii. 30). The Sacred Way did not pass through the Arch of Titus, as is generally supposed, but passing by it led up to the Palatine—this can be seen by examining the stones—and was then called Clivus Palatinus. A large piece of the pavement still exists on the Palatine, leading up to the Ædem Larum, and which road is miscalled Nova Via. The road leading from the Arch of Titus to that of Constantine was called the Clivus Triumphalis.

Hence the furrow must have passed under the north side of the Palatine, and down the west side to where it began; for Tacitus's account says, "Hence to the Forum which was added by Tatius." This furrow marked the bounds of the city, within which were the walls, the city itself occupying the hill above.

The remains of the walls of Roma Quadrata existing are sufficient to show us their exact line, for we have remains on four different sides, and, curious enough, at three of the angles. On the west and east sides it appears to have been built up to support the scarped cliff and above it; but on the south it ran along the edge on the top of the cliff—the valley below, beyond the pomœrium, being then the Murzian Lake. Along the southern cliff it was not a solid wall, but had embrasures, through which a *balista* or *catapult* might be fired upon an enemy below—the remains of which are still existing. These are the oldest Roman arches, being older than the Cloaca of Tarquin or the arches of Ancus Martius.

"But Romulus had formed the *idea* of a city rather than a *real* city; for inhabitants were wanting" (Florus, i. 1).

The principal roadway upon the Palatine was the Nova Via, a new way, evidently made after the Via Sacra, and simply called Nova Via without any distinguishing name being given to it. It commenced at the Porta Mugonia on the east, outside Roma Quadrata, and was here called Summa Nova Via. "Tarquinius Priscus ad Mugoniam Portam supra Summam Novam Viam" [habitabat] (Solinus, i. 24). From this point it went along the north and down the west side past the gate—there being steps down from the gate to the road. The descent off the hill was called the Hill of Victory. "Sed Porta Romana instituta est a Romulo infimo Clivo Victoriæ" (Festus). "Quæ habet gradus in Nova Via" (Varro). Passing by the Porta Romana it turned to the left, or west, under the Palatine to the Velabrum, where it ended. This part was called Infima Nova Via. "Aius Loquens in Infima Nova Via" (Varro, "Ap. Gell." xvi. 17). This altar still exists at the south-west corner under the Palatine. "Hoc Sacrificium [to Larentia] fit in Velabro, qua in novam Viam exitur" (Varro, "Ling. Lat." vi.).

## ROMA QUADRATA.

5, 6, 7, 8, 13, 19, 36, 37, 38, 39, 40, 41.

Romulus, the son of Rhea Silvia and Mars, founded Rome on the Palatine Hill, above the Tiber, 753 B.C., on the site of the Arcadian city of Evander, near the Lupercal, where Lupa had given him suckle. The city was built after the Etruscan rites, and surrounded by a massive wall, in a quadrangular form, whence it was called Roma Quadrata. See "Walls of Rome," page xvii.

Pliny (iii. 9) informs us that the city was entered by three gates.

PORTA MUGONIA (14),

situated on the east of the hill, the site of which has been identified by Varro ("L. L." 164):—

"Moreover, I observe that the gates within the walls are thus named; that at the Palatine 'Mucionis' (from 'mugitus,' lowing), because through it they used to drive out the cattle into the pastures around the old town."

PORTA ROMANA (40).

At the middle of the western side, at the commencement of the ascent on the Via Nova, called the Clivus Victoriæ in commemoration of the victory of Romulus over Acron. The remains were discovered March 1886. Varro says:—

"The other, called Romulana, was so called from Rome, the same which has steps into the Nova Via at the shrine of Volupiæ."

Festus, speaking of the same gate, says:—

"But the Porta Romana was set up by Romulus above the foot of the Hill of Victory, and this place is formed of tiers of steps disposed in a square. It is called Romana by the Sabines in particular, because it is the nearest entrance to Rome from the side of the Sabines."

PORTA CARMENTA (5).

Authorities on the subject say that the name and position of the third gate are lost.

Now we contend that the mass of ruins called the Scali Caci are the remains of the third gate, and that that gate was the Porta Carmenta, as distinctly stated by Virgil in his description of the meeting of Æneas and Evander, "without the gates." "Thus, walking on, he spoke, and showed the gate, *since* called Carmenta by the Roman state; then stopping, through the narrow gate they pressed" (Virgil, "Æn.," viii.). The position corresponds with his description, and is just the spot where a gate would be required. The remains consist of two different early periods—immense blocks of soft tufa of the Arcadian period, and blocks of hard brown tufa of the time of Romulus, corresponding with the material of which his wall is built.

The Porta Carmenta was to the south, and is thus mentioned by Propertius (iv. 1):—

" Where rose that house of Remus upon tiers of steps, a single
hearth was once the brothers' modest reign."

We suppose he uses the name of Remus here instead of Romulus
on account of the rhythm.

Solinus gives this description of it :—

" It [Roma Quadrata] begins at the wood which is in the area of
Apollo, and ends at the top of the stairs of Caius, where was [once]
the cottage of Faustulus."

Plutarch says ("Romulus," xx.) :—

" Romulus dwelt close by the steps, as they call them, of the fair
shore, near the descent from the Mount Palatine to the Circus
Maximus.  There, they say, grew the holy blackthorn tree, of which
they report that Romulus once, to try his strength, threw a dart
from Mount Aventine, which struck so deep that no one could pluck
it up, and grew into a trunk of considerable size, which posterity
preserved and worshipped as one of the most sacred things, and therefore walled it about.

" But, they say, when Caius Cæsar was repairing the steps about
it, some of the labourers digging too close, the root corrupted, and
the tree quite withered."

Now, in this passage, we think we have an explanation of why it
is called the Stairs of Caius, *not* Cacus.  This name does not refer to
Cacus, the shepherd robber, who had his cave on the Aventine, but,
as we learn from the above passage from Plutarch, to Caius the
emperor, who was nicknamed Caligula from his having worn
the sandals so-called of the Roman troops—he having been brought
up in the camp on the banks of the Rhine, Caius being his proper
name.  He, as we have seen, repaired these steps, and so they were
called after him ; but that was not their previous name.  The ques-
tion arises, What was that name?  Why, none other than the Porta
Carmenta, the missing third gate of Roma Quadrata, " the gate *since*
called Carmenta by the Roman state."

It was up this gateway that the Romans brought the Sabine
women when they ran off with them in the Circus Maximus.
Valerius Antias says they were five hundred and forty-seven in
number ; Plutarch says there were six hundred and eighty-three,
and that the event took place on the 18th of August.

But before this the gate had another name, the original name in the
Arcadian period.  We know from Virgil and Diodorus Siculus that it
existed before the time of Romulus, and was incorporated by him
into his city.  Let us see what that name was.

" Hercules, after he had gone through Liguria and Tuscany, encamped on the banks of the Tiber, where Rome now stands, built many ages after by Romulus, the son of Mars. The natural inhabitants at that time inhabited a little town upon a hill, now called Mount Palatine. Here Potitius and Pinarius, the most eminent persons of quality among them, entertained Hercules. There are now at Rome ancient monuments of these men; for the most noble family, called the Pinarii, remains still among the Romans, and is accounted the most ancient at this day. And there are Potitius's stone stairs to go down from Mount Palatine (called after his name), adjoining to that which was anciently his house" (Diodorus Siculus, iv. 1). Thus we see that the spot was originally called the Stairs of Potitius.

Virgil (" Æn.," viii.) informs us that Potitius, the Arcadian high priest, instituted the worship of Hercules; and that the priests were selected from the Pinarian house.

When the new walls were built by Servius Tullius, one of his gates was named Carmentalis after the above tradition; the original Porta Carmenta having become obsolete.

The valley between the Palatine and Aventine, the site of the Circus Maximus, was formerly the Murzian Lake or bay, formed by an arm of the Tiber, and these stairs led down to the fair shore (Pulcrum Littus, Καλὴ 'Ακτή)—that is, to the shore of the lake, where Æneas landed—and this had nothing to do with the banks of the Tiber, which would hardly be called a fair shore by Plutarch. Virgil calls it " the strand."

*The above name was also given to one of the temples.*

## THE TEMPLE OF ROMA QUADRATA (6).

" A certain hallowed place on the Palatine before the Altar of Apollo Rhamnusii (5), which every city built with Etruscan rites contained, and in which were placed those things considered of good omen in founding a city" (Festus). This hallowed place, as well as the city, was called by Romulus Roma Quadrata.

## ALTAR OF APOLLO RHAMNUSII (5),

called the Altar of Apollo of the Blackthorn. Erected in commemoration of the blackthorn tree that sprang from the staff of Romulus. The large tufa blocks of the altar, and in front of it the Temple of Roma Quadrata, still remain, and by their side the Porta Carmenta.

### THE CURIÆ VETERES (19).

Romulus divided the people into three tribes, and each tribe into ten curiæ (Dionysius, ii. 8), thus making thirty curiæ in all. Each curia had its own priests and separate dining-room and chapel, which were also called curiæ (*Ibid.*, ii. 23). The only one of these which we have mentioned as existing at a late period is the one connected with the Palatine: as we have seen, it is one of the objects Tacitus gives us for the line of the plough. Now, on the Palatine, on that line, we have a ruin below the present surface agreeing with the time of Romulus in its construction, to which no name has been given by the topographers, but which we consider as the Curiæ Veteres mentioned by Tacitus. It now supports the Auditorium of Domitian.

### THE HOUSE OF ROMULUS

"was where the Roma Quadrata ended, at the corner as you turn from the Palatine Hill to the Circus" (Dionysius). It was upon that part of the hill called Germalus from the twins being left there when the flood went down. This would be the shelf at the south-west corner of the Palatine.

### THE TEMPLE OF JUPITER STATOR (13),

vowed by Romulus when his army was fleeing before the Sabines, if Jupiter would stay their flight; hence the name. "Romulus built a temple to Jupiter near the Porta Mugonia" (Dionysius, ii. 30). It was restored by Regulus, A.U.C. 459 (Livy, x. 37). It was in this temple that Cicero made his first oration against Catiline (Plutarch). Cicero says that here the goods of Pompey were offered for sale.

### UNDER THE REPUBLIC.

It was not till the glories of the republic outshone the memory of the kings that the Palatine became the favourite residence of the wealthy. We have record of the houses inhabited by Vaccus, Catulus, Crassus, the Gracchi, Ceneus, Cicero, Scaurus, Mark Antony, and other notorious republicans. Some slight remains of republican walls can be seen at various points.

### THE TEMPLE OF CYBELE (4).

Dedicated by M. J. Brutus, B.C. 191, under the name of Mater Idæa, Mother of the Gods (Livy, xxxvi. 36). "Cybele was not worshipped in Rome till A.U.C. 550, when the goddess, a stone, was brought from Pessinus, a city of Phrygia, by Scipio Nasica" (Strabo). The vessel containing it having grounded at the mouth of the Tiber, remained immovable till Claudia Quinta, to prove her chastity, after calling upon the goddess, drew the ship with slight effort to Rome (Ovid, " Fasti," vi. 300). This event is commemorated upon an altar in the Capitoline Museum. The form of the temple remains, and part of the seated statue of the goddess, a beautiful fragment, corresponding with her figure as represented on coins. The remains are of *opus insertum*.

## THE TEMPLE OF VICTORY (9).

The remains of this are just inside the Porta Carmenta. It was founded originally by the Greek settlers, and restored under the republic; the construction agrees with this supposition, for here we have the two different stones used in these periods, soft tufa and peperino.

" Upon the top of the hill they set apart a piece of ground, which they dedicated to Victory, and instituted annual sacrifices to be offered up to her also, which the Romans perform even in my time" (Dionysius, i. 32), A.U.C. 458. "They carried the statue of Cybele into the Temple of Victory on the Palatine Hill " (Livy, xxix. 14).

*Near this ruin, on the other side of the road, are the remains of*

## THE SHRINE OF MAIDEN VICTORY (9A).

In A.U.C. 560, " Marcus Portius Cato dedicated a chapel to Maiden Victory, near the Temple of Victory, two years after he had vowed it " (Livy, xxxv. 9).

## ALTAR TO AIUS LOQUENS (35).

Still standing ; was erected 124 B.C., near the site where Camillus had erected the original, in the undetermined state, to the unknown voice that warned Marcus Cedicius of the approaching Gauls, 391 B.C.

" In the Via Nova, where now is the shrine, above the Temple of Vesta" (Livy, v. 23). "A voice was heard in the Grove of Vesta, which skirts the Nova Via at the foot of the Palatine" (Cicero, "Div." i. 45).

## TEMPLE OF JUPITER VICTOR (21).

Founded during the third Samnite war by Fabius Maximus (Livy, x. 29)—299-296 B.C.—overlooking the Circus Maximus. The remains consist of tufa substructions, steps leading up to the temple, and some peperino fragments.

The circular altar on the steps, found close by, bears an inscription to Calvinus, consul B.C. 53-40.

## THE HOUSE OF GERMANICUS (10),

*(See plan, page 8?)*

called erroneously by various authorities the House of Claudius Nero, of Livia, of Augustus. It was incorporated into the Imperial Palace by Tiberius, though for very many years it preserved its distinctive title. Josephus tells us that " Caligula was killed in a private narrow passage within the palace as he was going to the bath, having turned from the direct road along which his servants had gone. The passages also were narrow wherein the work was done, and crowded with Caius's attendants, whence it was that they went by other ways, and came to the house of Germanicus, which house adjoined to the palace." A crypto-portico still connects this house with the Palace of Caligula, another going off at right angles to the House of Augustus.

We have here a good specimen of a Roman house. In the vestibulum are remains of the mosaic floor and frescoed walls. The atrium still shows the pattern of its pavement. The tricliniarium is ornamented with frescoes of arabesque work, animals and fountains, also with mosaic pavement. The tablinium, in three parallel halls, painted with beautiful arabesque groups ; wreaths of flowers and fruit ; a group of Galatea and Polyhymnia ; another of Mercury, Io, and Argus ; a view of a Roman house; a lady at her toilet, &c. Behind these is the peristylium, out of which open the bedrooms, bath, kitchen, &c. In the centre tablinium are some leaden pipes, found in the excavations, stamped with the names of Julia, Domitian, and Niger,—the daughter of Augustus, the emperor, and the insurgent.

## THE PALACES OF THE CÆSARS

gradually incorporated the whole of the Palatine buildings; and when we speak of the Palace of the Cæsars, it is not meant that it was one, but different palaces, built by different emperors, called after them, and connected with those previously erected by crypto-porticoes.

## THE HOUSE OF AUGUSTUS (18).

" He resided in a small house formerly belonging to Hortensius. This was destroyed by fire, and rebuilt by contributions of the public " (Suetonius). The palace was destroyed by fire, under Titus, A.D. 80 ; the ruins were filled in by Domitian in the second year of his reign, and upon the top he built his celebrated palace. The remains of the Palace of Augustus—not now accessible, being under the convent— were explored and partly excavated some years ago.

From the PALACE OF DOMITIAN (17) we can descend into some of the small chambers, the vault of one being adorned with a fresco representing Victory.

### THE GELOTIANA (32),

mentioned by Suetonius as the place from which Caligula viewed the games in the Circus Maximus, is supposed to have been a house occupied by the guard and servants of the palace. Its ruin consists of chambers at the base of the hill, under the convent. It was here that the skit of the Crucifixion, now in the Museum of the Collegio Romano, was found. (See page 10.) The walls are still covered with names,&c., scratched by the soldiers.

### THE HOUSE OF TIBERIUS (3).

We learn from Suetonius and Tacitus that it was situated on the western side of the Palatine, overlooking and communicating with the Velabrum. The remains consist of vast halls and substructions, and a row of arches supposed to have been the guard's quarters. This palace has yet to be excavated.

### THE PALACE OF CALIGULA AND HADRIAN (2).

"Having continued part of the Palatine as far as the Forum, he converted the Temple of Castor and Pollux into the vestibule of his house." "He built a bridge over the temple of the deified Augustus, by which he joined the Palatine to the Capitol" (Suetonius). He connected his palace with that of Tiberius by means of porticoes. The remains consist of a suite of rooms, portions built over the Clivus Victoriæ, chambers with fresco and stucco decorations, and mosaic pavements, also a portion of the beautiful marble balustrade of the solarium. Suetonius tells us that this palace was destroyed by fire : in fact, most of the remains show the construction of Hadrian, who must have rebuilt it and used it as his palace.

The remains of this palace have been recently uncovered at the northern side of the Palatine. It appears that the palace was built in a series of terraces against the Palatine Hill, the construction showing work of Caligula, Hadrian, and Septimius Severus. There are some chambers which were warmed with hot air in terra-cotta pipes, and containing fragments of statuary on the lowest level excavated. Then, on the terrace above, there is an arcade paved with blocks of silex, and on one side shops. A flight of travertine steps conducts to some small chambers above, with mosaic pavements and frescoes, which were built by Hadrian against a wall of Caligula having frescoes on yellow and white grounds. The side walls and vaults are decorated with frescoes of the time of Hadrian.

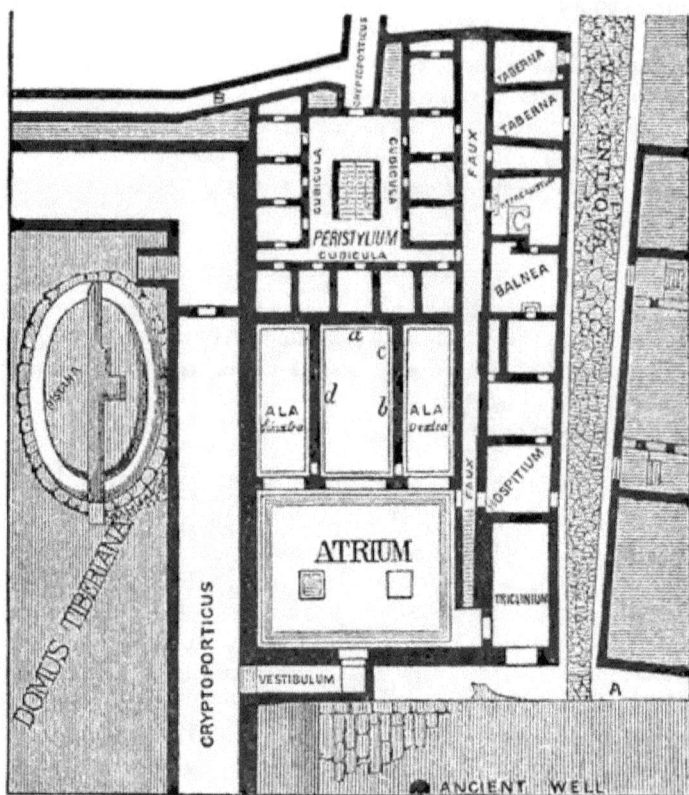

PLAN OF HOUSE OF GERMANICUS, A.D. 1.

## THE PALACE OF DOMITIAN (17).

He used the remains of Augustus's palace, destroyed by fire in the second year of the reign of Titus, filling in the chambers of the earlier buildings with earth, so that they formed a solid foundation. "He embellished the portico, in which he took his airing, with polished stone, so that he might observe if any one approached him" (Suetonius). The remains consist of the tablinium, or summer-parlour; the lararium, or chapel of the household gods; the bed-chamber where he was assassinated; the tricliniarium, or dining-room; the peristylium, or open court; nymphæum, or aquarium; the vometarium; auditorium; and the crypto-porticoes connecting it with the other palaces.

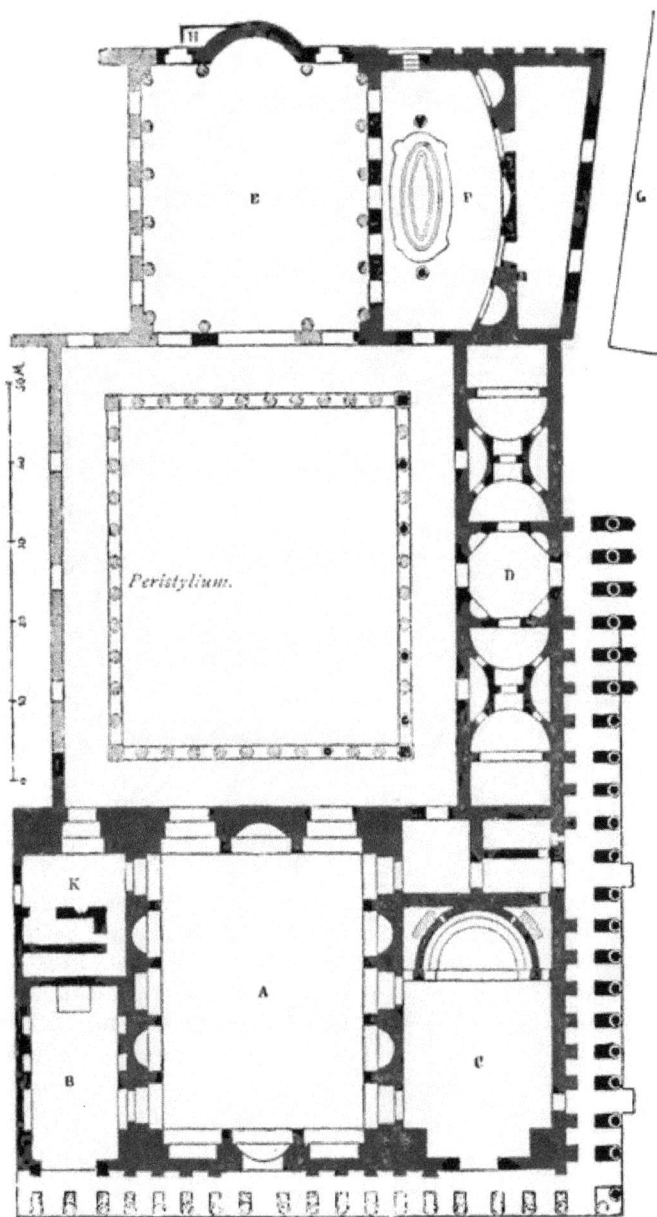

PLAN OF THE PALACE OF DOMITIAN, A.D. 81-96.

A. Tablinium.    F, Lararium.    C, Basilica.    D, Vestibule.    E, Triclinianum.    F, Nymphæum.
G, Temple Jupiter Victor.    H, Vometarium.    K, Cubiculum.

## THE BASILICA (16).

When the Palace of Augustus and the other edifices were burned down, Domitian filled them in with earth, and on the top of the platform built his palace. But some of the destroyed edifices were consecrated: as he could not do away with them, he rebuilt them upon the higher level, over their old sites. The basilica and chapel of the household gods were both treated in this way. As this was the only basilica on the Palatine, we may presume that it was the court of appeal unto Cæsar himself. If so, on this site S. Paul appeared before Nero; but not in this identical building, which was erected by Domitian, A.D. 81–96, after Paul's death, A.D. 64.

The Basilica was the hall of justice, coming from a Greek word signifying "the regal hall." It consisted of a tribunal, nave, and aisles. The form was oblong; the middle was an open space, called *testudo*, and which we now call the nave. On each side of this were rows of pillars, which formed what we should call the aisles, and which the ancients called *porticus*. The end of the testudo was curved, and was called the *tribunal*, from causes being heard there. A rail separating the tribunal from the body of the hall was called *cancelli*, because it was of open work. Not far from the entrance was a round stone in the pavement, on which the prisoner stood to be tried. Between the judge's seat on the tribunal and the rails stood the altar of Apollo. These halls were likewise used as places of exchange by business men. Being the largest halls the Romans had, the form of them was copied by the early Christians for their churches. The tribunal was called the apse; in some churches it is still called the tribunal. The judge's seat gave place to the bishop's throne; the altar of Apollo to the communion table; the cancelli to the chancel; and the fountain in the court in front to the holy-water basins; and so the name was handed down and given to Christian churches,

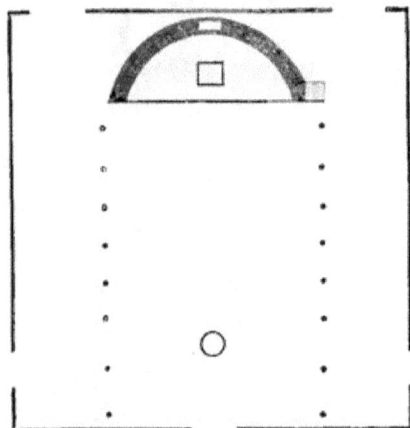

PLAN OF THE BASILICA ON THE PALATINE.

though there is not a single church in Rome that was once a pagan basilica, or hall of justice. Many of the so-called basilicas are not true basilicas, for they have introduced the transept to give them the form of a cross.

## THE STADIUM (26).

On the east side of the Palatine, built by Domitian, and only partly excavated. Used for races both for men and women. "Young girls ran races in the Stadium, at which Domitian presided in his sandals, dressed in a purple robe made after the Grecian fashion, and wearing upon his head a golden crown bearing the effigies of Jupiter, Juno, and Minerva; with the flamen of Jupiter and the college of priests sitting at his side in the same dress, excepting only that their crowns had also his own image on them" (Suetonius).

The work of excavating the Stadium is not yet completed. It appears that the portico surrounding it originally consisted of cipollino columns, with composite capitals. This was rebuilt in the third century in two tiers, supported with half-columns of brick, coated with slabs of marble, having Ionic bases and Doric capitals. A brick stamp informs us that the Imperial tribune was rebuilt in the third consulship of Ursus Servianus, under Hadrian, 134. At the edge of the foot-course, below the portico, was a marble channel to carry off the rain-water. Traces of the spina still remain. The Stadium seems to have been altered into a hippodrome in the time of Diocletian by building elliptical walls upon its surface. The following stamp was found on some of the bricks,—A.D. 500 OFFS R. F. MARCI HIPPODROME THEODORIC REGNANTE DN THEODERICO FELIX ROMA,—evidently some of the repairs ordered by the great king during his six months' visit to Rome.

## THE EXEDRA, OR ODEUM (27).

On the right of the Stadium, for musical performances, with three chambers underneath decorated with fresco work.

## THE NYMPHÆUM OF MARCUS AURELIUS (30).

We claim the honour of having discovered the use of these imposing ruins, whose summit is climbed by many visitors to enjoy the fine view over the Campagna. It was built by the best of the Roman emperors as a large reservoir for the supply of water to the Palatine Hill, acting as the Trevi Fountain does at present. We have traced the specus of the aqueduct to it; and the top is covered

6

with *opus signinum*, the peculiar cement used by the Romans whenever they conducted water.

The brickwork shows signs of careful construction; the courses of cement carefully laid between the bricks being of the same thickness as the bricks themselves, seven of which measure a foot. The Nymphæum probably took its name from the female statues which decorated it, handing down the custom of the ancient Romans in peopling the springs with nymphs.

It is thus mentioned by Marcellinus (xv. vii. 3):—"The Emperor Marcus built the Nymphæum, an edifice of great magnificence, near the well-known Septemzodium," which was built by Septimius Severus at the corner of the Palatine, where slight traces of it remain; it having been destroyed by Pope Sixtus V.

The spot now forms a pleasant terrace, from which a splendid prospect of the southern part of ancient Rome, the Campagna, and the distant Alban Hills may be enjoyed. In fact, a vast study is spread, like a map, before the visitor.

## THE PALACE OF COMMODUS (25, 29)

stood on the south-east side of the hill. He constructed a passage from the Palatine to the arena of the Colosseum. He was strangled in his chamber; and his successor, Pertinax, was stabbed in the same palace. This was destroyed by fire, and on the top of the ruins was erected the Palace of Septimius Severus, Caracalla, and Alexander Severus. The remains consist of numerous chambers, corridors, and vaults, still retaining some of their mosaic pavements and stucco roofs, with walls built into them in a very confused manner, showing different alterations. The palace is to be cleared out.

## THE PALACE OF THE CÆSARS.

After the death of Alexander Severus, A.D. 235, we have little or no history of buildings upon the Palatine, and there are no remains the construction of which shows a later date. Indeed the emperors reigned but a short time down to Diocletian, except Gallienus, who, we know, had a palace and gardens on the Esquiline. Fifty years after Alexander Severus died a great blow was struck at the grandeur of Rome; for the colleagues in empire, Diocletian and Maximian, made new capitals at Milan and Nicomedia, and thus divided the seat of power and empire. In A.D. 302, eighteen years after his declaration, Diocletian came to Rome for the first time, to celebrate his triumph, making a short stay of two months. The year 312 witnessed a great change. On October 28 the great Constantine, the first Christian emperor, and a Briton, made his entry into the imperial city, which for years had ceased to give rulers to the empire, and was now to be the seat of government no longer. Constantine did not make a long stay in the city; and, after he had secured his power, removed in 330 the capital of the empire to Byzantium, which was named Constantinople, to decorate which Rome was stripped of statues, marbles, and works of art. In 356 Constantius visited Rome, which had been abandoned by her rulers and denied the splendours of the imperial court. "After his entry he retired into the imperial palace, where he enjoyed the luxury he had wished for." " He quitted Rome on the thirtieth day after his entry (29th May)" (Marcellinus). The same historian informs us that, "on the night of the 18th of March 362, the Temple of Apollo, on the Palatine, was burned down." Theodosius, in 394, entered Rome in triumph. Honorius, his son, in 403 celebrated the grandest triumph since that of Diocletian, one hundred years before. Indeed, during this long period but four emperors had paid flying visits only to their ancient capital, and the Palace of the Cæsars was falling into decay, as Claudian, the last of the Roman poets, sings. Honorius for a short time revived the glories and memories of the past; the curule chairs once more surrounded the rostra, and their emperor's voice was once more heard by the *plebs*, whilst they gazed with awe at the lictors with their gilt fasces. After Honorius's departure, Alaric, and the barbarians that were with him, in 410, "took Rome itself, which they pillaged, burning the greatest part of the magnificent structures and other admirable works of art it contained" (Socrates, " E. H." v. 10). In 417 Honorius again entered Rome in triumph, and endeavoured to restore the city, and invited fugitives from all parts to people it. This benefactor of the city was buried near the supposed remains of S. Peter in the Vatican basilica. In 425 Valentinian III., whilst still a boy, received the imperial purple in the ancient Palace of the Cæsars, at the hands of an ambassador of Theodosius; and, although Ravenna was the seat of his government, he frequently visited Rome and inhabited the imperial palace. During one of these visits, in 454, Aetius, the general, fell in the imperial palace, stabbed by the hand of the licentious emperor, who drew his sword for the first time to kill the general who had saved his empire. In the following year, March 27, he was himself assassinated in the Campus Martius during a review; and Petronius Maximus was declared emperor, but was in his turn soon after murdered.

The third day thereafter, Genseric and his Vandals entered Rome, and plundered it of everything they could carry off, from the seven-branched candlestick to the common utensils of Cæsar's Palace, which they completely stripped. Avitus, a Gaul, the successor of Petronius, visited Rome for a short time, and was murdered on his return to Auvergne. After the throne had been vacant for ten months, Majorianus was made emperor by Ricimer, 457. He published an edict from Ravenna against destroying the ancient monuments of Rome and using the materials for building. Severus Libius was his successor, and he was poisoned within the walls of the Palatine, August 465. Anthemius entered Rome in a triumphal procession in April 467, and revived the Lupercalia games; he was put to death in the palace by Ricimer, who captured Rome, July 11, 472. From 472 to 476 there were four emperors, the last of whom, Romulus Augustus, abdicated in presence of the senate, who proclaimed the extinction of the Western Empire.

In A.D. 500 King Theodoric paid a visit of six months to Rome. After addressing the people from the Rostra ad Palmam, which stands at the head of the Forum, he took up his residence at the Palace of the Cæsars, and appointed officers to take care of the ancient monuments. After his death, Athalaric and his mother governed till the former's death in 534. Theodatus, his successor, was murdered on the Flaminian Way, as he was retreating before Belisarius, the general of the Eastern emperor Justinian, who fixed his quarters at the Pincian Palace. In 549 Totila captured the city, and resided in the Palace of the Cæsars, exhibiting games in the Circus Maximus for the last time. During the winter of 552–553 Narses, the Eastern general, took Rome, and resided there, Rome being again united to the Eastern Empire, governed by an exarch, who generally resided at Ravenna. The history of the Palatine is a blank till the time of Heraclius 1. Though not present himself, a coronation ceremony was held with great pomp in the Palace of the Cæsars, 610. A great event for Rome took place in 663. Then, for the last time, she received within her walls her emperor, Constans II., who contemplated again making her the capital of the empire. He was received by Pope Vitalianus at the Porta Appia with a procession of priests with tapers, banners, and crosses,—a curious contrast with former usages. Constans was the last emperor who resided in the Palace of the Cæsars, which was even then in a dilapidated condition; and his time seems to have been occupied with church ceremonies. His visit lasted twelve days, when he carried off what plunder he could, besides the gilt bronze tiles of the roof of the Pantheon. A blank again occurs till Justinian II., in 709, created the first Duke of Rome,

ARCH OF TITUS, BEFORE RECENT EXCAVATIONS.

who was afterwards elected by Pope and people, and resided in the Palace of the Cæsars. For many years the power of the Church of

Rome had been increasing, and in 772 Pope Adrian I. threw off the nominal sovereignty of the Eastern Empire, and, calling upon Charlemagne to free him from the Lombard kings, he entered Rome on Saturday, April 2, Easter eve. Charlemagne confirmed Pepin's gifts to the Holy See. He again visited it, and on Christmas day A.D. 800 Pope Leo III. crowned him emperor in S. Peter's, with the title of Emperor of the Romans. From thence commenced the Holy Roman Empire.

*Leaving the Palatine, we turn to the right, and by the newly-excavated Vicus Vestæ, on the north side of the hill, reach*

### THE ARCH OF TITUS.

On the ridge of the Velia hill, which forms a continuation of the Palatine, and separates the hollow of the Forum from that of the

BAS-RELIEF ON THE ARCH OF TITUS.

Colosseum, a triumphal arch was erected (though not till after his death and deification) to Titus, the conqueror of Jerusalem. The reliefs, still preserved within the arch, are among the most remarkable of the kind existing in Rome as to the position they occupy in the history of art and of the world. We find here not only the emperor standing in the triumphal chariot in which he advanced to the Temple of Jupiter Capitolinus, but also the table of the shewbread, and the seven-branched candlestick, borne in this triumphal procession as the most precious spoils of the Jewish temple.

"There was a golden table, which weighed many talents; also a golden candlestick, which was constructed upon a different principle from anything in use amongst us now. In the middle was the main stem, which rose out of the base ; from this proceeded smaller branches, very much resembling the form of a trident ; and on the top of them was a lamp, worked in brass. There were seven such in all, emblematic of the seven days of the Jewish week. The Law of the Jews was the last of those spoils in the procession" (Josephus, "Wars of the Jews," viii. v. 5). "The legs of the table were perfectly finished in the lower half, like those the Dorians put upon their couches, but the upper half of them was worked square" (Josephus, "Antiquities of the Jews," iii. vi. 6).

Two censers were placed upon the table ; in front of the table are two trumpets crossed. (See Exodus xxv. 26).

These spoils were deposited by Vespasian in the Temple of Peace. After the sack of Rome, A.D. 455, the Vandal king Genseric carried them to Carthage. Belisarius recovered them, A.D. 535, and took them to Constantinople ; and they were transferred from there to the Christian Church in Jerusalem (Procopius, "De Bell. Vand.," i. 5 and ii. 4).

Evagrius (iv. 17) relates that when Khosroes, king of Persia, took Jerusalem in 614, they passed into his hands ; and all trace of them has been lost since then. It is altogether erroneous to suppose they were thrown into the Tiber.

*On the opposite side* is the Emperor Titus in a chariot drawn by four horses, preceded by Romans wearing laurel wreaths and carrying the fasces. Behind the chariot, Victory is in the act of placing a crown on the emperor's head. The vault is ornamented with square coffers and roses, and in the centre the apotheosis of Titus, in square relief.

At this point the Via Sacra was sometimes called the Clivus Palatinus, as it led up to the Palatine, *on the right.*

"Clœlia had her statue in the Via Sacra, as you go up to the Palatine" (Plutarch, in "Publicola").

*Passing through the Arch of Titus,*

*On our right* are some remains of the Frangipani fortress, a tower of the middle ages ; a piece of the second wall of Rome ; some substructions and walls, as it were supporting the Palatine Hill; and remains of the Baths and

### TEMPLE OF THE SUN,

" built by Elagabalus, on the slopes of the Palatine, for the worship of the Syro-Phœnician sun-god, which was represented by a black conical stone, set with gems. Elagabalus broke into the Temple of

ARCH OF TITUS, WITH THE META SUDANS, AND BASILICAE OF THE FORUM OF CUPID.

Vesta, intending to remove the Palladium to his Temple of the Sun, but the virgins, by a pious fraud, defeated his object, on discovering which he broke into their sanctuary, and carried off one of the virgins to add to his list of wives " (Lampridius).

The temple was built for the worship of the Sun. Around it was the Lavacrum, or gratuitous baths, A.D. 218–222. The temple was converted in A.D. 800 into the Church of S. Maria, by Pope Leo III. The remains of the altar can be seen at the east end; at the west end is the baptistery, in the form of a Greek cross, with an apse at the top containing the raised platform with the depressed basin of the font in which the person about to be baptized stood, whilst the minister occupied the platform above it and poured the water over his head.

*On our left is*

## THE FORUM OF CUPID AND ITS BASILICÆ,

miscalled the Temple of Venus and Rome. The platform upon which it stands is partly the Velia ridge and partly artificial.

When a building was inaugurated after consecration it was called a *templum*. A *delubrum* was an isolated building, surrounded with an area, dedicated to religious purposes. This—because it was double, having two aspects, two distinct apses or tribunals—we call, in the plural number, *delubra*, or the double basilica.

The remains consist of two large tribunals, back to back, with a portion of the lateral walls and vaults. The wall in the monastery gardens can be seen on application to the guard.

The name of this building is entirely lost. All we know about it is, that it is of the time of Maxentius and Constantine, A.D. 306–337, the construction showing it to be of that time; besides, Nibby found in the walls bricks stamped with the name of Maxentius.

Nearly all late authorities have called this ruin the Temple of Venus and Rome. Now, it could not possibly be that temple, for we are told distinctly, as we have related, by Apollodorus, that the Temple of Rome was NOT built on a platform. Again, the Temple of Rome was built by Hadrian, A.D. 118–138, and these remains are of the time of Maxentius and Constantine, A D. 306–337 ; besides, Roman temples had no tribunals or apses.

These basilicas were surrounded by a colonnade of gray granite, numerous fragments of which still lie about, and there was probably originally a forum or market-place for the sale of fruit and toys.

Varro (L. L. 532, R. R. i. 2), Ovid (A. A. ii. 265), Propertius (iii.

xvii. 11), Terence, Eunuchus, contemporary writers, all speak of a macellum and forum of Cupid upon the Via Sacra.

Festus, who lived in the fourth century, speaks of them under the same name; so we may conclude that the ruins before us are the basilicas of the Forum of Cupid, restored by Maxentius, and dedicated by Constantine.

The front of this platform, towards the Colosseum, was discovered in 1828 to have been used during the middle ages as a cemetery, several coffins of terra cotta being exhumed.

At the corners are the remains of steps which led from below up to the delubra. Near the left-hand steps, in descending, are the remains of the

## PEDESTAL OF NERO'S COLOSSUS,

which, as we have seen, first stood in the vestibule of his house; then where the atrium was; thence it was removed by Hadrian with twenty-four elephants to this spot, as is shown on a coin of Alexander Severus. It was 120 feet high. Vespasian radiated the head to make it represent the sun; Commodus took off Nero's head, and replaced it with his own. The popular quotation from Bede refers to this Colossus, not to the Colosseum.

*In a line with Nero's Pedestal is the*

## META SUDANS,

the remains of a fountain, erected by Titus, and repaired by Domitian and Gordianus, which stood in the centre of a large circular basin. Popular tradition narrates that the gladiators used to wash here after combat: it is certainly possible, but not very probable, that they would come outside to wash at an open fountain. The epithet Meta Sudans, or "sweating-goal," is supposed to be taken from the perpetual issue of foaming water, or because it contributed to satisfy the thirst of the audience at the Colosseum; or *meta*, because it was built in the form of a goal, and *sudans*, because the water trickled out.

*To the right is*

## THE ARCH OF CONSTANTINE,

dedicated by the senate and people of Rome to commemorate the victories of the first Christian emperor, to do which they took reliefs from the Arch of Trajan, and built them into an attic which they erected upon the top of the Arch of Isis, re-dedicating the conglomeration as the Triumphal Arch of Constantine. The reliefs which

ARCH OF CONSTANTINE.

refer to Trajan can be easily distinguished from those of Constantine (which are very bad) owing to their superior style and the subjects represented.

The designs commence, *on the left side*, with the triumphal entrance of Trajan by the Porta Capena, after the first Dacian war; then, secondly, commemorate his services in carrying the Appian Way through the Pontine Marshes; thirdly, founding an asylum for orphan children; fourthly, his relations with Parthamasiris, king of Armenia. *On the opposite side*, dedication of the aqueduct built by Trajan (*seen on the left*); secondly, audience with the Dacian king Decebalus, whose hired assassins are brought before him; thirdly, with a representation of the emperor haranguing his soldiers; and, fourthly, the emperor offering the *suovetaurilia* sacrifice of a boar, ram, and bull.

Corresponding with these reliefs, two medallions, representing the private life of the emperor in simple and graceful compositions, are introduced over each of the side arches. The first represents his starting for the chase; the second, a sacrifice to Silvanus, the patron of silvan sports; the third displays the emperor on horseback at a bear-hunt; and the fourth a thank-offering to the goddess of hunting. On the side facing the Colosseum, a bear-hunt, a sacrifice to Apollo, a group contemplating a dead lion, and lastly a consultation of an oracle. Most of these refer to Trajan; we think some refer to Hadrian, because on one of them Antinoüs is represented. On the inside of the arch is a battle-piece, assigned to Constantine by the inscriptions, "To the founder of peace," "To the deliverer of the city." They refer to Alexander Severus. Over the side arches are some narrow reliefs referring to Constantine, one of which is peculiarly interesting, as it represents that emperor addressing the people from the Rostra ad Palmam, with some of the principal monuments in the Forum in the background.

## THE COLOSSEUM.

"A noble wreck in ruinous perfection."—BYRON.

The vast amphitheatre erected in the centre of ancient Rome by Vespasian was known to the ancient Romans as the Flavian Amphitheatre. It was begun by the Flavian emperors A.D. 72, and dedicated A.D. 80. It is 157 feet high, and is 1900 feet in circumference, and was built by the captive Jews after the fall of Jerusalem. Originally the upper story was of wood, but this was burned down, and it was rebuilt with travertine stone like the rest of the edifice. Martial tells us that its site was formerly occupied by the artificial lakes of Nero; and Marcellinus (xvi. x. 14) says, "The vast masses of the amphitheatre so solidly erected of Tiburtine stone, to the top of which human vision can scarcely reach." All the brickwork we now see are repairs at various dates after the dedication; but there is enough travertine left at different points to show that it was originally built of this stone, as recorded by the historian. For nearly five hundred years it was the popular resort of the Roman populace and their betters. There were eighty arches of entrance, and it held one hundred thousand people, and could be emptied in ten minutes; such were the order kept and regulations observed that there was no confusion. It was devoted to the exhibition of wild beasts, their fighting together, gladiators fighting together, or with beasts, and naval fights. On these latter displays the stage or arena was moved, water let in, and naval fights represented in real earnest.

Suetonius ("Vespasian," vii.), says, "He began an amphitheatre in the middle of the city, upon finding that Augustus had projected such a work." *Ibid.* ("Titus," vi.): "He entertained the people with most magnificent spectacles, and in one day brought into the amphitheatre five thousand wild beasts of all kinds."

The last display was given by Theodoric in 523; and in 555 the lower part was destroyed by a flood from the Tiber, when the whole of Rome was under water for seven days. From then we must date the ruin of the Flavian Amphitheatre—the Romans themselves hastening on the work, using the material for building purposes.

> " Which on its public shows unpeopled Rome,
> And held uncrowded nations in its womb."—JUVENAL.

It is held by the Roman Church, on the authority of an inscription found in the Catacombs, that the architect of the Colosseum was one Gaudentius; but that inscription only says that he was employed there. We believe the architect to have been Aterius, whose monument is now in the Lateran, and upon which several buildings are represented of which he was no doubt the architect, also the machine used to raise the stones into their places. He flourished at the end of the first century, and, no doubt, these buildings shown in relief upon his tomb were erected by him, the dates agreeing; for if not, why should they be there represented?

First, we have an arch which says on it, "Arcus ad Isis." Now if we compare this with the Arch of Constantine, we find it is the same

without the attic. Then we have the amphitheatre without the
upper story; then an arch (query, Arch of Domitian?). Then
another arch with the words, " Arcus in Sacra Via Summa:" compare this with the Arch of Titus, and, minus the restorations, it will
be found to be the same. Then there is a temple agreeing with the
descriptions of that of Jupiter Stator upon the Palatine. All these
buildings were erected or rebuilt about this time, and from being
recorded on this monument of the Aterii, tend to show that Aterius
was the architect of them.

When perfect, the Colosseum consisted of four stories—the
lowest, of the Doric order, 30 feet high; the second, Ionic, 38 feet
high; the third, Corinthian, about the same height; and the fourth,
also Corinthian, 44 feet high. The holes in the cornice with the
corbels below them were to receive the masts that supported the
*velaria* on the outside.

The numerous holes in the stone were made in the middle ages for
the purpose of extracting the iron cramps that kept the stones from
shifting. The long diameter is 658 feet, the shorter 558 feet; the
arena is 298 feet by 177 in its widest part.

The last performance was a bull-fight, held at the expense of the
Roman nobles, in the year 1332. Many martyrs are said to have
perished in the Colosseum during the persecutions of the early
Christians, and among others S. Ignatius, who was brought from
Antioch to be devoured by wild beasts. Benedict XIV. consecrated
the building to the Christian martyrs, A.D. 1750.

In excavating the Basilica of S. Clement, the Rev. Father Mullooly found (1870) the remains of S. Ignatius, and had them carried
with great ceremony over the scene on the anniversary of his
martyrdom.

At the present day there remains sufficient to indicate the construction of the building, though but a small portion of the immense
outer shell, which originally both adorned and formed an impene-
trable girdle round the whole, has been preserved. In the interior,
a great deal of rebuilding has been necessary for its preservation.

Vast as the building is, its construction is easily understood; a
simple segment of the whole serving to show how all the others succeed one another like the cells of a bee-hive.

The upper part was originally of wood only, and was burned, having
been set on fire by lightning. The three lower stories only are of
the time of the Flavian emperors; the upper story was rebuilt
and added in the third century, and only finished in the time of the

THE COLOSSEUM.

Gordiani, as is shown by the coins representing it. The imperial entrance was from the Esquiline side, between the arches Nos. 38, 39, which is without number. Commodus constructed an underground passage from the arena to the Palatine, which has not yet been discovered, his so-called passage (*on the right in entering*) being that by which the dead bodies were carried from the arena. Dion Cassius says: "Upon the last day of the sports his helmet was taken off and fell through the door where the dead used to be carried out."

The area, basement, or ground-floor, was flooded for the naval fights. Surrounding this were the dens, in front of which was a channel for fresh water for supplying the animals with drink—a spring still supplies it; about ten feet above was the movable stage, sprinkled with sand for the combats, and hence called the arena. A few feet above the arena was the podium, or seat of the emperor, vestal virgins, &c., protected from the arena by iron bars. Behind the podium was a double portico, which ran round the whole building. Fragments of the marble chimeras, with long wings, that ornamented the seats of the podium have been found.

The three successive tiers were called *cavea*. Above these was a tier for the people; above this one for the "gods;" thus making six in all. The amphitheatre seated eighty-seven thousand people, and there was standing room for thirteen thousand more.

The walls standing upon the area, composed of tufa, travertine, and brick, old material re-used, were built at a period long after the building was dedicated, when the naval fights being abandoned there was no longer any occasion for a movable stage or arena as before. They contained the machinery for the stage above, and for the lifts or *pegmata* to send men or beasts from the area to the arena. Probably these are the walls thus alluded to by Dion Cassius: "He [Commodus] divided the theatre into four parts by two partitions that cut through diametrically, and by right angles, to the end that from the galleries that were round about he might with greater ease single out the beasts he aimed at."

"The emperor having employed himself in shooting from above ......descended afterwards to the bottom of the theatre, and there slew some other private beasts, whereof some made toward him, others were brought to him, and others were shut up in dens. Returning after dinner, he used the exercises of a gladiator, with a shield in his right hand, and in his left a wooden sword. After him fought those whom he had chosen in the morning at the bottom of

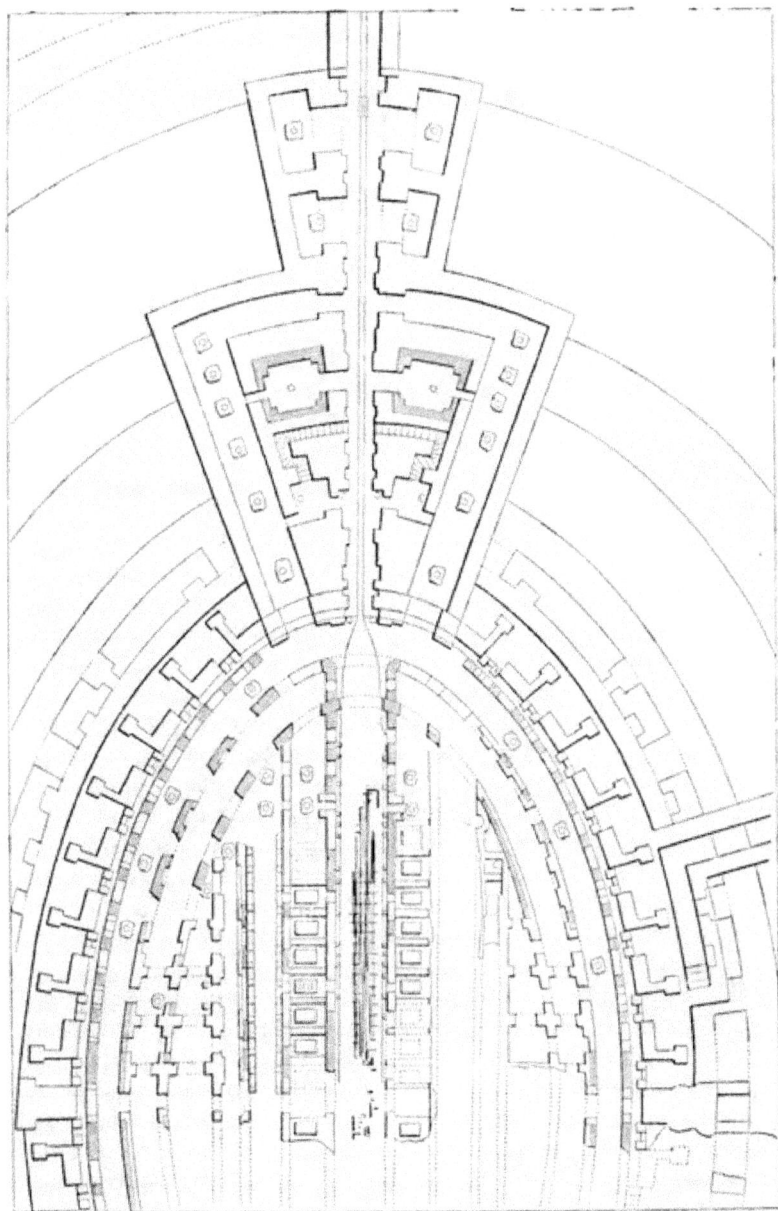

PLAN OF THE EXCAVATIONS BELOW THE ARENA OF THE COLOSSEUM.

the theatre." Also, in his life of Septimius Severus, he says: "There was a kind of cloister made in the amphitheatre, in the form of a ship, to receive them [the wild beasts]. On a sudden there issued out bears, lions, ostriches, wild asses, and foreign bulls."

The walls before us are of very bad construction, evidently repairs of a late date: they are the work of either Lampridius, prefect of Rome under Valentinian III., 425–455, who repaired the steps and renewed the arena; or of Basilius, who restored the podium and arena after their destruction by an earthquake in 486—this we learn from two inscriptions standing at the entrance. Half way, on each side, two large passages have been discovered choked up with mud : they were the aqueducts to bring the water for the *naumachiæ* from the reservoirs upon the Esquiline and Cælian Hills respectively ; from the small openings in the blind arches the water also poured out over the top of the dens, thus forming cascades all round. At the end opposite the present entrance a long passage has been opened, above the level of the area floor; below this passage is the great drain, with the remains of the iron grating* to prevent large objects going down : this and the passage were closed by flood-gates on naval representations, which can be clearly seen in the construction. On the right and left of this passage, connected with it, but at a lower level, two dens have been cleared out, 27 yards long by 5 wide, containing six holes in the floor, in the centre of square blocks of stone, and these holes are faced with bronze, evidently the sockets into which metal posts were fixed to which the beasts were chained. On the fragments depicting scenes from the arena, the animals are shown with a long piece of rope or chain dangling from their necks, which seems to bear out our idea that they were attached to posts fixed in these sockets, and that as they were wanted the chain or rope was cut, and they were free to rush upon the arena.

The corbels round the front of the line of arches under the podium are in pairs, and between them the masts were inserted to support the awning on the inside, as the holes and corbels supported the masts on the outside ; for we find on examination that those inside are exactly in a line with those outside at the top of the building. These corbels are 29 inches deep, and from them to the level of the area is 10 feet, and to the present surface 11 feet; between each pair of corbels are chases 19½ inches wide, ending on a block of travertine for the masts to rest on, the chases coming down 1½ yard below the corbels, which are 15 feet apart. They probably helped to

* Recently removed to clean out the drain.

support the arena, and show what the height of this wooden arena must have been, and that from its vast size it must have had a framework and supports : the numerous holes on the area, in travertine, were for the heels of the supports; one of these, a square one, has remains of the decayed timber in it.

In the central passage, resting on the area and extending as far as the excavations, is an ancient wooden framework in a decomposed state. Various suggestions have been made as to its use,—we suppose it to be the framework and joists of the flooring covering the central passage ; others, a sort of tramway for running the cages along,—but till the whole space has been cleared out it is impossible to arrive at a correct estimate of its use.

Honorius, A.D. 404, having abolished the gladiatorial combats, probably the last display of wild beasts was that given by King Theodoric at the beginning of the sixth century.

The soil cleared out in the passage, dens, galleries, and area was found to be composed of mud deposited during a flood or floods by the Tiber, the composition of which may still be seen in parts of the long passage not yet cleared. The most remarkable of these floods, which lasted some days and did immense damage to the city, were those of A.D. 555, 590, 725, 778, 1476, 1530, 1557, and 1598.

We may presume, from the nature of the soil, that at some early date, probably A.D. 555, one of those terrible floods reached the Colosseum, and on the waters retiring a great deposit of mud was left, covering the old area floor and filling up the various passages and galleries, and that the authorities, instead of clearing out this deposit, added to it to make a solid floor, and used the arena above; for after that date we have no record of its being used, with the exception of the bull-fight.

*On the left of main entry, fee 50 c., the visitor can ascend to the top,* where a most magnificent view is enjoyed, the only way to get a good idea of its size and oval shape, and where the construction of the upper galleries can be studied. It will be seen that the arches forming the tiers of seats have at some date been filled in with brickwork, of the time of Alexander Severus and the Gordiani. The water-courses for keeping the building cool in hot weather can also be traced. The highest wall of all, the inside brick casing of which is partly gone, is built of fragments evidently not originally intended for the purpose for which they are used, corresponding to a great extent with the construction of the walls upon the area.

The Colosseum was for a long time used as a quarry, from which several of the palaces in Rome were built.

Should the visitor be fortunate enough to see the ruin under moonlight, or when it is illuminated with Bengal lights, he will see it in its grandeur, for "it will not bear the brightness of the day."

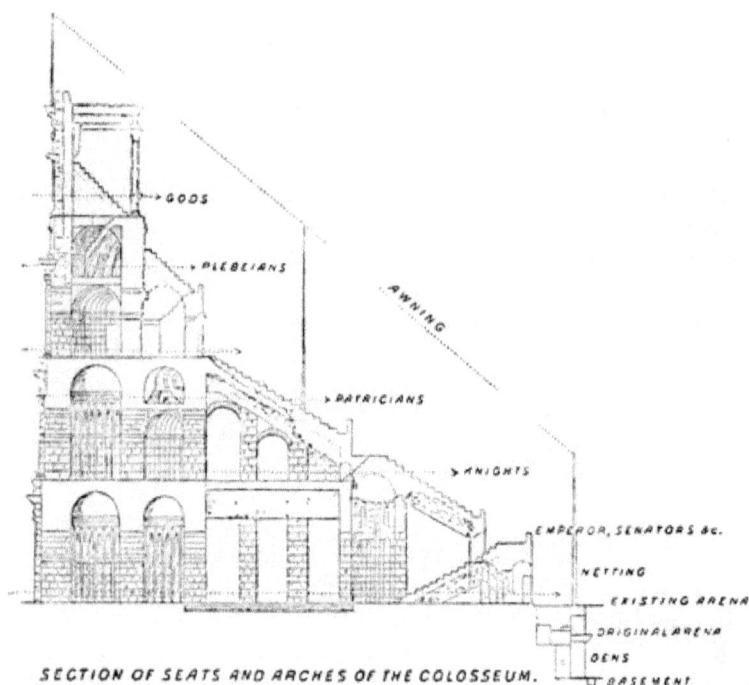

GODS

PLEBEIANS

AWNING

PATRICIANS

KNIGHTS

EMPEROR, SENATORS &c.

NETTING

EXISTING ARENA

ORIGINAL ARENA

DENS

BASEMENT

SECTION OF SEATS AND ARCHES OF THE COLOSSEUM.

# RAMBLE II.

---

---

## IN TRASTEVERE.

(*Over the Tiber.*)

### THE ROUTE.

*From the Piazza del Popolo the Via Ripetta leads towards S. Peter's,
turning off to the right, past the bridge, by the Via Monte Brianzo.
The new Ponte Margherita and Via Cola di Rienzo is the direct road.*

*From the Piazza di Spagna we take the Via Condotti to the Via
Monte Brianzo and Tor di Nona.*

Considerable changes are taking place along this line of streets
in the works for the new Tiber embankment. The Ponte S. Angelo
is closed to be elongated. *On the left, opposite the entrance to the
bridge,* is the Italian Free Church, founded by the late Father
Gavazzi.

*We cross the river by a temporary iron bridge.*

### THE BRIDGE OF S. ANGELO

(*Ponte S. Angelo*)

is decorated with ten angels standing on the parapet, bearing the instruments of our Lord's passion ; and SS. Peter and Paul, an addition made in 1668 by Clement IX. It is the finest bridge in Rome, and was built by Hadrian.

### TOMB OF HADRIAN, NOW THE CASTLE OF S. ANGELO.

(*Castel S. Angelo. Permissions required: see page 361.*)

It was covered with white Paros marble, and decorated with statues of the gods and heroes, the works of Praxiteles and Lysippus, which were hurled upon the heads of the Goths. Erected by Hadrian, A.D. 130. The porphyry sarcophagus, which is supposed to have contained his remains, is now used as the font in the chapel on the left in S. Peter's.

Procopius thus describes it : " The tomb of the Emperor Hadrian is situated outside the Porta Aurelia. It is built of Parian marble, and the blocks fit close to one another without anything to bind them. It has four equal sides, about a stone-throw in length ; its altitude rises above the city walls ; on the top are statues of the same kind of marble, admirable figures of men and horses."

Lucius Verus, Antoninus Pius, Marcus Aurelius, Commodus, were all buried here. It was first turned into a fortress A.D. 423. Popes John XXIII. and Urban VIII. built the covered way connecting it with the Vatican. One of the barrack-rooms contains frescoes by Pierino del Vaga and Sicciolante, another by Giulio Romano. A circular room, surrounded with carved wood cases, once contained the archives of the Vatican. A large iron-bound chest contained the treasury. Some dark cells built in the thickness of the walls are shown as the prisons of Beatrice Cenci (?). Cellini, Cagliastro, and others. Tradition asserts that Gregory the Great saw S. Michael standing over the fortress sheathing his sword as a sign that a pestilence was stayed; to commemorate which the castle is now surmounted by a figure of the archangel in the act of sheathing his sword. This old castle served for a fortress during several ages, and its first cannon were cast out of part of the bronze taken from the roof of the Pantheon.

*The Borgo Nuovo leads to* the Cathedral, passing, *on the right*, the Church of S. Maria, built on the site of a pyramid to Honorius, 423 A.D., which is represented on the doors of S. Peter's.

## S. PETER'S.

(*S. Pietro.*)

EXTERIOR.

Before the era of railways, the traveller in approaching Rome, across the Campagna, was generally electrified by the first glimpse of S. Peter's dome looming in the distance. Then he had full time, in advance of entering the gates of the city, to ponder over all the recollections which the magical word "Roma" might suggest to him. At present he is rapidly borne into the city, and sometimes before he is aware of having arrived even in its neighbourhood; yet the dome is plainly visible from afar by the railway approach of to-day. Now, as then, the first sight of Rome is always her unequalled cathedral; now, as then, the latter is the great object which the tourist eagerly hastens to visit. The present Church of S. Peter is relatively modern, having been first conceived by Pope Nicholas V. about the year 1450. It is built upon the site of the religious edifice erected in the time of Constantine, and consecrated as the "Basilica of S. Peter." The old basilica stood on part of the Circus of Nero, and occupies the spot consecrated by the blood of the martyrs slaughtered by order of that tyrant. Tradition supposes that the basilica held possession of the body of the apostle after his crucifixion,—a circumstance which reflected high credit upon it, and dignified its entrance with the appellation of the "limina apostolorum" (threshold of the apostles). After enjoying the veneration and tributes of all Christendom during eleven centuries, the walls of the old basilica began to give way, and its approaching ruin becoming visible about the year above stated, Nicholas V. conceived the project of taking down the old church, and erecting in its stead a new and more expensive structure. The project was begun, and resulted, after a long series of experiments made by various architects, in the splendid fabric which is now regarded by the world as the chief glory of modern Rome. The work made slight progress until the epoch of Julius II., who resumed the great task, and found in Bramante an architect capable of comprehending and executing his grandest conceptions. The walls of the ancient basilica were then wholly removed, and on the 18th of April 1508 the foundation stone of one of the vast pillars supporting the dome, as we now see it, was laid by Julius with great pomp and ceremony. From that period the work, though carried on with ardour and perseverance, continued during one hundred years to

occupy the attention and absorb much of the incomes of eighteen
pontiffs. The most celebrated architects of the times displayed
their talents in its erection—namely, Bramante, Raphael, San Gallo,
Michael Angelo, Vignola, Carlo Maderno, and last, though not least,
Bernini, who gave it the finishing touches of ornamentation, and
who built the enclosing colonnade. It is estimated that its cost,
after completion, was no less than £12,000,000 sterling—a sum
representing a far greater value than it does in our day. Colossal
statues of Peter and Paul, erected by Pius IX., guard the approach
at the foot of the steps on either side.

Eustace says: "Entering the piazza, the visitor views four rows
of lofty pillars, 70 feet high, sweeping off to the right and left in a
bold semicircle. ('A tabernacle for a shadow in the day-time from
the heat, and for a place of refuge, and for a covert from storm and
from rain,' Isa. iv. 6.) In the centre of the area formed by this immense colonnade, an Egyptian obelisk, of one solid piece of granite,
ascends to the height of 130 feet; two perpetual fountains, one on
each side, play in the air, and fall in sheets round the basins of
porphyry that receive them. Raised on three successive flights of
marble steps, extending 379 feet in length, and towering to the
elevation of 148, you see the majestic front of the basilica itself.
This front is supported by a single row of Corinthian pillars and
pilasters, and adorned with an attic, a balustrade, and thirteen colossal
statues. Far behind and above it rises the matchless dome. Two
smaller cupolas, one on each side, add not a little to the majesty of
the principal dome."

Five lofty portals open into the vestibule; it is 468 feet in length,
66 in height, and 50 in breadth, paved with variegated marble,
covered with a gilt vault, adorned with pillars, pilasters, mosaic, and
bas-reliefs, and terminated at both ends by equestrian statues, one
of Constantine, the other of Charlemagne.

### THE OBELISK

is the only one near its original site, the *Spina* of Nero's Circus,
which was near the Sacristy, on the left of S. Peter's. An inscription
in the pavement marks the place. Pliny (xxxvi. 14), says: "The
third obelisk at Rome is in the Vatican Circus, which was constructed by the emperors Caius [Caligula] and Nero; this being the
only one of them all that has been broken in the carriage. Nun-
corcus, the son of Sesoses, made it [*the original, this is probably a
copy*], and there remains [in Egypt] another by him, 100 cubits in

S. PETER'S AND THE VATICAN.

height, which, by order of an oracle, he consecrated to the sun, after
having lost his sight and recovered it." Herodotus says: " It was
dedicated by Phero, son of Sesostris, in gratitude for his recovery
from blindness." It has no hieroglyphics, so if this was the original
how could they know who erected it ? but it bears this inscription of
Caligula—

DIVO. CAES. DIVI. JULII. F. AUGUSTO.—TI. CAESARI.
DIVI. AUG. F.—AUGUSTO. SACRUM.

[To the divine Augustus, son of the divine Julius, and to the divine
Tiberius, son of the divine Augustus.]

The Nuncoreus of Pliny is supposed to stand for Menophtheus,
the king Meneph-Pthah.

Pliny (xvi. 76) gives the following particulars of how it was
brought over :—

" A fir tree of prodigious size was used in the vessel which, by the
command of Caligula, brought the obelisk from Egypt, which stands
in the Vatican Circus, and four blocks of the same sort of stone to
support it. Nothing certainly ever appeared on the sea more
astonishing than this vessel ; 120,000 bushels of lentils served for its
ballast ; the length of it nearly equalled all the left side of the port of
Ostia—for it was sent there by the Emperor Claudius. The thickness
of the tree was as much as four men could embrace with their arms."

Suetonius ("Claudius," xx.) says: " He sank the vessel in which
the great obelisk had been brought from Egypt, to secure the foundation of the mole at Ostia."

Pliny (xvi. 76), says: "As to the one in which, by order of the
Emperor Caius, the other obelisk had been transported to Rome, it
was brought to Ostia, by order of the late Emperor Claudius, and
sunk for the construction of his harbour."

Marcellinus says: " Subsequent ages to Augustus brought also
other obelisks, one of which is in the Vatican."

### VESTIBULE.

Over the entrance *outside* is a relief of Christ giving the keys to
Peter; *inside* the vestibule is Giotto's (1298) celebrated mosaic,
representing our Lord sustaining Peter when he was about to
sink whilst walking on the sea. Opposite are the great bronze
doors, opened only on special occasions, the work of Antonio
Filareto and Simone Donatello in the fifteenth century. The upper
panels represent in relief our Saviour and the Virgin, below whom are

SS. Peter and Paul; Peter is giving the keys to Pope Eugenius IV. Beneath are the martyrdoms of Peter and Paul: in the former is represented the pyramidal tomb which stood in the Borgo Nuovo, and which was destroyed by Alexander VI. The smaller reliefs represent scenes from the life of the Emperor Sigismund—his coronation, the council of Florence, and his entry into Rome. The framework represents satyrs, nymphs, fauns, Leda and the Swan, Ganymede, the Fox and the Stork, with reliefs of fruit and flowers, and medallions of Roman emperors. The walled-up side door, on the right, is the Porta Santa, which was formerly opened on Christmas-eve of the years of jubilee—every twenty-fifth year.

*The first* inscription relates the gift of olive-yards to provide oil for the lamps given by Gregory II.

*The second*, the Bull of Boniface VIII., of the indulgence granted at jubilee.

*The third*, Panegyric of Charlemagne on Pope Adrian I.

### INTERIOR.

Five portals give access to the edifice, which faces east.

" Enter, its grandeur overwhelms thee not."—BYRON.

" The most extensive hall ever constructed by human art expands in magnificent perspective before you. Advancing up the nave, you admire the beauty of the variegated marble under your feet, and the splendour of the golden vault overhead, the lofty Corinthian pilasters with their bold entablature, the intermediate niches with their statues, the arcades with the graceful figures that recline on the curves of their arches. But how great your astonishment when you reach the foot of the altar, and, standing in the centre of the church, contemplate the four superb vistas that open around you; and then raise your eyes to the dome, at the prodigious elevation of 440 feet, extended like a firmament over your head, and presenting, in glowing mosaic, the companies of the just and the choirs of celestial spirits......

" Around the dome rise four other cupolas, small, indeed, when compared with its stupendous magnitude, but of great boldness when considered separately; six more, three on either side, cover the different divisions of the aisles; and six more of greater dimensions canopy as many chapels. All these inferior cupolas are, like the grand dome itself, lined with mosaics. Many, indeed, of the masterpieces of painting which formerly graced this edifice have been removed [to the Church of S. Maria degli Angeli, see page 265], and

replaced by mosaics, which retain all the tints and beauties of the
originals, impressed on a more solid and durable substance. The
aisles and altars are adorned with numberless antique pillars that
border the churches all around, and form a secondary order " (Eustace).

The variegated walls are in many places ornamented with festoons,
wreaths, crosses, and medallions representing the effigies of different
pontiffs. Various monuments rise in different parts of the church,
of exquisite sculpture, and form very conspicuous features in the
ornament of this grand temple.

Below the steps of the altar, and, of course, some distance from it,
at the corners, on four massive pedestals, four twisted pillars, 50 feet
in height, rise and support an entablature, which bears the canopy
itself, topped with a cross. The whole is 95½ feet from the pavement. This brazen edifice—for so it may be called—was constructed
of bronze stripped from the dome of the Pantheon, and is so disposed
as not to obstruct the view by concealing the chancel and veiling the
chair of S. Peter. This ornament is also of bronze, and consists of
a group of four gigantic figures, representing the four principal
doctors of the Greek and Latin Churches, supporting the chair at an
elevation of 70 feet. Under the high altar of S. Peter's is the tomb
of that apostle, the descent to which is in front, where a large open
space leaves room for a double flight of steps. The rails that surround this space above are adorned with one hundred and twelve
bronze cornucopiæ, which support as many silver lamps, burning
during the day in honour of the apostle. Upon the pavement of the
small area enclosed by the balustrade is the kneeling statue of Pius
VI., by Canova.

### DIMENSIONS.

#### Interior.

613½ feet long.
152½ feet, height of Nave.
87½ feet, width of Nave.
33¾ feet, width of Aisles.
197¾ feet, width of Basilica.
446½ feet, length of Transepts.
95¼ feet, height of Baldacchino complete.
139 feet Cupola, interior diameter.
179 feet Cupola high.
277 feet above Floor.
440 feet from Pavement to Base of Lantern.

#### Area.

240,000 square feet.

INTERIOR OF S. PETER'S.

### A PROMENADE IN S. PETER'S.

On entering, the size of objects may be judged by noticing the cherubs that support the holy water basins; they present no extraordinary appearance, but stand by them and their immense size will be appreciated. The first chapel, on the right, contains Michael Angelo's Mary with the Dead Christ; hence it is called the Chapel of La Pietà. It was executed by the great master when only twenty-four, and bears his name across Mary's girdle. This work of art is unfortunately very badly placed for proper observation. Opening out of this chapel are two side chapels, kept closed: in that of the left are kept the relics belonging to the basilica; and in the right, a column, ornamented with flutings and reliefs, and said to be the column against which Jesus leaned when disputing with the doctors.

Proceeding up the aisle, on the right, is Fabris's statue of Leo XII.; and opposite, Carlo Fontana's monument to Christina, Queen of Sweden, who died in Rome in 1689, after her abjuration of Protestantism. The chapel beyond contains a beautiful mosaic copy of the Martyrdom of S. Sebastian; the original was by Domenichino. Next is the monument to Innocent XII., supported by Charity and Justice, by Filippo Valle; and opposite is one to the Countess Matilda, by Bernini; the relief is Gregory VII. giving absolution to Henry IV.

The Chapel of the Sacrament contains, above the altar, a fresco by Cortona; over the side-altar is a mosaic copy of Caravaggio's Entombment. The principal altar is formed with a model in lapis lazuli and gilt bronze of Bramante's chapel; the original is erected over the spot pointed out as the scene of Peter's martyrdom. Before the side-altar is the bronze tomb of Sixtus IV., with reliefs by Antonio del Pollajuolo; near by is interred Julius II., whose monument, now in S. Pietro in Vincoli, was to have been the grand masterpiece of Michael Angelo.

Beyond, on the right, is the monument to Gregory XIII., supported by Religion and Power, with a relief representing the correction of the calendar, the work of Rusconi. Opposite is Gregory the Fourteenth's simple marble urn.

The next chapel is named Madonna del Soccorso, containing the monument to Gregory XVI., erected by the cardinals he had made. On the left is a mosaic copy of Domenichino's Last Communion of S. Jerome. In the aisle, proceeding on the right, is the monument to Benedict XIV. (with figures of Science and Charity), by Pietro Bracci. Opposite is a mosaic copy of S. Basil Celebrating Mass before the Emperor Valens, after Subleyra's picture.

In the transept are mosaic copies of S. Wenceslaus, king of Bohemia, by Caroselli; Martyrdom of SS. Processus and Martinianus, after Valentin; and that of Erasmus, after Poussin. In the aisle, leading out, is Canova's celebrated tomb of Clement XIII. It took eight years to execute. The pope is represented praying: on one side is the genius of Death with inverted torch (the finest piece of sculpture in S. Peter's), and on the other Religion with the cross; at the angles are a wakeful and a sleeping lion. Opposite is a mosaic of S. Peter Walking on the Sea, after Lanfranco. In the next chapel is a mosaic of Guido's S. Michael and Guercino's S. Petronilla. On the left, coming towards the apse, S. Peter Resuscitating Tabitha, from Costanzi's painting; and opposite is the tomb of Clement X., by Ferrata.

In the centre of the apse is S. Peter's chair. January 18th is the feast of the chair of S. Peter in Rome. Some remarks on the chair which does duty for S. Peter's may be of interest to our readers. A photograph of this famous object was taken in 1867, when it was last exposed to view, and can be had at any of the shops in Rome. Visitors must be content with looking at the photograph, for the chair itself is not to be seen. At present it is enclosed in the bronze covering which is supported by the four colossal figures of the doctors of the Church—SS. Gregory, Jerome, Ambrose, and Augustin.

It is encased in a framework, in which are the rings through which the poles were inserted in order to carry the person seated. This casing, consisting of four posts and sides, is made of oak, and is very much decayed. The straight vertical joints are easily distinguished where the frame is attached to the chair itself, which is composed of dark acacia wood. The front panel is ornamented with three rows of square plates of ivory, six in a row, eighteen in all, upon twelve of which are engraved the labours of Hercules, and on the other six, constellations, with thin *laminæ* of gold let into the engraved lines. Some of the ivories are put on upside down, and had evidently nothing to do with the original chair: they are Byzantine in style, of the eleventh century. The ivory band decorations of the back and sides evidently belonged to the chair, and correspond with its architecture and fit into the woodwork. They are sculptured in.

relief, representing combats of men, wild beasts, and centaurs. The centre point of the horizontal bars has a portrait of Charlemagne crowned as emperor. In his right hand is a sceptre (broken), and in his left a globe ; two angels on either side offer him crowns and palms, they having combatants on each side. The chair is 4 feet 8¾ inches high at back, 2 feet 10½ inches wide, 2 feet 2½ inches deep, and 2 feet 1½ inch high in front. Fancy Peter using such a chair as this !

It is asserted by the Roman Church that this chair was used by S. Peter as his episcopal throne during his rule over the Church at Rome. Even if we grant, for argument's sake, that he was bishop in Rome, there is no evidence to prove that this was his chair ; in fact, every evidence to the contrary. All the primitive episcopal chairs are of marble, and as unlike this one in construction as possible ; for it is not an episcopal throne, but a *sella gestatoria* or cathedra, similar to the chairs introduced into Rome in the time of the Emperor Claudius, mentioned by Suetonius (" Nero," xxvi.), and Juvenal (i. 64, vi. 90). It is not unlike in shape the one used to carry the Pope in grand ceremonies in S. Peter's. Some early authors speak of a *sella gestatoria* which was placed in the baptistery of old S. Peter's by Damasus, and which, formerly on the 22nd of February, was carried hence to the high altar, where the Pope, with much ceremony, was enthroned upon it.

The chair which was originally assigned as that of S. Peter was eventually passed on from one chapel to another, till, it is said, that, when Rome was sacked by the imperialists in 1527, they stripped it of its ornaments and covering, for the sake of their value ; and that beneath they found an old carved wooden chair, with the inscription, " *There is only one God, and Mohammed is his prophet*"—which same formula is engraved upon the back of the marble episcopal chair in the Church of S. Pietro in Castello at Venice. In 1558, the feast of the chair of S. Peter was fixed in Rome for the 18th of January, and in Antioch for February 22nd ; and in 1655 Pope Alexander VII. placed this chair where it now stands. The present chair is medieval, ninth century, and is unlike early representations in art of the chair used by the Apostle Paul, which we may look upon as episcopal.

The ivory diptych of St. Paul (A.D. 400), the property of Mr. Carrand of Lyons, engraved by the Arundel Society, represents Paul seated on a chair, holding in his left hand a roll, the symbol of apostleship, whilst the right hand is raised in the act of blessing Linus, who carries a book in his hand. At the back of the chair is S. Mark, holding a roll in his left hand. The chair is light, and not unlike a modern library one in shape. Later art agrees with the present chair. A fresco at S. Clement's, Rome (1050), represents Peter installing Clement into the Papal chair—a chair, so far as can be seen, not unlike the present one of S. Peter, which was made after the coronation of Charlemagne as Emperor of the Holy Roman Empire (A.D. 800).

Upon our right is the tomb of Urban VIII. His bronze statue is by Bernini, with Justice and Charity in marble. On our left is Della Porta's monument to Paul III.; likewise a bronze figure, with Prudence (the Pope's mother, Giovanna Gaetani) and Justice (his sister, Giulia Farnese). Justice is a beautiful figure, but the tin drapery put on to cover its nakedness by Bernini destroys its beauty. It is necessary to re-paint the tin every now and then. There is a deal of this mock modesty in S. Peter's.

Turning into the south aisle, on our right, is the tomb of Alexander VIII. The bronze statue is by Arrigo, and the figures of Religion and Prudence by Rossi. The relief represents the Pope canonizing five saints. Opposite is the mosaic of S. Peter at the Gate of the Temple. It is said that this scene, here represented, gave to President Lincoln the idea for his proposed motto for the greenbacks. When the commission applied to him for a motto to put upon the notes, he said, "I can think of nothing better than what Peter said to the sick man at the gate of the temple—'Silver and gold have I none, but what I have that give I unto thee.'"

Beyond, upon the right, is a splendid alto-relief by Algardi, representing Leo threatening Attila with the vengeance of Peter and Paul if he should attack the holy city of Rome. It is the largest relief ever executed. A circular marble slab below it marks the tomb of Leo XII. Upon the right, coming down the aisle, is the tomb of Alexander VII., by Bernini. Justice, Prudence, Charity, and Truth surround the kneeling pontiff. A bronze gilt figure of Death supports the marble canopy. The naked Truth was clothed in tin by Innocent XI. Opposite is Vanni's oil-painting, the Fall of Simon Magus. The south transept contains mosaics of S. Thomas by Camuccini, the Crucifixion by Guido, and S. Francis by Domenichino. On the left is the chair of the Grand Penitentiary, where great princes have to make their public confession as pilgrims

Returning to the aisle, on the right is the tomb of Pius VIII., by Tenerani. Our Saviour is blessing the Pope; Peter and Paul are on either side; Justice and Mercy are represented in relief below. Opposite is a mosaic of Ananias and Sapphira after Roncalli. Beyond is the Miracle of Gregory the Great, by Sacchi. Facing us is the tomb of Pius VII., by Thorwaldsen. History and Time support him on either side, with Power and Wisdom below. On the left, nearly opposite, is a mosaic copy of Raphael's Transfiguration. Proceeding down the aisle, on our right, is the tomb of Leo XI., with a relief, by Algardi, representing the abjuration of Henry IV. of France. Opposite is the tomb of Innocent XI., with relief of the raising of the siege of Vienna by John Sobieski, with figures of Religion and Justice, by Monot.

On our right is the Chapel of the Choir, decorated by Giacomo della Porta. The mosaic altar-piece of the Conception is after Pietro Bianchi. Over the door, in the pier on the left of the chapel, is a niche closed with a wooden sarcophagus; here the body of the Pope is placed till his tomb is prepared. Opposite is the bronze memorial to Innocent VIII. by the brothers Pollaiolo. The spear-head held in the hand of the Pope refers to the spear which pierced our Saviour's side, it being presented to this Pope by the Emperor Bajazet II. On our right is a fine mosaic by Romanelli, the Presentation of the Virgin in the Temple. Beyond, on the left, is Canova's memorial to the "last of the Stuarts," who died in Rome, and are buried in the crypt below. It takes the form of an entrance to a tomb, which is guarded by beautiful genii. Over the door are the words—"BLESSED ARE THE DEAD THAT DIE IN THE LORD." Above are medallions of the Chevalier S. George, Prince Charlie, and the Cardinal York, the whole being surmounted by the British coat-of-arms, in which is quartered that of France. This monument was erected by George IV. Opposite, over the door leading to the dome, is the monument to Maria Clementina, wife of the Chevalier S. George, whose portrait in mosaic is by Barigioni. Beyond is the baptistery. The font is of red porphyry, which was once the top of the tomb of Otho II., and originally, it is said, of Hadrian. In front is Carlo Maratta's Baptism of Christ in mosaic; upon the left Peter baptizing the jailers in the Mamertine prison, a fiction from Passeri; and opposite is Procaccini's Baptism of the Centurion. This baptistery is said to be on the site of a temple to Apollo, upon what authority we cannot say.

The nave has marked in the centre of its pavement the measurement of all the principal churches in the world, whereby it can be seen that S. Peter's is 93 feet longer than S. Paul's, London. The large porphyry circular slab is that upon which the holy Roman emperors were crowned, and where the priest who is made judge of ecclesiastical matters in the Roman Church is ordained. In a niche in each of the piers supporting the vault are colossal statues, 16 feet high, of the founders of the various religious orders; and in the piers of the dome are S. Longinus, the soldier who pierced our Saviour's side, S. Helena, who found the cross, S. Veronica, who wiped his face, and S. Andrew. Above are kept the relics of these saints, which are only shown to those who hold the title of a canon of the church. On the spandrels of the arches of the dome are four large mosaics, representing Matthew, Mark, Luke, and John, with their emblems. S. Luke's pen is 7 feet long, and the letters on the frieze are 6 feet high.

The great piers are 253 feet in circumference; which space is exactly occupied by the church and house of S. Carlo, in the Via Quattro Fontane. Near the first pier of the right side is the celebrated bronze seated statue of S. Peter, with the keys in one hand, the other raised in the act of blessing, under a canopy erected by Pius IX., whose portrait in mosaic surmounts it. It is asserted by some that this was a statue of Jupiter, supremely good and great, that stood in the Capitoline temple, and that it was altered into S. Peter; others say they recast Jupiter into the " Jew Peter."

### THE SACRISTY

is connected with S. Peter's by a long gallery, and is adorned with pillars, statues, paintings, and mosaics. It is entered by passing through a door under the monument to Pius VIII., in the left aisle. There is a very rich collection of church plate and vestments kept in the *guardaroba*, which visitors should not fail to see.

### THE CRYPT.

*Orders must be obtained of Cardinal Ledockowski, Palazzo Cancelleria. It must be visited before* 11 A.M. The entrance is at the side of the statue of S. Veronica. It contains the tombs of the early Popes, and also some old bas-reliefs, and some very ancient statues of S. Peter. Adrian IV., the only English Pope, is buried here, and also several distinguished historical characters, including " the last of the Stuarts."

## THE DOME.

*Orders must be obtained at 8 Via della Sacrestia for visiting the dome, which is only open without an order on Thursdays, between 8 and 10 A.M.*

It is reached by a winding ascent, the entrance being opposite the Stuart monument. On the platform of the roof the cupolas, domes, and pinnacles are seen to advantage; and hence, by different staircases between the walls of the cupola, the ball is reached. During the ascent, a fine view may be obtained of the lower parts of the church, as well as of the mosaics and stuccoes which embellish the interior of the dome.

On reaching the summit, a panoramic view of Rome and the Campagna is had, quite repaying the labour of the ascent.

## THE VATICAN.

From the vestibule of S. Peter's we see, to the fullest advantage, the fine piazza, with the Vatican on our left, which presents very much the appearance of a large factory. Having been erected by different architects in various eras, it has no systematic design, and is, in fact, a collection of palaces built by different Popes. The entrance is at the end of the right-hand colonnade in approaching. The Pope's Swiss Guard, whose uniform was designed by Michael Angelo, permit visitors to pass up the corridor. *Halfway up on the right, at a desk, the necessary pass to visit the collections must be obtained. All sticks and umbrellas must be left at the cloak-room on the top of the stairs, left. We proceed up*

## THE SCALA REGIA,

built in the pontificate of Urban VIII., from the design of Bernini. The first flight is composed of Ionic columns, the second of pilasters. The ornamental stucco work is from the designs of Algardi. The equestrian statue of Constantine is by Bernini. On the first landing is the cloak-room; then follow up flight of steps. *At the top, on the left, through a small awkward door, is the entrance to*

## THE SISTINE CHAPEL,

built by Sixtus IV. in 1473. It is celebrated for its paintings in fresco by Michael Angelo; the roof alone occupied twenty months in the painting.

The Roof.—On the flat part are nine compartments illustrative of —(1) The Separation of Light from Darkness; (2) Creation of the Sun and Moon; (3) Land and Sea; (4) Adam; (5) Eve; (6) the Fall and Expulsion (the figure of Eve is considered to be the most perfect painting of the female form in existence); (7) the Sacrifice of Noah; (8) the Deluge; (9) Noah inebriated. These are bordered by sitting figures of prophets and sibyls: *over the altar*, Jonah; *on the left*, Joel, the Sibyl Erithræa, Ezekiel, the Sibyl Persica, Jeremiah and Zechariah; *on the right*, the Sibyl Lybica, Daniel, the Sibyl Cumæa, Isaiah, and the Sibyl Delphica. In the four corners are—Moses lifting up the Brazen Serpent, King Artaxerxes, Esther and Haman, David and Goliath, Judith and Holofernes. In the arches over the windows, and in the recesses, Genealogy of Christ from Abraham to Joseph.

The Walls.—Behind the altar is the great fresco of Michael Angelo, representing the Last Judgment, designed by him when in his sixtieth year, and completed in eight years (1540). *At the top* is our Saviour, with the Virgin seated on his right, above angels bearing the instruments of the passion. *On one side* of our Lord are saints and patriarchs, and on the other martyrs. *Below*, a group of angels sounding the last trump and bearing the books of judgment. *On the right* is represented the fall of the condemned; Charon ferrying some of them across the river Styx, striking the tumultuous with his oar. The figure in the right-hand corner, representing Midas with ass's ears, is Messer Biagio of Casena, the Pope's master of the ceremonies, who said the nude figures were indecent; on which account the Pope ordered Daniele da Volterra to cover them with drapery, which obtained for him the cognomen of *Braghettone* (breeches-maker). Michael Angelo said, "Let the Pope reform the world, and the pictures will reform themselves." And to spite Biagio, he represented him in hell, whereat he complained to the Pope in order to have his figure removed. The Pope replied that as he was in hell he must stop there, as he had no power to release from hell, but from purgatory! *On the left*, the blessed are ascending to heaven assisted by angels and saints.

*Between the windows*, portraits of the Popes of the time, by the artist of the subject below. The lower part of the walls is painted in imitation of drapery, over which were hung on grand ceremonies tapestries from Raphael's cartoons.

*On the side walls* are scenes from the life of Moses typical of the life of our Lord. *From altar, to the right—*

| TYPE. | FULFILMENT. |
|---|---|
| Moses and Zipporah going down into Egypt. By Luca Signorelli. | Baptism of Christ in Jordan. By Perugino. |
| Moses slaying the Egyptian. Driving away the shepherds. The Lord appearing in the burning bush. By Sandro Botticelli. | Our Lord being tempted. By Sandro Botticelli. |
| Pharaoh overwhelmed in the Red Sea. By Cosimo Rosselli. | Christ calling Peter and Andrew. By Dom Ghirlandajo. |
| Moses receiving the tables of the law. Destruction of the Golden Calf. By Cosimo Rosselli. | The Sermon on the Mount. By Cosimo Rosselli. |
| Destruction of Korah, Dathan, and Abiram, and the sons of Aaron. By Sandro Botticelli. | Christ giving unto Peter "the keys of the kingdom of heaven" (Matt. xvi. 19). By Perugino. |
| Death of Moses. Reading of the law. By Luca Signorelli. | The Last Supper. By Cosimo Rosselli. |
| The Archangel contending about the body of Moses.* By Francesco Salviati. | Christ's Resurrection. By Dom Ghirlandajo. |

*Apply to the custodi of the Sistine Chapel to visit the Pauline Chapel, which is entered from the*

### SALA REGIA,

built as an audience hall for the ambassadors to the Papal Court. It is decorated with frescoes representing different important events in Papal history.

### THE PAULINE CHAPEL

was erected by Paul III. Its walls are painted in fresco, the conversion of S. Paul and the execution of S. Peter being by Michael Angelo. The painted roof and the portraits of twenty-eight Popes are by Lorenzo Sabatini and Frederigo Zucchero.

*Ask the custodian to let you out by the door under the Last Judgment. Upstairs, we reach the*

### GALLERY OF MODERN PAINTINGS.

#### (*First Room, right.*)

1. Beatitude of Benedict of Urbino (Capuchin).—Guido Guidi, 1875. He is being presented, with other missionaries, to Clement VIII.

* "And he buried him in a valley in the land of Moab, over against Beth-peor: but no man knoweth of his sepulchre unto this day" (Deut. xxxiv. 6). "Yet Michael the archangel, *when* contending with the devil he *disputed about* the body of Moses" (Jude 9).

2. Beatitude of John Sarcander, who is led to the torture by the Dutch Calvinists.—By F. Grandi. 3. S. Giovanni della Salle, founder of the Christian Brothers' Schools.—By C. Manani, 1888. 4. Jesuits Martyred in Japan.—By Peter Gagliardi. 5. John Berchmans' Vision of the Virgin.—Gagliardi. 6. Peter of Arbues, Grand Inquisitor of Spain, murdered at the altar.—G. Mauretta. *At the end* of this hall is a piece of tapestry designed by Raphael. It represents S. Paul striking Bar-jesus (Elymas) blind before the pro-consul Sergius Paulus at Paphos in Cyprus.—Acts xiii. 6. *Returning up the hall.* 7. Paul of the Cross, founder of the Passionist Order.—Coghetti. 8. Declaration of the Dogma of Immaculate Conception by C. de Paris. 9. The Virgin with the Infant Jesus appearing to Maria degli Angeli, a Carmelite nun.—De Rohden.

The entry and the connection between the first and second hall were once the chapel of Pius V. The richly-painted window, by Ludovic Gesta of Toulouse, represents Germana Cousin, the Shepherdess of Pibrac, crossing a stream, and portraits of Pius IX. and French ecclesiastics. The cupola is the work of Federico Zuccheri; the subjects are the Fall of Satan and scenes from the Life of Tobit. In the lunettes below are the four doctors of the Latin Church, by Paoletti.

(*Second Room, left.*) 10. Saints Martyred in Gorcum in the Netherlands.—Cæsar Fracassini. His masterpiece; a very fine work of art. 11. A fine large painting, the gift of the Polish Roman Catholics. It represents John Sobieski, King of Poland, relieving Vienna from the Turks: the work of Matejko, 1883. 12. S. Grata of Bergamo, with the Head of her Lover, S. Alexander, of the Theban Legion.—By P. Loverini, 1887. 13. S. Michael de' Sanctis.—Jojetti. 14. Beatitude of the Canon John de' Rossi.—Dies. *Passing from these we go into the* SALOON OF PODESTI, containing frescoes relating to the Dogma of the Immaculate Conception. *On the end wall* is represented the supposed Vision of the Virgin to Pius IX.; *opposite*, the Discussion of the Dogma; *on the right wall*, Proclamation of the Dogma. They were done in 1870, in commemoration of the Vatican Decrees. *Thence we pass into the*

### STANZE OR CAMERE OF RAPHAEL,

consisting of four rooms designed by Raphael, and completed by his pupils after his death, to illustrate the triumphs and establishment of the Catholic Church. The principal frescoes are :—

IN THE FIRST ROOM.—*On the right*, the Incendio del Borgo, A.D.

847; *over the window*, Justification of Leo III.; *in front*, Victory of Leo IV. over the Saracens at Ostia; and *opposite*, Coronation of Charlemagne. The chiaro-oscuro portraits, *below*, by Caravaggio, represent the princes who first gave tribute to the Church. The roof is by Perugino, Raphael's master.

SECOND ROOM.—Illustrative of Theology, *on the entry wall;* Poetry, *over the window;* Philosophy, *in front;* and Jurisprudence, *on the right.* Representations of the Fall of Man, the Flaying of Marsyas, the Study of the Globe, the Judgment of Solomon, *on the ceiling. On the walls* corresponding—the Dispute on the Sacrament, Mount Parnassus, the School of Athens (a portico crowded with philosophers, which gives its name to the room), Prudence, Fortitude, and Temperance.

THIRD ROOM.—*In front*, the Miraculous Expulsion of Heliodorus from the Temple; *on the right*, the Mass of Bolsena; *on the entry wall*, Attila driven back from Rome by Leo I.; *over the left window*, S. Peter's Release from Prison (notice the four different lights here). *The ceiling* represents subjects from the Old Testament.

FOURTH ROOM.—*On the right*, Battle between Constantine and Maxentius at the Ponte Molle; *entry wall*, Baptism of Constantine; *left wall*, Rome presented by Constantine to Silvester; *in front*, the Cross appearing to Constantine (the dwarf is Gradasso da Norcia, from Berni's Poetry; *on the vault*, the pagan statue thrown down represents the Triumph of Faith, by Lauretti (notice the wonderful bit of perspective here); *on the right-hand corner, a door leads into the* ANTICAMERA OF THE STANZE, originally painted by Raphael, restored by Carlo Maratta. *Out of this room is*

### THE CHAPEL OF S. LORENZO.

The frescoes are by Fra Angelico, representing events in the lives of SS. Stephen and Laurence. *On the ceiling* are the four Evangelists. It was built as the private chapel of Nicholas V., and is the oldest decorated portion of the Vatican. *We now pass into*

### THE LOGGIE OF RAPHAEL.

*to the right on entering.*

"It is impossible either to execute or imagine a more beautiful work" (Vasari). It is called Raphael's Bible. It is divided into thirteen arcades, each containing four subjects of Scripture history—1. The Creation of the World, by Raphael; 2. History of Adam and Eve; 3. The History of Noah, by Giulio Romano; 4. Abraham and

Lot; 5. History of Isaac, by Penni; 6. Jacob, by Pellegrino; 7.
Joseph; 8. Moses, by Giulio Romano; 9. Moses, by Raffaello del
Colle; 10. Joshua; 11. David, by Pierino del Vaga; 12. Solomon,
by Pellegrino; 13. From the New Testament, by Giulio Romano.
The stucco ornaments and arabesque work are by Giovanni da
Udine, from Raphael's designs, who took the idea from the Golden
House of Nero. The weather has very much damaged them. Pius
IX. put the glass windows in.

*The other sides* were built by Gregory XIII., and executed by
Giovanni da Udine; they have recently been restored by Mantovani.
*The farther one,* parallel with the Papal apartments, is where his holi-
ness gives audience.

*A flight of stairs on the left leads to the* Upper Loggia, painted with
maps and landscapes. *Entrance to the Picture Gallery—ring the bell
at the second door on the left of the Central Loggia.*

### THE PICTURE GALLERY.
#### (*The Pinacotheca.*)

Formed by Pius VII. As the artist's name and the subject are
painted on the frame of each picture (a hint some of the other galleries might adopt), it will be only necessary to mention the most
important.

FIRST ROOM.—The Christian Mysteries, one of Raphael's earliest
paintings; Faith, Hope, and Charity, three medallions, by Raphael;
Doubting Thomas, by Guercino; Marriage of S. Catherine of Alexandria with the Infant Christ, by Murillo; Adoration of the Shepherds, by Murillo.

SECOND ROOM.—The Last Communion of S. Jerome, by Domenichino; Madonna di Foligno, by Raphael; The Transfiguration, Raphael's masterpiece; Plan of Bologna; Gregory XIII.; Boniface VIII.

THIRD ROOM.—S. Sebastian, by Titian; The Assumption of the
Virgin, in two parts—the Crowning, by Giulio Romano, and the
Apostles round the Tomb, by Francesco Penni; Virgin and Child,
by Sassoferrato; The Entombment, by Caravaggio.

FOURTH ROOM.—S. Peter's Crucifixion, by Guido; Annunciation,
by Baroccio; Christ Enthroned, by Correggio.

### THE MOSAIC MANUFACTORY.

*Orders must be obtained from the Ufficio Tecnico, 8 Via della
Sacrestia.*

*It is entered by a corridor from the ground floor at the left-hand corner of the Court of S. Damaso.* The mosaics in S. Peter's, S. Paul's, and other churches, were manufactured here. Some mosaics take a long time to execute, as great patience and art are required in blending the shades, &c., upwards of 27,000 different shades of the coloured *vetri* being kept in stock.

A plate, generally of metal, of the required size, is first surrounded by a margin rising about three-quarters of an inch above the surface. A mastic cement, composed of powdered stone, lime, and linseed oil, is then spread over as a coating, perhaps a quarter of an inch in thickness. When set, this is again covered with plaster-of-Paris rising to a level with the margin, upon which is traced a very careful outline of the picture to be copied, and just so much as will admit of the insertion of the small pieces of smalto or glass is removed from time to time with a fine chisel. The workman then selects from the trays, in which are kept thousands of varieties of colour, a piece of the tint which he wants, and carefully brings it to the necessary shape. The piece is then moistened with a little cement, and bedded in a proper situation, the process being repeated until the picture is finished, when the whole, being ground down to an even face and polished, becomes an imperishable work of art. The process is the same for making the small mosaics so much employed at the present day for boxes, covers, or articles of jewellery, and this work is sometimes upon almost a microscopic scale. The Florentine mosaic, which is chiefly used for the decoration of altars and tombs, or for cabinets, tops of tables, coffers, and the like, is composed of precious materials, in small slices or veneers, and by taking advantage of the natural tints which characterize the marble, the agate, or the jasper, very admirable effects may be produced in imitation of fruits, flowers, or ornaments. The use of this kind of mosaic is extremely restricted, on account of the great value and expense, not only of the materials, but of the labour employed upon them. None but the hardest stones are used ; every separate piece must be backed by thicker slices of slate or marble to obtain additional strength ; and every minute portion must be ground until it exactly corresponds with the pattern previously cut.

## THE VATICAN MUSEUM.

*Open daily, except Sundays and festas, from September 15th to June 14th, from 10 to 3. From June 15th to September 14th, from 9 till 1. The entrance fee is one lira each person, which covers all the museums.*

*Entrance* is obtained by going round to the back of S. Peter's, thus enabling us on our way to admire the vast proportions of the latter. The Vatican Museum was founded by Julius II., and consists of those objects of art that have been discovered, and which once graced the principal buildings of ancient Rome. Many of the titles recently put on the statues are not to be trusted. For the convenience of visitors, we have published a complete work on all "The Museums of Rome," which is not merely a catalogue, but treats of the historical and mythological interest, as well as of the great masters who executed them. *Price 2 lire. Entering on the left by the iron gates, filled in with glass, and ascending the marble stairs, we enter*

### THE HALL OF THE GREEK CROSS.

In the centre of the floor is a splendid mosaic, found at the Villa Ruffinella. A bust of Minerva forms the centre, around which are twelve planets and various phases of the moon. The outer circle (modern) is composed of masks and figures. The principal statues are—582, *right*, Apollo Palatinus, by Scopas ; 574, *left*, is a copy of Praxiteles's Venus of Cnidos ; 566, *left*, red porphyry sarcophagus, which contained the remains of Constantia, the daughter of Constantine the Great ; 589, *opposite*, generally attributed to Helena, the mother of the Christian emperor. (See page 330.) Before the door is a fine mosaic representing a faun watering a flower. At the foot of the stairs, by two sphinxes, is a beautiful basket of flowers in mosaic. *We now enter*

### THE ROTUNDA.

Erected by Simonetti, by order of Pius VI. In the centre is a magnificent vase of red porphyry, 46 feet in circumference, found in the House of Titus. The large mosaic represents combats between Centaurs and Lapithæ, and nymphs carried on the backs of monsters ; in the centre, under the vase, is the head of Medusa. The border represents the adventures of Ulysses, Neptune, and monsters. The principal statues are 537, 538, Tragedy and Comedy ; 539, Bust of Jupiter ; 540, Colossal statue of Antinoüs ; 546, Statue of Ceres, a copy of Praxiteles ; 544, Hercules, in gilt bronze, an original bronze by Myron, and was placed by Pompey in the Round Temple of Hercules, near the Pons Palatinus. It was consulted as an oracle, a boy passing in at the head to speak. It is fifteen feet high. 542, Colossal Juno, after Praxiteles ; 548, Nerva, a seated statue crowned with bronze oak wreath ; 552, Juno Quiritis, by Polycletus ; 555, The Genius of Augustus. *We now pass into*

### THE HALL OF THE MUSES.

It contains statues of muses, busts of Greek philosophers, poets, and statesmen, all of which deserve special attention. *Left.* 525, Bust of Pericles; 524, Seated Statue of Sappho; 523, Bust of Aspasia. *Right.* 535, Mnemosyne, the mother of the muses; 511, Erato, muse of love song ; 514, Bust of Socrates ; 515, Calliope, muse of epic poetry ; 516, Apollo, as leader of the muses ; 517, Terpsichore, muse of dancing ; 520, Euterpe, muse of melody. *Left.* 508, Polyhymnia, muse of sacred poetry; 505, Clio, muse of history; 506, Bust of Demosthenes; 504, Urania, muse of astronomy; 503, Thalia, comic and pastoral muse; 499, Melpomene, muse of tragedy. *Beyond, left.* 492, Sophocles ; 491, Silenus ; 490, Diogenes. *Right.* 498, Epicurus ; 496, Homer. *Now pass into*

### THE HALL OF THE ANIMALS.

The principal objects of interest are—124, Mithraic Sacrifice found at Ostia, in the temple dedicated to the worship of the Persian deity ; 139, Commodus on Horseback ; 143, Sleeping Shepherd ; 228, Triton carrying off a Nereid. *We next enter*

### THE GALLERY OF STATUES.

In the centre of the gallery is a magnificent bath of the finest Oriental alabaster. *Right-hand side on entering.* 248, Clodius Albinus, governor of Britain under Commodus; 250, Cupid, by Praxiteles, the "Genius of the Vatican;" 255, Paris; 259, Minerva as the Peace-bearer; 261, Penelope; 262, Caligula; 264, Apollo with the Lizard ; 267, Drunken Faun ; 270, Urania; 271, Posidippus, the master of Greek comedy. *Entrance to Hall of Busts (see below).* 390, Menander; 391, Nero as Apollo; 392, Septimius Severus; 393, Dido; 394, Neptune; 396, Narcissus; 398, Macrinus; 399, Æsculapius and Hygeia; 401, Fragment of Æmon and Antigones; 402, Seneca ; 405, One of the fifty daughters of Danaus drawing water from Lethe; 406, Faun, repetition of Praxiteles. *Entrance on left to Cabinet of Masks.* 414, Sleeping Ariadne; 417, Mercury, by Ingenui; 420, Lucius Verus.

### THE HALL OF BUSTS.

273, Augustus : 272, Cæsar ; 292, Caracalla ; 307, Saturn, colossal veiled head ; 311, Menelaus; 326, Jupiter seated ; 333, Crispina; 352, Livia as Piety, or Diana, or Surprise ; 366, Scipio.

So called from the mosaic pavement found in Hadrian's Villa. The ceiling is by Domenico de Angelis, representing the marriage of Bacchus and Ariadne, Diana contemplating Endymion, Paris refusing Minerva the apple, Adonis and Venus. 425, Replica of the Venus of Cos, by Praxiteles. The head does not belong to this statue. 427, the Crouching Venus, a copy after Heliodorus, by Bupalus ; 429, the Empress Sabina, Hadrian's wife, as Venus Genetrix, after Arcesilaus (the head and arms have been inserted in an older statue); 432, Faun in *rosso antico* ; 433, Venus rising from the Sea, after Alcamenes ; 441, Venus anointing herself, after Polycharmes ; 436, Venus of Cnidos, by Praxiteles ; 443, Apollo.

*We now proceed to the Court of the Belvedere,* which is supported by sixteen columns, having a fountain in the centre. The court is adorned with baths, urns, sarcophagi, statues, columns, bas-reliefs, and medallions. The four corners of the court are occupied by cabinets *in the following order, commencing on the left :—*

### MERCURY OF THE BELVEDERE.

Hermes, by Polycletus ; the masterpiece of the Vatican ; found at the Baths of Titus in 1779. On the walls are bas-reliefs representing a combat between Amazons and Athenians, and a sacred procession ; 56, Priapus, the god of orchards ; 57, Hercules.

### CANOVA'S CABINET.

It contains three splendid works by this great modern master : Perseus with the Head of Medusa ; the Two Boxers, Kreugas (defence), Damoxenus (attack).

### APOLLO BELVEDERE.

A copy, in Carrara marble, of Baton's original, 270 B.C. ; discovered at Porto d'Anzio towards the close of the fifteenth century—Apollo in the attitude of turning the army of the Gauls into stone, with the head of Medusa, B.C. 278, as we are informed by the inscription in bronze ; it was restored erroneously. It is beautifully described by Byron in "Childe Harold."

### CABINET OF THE LAOCOON.

Found in the Baths of Titus in 1506. Pliny (xxxvi. 4) thus describes it :—"A work which may be considered superior to all others both in painting and statuary. The whole group—the father, the boys, and the awful folds of the serpents—were formed out of a single block by Agesander, Polydorus, and Athenodorus, natives of Rhodes.   Michael Angelo said, however, and it has since been proved, that it is in three pieces."

> " Two serpents.....their destined way they take,
> And to Laocoön and his children make :
> And first around the tender boys they wind,
> Then with their sharpened fangs their limbs and bodies grind.
> The wretched father, running to their aid
> With pious haste, but vain, they next invade ;
> Twice round his waist their winding volumes rolled.
> And twice about his gasping throat they fold.
> The priest thus doubly choked, their crests divide,
> And towering o'er his head in triumph ride."
>
> VIRGIL, " Æn.," ii. 209 : DRYDEN.

*We now enter the*

### ROOM OF THE MELEAGER,

a replica of the bronze, by Lysippus.   Found in the year 1500 outside the Porta Portese.   20, The Loves of Æneas and Dido ; 17, Inscription relating to the foundation of the temple of Hercules Victor by the consul Mummius.

### THE ROUND VESTIBULE.

In the centre is a basin of pavonazzetto ; on the balcony a very rare ancient sun-dial, found in 1770 near the Colosseum.   The view from here has given to this balcony the name

### BELVEDERE.

It commands a beautiful panoramic scene of Rome and the Campagna, bounded by the distant Alban and Sabine Hills.

### VESTIBULE.

The gray peperino sarcophagus was discovered in the tomb of the Scipios on the Via Appia in 1780.   It contained the remains of Scipio Barbatus.   When it was opened, two thousand years after his death, the skeleton was found entire, with a ring upon one of the fingers. The ring passed into the hands of the Earl of Beverley, and the bones were removed to Padua by the Venetian senator, Angelo Quirini. On the wall are inscriptions found in the tomb.   A bust of the poet Ennius surmounts the sarcophagus.   .

### THE TORSO

of Hercules.   The work of Apollonius, son of Nestor of Athens. Found near the Theatre of Pompey.   It is considered to be the most perfect resemblance to human flesh, and was greatly admired by Raphael and Michael Angelo, the latter declaring that he was its pupil. *Descending the stairs we reach*

## THE CHIARAMONTI CORRIDOR,

containing numerous monuments of Greek and Roman art. *On the left going down.* 733, Recumbent Statue of Hercules ; 698, Cicero ; 682, Antoninus Pius; 681, Minerva; 636, Hercules with Ajax, found near Pompey's Theatre ; 589, Mercury ; 588, Group of Bacchus and Ampelus ; 544, Silenus ; 495, A Cupid, by Praxiteles ; 494, Tiberius ; 493, Diadumenianus ; 450, Mercury ; 422, Bust of Demosthenes ; 419–417, Busts of Caius and Lucius, nephews of Augustus ; 418, Julia, his daughter ; 372ᵃ, A fragment, by Phidias ; 401, Colossal Head of Augustus ; 400, Tiberius ; 399, Head of Tiberius ; 353, Nymph on a Rock ; 294, Hercules Resting ; 263, Bust of Zenobia ; 242, Apollo Citharœdus; 241, Juno suckling Mars; 240, Britannicus; 197, Minerva, with modern helmet and enamelled eyes; 177, Polyhymnia ; 176, The Headless Niobid, either by Scopas or Praxiteles; 135, Bust of Cæsar; 121, Clio, the historical muse and guardian of truth ; 120, Priestess of Vesta; 85, The God of Sleep; 62, Hygeia, the goddess of health ; 61, Urania ; 15, A consular statue ; 6, Autumn.—*Gates to Corridor of Inscriptions.—Returning.* 13, Winter ; 19, Paris ; 18, Apollo ; 17, A Faun. *Entrance to the Nuovo Braccio.* 106, A Relief of Masks ; 124, Drusus ; 181, Hecate ; 179, Myth of Alcestis ; 245, Polyhymnia ; 244, Ocean ; 287, Sleeping Fisher Boy ; 298, Bacchus ; 297, Athlete : 343ᵃ, Brutus who stabbed Cæsar ; 355–357, Figures found at Tusculum ; 356, Captive ; 453, Meleager ; 498, Clotho ; 497, Sarcophagus, with Corn-mills ; 383, Cupid ; 547, Isis ; 548, A Vestal ; 580, Præfica ; 591, Claudius ; 627, Venus and Mars ; 639, Julia Sœmia ; 686, Tuccia, the vestal virgin, carrying water in a sieve from the Tiber to the Forum. (See Dionysius, ii. 69.) On the border is S. K. Pello, " By this proof a sepulchre and a calumny are removed from me." 685, Sarcophagus, representing the manufacture of oil ; 684, Æsculapius.

## THE NUOVO BRACCIO.

Built by Pius VII., in 1817, from the designs of Stern. The floor is composed of ancient mosaics, and is worthy of notice. The chief objects of interest are—5, Caryatide, supposed to be one of those which supported the portico of the Pandrosium at Athens, by Phidias ; 8, Commodus ; 9, Captive Dacian King ; 11, Silenus ; 14, Augustus. found in 1863 in the ruins of the Villa of Livia at

Prima Porta; 17, Antonius Musa, the physician of Augustus; 20, Nerva; 23, Prudence; 26, The Roman poet Quintus Horatius Flaccus. This statue shows Horace as he describes himself, "short and fat." He is evidently reciting the verses written in the roll. The honey-comb at his foot denotes the goodness and sweetness of his verse. 38*, Ganymede, by Phidimos; 44, Copy of the Wounded Amazon, by Cresilas; 47, Caryatide, by Diogenes, from the Pantheon; 50, Diana Lost in Wonder, after Euphranor; 53, Euripides; 56, Julia, daughter of Titus; 62, Demosthenes; 67, Athlete Using the Scraper, a copy of the bronze, by Lysippus; 71, Amazon, after Polycletus; 77, Daughter of Mark Antony, wife of Drusus; 83, Ceres, copy of the original, by Praxiteles; 86, Fortune; 97*, Bust of Mark Antony; 109, The Nile—the sixteen children are allegorical of the cubits at which the rise of the river begins to irrigate the land; 112, Fine Bust of Juno Regina, with the disk, an emblem of royalty; 114, Minerva, after Phidias; 120, A copy of the Faun, by Praxiteles; 126, The Spear-Bearer, copy of Polycletus; 129, Domitian, by Carus.

*Special permission must be obtained of the majordomo for strangers to enter the* CORRIDOR OF INSCRIPTIONS. *Off it, on the right, is the entry to*

## THE LIBRARY.

(*This is also entered from the entrance to Museum. Fee, 50 c. each.*) It was founded by Sixtus V., and contains 120,000 volumes, of which 25,000 are manuscripts. The magnificent great hall is 220 feet long, and contains many objects of interest, notably two fine candelabra of Sèvres china presented to Pius VII. by Napoleon I.; a vase of malachite and another of immense size, presented by Prince Demidoff; two vases of Meissen porcelain, presented by the Emperor of Germany; a large vase of porcelain china, presented by Napoleon III. to Pius IX. after it had been used as the font in the baptism of the Prince Imperial; a beautiful basin of Aberdeen granite, presented by the Duke of Northumberland.

## THE CHRISTIAN MUSEUM.

The contents comprise a collection of lamps, glass vessels, gems, &c., found in the Catacombs. In the room beyond is a very interesting collection of Byzantine and medieval Italian paintings, a Russian calendar, and other interesting objects. At the end of this vista of rooms is a full-length seated portrait of Pius IX., painted on glass at Aix-la-Chapelle.

*From the Hall of the Greek Cross, left of stairs, we enter*

## THE EGYPTIAN MUSEUM.

Formed by Gregory XVI. from Egypt, and from Egyptian remains dispersed in the several museums of Rome. It comprises a hall of monuments, hall of the imitations executed by Roman and Greek artists, and several cabinets containing many interesting objects.

*Ascending the stairs we reach, on the right,*

## THE HALL OF THE BIGA,

adorned with several beautiful works of ancient art, the principal of which is the Biga or chariot, only the body of which is ancient. The Biga for a long time served as an episcopal throne in the Church of S. Mark in Rome. The torso of the right horse was a gift of Prince Borghese; the additions and restorations are by Franzoni. No. 611, Alcibiades, after Nycerates; 615, Discobolus, after Naukides; 616, Phocion; 618, Discobolus, after Myron.

*The long corridor is called*

## THE GALLERY OF THE CANDELABRA,

and is divided into six compartments, containing cups, vases, sarcophagi, statues, candelabra, &c. It has recently been restored by Leo XIII., the floors and ceilings being masterpieces of modern art. The most important objects of interest are: 19, a Child Playing at *Capita et Navia* (heads or tails); 74, Faun Extracting a Thorn from a Satyr's Foot; 81, Diana of Ephesus—her sixteen breasts signify the sixteen cubits at which the Nile overflows; the various half figures of sphinxes, lions, bulls, stags, bees, and flowers are her attributes as the nurse of all things living; the disk ornament refers to the sun; the four seasons, the signs of the zodiac, and a necklace of acorns adorn her neck: the statue was found at Hadrian's Villa. 88, Mercury seated amidst his Symbols; 134a, a Well Head; 134c, statue of the Sabine God Semoni Sanco, found in 1879 on the slopes of the Quirinal Hill, presented by Leo XIII.: 134b, Well Head; 135, seated statuette of Sophocles; 177, an Old Fisherman; 183, Saturn (rare); 184, Personification of Antioch on the Orontes, by Eutychides; 222, a Spartan Virgin Racer, earlier art than that of Phidias; 231, Actor, with mask; 257, Ganymede and the Eagle. *Returning*—269, a Warrior; 194, Child and Swan; 204, sarcophagus representing Diana and Apollo Shooting at the Niobides; 149a, Somnus (Sleep); 148, a Faun Carrying the Infant Bacchus; 118a, the Eagle carrying off Ganymede, a replica of the bronze original, by Leochares; 112, sarcophagus illustrating the Story of Protesilaus and Laodamia. This should be compared with the relief, No. 269, in the Gallery of Statues. On the sides are the myths of Ixion, Sisiphus, and Tantalus. 52, a Drunken Faun, in green basalt.

## THE GALLERY OF TAPESTRIES

contains copies of Raphael's cartoons which are at the South Kensington Museum : they were woven in Flanders by order of Leo X. to adorn the Sixtine Chapel. *Right side going down.* Our Saviour giving the Keys to Peter—*the border* represents the Medici fleeing from Florence ; Peter healing the Man at the Beautiful Gate of the Temple—*border*, Cardinal Medici at the Battle of Ravenna; Conversion of Saul—*border*, the Taking of Prato in 1512; in three pieces, Slaughter of the Innocents; The Resurrection; Stoning of Stephen—*border*, Cardinal Medici entering Florence, allegorical of the Papal power; the Earthquake during Paul's imprisonment at Philippi. *Right in returning.* Descent of the Holy Ghost; Adoration of the Wise Men; Our Lord's Ascension; Adoration of the Shepherds; The Presentation in the Temple; Christ as the Gardener; Scenes from our Lord's Passion ; *small*, Paul on Mars' Hill—*border*, Scenes from the Acts; Paul and Barnabas at Lystra—*border*, Scenes from the Life of Paul ; Miraculous Draught of Fishes; Death of Ananias—*border*, Faith, Hope, and Charity.

*Retracing our way through the Gallery of the Candelabra, a small flight of steps at the end leads to a balcony where there is a good view of the lower halls. On the right is the entrance to*

## THE ETRUSCAN MUSEUM,

which contains various works of art brought from the ancient towns of Etruria and Magna Græcia. These works are generally mixed up in the Roman museums.

FIRST ROOM.—Three terra-cotta sarcophagi, with reclining figures on the covers; two horses' heads in tufa from Vulci.

SECOND ROOM.—Cinerary urns from Volterra, in Volterra alabaster.

THIRD ROOM.—A large peperino sarcophagus, found at Corneto, the ancient Tarquinii : an Etruscan king-priest, *Lucumo*, reclines upon it, and on its sides are Greek myths. A travertine slab, with a Latin and Umbrian inscription, from Todi ; frieze of terra-cotta from Cervetri. In the corners of the room cinerary urns, found beneath a volcanic stratum between Albano and Marino: they are in the form of huts, and still contain ashes.

FOURTH ROOM.—A Roman Mercury in terra-cotta, found at Tivoli; a wounded youth reclining on a couch, generally called Adonis.

FIFTH, SIXTH, SEVENTH, and EIGHTH Rooms contain terra-cotta vases, glass beads, and ornaments.

NINTH ROOM (*entered from Sixth Room*).—Hall of bronzes and jewellery; a bronze statue of a warrior, found at Todi in 1835; shields, arrows, helmets, spurs, mirrors, &c.; a funeral bier from Cære; a bronze child with a bulla, supposed to represent Tages, the boy-god who sprang from a clod of earth at Tarquinii; a Roman war-chariot, found at the Villa of the Quintilii on the Appian Way; bronze toilet-cases (*cista mistica*); brazier with tongs on wheels; a rake with a hand for its handle; shovel—two swans bearing a boy and a girl form the handle. *In the centre of the hall*, Jewel-case of objects found in the tomb of *Mi Larthial* ("I, the great lady") and of an Etruscan priest at Cervetri (Cære), from which town and its customs we get the word "ceremony."

TENTH ROOM.—Bronze figure of a boy; and Roman lead pipes.

ELEVENTH ROOM.—Copies of the frescoes found in the tombs at Vulci and Tarquinii; Etruscan vases.

TWELFTH ROOM.—Imitation Tomb, with genuine peperino lions.

## THE INQUISITION.

Returning from the Museum, on reaching the colonnade of S. Peter's, *turn off to the right*, through the middle of the colonnade. Opposite is the Palazzo del S. Uffizio,—the Inquisition, which was established here in 1536, and abolished by the Roman Republic in 1849. It is now used as a barrack, and the Inquisition holds its meetings in the Vatican.

Passing at the back of the columns into the Borgo S. Michaele, and *turning to the right*, we enter the Borgo S. Spirito. *On the left* is the fine tower of the Church of S. Michaele in Sassia, in which Raphael Mengs is buried. This name, Sassia, commemorates the Saxon settlement founded in 727, and the word "borgo" comes from the Saxon "burgh." *Beyond is*

## THE PORTA S. SPIRITO,

a massive gateway built by San Gallo in the walls erected by Leo IV. round S. Peter's and the Vatican, whence the district inside is called the Leonine City. *Outside the gate a steep ascent leads up to*

## S. ONOFRIO—TASSO'S TOMB.

This convent is for ever memorable in the history of Italian literature as the place where Tasso died. The adjoining church, called Girolmini, or Brothers of S. Jerome, built for the use of the monks, was erected in 1429 A.D., during the reign of Eugene IV. Tasso, summoned to the Capitol to be crowned there as king of bards, died in 1595, a short time after his arrival in Rome. He was buried in the church without much ceremony, and his remains lay undisturbed in a simple tomb on the left of the entrance until the year 1857, when they were transferred to a chapel in the church expressly built for their reception at the public expense. A fine statue of the poet by Fabris is shown. In the convent garden is a tree called Tasso's Oak,* under which the author of "Jerusalem Delivered" used to sit in pious meditation. The view of Rome and of the Sabine and Alban Hills, with Soracte in the distance, is magnificent. The fresco of the Virgin and Child over the door of the church, and three paintings under the portico illustrating the life of S. Jerome, are the work of Domenichino. In the convent is a Virgin and Child by Leonardo da Vinci; and in the same building are preserved several relics of Tasso, in the room where he died—his crucifix, his inkstand, and the leaden coffin in which his bones reposed for two hundred and sixty-two years—namely, till the time of his second burial. Two other distinguished men were buried in S. Onofrio—Guidi, the poet, and Cardinal Mezzofanti, the famous linguist.

*At the bottom of the ascent, turn to the right, down the Via Lungara. Some little distance down on the right is the*

### PALAZZO DEI LINCEI.

(*Formerly Corsini.*)

*Open Monday, Thursday, and Saturday, from 9 to 3.*

As this palace, now the home of the Academy of the Lincei, is again open to the public, and as the paintings were generously presented by Prince Corsini to the city of Rome, it may be of advantage to visitors in Rome if we enumerate the paintings most worth inspection. At the same time we would inform our readers that there are full catalogues, on cards, in Italian and French in each room.

FIRST ROOM.—*In glass case on stand at window*, Birth of Christ, by Batoni; 6, Sacred Family, by Barocci; 23, S. Catherine of Sienna, by Zobole.          * Blown down in the storm of October 29, 1891.

SECOND ROOM.—*In glass case on stand at first window*, Mater Dolorosa, by Guido Reni. *In second window*, Madonna and Infant Jesus, by Carlo Dolci; 11 and 27, Fruit, by Mario di Fiori; 15, a Landscape, by Poussin; 20, Pietà, by Caracci; 41, Andrea Corsini, by Gessi, copied in mosaic in the Corsini Chapel in S. John's Lateran.

THIRD ROOM.—89, Ecce Homo, by Guido Reni; 1, Ecce Homo, by Guercino; 9, Madonna, by Sarto; 10, Birth of the Virgin, by Caracci; 15, Madonna, by Sarto; 17, Madonna, by Caravaggio; 21, Virgin and Child, by Vandyck; 22, The Players, by Rubens; 23, Sunset, by Botti; 26, Sacred Family, by Fra Bartolomeo; 27, Peter Paying the Tribute Money, by Caravaggio; 33, Flight into Egypt, by Perugino; 36, Holy Family, by Garofalo; 40, The Sleep of Jacob, by Massow; 44, Julius II., by Raphael; 45, Birth of the Virgin, by Berettini of Cortone. *Under glass in last window*, a Hare, by Albert Durer; 55, Butcher's Shop, by Teniers; 82. John the Baptist, by Carlo Maratta; 88, Ecce Homo, by Carlo Dolci.

FOURTH ROOM.—*In the centre*, an ancient marble chair, with low reliefs, found at the Lateran. 1, Ancient mosaic, a Man Binding Bulls; 4, Cupid Asleep, by Guido; 11, The Daughter of Herodias, by Guido; 16, Madonna, by Guido; 20, The Baptist, by Guercino; 31, Peter and Agata, by Lanfranco; 33, Death of S. Stephen, by Domenichino; 40, Faustina Maratta, by Carlo Maratta; 41, the Fornarina, by Giulio Romano, after Raphael; 42, an Old Man, by Guido; 43, Holy Family, by Carlo Maratta; 45, Magdalen, by Carlo Dolci.

FIFTH ROOM.—8, The Annunciation, by Michael Angelo—one of his few easel pictures; 12, S. Agnese, by Carlo Dolci; 16, The Sacred Family, by Schidone; 21, Madonna, by Carlo Maratta; 22, Marriage of S. Caterina, by Domenichino; 24, Christ at the Well, by Guercino; 26, Madonna, by Sassoferrato; 29, Madonna and Infant, by Guercino; 32-40, Annunciation, by Guercino; 34, The Forum Romanum, by Pannini; 38, Ecce Homo, by Guido; 39, S. John, by Guido.

SIXTH ROOM.—21, The Children of Charles V., by Titian; 22, a Woman, by Rembrandt; 37, Mrs. Martin Luther, by Holbein; 31, Martin Luther, by Holbein; 47, Rubens's Portrait, by himself; 50, Cardinal Farnese, by Titian.

SEVENTH ROOM.—11, Landscape, by Poussin; 15, S. Sebastian, by Rubens; 19-27, Annunciation, by Carlo Maratta; 21, The Dispute, by Giordano; 23, 24, Last Judgment and Ascension, by Fra Angelico; 30, "Let him who is without sin cast the first stone," by Titian; 42, Magdalen, by Franceschini.

EIGHTH ROOM.—2, Sacred Family, by Francia; 8, Christ before Pilate, by Vandyck; 9, The Baptist, by Caravaggio; 12, St. George and the Dragon, by Grandi; 13, Contemplation, by Guido; 15, Landscape, by Poussin; 16, a Sea Piece, by Salvator Rosa; 18, Susanna, by Domenichino; 19, Seneca Dying in the Bath, by Caravaggio; 24, S. Jerome, by Guercino; 29, Christ in the Garden, by Correggio; 32, Peter Raising Tabitha, by Placide Costanzi, copied in mosaic in S. Peter's; 37, Woman and Child, by Murillo.

NINTH ROOM.—2, Village Interior, by Teniers; 9, Triumph of Ovid, by Velasquez; 10, an Old Man Reading, by Guido; 12, Prometheus, by Salvator Rosa; 58, Death of S. Joseph, by Giuseppe del Sole. *Opposite is*

## THE FARNESINA PALACE.

*Open on the 1st and 15th of the month.*

It contains the famous frescoes of Raphael. On the ceiling of the first room that of the fable of Cupid and Psyche, designed by Raphael, and painted by Giulio Romano. This charming fable is described by Kugler in his "Handbook on the Italian Painters."

*Commencing on the left*, the first is Venus ordering Cupid to punish Psyche; second, Cupid showing Psyche to the Three Graces; third, Juno and Ceres pleading for Psyche; fourth, Venus in her Car going to claim the interference of Jupiter; fifth, Venus pleading before Jupiter; sixth, Mercury flying to execute the Order of Jupiter; seventh, Psyche with the Vase of Beauty-Paint given by Proserpine to appease Venus; eighth, Psyche giving the Vase to Venus; ninth, Cupid complaining to Jupiter; tenth, Mercury taking Psyche to Olympus. *On the vault*, Council of the Gods, by Giulio Romano; Banquet of the Gods, on the Marriage of Cupid, by Francesco Penni. *On the wall of the second room*, Raphael's Galatea; on the ceiling, Diana in her Car drawn by Oxen, by Peruzzi, and the fable of Medusa, by D. Volterra. The landscapes are by Poussin.

On the opposite side of the street, just beyond the Corsini Palace entrance, in the Vicolo Stalle d'Corsini, is the

## TORLONIA MUSEUM.
### (*Museo Torlonia.*)

*Permission must be obtained from Prince Torlonia. Written application should be made to the prince at his palace in the Piazza di Venezia.*

A full catalogue of the Torlonia Museum has been written and printed by Signor P. E. Visconti. Copies are lent for the use of visitors. This grand collection of sculptures has been in course of formation by Prince Torlonia during many years. Some of the objects were found on his own property, others have been purchased by him, and many of the most valuable works formerly belonged to the Mosca, Cambral, Giustiniani, Ruspoli, and Randanini collections. As containing works of art, it ranks next to the Vatican collection, and is the finest private gallery in the world.

Amongst so many valuable and beautiful works of art it is almost impossible to say what the casual observer should more particularly notice. A day may be well and profitably spent amongst this admirable collection. The lover of art will gain every information from Visconti's excellent catalogue, whilst ordinary visitors can stroll through and consult it for those objects which strike them most. Venuses, the Muses, gods and goddesses, heroes and tales of mythology, the emperors and their wives,—all are amply illustrated here. Many of the objects are unique, and as there is such a good printed catalogue lent, it is unnecessary for us to enumerate the different objects.

*Continuing down the Via Lungara, at a short distance is*

### THE PORTA SETTIMIANA,

said to have been an archway leading into a villa of Septimius Severus. It was incorporated by Aurelian into the line of his walls, and fortified by Honorius. Passing under the arch, the VIA GARIBALDI *on the right* leads to the garden-crowned height of

### S. PIETRO IN MONTORIO,

which commands a magnificent view of Rome, its surroundings, and the windings of the Tiber. The church was erected by Ferdinand and Isabella of Spain, and is still under the protection of the crowned head of Spain. In the court of the monastery is a small temple formed of sixteen Doric columns, said to be erected over the spot where the cross on which S. Peter was executed stood. Raphael's Transfiguration was painted for this church, whence it was taken by the French to adorn the Louvre. On its restoration to the Papal authorities it was placed in the Vatican. The tomb of Beatrice Cenci is to our left of the high altar, but no name is recorded on the stone. The new Spanish Academy adjoins the church.

## MARTIAL'S VILLA

The Government has recently acquired and thrown open to the public these grounds, known as the Corsini Villa, which for its view is one of the most charming sites in Europe, formerly the villa of Julius Martialis described by his nephew ("Ep." iv. 64) :—

> "The few acres of Julius Martial,
> More blest than the Hesperides' gardens,
> Lie on the long ridge of the Janiculum.
>
> It is possible hence to see the seven ruling mounts,[*]
> And to estimate all Rome,—
> The Alban hills, and those of Tusculum ;
> And whatsoever cool shade lies under the city ;
> Old Fidenæ,[†] and little Ruba ;[‡]
> And, that which delights in virgins' blood,
> The apple-bearing grove of Anna Perenna.[§]
> From thence, on the Flaminian and Salarian ways,[‖]
> The rider is manifest, his chariot-wheels being silent,
> Whose gentle sleep may not be molested,
> Neither to break it by nautical shouts,
> Nor the clamour of the vigorous bargee,
> Although the Mulvian bridge [¶] may be so near,
> And keels glide swiftly on the Sacred Tiber."

## THE JANICULUM.

The long narrow ridge which commands Rome on its western side took its name from Janus (Virgil, " Æn." vii. 358), but, although fortified by Ancus Martius, was not reckoned in the city. It was sometimes called Mons Aureus, from the golden colour of its sandy soil. From the fort on the summit a flag flying denoted that all was well ; but if the flag was hauled down, the enemy were in view. It was this fort that Lars Porsena seized when Horatius defended the bridge below.

*Above the church of S. Pietro in Montorio is*

[*] The hills of Rome. She ruled the world.
[†] Five miles on the Salarian Way.
[‡] Sax Ruba, eight miles on the Flaminian Way.
[§] On the Ides of May a popular carousal was held to this goddess, on the fields of Aqua Acetosa, by the banks of the Tiber, whereat many were espoused. (See Ovid. "F." iii. 523.)
[‖] Northern roads, one on either side of the Tiber.
[¶] Now Ponte Molle.

THE PAULINE FOUNTAIN.

### THE PAULINE FOUNTAIN,

*(Fontana Paolina,)*

supplied by the ancient Aqua Trajana, which has its source in the
Lago di Bracciano, thirty-five miles from Rome. The fountain was
built out of the remains of the Temple of Minerva which stood in
the Forum of Domitian. The Corsini Villa is entered through the
gate on the right. *The road through the* PORTA S. PANCRAZIO *leads
to the*

### VILLA PAMPHILI DORIA.

*Open on Monday and Friday afternoons; one-horse carriages not
admitted.*

The villa—the most extensive and delightful of the Roman villas,
abounding in avenues and woods, fountains and cascades—is situated
on the summit of the Janiculum, it is supposed upon the site of a villa
of Galba. From the ilex-fringed terrace there is one of the best
views of S. Peter's ; a lake supporting swans ; a temple to the slain
amongst the besiegers of Rome in 1849—all of which must be seen to
be appreciated. "Galba was buried in his gardens, which are situated on the Aurelian Way, not far from the city" (Eutropius, vii. 16).

*Re-entering the city, and descending the hill by the new road, thence
by the Via delle Fratte, we reach the*

### CHURCH OF S. CECILIA,

originally the house of the saint. To the right, on entering, is the
tomb of Adam Hereford, Bishop of London, who died in 1398. The
second chapel on the right is said to have been the bath-room, and
pipes may still be seen in the wall. Beneath the high altar is the
statue of S. Cecilia, representing her body as found in the Catacombs of S. Calixtus, "not lying upon the back, like a body in a
tomb, but upon its right side, like a virgin in her bed, with her
knees modestly drawn together, and offering the appearance of sleep."
A golden circlet conceals the wound in her throat that caused her
death. The inscription is as follows: "Behold the body of the most
holy virgin Cecilia, whom I myself saw lying incorrupt in her tomb.
I have in this marble expressed for thee the same saint in the very
same posture of body.—Stefano Maderno." Thus, when Cardinal
Sfondrati restored the church, in 1599, was the body found in her
tomb just as it had been deposited there eight hundred years before,
after being found in the Catacombs by Paschal I. (See page 289.)

*By the Via dei Vascellari and Via Lungaretta we reach the*

## CHURCH OF S. CHRISOGONO.

Founded by Pope Sylvester, and rebuilt 1623. It has a fine old *opus Alexandrinum* pavement, and the aisles are formed by twenty-two columns, two in porphyry supporting the arch. A mosaic in the tribune represents the Madonna and Child enthroned between SS. James and Chrisogono. The ceiling was painted by Arpino. *On the left of the piazza is the small street,* MONTE DI FIORE, *in which is the*

### STAZIONE VII COHORTI DEI VIGILI

(Roman firemen), remodelled and formed into seven watches by Augustus. The building was discovered in 1866. *The custodian conducts the visitor over, fee half a franc.* Descending the stairs we enter a mosaic paved courtyard, with a well in the centre, and on the right a small altar with mural paintings. There are several other chambers, and a bath, with numerous inscriptions on the walls scratched by the firemen during their idle moments.

*Going down the* VIA LUNGARETTA, *we enter the* PIAZZA OF S. MARIA, in which are a fine fountain and the

### CHURCH OF S. MARIA.

The façade is covered with mosaics representing the Virgin and Child enthroned, surrounded by ten virgins, and on either side the figure of a bishop (Innocent II. and Eugenius III.); above this are palms, the twelve sheep, and the mystic cities, and our Lord enthroned between angels. The interior contains twenty-two columns. The Assumption, on the ceiling, is by Domenichino. Beneath the high altar are the remains of five early popes. In the upper part of the tribune are mosaics of the Saviour and a female figure (representing the Church, the bride of Christ, and not the Virgin, as is generally said) seated on thrones, surrounded by S. Peter and six other saints ; twelfth century. Below, the scenes from the life of Mary are by Pietro Cavallini ; also the Virgin, between S. Paul and S. Peter, over the bishop's throne. S. Peter is presenting Bertoldo de' Stefaneschi, who had the mosaic done in 1290, to Mary.

On the face of the arch are Isaiah and Jeremiah, with the symbols of the four evangelists. The large frescoes on either side of the Virgin are by Ciampelli.

The Chapel of the Madonna di Strada Cupa, left transept, was designed by Domenichino, and restored by the Cardinal York, hence the British arms. At the entry is the sarcophagus of Alexander

Campeggio, legate from Leo X. to Henry VIII. : the Campeius of Shakespeare.

A tradition says that this church was founded on a spot where a fountain of oil sprang out of the ground and ran down to the Tiber on the birth of our Saviour ; and it is connected by some with the squabble that occurred between some Christians and tavern-keepers as to the ownership of the site, which Alexander Severus decided was to be given to the Christians, as it was better that God should be worshipped, in whatever form, than that it should be devoted to tavern-keepers (Lampridius, " Alexander Severus," 49).

*Leaving the church, and going down the* VIA DELLA SCALA, *hence turning to the right into the* VIA DI PONTE SISTO, the house on the left, a baker's shop, with Gothic upper windows, was the HOUSE OF RAPHAEL'S FORNARINA. RAPHAEL'S HOUSE was at No. 124 Via dei Coronari, near the S. Angelo Bridge. *A short distance, and we reach*

## THE PONTE SISTO.

The present bridge was built by Pope Sixtus IV., who laid the foundation stone, April 29, 1473, on the site of an older bridge which was destroyed in the flood of A.D. 792, it having been built by Symmachus, prefect of Rome under Valentinian (A.D. 365), "under whose government the most sacred city enjoyed peace and plenty in an unusual degree ; being also adorned with a magnificent and solid bridge which he constructed, and opened amid the great joy of his ungrateful fellow-citizens" (Ammianus Marcellinus, xxvii. iii. 3). In 1878, in making the new embankment for the Tiber, the remains of the left arch were found at the bottom of the river, upon which was part of the inscription, one foot seven inches high—VALENTINIAN. Pedestals which formed part of the decorations were also found, and part of an inscription—VALENTINIANI AU COSTI. At the Campus Martius end was a triumphal arch dedicated to Valens and Valentiniani—

DEDICANDI . OPERIS . HONORE . DELATO . INDICIO . PRINCIPUM .
MAXIMORUM . LUCIO . AURELIO . AVIANIO . SYMMACHO . VIRO .
CLARISSIMO . EX . PREFECTIS . URBI .

Remains of a bronze statue were also found.

# RAMBLE III.

## BY THE TIBER.

### THE VIA RIPETTA.

From the Piazza del Popolo the line of the Ripetta runs between
the Corso and the Tiber. A new bridge, Ponte Margherita, leads
through the new quarter of the Prati Castello to S. Peter's. Down
the Via Ripetta another bridge spans the river, Ponte Ripetta; this
leads to the New Law Courts, now in the course of erection. On the
right bank, now built over, was the farm of Cincinnatus (Livy, iii. 26).

## THE MAUSOLEUM OF AUGUSTUS.

*Turning out of the Ripetta on the left into the Via dé Pontefici, through a gateway on the right,* are the remains of this once handsome tomb; only the double reticulated wall, on which the tumulus with its trees formerly stood, remains. This ruin has been converted into a modern theatre, and thus the original finely-proportioned arrangements can no longer be traced. A part of the enclosure wall may be best seen from the court of the Palazzo Valdambrini, *102 Via Ripetta.* The mausoleum was built by Augustus, B.C. 27. Marcellus, Agrippa, Drusus, and Germanicus were buried there. Strabo describes it as standing upon a lofty substruction of white stone, and shaded up to the top with trees. The summit was crowned with the statue of Augustus in bronze, and there were two Egyptian obelisks at the entrance, brought over by Claudius. They are mentioned likewise by Marcellinus.

*It stood in*

## THE CAMPUS MARTIUS,

which Strabo thus describes: "The plain, adorned by nature and art, is of wonderful extent, and affords an ample and a clear space for the running of chariots, and other equestrian and gymnastic exercises. It is in verdant bloom throughout the year, and is crowned by hills which rise above the Tiber and slope down to its very banks. The whole affords a picturesque and beautiful landscape, which you would linger to behold. Near to this plain is another of less magnitude; and all around it are innumerable porticoes and shady groves, besides three theatres, an amphitheatre, and various temples contiguous to each other, so that the rest of the city appears only an appendage to it." This lesser plain occupied the space between the Mausoleum of Augustus and the Theatre of Marcellus — the plain from the tomb to the modern Ponte Molle. "Sylla's monument stood in the Campus Martius" (Plutarch).

*Just past the bridge, a street on the left leads to the* BORGHESE PALACE, *the Picture Gallery of which has been removed to the Museum in the Villa. Keeping straight on down the Via della Scrofa, in the third turning on the right, at Via Portoghesi, is the* TORRE DELLA SCIMMIA, better known to Hawthorne's readers as

## HILDA'S TOWER.

It is one of those medieval watch-towers that come upon one so unexpectedly in all sorts of out-of-the-way places in Rome. The Romans call it the Tower of the Monkey, from a legend that years ago the proprietor kept a monkey. This monkey one day seized upon a baby in the street below, and carried it to the top of the tower, to the agony of the parents, who vowed a shrine to the Virgin if the child were safely restored. No sooner was the vow uttered than the monkey brought down the baby by means of the water-pipe. The shrine was forthwith erected, and every evening the lamp is lighted at *Ave Maria*, and shines like a bright star till dawn.

*Proceeding down the street, the next turning on the right leads to the*

## CHURCH OF S. AGOSTINO,

built out of the Colosseum in 1483. At the entrance is a popular statue of the Madonna and Child, by Jacopo da Sansavino. On the third pilaster of the left nave is Raphael's fresco of Isaiah, and Two Angels holding a Tablet, 1512. It was restored by Daniele da Volterra. In the first chapel on the left is the Madonna di Loreto, by Caravaggio. In the second, a marble group of S. Anna and the Virgin, by Andrea da Sansavino. In the chapel of the right transept is Guercino's S. Augustine. The second chapel of the right aisle contains a copy of Raphael's lost painting, the Madonna della Rosa. By the side of the church is the Biblioteca Angelica, open from 9 to 2.

*Regaining the Via della Scrofa, turning to the right, on the opposite side of the street, is the* ITALIAN WESLEYAN CHURCH ; *then on the left is*

## S. LUIGI DEI FRANCESI.

The Chapel of S. Cecilia, second on right, contains Domenichino's fine frescoes of the saint. Above the altar, fourth on right, is a copy by Guido of Raphael's S. Cecilia at Bologna. Over the high altar is the Assumption, by Francisco Bassamo. On the left of this is the Chapel of S. Matthew, with three pictures of that saint's life, by Caravaggio. Amongst other monuments to eminent Frenchmen is one to Claude Lorraine, who was buried in the Church of Trinità dei Monti, but whose tombstone has been placed at the foot of this monument.

*The Via Giustiniani, opposite, leads to the Piazza Rotonda.*

## THE OBELISK

surmounts a fountain. This obelisk and the one in the Piazza Minerva were erected as pairs in Rome. They stood before the Temple of Isis and Serapis in the Campus Martius. There is a small relief in the Villa Ludovisi, representing in its background a temple with

four Ionic columns, and to the left an Egyptian obelisk. In the
foreground, to the left, is the figure of Minerva, fronting a reclining
female figure holding a vessel full of ears of corn (Isis?). By her side
is Cupid, and at their back a figure holding something in a spread-
out cloth. May not the temple in the background represent the
Temple of Isis and Serapis?

## THE PANTHEON.

This incomparable circular edifice, originally intended by Agrippa
to form the conclusion of his thermæ,* with which it is intimately
connected, is one of the noblest and most perfect productions of that

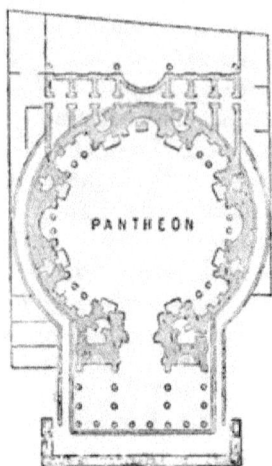

PANTHEON

style of architecture specifically denominated Roman. When the first wonderful
creation of this species came into existence,
the founder of this glorious dome appears
to have himself shrunk back from it, and
to have felt that it was not adapted to be
the every-day residence of men, but to be
a habitation for the gods.

The Church of S. Maria ad Martyres
was originally the sudatorium, or sweating-room, of the Baths of Agrippa, being
similar in construction to all the sweating-
rooms now existing, notably one in the
Villa of Hadrian at Tivoli. It exactly
answers Vitruvius's description of this
department of the baths. It seems after-
wards to have been dedicated as a temple of the gods, or Pantheon
of the Julian line, according to Dion Cassius (liii. 27), when the
portico was added in the third consulship of Agrippa.

M. AGRIPPA . L. F. COS . TERTIUM . FECIT.

The straight vertical joint where the Greek portico has been built
up to the Roman body can be distinctly seen, and the pediment and
entablature can be observed behind the portico. It was burned in
the fire under Titus; and was restored, as the inscription on the
architrave tells us, by Septimius Severus and Caracalla—

PANTHEUM VETUSTATE CORRUPTUM CUM OMNI CULTU RESTITVERUNT.

* Warm baths which were destined for public use only.

INTERIOR OF THE PANTHEON.

Recent explorations have shown that in front of the Pantheon was a large enclosure surrounded by a covered arcade, somewhat after the manner of the colonnade at S. Peter's, and entered by an arch of triumph. Remains of this arch exist under the houses in front of the Pantheon, which are to be pulled down.

When Agrippa dedicated the Pantheon as a temple, it was consecrated to Jupiter the Avenger. "Some of the finest works that the world has ever beheld...the roofing of the Pantheon of Jupiter Ultor that was built by Agrippa" (Pliny, "N. H.," xxxvi. 24). The repairs commenced by Septimius Severus and Caracalla were completed by Alexander Severus, who built his baths close by. We call attention to a coin of this emperor, which represents the temple and its enclosure on the reverse ; on the obverse is the emperor's portrait, and the legend IMP . C . M . AVR . SEV . ALEXANDER . AUG. On the coin the columns are placed close on either flank, and two are omitted, to show the seated statue of Jupiter in the temple, which statue is now in the Hall of Busts in the Vatican Museum, and is a copy of the celebrated Jupiter of Phidias.

THE PANTHEON.
(From a Coin.)

The fact that the Pantheon was originally built as a sudatorium has been proved to a certainty by the excavations made in the sudatorium of the Baths of Caracalla. There we have, as it were, the Pantheon in ruins. It is slightly smaller, the diameter being 125 feet—17 less than the Pantheon. Opposite to the entrance is an apse, and on each side there are three recesses, as at the Pantheon, which were used as caldaria, but are now, in the Pantheon, chapels of the saints.

The portico is 110 feet long, and 44 feet deep. Sixteen Corinthian columns, 46½ feet high and 5 feet in diameter, support the roof. The Pantheon was converted into a church by Boniface IV. in 609, by permission of the Emperor Phocas, and it was dedicated to the martyrs on November 1st (All Saints' Day), 830. The doors and grating above, of ancient bronze, with the rim round the circular opening in the vault of the interior, are all that is left of the ancient metal work. The interior is 142 feet in diameter, and 143 feet high, and is lighted by an open space of 28 feet in diameter. It is the burial-place of Raphael (*left*) and of Victor Emanuel II. (*right of high altar*).

Pliny says ("Nat. Hist." xxxvi. 4): "The Pantheon of Agrippa has been decorated by Diogenes of Athens, and the caryatides by him, which form the columns of that temple, are looked upon as masterpieces of excellence. The same, too, with the statues that are placed upon the roof, though, in consequence of the height, they have not had an opportunity of being so well appreciated." "The capitals, too, of the pillars which were placed by M. Agrippa in the Pantheon, were made of Syracusan metal" (*ibid.*, xxxiv. 7). Marcellinus (xvi. x. 14) says: "The Pantheon, with its vast extent, its imposing height, and the solid magnificence of its arches, and the lofty niches rising one above the other like stairs, is adorned with the images of former emperors."

An inscription on the left of the door records the destruction of the bronze plates of the roof by Urban VIII. : "That the useless and almost forgotten decorations might become ornaments of the apostle's tomb in the Vatican temple, and engines of public safety in the fortress of S. Angelo, he moulded the ancient relics of the bronze roof into columns and cannons, in the twelfth year of his pontificate" (Inscription).

"What the barbarians did not the Barberini have done" (Pasquino).

Raphael's tomb is in the third chapel on the left.

> "Living, great Nature feared he might outvie
> Her works; and, dying, fears herself to die."
> CARDINAL BEMBO: *translated by* POPE.

A bust, by Nardini, of Raphael was originally placed near here, but was removed in 1820, in consequence of people offering their devotions to it. Another bust has now been placed here. Annibale Caracci is buried on the right of the altar, which was designed by Raphael, and erected by his intended bride, niece of Cardinal Bibiena.

## THE BATHS OF AGRIPPA.

The houses built amidst the ruins of the Baths of Agrippa at the back of the Pantheon have been demolished, and part of a large hall has been exposed to view. Nothing that has been discovered is new to those who have studied the subject. It has long been known that these houses were built on the old walls and vaults of the Thermæ. In fact, the sacristy of the Pantheon was made out of a vaulted chamber, a floor being inserted about half-way above its base. Besides the vaults and walls now cleared, pavements, pipes, and fragments of pavonazzetto columns have been found ; also an earthenware jar containing 1,200 debased silver coins—provincial money of the thirteenth century, with the motto, *Roma caput mundi.* Portions of a beautiful frieze, formed with tridents, shells, dolphins, and acanthus leaves, blended harmoniously together, were found, and skilfully replaced in their ancient position. It is almost impossible to say for what purpose this hall was used, as nearly the whole of these baths are buried under the surrounding houses ; but judging from its relative position to the circular hall, and from the plans of other thermæ, it was most probably the tepidarium. The hall was 150 feet long by 70 feet wide. Oriental marbles decorated the floor and walls, the latter being relieved with niches containing statues.

BATHS OF AGRIPPA.

Through the central apse was the original entry into the circular hall behind. The wall now exposed to view has a large apse in the centre, with the platform, on which stood a statue ; and on either side are three niches for statues. Agrippa served his first consulship in A.U.C. 717. He was ædile in 719–20. In this service he built his baths (Dion Cassius, in "Augustus ;" Pliny, xxxvi. 24). In 726 he was consul for the second time. In 727 he was consul for the third time, when the circular hall of his baths was turned into a temple, as we are informed by the inscription *in situ.*

These were the first large baths erected in Rome. Only small fragments of them remain, built into the houses at the back of the Pantheon, and so difficult to see. In the VIA DELL' ARCO DELLA CIAMBELLA, some little distance back, are the remains of a circular hall.

*The Via Minerva, to the left of the Pantheon, leads to the Piazza Minerva.*

### THE OBELISK,

standing upon an elephant, stood, with the one in the square of the Pantheon, in front of the Temple of Isis. The elephant upon which it stands is the work of Ercole Perrata, and of course had nothing to do originally with the obelisk. *On the left is the*

## CHURCH OF S. MARIA SOPRA MINERVA,

so named from being on the site of the Temple of Minerva dedicated by Pompey. It is one of the few Gothic churches in Rome.

The interior is highly decorated in the Gothic style. Second chapel on right, tomb of Princess Colonna. Fourth, the Chapel of the Annunciation. Fifth, Aldobrandini Chapel. The Caraffa Chapel contains a slab to a son of the late Bishop of Winchester, who joined the Roman Catholic Church, and died at Albano in 1857. The pictures of the Annunciation over the altar, the S. Thomas, and the Assumption are fine.

The roof represents four sibyls surrounded by angels, by Raffaelino del Garbo. The Altieri Chapel contains an altar-piece by C. Maratta. Next is the tomb of Guillaume Durand, with a very fine mosaic. Interesting to English visitors is the tomb of Cardinal Howard, Great Almoner of England, who died at Rome in 1694. The body of S. Catherine of Sienna reposes beneath the high altar. *On the right* is Obicci's statue of S. John ; and *on the left* Michael Angelo's celebrated statue of the Saviour (the bronze drapery is an addition). In the sacristy is a chapel formed from the walls of the room in which S. Catherine died (1380). The festivals of S. Thomas Aquinas (March 7th) and of the Annunciation (March 25th) are celebrated here with great ceremony.

*On the left of the high altar* is the tomb of Fra Angelico, a monumental slab of the artist-monk, standing, with clasped hands, within an arch, in low relief.

HIC . JACET . VENELIS . PICTO . TE . JO . ORDIS . PREDICATO . 1455.

The monument was executed by Nicholas V., who is said to have written the inscription—

> "Let me not gain praise because I was a second Apelles,
> But because, O Christ, I gave all my gains to the poor.
> Seeing some of my works are extant on earth, others in heaven,
> The City of Flowers of Etruria reared me."

The MONASTERY attached was the headquarters of the Dominicans, and in it Galileo was tried "for asserting that the world revolved round the sun, in opposition to Holy Writ."

The LIBRARY is open every day from 7.30 to 11 A.M., and from 3 to 5 P.M.

On the façade are some curious inscriptions, referring to the height of the floods caused by the Tiber from 1422.

## THE TEMPLE OF MINERVA CAMPENSIS

was erected by Pompey the Great in celebration of his Eastern victories. The cella was destroyed in the sixteenth century. In making some alterations, in April 1874, in the houses to the right of the church above, some remains of walls six feet thick, and having stamps of repairs A.D. 123, were found.

*Either of the lines of streets at the sides of the Pantheon leads into the fine new thoroughfare, CORSO VITTORIO EMANUELE. Turning to the right, on the opposite side, is the*

## CHURCH OF S. ANDREA DELLA VALLE.

The work carried on for the new street, Corso Vittorio Emanuele, has fully exposed to view the fine front of this church, which was designed by Olivieri, and finished in 1591 by Carlo Ranaldi, the statues being by Domenico Guidi, Ercole Ferrata, and Fancelli. The interior is pleasing, and worth visiting for its works of art. The first chapel on the right contains monuments of the Ginetti family, whilst opposite is the Barberini Chapel. The beautiful Assumption, over the altar, is by Domenico Passignani. The four statues on the sides are beautifully executed—Martha, by Mochi; S. John, by Buonvicino; the Baptist, by Bernini; and the Magdalen, by C. Santi.

The next chapel contains the tomb of Giovanni Casal, Archbishop of Benevento, 1556. The altar of S. Sebastian, in the chapel beyond, is by Giovanni dei Vecchi. In the opposite chapel are copies of Michael Angelo's Leah, Pieta, and Rachel. In the pier adjoining is the tomb of Pius II.; and opposite, that of Pius III., both from old S. Peter's, by Paolo Romano and Pasquino of Montepulciano.

The frescoes on the walls of the choir are by Il Calabrese, those of the vault by Domenichino; both sets refer to the martyrdom of Scotland's patron saint.

The dome was painted by Lanfranco, whilst the Four Evangelists, on the spandrels, are by Domenichino—that of S. John being very fine. The great star on the pavement beneath the cupola marks, as near as possible, the site where Cæsar was murdered in the Senate House of Pompey, and which was dedicated to Victory, for the church is built partly over the site of Pompey's senate house.

*The street on the right hand, facing the church, VIA CHIAVARI, forms a bow to the right. It will be noticed that the fronts of the houses are circular; this is because they are built on the curve of*

## THE THEATRE OF POMPEY.

"Pompey also built that magnificent theatre, which is standing at this day, at whose dedication five hundred lions were killed in five days, and eighteen elephants having fought against armed men, part of them died upon the place, and the rest soon after" (Dion Cassius, "Cæsar"). Plutarch relates the same. The same author, in his "Life of Nero," speaking of the reception of Tiridates, says : "There was a great assembly in the Theatre of Pompey by order of the senate. Not only the scene, but all the inside of the theatre, and everybody that came into it, were covered with gold, which made that day be named Golden Day. The covering which was spread over it to defend the spectators from the heat of the sun, was of rich stuff, the colour of purple, representing the heavens, in the midst of which was Nero driving a chariot." (See Pliny, xxxiii. 16.) "Tiberius undertook to restore the Theatre of Pompey" (Suetonius, "Tiberius," xlvii.). "Tiberius undertook to rebuild the Theatre of Pompey, which was accidentally burned, because none of the family was equal to the charge ; still, however, to be called by the name of Pompey" (Tacitus, "Ann." iii. 72). "Caligula completed it" (Suetonius, "Caligula," xxi.). It was burned ; and again rebuilt by Caracalla, as we learn from an inscription found at Ostia in 1881. "In the games which Claudius presented at the dedication of Pompey's theatre, which had been burned down, and was rebuilt by him, he presided upon a tribunal erected for him in the orchestra ; having first paid his devotions in the temple above, and then coming down through the centre of the circle, while all the people kept their seats in profound silence" (Suetonius, "Claudius," xxi.). It accommodated forty thousand (Pliny, xxxvi. 24). It was built B.C. 55, "in his second consulship" (Vel. Paterculus, ii. 48) ; but afraid of the criticism of the people, he erected at the top of the seats a temple to Venus.

### THE SPOT WHERE CÆSAR FELL.

In the neighbourhood of his theatre Pompey built a house for himself (Plutarch) ; and from the back of the stage a portico (Vitruvius), which, according to Propertius (ii. 32), must have been a beautiful place.

"Pompey's portico, I suppose, with its shady columns, and magnificently ornamented with purple curtains, palls upon you ; and the thickly-planted, even line of plane-trees, and the waters that fall from a sleeping Maro, and in streams lightly bubbling all over." In the centre of this portico Pompey erected a large hall, which he presented to the Roman people for the use of the senate. At the time of Cæsar's assassination the senate house on the Forum was being rebuilt. Suetonius ("Cæsar," lxxx.) says : "Public notice had been given, by proclamation, for the senate to assemble upon the ides of March (15th) in the senate house built by Pompey : the conspirators approved both time and place as most fitting for their purpose." "They killed him in the hall of Pompey, giving him twenty - three wounds" (Livy, "Ep." cxvi.). "The conspirators having surrounded him in Pompey's senate house, fell upon him all together, and killed him with several strokes" (Dion Cassius, "Cæsar." See Suetonius, "Cæsar," lxxxii.).

"The place, too, where the senate was to meet seemed providentially favourable for their purpose. It was a portico adjoining the theatre ; and in the midst of a saloon, furnished with benches, stood a statue of Pompey, which had been erected to him by the commonwealth when he adorned that part of the city with those buildings. The senate being assembled, and Cæsar entering, the conspirators got close about Cæsar's chair. Cassius turned his face to Pompey's statue, and invoked it, as if it had been sensible of his prayers" (Plutarch. See Florus, iv. 2).

"The senate house in which he was slain was ordered to be shut up, and a decree was made that the ides of March should be called parricidal, and that the senate should never more assemble on that day" (Suetonius, "Cæsar," lxxxviii.).

On the marble plan of Rome, in the Capitoline Museum, a fragment shows Pompey's theatre, portico, and senate house. With the given remains of the theatre and the plan it is easy to find the site of the Curia, which is shown on the plan in the form of a basilica : this will bring the curve exactly at the apse of the Church of S. Andrew. Now, we are told that Cæsar was seated in the chair where in the morning Brutus dispensed justice, so he was, no doubt, seated on the tribunal ; and as the tribunal of the church and curia exactly correspond,

HERE CÆSAR FELL !

*From here we retrace our steps down the Via Chiavari, crossing the Via Giubbonari, passing, on our left, the* MONTE DI PIETÀ (Uncle to Rome) ; *turn to left Via Pettinari; the first turning on the right leads*

*to the Piazza Capo di Ferri.* On the left, decorated with statues, is the Spada Palace. In the vestibule of the palace, upstairs, is

## THE STATUE OF POMPEY,

at whose feet great Cæsar fell.

"There was a statue of Pompey, and it was a work which Pompey had consecrated for an ornament to his theatre."

"Either by accident, or pushed hither by the conspirators, he expired at the pedestal of Pompey's statue, and dyed it with his blood" (Plutarch).

"Augustus removed the statue of Pompey from the senate house, in which Julius Cæsar had been killed, and placed it under a marble arch, fronting the curia attached to Pompey's theatre" (Suetonius, "Aug." xxxi.).

The statue is eleven feet high, and was found in 1553 in the Vicolo di Lentari; it was under two houses, and the proprietors could not agree as to whom it should belong to, when Pope Julius II. gave them five hundred gold dollars for it, and presented it to Cardinal Capodiferro. In 1798-99 the French carried this statue to the Colosseum, where they performed Voltaire's "Tragedy of Brutus" to the original statue. To facilitate moving it, they cut off the extended arm; hence the join.

## THE SPADA PALACE.

The Picture Gallery of the Spada Palace has now been closed to the public for some years, but the porter will allow visitors to see the statue of Pompey for a fee.

The Museum has been broken up, but the fine reliefs are arranged on the wall of the corridor leading to the Council Chambers upstairs. *On the left:*—1. Paris seated on Mount Ida. 2. Adrastus and Hypsipyla finding the body of Archemorus, who was killed by the serpent. 3. Paris and Œnone on the Plains of Troy. The rivergod is Xanthus of the Scamander stream. 4. Ulysses and Diomedes stealing the Palladium. 5. Adonis Wounded. *Returning:*—6. Bellerophon watering Pegasus. 7 and 8 are casts of originals in the Capitoline Museum—Perseus and Andromeda, Endymion. 9. Dædalus and Pasiphæ. 10. Amphion and Zethus.

*Turning to the left in leaving the palace, we reach* PIAZZA FARNESE.

## THE FARNESE PALACE.

In the piazza are two fountains, the granite basins of which were found in the Baths of Caracalla. The palace is not now to be visited,

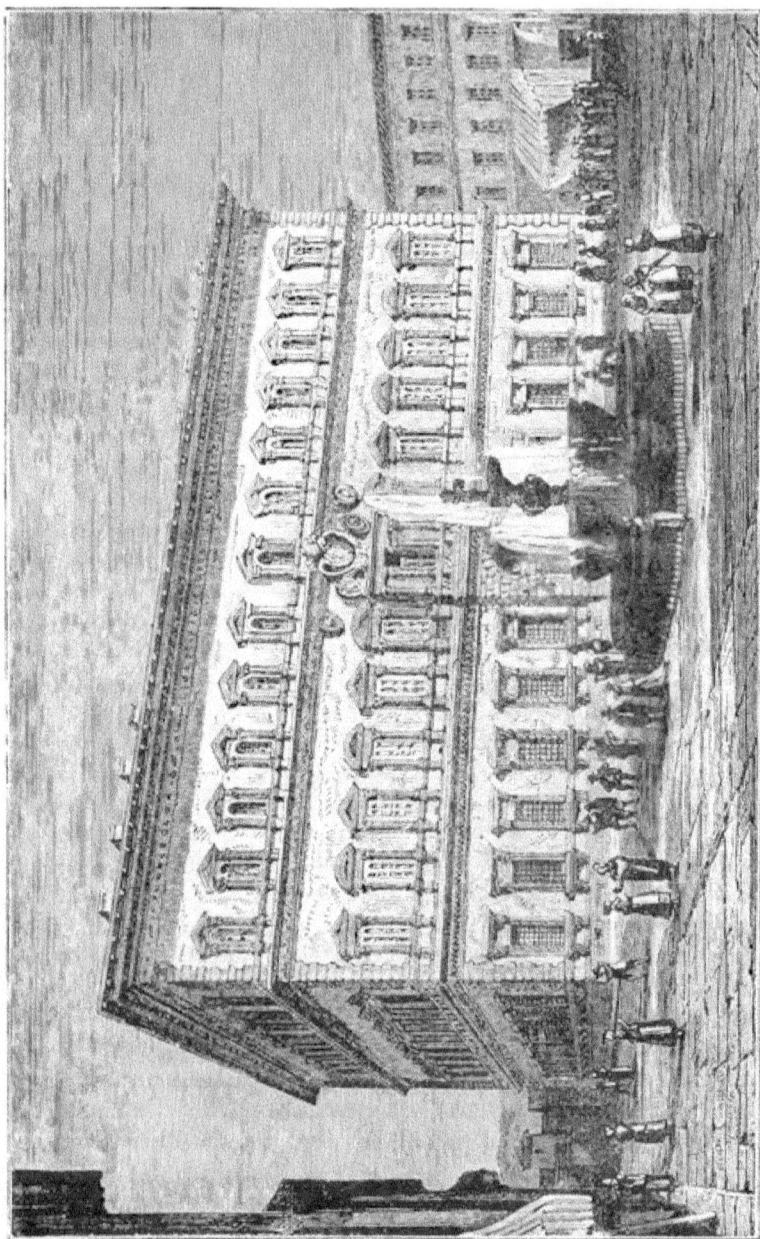

THE FARNESE PALACE.

as it is occupied by the French Embassy. Its architecture is more admired than that of any other palace in Rome : it was built by Pope Paul III. with materials taken from the Colosseum. Its rooms are adorned with frescoes of Annibale Caracci, his finest works, consisting of mythological subjects. The centre piece represents the Triumph of Bacchus and Ariadne.

*The street in front of the palace leads into*

## THE PIAZZA CAMPO DI FIORE,

in which neighbourhood a fair is held every Wednesday. *In the centre is the statue of* GIORDANO BRUNO, *erected June 9, 1889, on the spot where he was burned on February 17, 1600.* The bronze statue stands on a lofty pedestal, and represents him as a Dominican. Reliefs on the sides represent his execution, condemnation, and lecturing at Oxford. Above these are medallions of reformers; amongst them is Wickliffe. It is the work of Ettore Ferrari.

*At the left corner of the square is*

## THE CANCELLERIA PALACE,

### (Palazzo della Cancelleria,)

one of the finest palaces in Rome, built out of the travertine taken from the Colosseum : the forty-four red granite columns which support the portico came from Pompey's Theatre. At the foot of the staircase Count Rossi was assassinated in November 1848.

Adjoining the palace is the CHURCH OF SS. LORENZO E DAMASO, lately restored. *A short lane, Vicolo de' Leutari, leads to the Braschi Palace, at the side of which is*

## THE STATUE OF PASQUINO,

a mutilated torso found here in the sixteenth century. It took its name from Pasquino, a tailor, who lived opposite, and whose shop was the rendezvous of the wits of the city, who wrote their jokes and stuck them on the statue : these were replied to by the statue of Marforio, now in the Capitol Museum.

Some of Pasquino's sayings were very witty, and have been published. Now, under a free government, he seldom speaks.

| PASQUINO'S REPLIES | IN REFERENCE TO THE |
|---|---|
| What the barbarians did not, the Barberini have done. | Barberini family having destroyed the antiquities. |

Public, thou liest; they were not public vows, but were vows of thy vain despotism.

Canova has this time made a mistake: he has clothed Italy, and she is stripped.

The Most High above sends us the tempest; the most high below takes from us that which remains; and between the two most highs we are very badly off.

The French are all rogues; not all—but a good part of them (Buona parte).

*Pasquino.* Beware, Cæsar, lest thy Rome become a republic.

*Cæsar.* Cæsar governs.

*Pasquino* Therefore he will be crowned. A heretic had the preference; after him, a schismatic; but now there is a Turk. Good-bye, Peter's Library!

Inscription put up over the door of the Sacristy of S. Peter's.

Statue of Italy by Canova exhibited during the French Invasion.

Some decrees of Napoleon's, and a severe storm which visited the city.

French occupation of Rome.

Marriage of a man named Cæsar to a girl named Roma.

Appointment of the librarians of the Vatican.

*The Via del Governo Vecchio leads to the*

## CHURCH OF S. MARIA IN VALLICELLA,

*(La Chiesa Nuova,)*

containing three paintings by Rubens; they are at the high altar.

*From the Statue of Pasquino, by the side of the Braschi Palace, we enter the*

## CIRCO AGONALE,

one of the finest squares in Rome, sometimes called Piazza Navona. It takes its name from being the site of the Circus Agonalis. *Fêtes* are held here during Carnival, and a fair at the Epiphany.

Notice the three fountains — the centre one by Bernini: four figures, representing four rivers, recline on a craggy rock; on its top stands an Egyptian obelisk, at its base a lion and a sea-horse.

## THE OBELISK.

This, from the inscription, was either made for, or the inscription was added to and imitated by, Domitian :—"Sun god. Son of the Sun god. Supporter of the world. Giver of life to the world. The man-god Horus. The son of the woman Isis, who is come to avenge the death of his ancestor Osiris. The king living for ever, Domitianus." From his Alban Villa, where it originally stood, it was transported, in A.D. 311, to the spina of the Circus of Maxentius on the Via Appia, thence to its present site.

*On the left is*

## THE CHURCH OF S. AGNESE,

said to have been built on the site where S. Agnes was exposed after her torture; the high altar in the subterranean chapel is said to stand on the very spot. In another part is shown her prison, and where she was beheaded and burned, the church occupying the side vaults of the circus. The upper church contains eight columns of red Cortanella marble; it is ornamented with stuccoes, statues, alto-reliefs, and pictures. Behind the high altar is the sepulchral chapel of Princess Mary Talbot, wife of Prince Doria, who died in 1857.

*A street on the left leads to*

### THE CHURCH OF S. MARIA DELLA PACE,

containing Raphael's Sibyls—the Cumæan, Persian, Phrygian, Tiburtine—on the face of the arch in the first chapel on the right.

Some statues in the Cesi Chapel were worked from pilasters found behind the Palace dei Conservatori, on the Capitol, from the Temple of Juno.

*Returning to the Corso Vittorio Emanuele, we turn to the left, and come to the Piazza S. Nicola a Cesarini, on the right. In the court of No. 56 (Red Cross) is*

### THE TEMPLE OF CASTOR,

spoken of by Vitruvius (iv. 7) as being similar to that of Minerva on the Acropolis at Athens, and being near the Circus Flaminius. Four fluted tufa columns still exist of this circular temple.

*Lower down the Corso Vittorio Emanuele, and facing up the street, is*

### THE CHURCH OF THE JESUITS (Il Gesu),

one of the finest in Rome. Its interior is rich in stuccoes, paintings, and sculptures. The frescoes of the tribune, the dome, and the roof are by Baciccio. The Chapel of S. Ignatius is very fine; the columns and ball over the altar are composed of lapis-lazuli. Beneath the altar, in an urn of gilt bronze, is the body of the saint. The small circular chapel close by is rich in paintings and stained-glass windows.

It is well worth a visit there to hear mass, vespers, or one of the fathers preaching. Festivals—July 31st, December 31st.

The wind generally blows in the piazza, which is thus accounted for. One day the wind and the devil were out for a ramble; and, on arriving at this square, the old gentleman asked the wind to stop a moment while he went into the church. The wind is still stopping for the devil, who has not yet come out.

*To the right of the church, the Via Ara Cœli leads up to*

It was originally called the Hill of Saturn (Dionysius, ii. 1), being occupied by Romulus as a defence for the Palatine Hill (Plutarch, in "Rom."), and was betrayed to the Sabines by Tarpeia, the daughter of the commandant of the fortress (Livy, i. 11). When the Palatine and Capitoline Hills were united into one city, and the two kings reigned together, the name of the hill was changed and called the Tarpeian Hill. In the 138th year after the foundation of Rome, when Tarquin the Great was making the foundations for the great Temple of Jupiter, they found a human head; and the oracle told them that the spot where the head was found should become the head of the world; and so they changed the name of the hill again, and called it the Capitoline Hill,—from caput, a head (Livy, i. 55; Pliny, xxviii. 4). The whole hill was the Arx or Citadel of Rome, just the same as at Athens, Veii, Tusculum, &c. Several ancient authors agree in this. The shape of the hill is a saddle-back,—the centre being depressed, with an eminence at each end. The one on our left is known as the Ara Cœli height, and the one on our right as the Caffarella height. On the Ara Cœli height stood the great Temple of Jupiter, facing south, and approached from the Area Capitolina (Piazza del Campidoglio) by a flight of steps. On the opposite or Caffarella height stood the Temple of Juno Moneta or the Mint, and the Temple of Concord, both built by Camillus; and the Temple of Jupiter Feretrius, founded by Romulus. Many other temples, altars, and shrines occupied the space inside the citadel, which was approached by three ascents upon its eastern side,—the Clivus Capitolinus, the Pass of the Two Groves, and the Hundred Steps. The ascents upon its western side date from 1348, when the marble stairs on our left, leading up to the Ara Cœli, were erected out of the stairs that led up to the Temple of Quirinus (Romulus) upon the Quirinal Hill. The ascent to the Square was made in 1536 for the entry of Charles V. The roadway on its right is quite recent. In forming it some remains of the tufa walls that protected the arx on this side were found, and can still be seen inside the iron gate.

On the balustrade at the bottom of the ascent to the Capitol are two Egyptian lionesses. At the top of the ascent are two colossal statues of Castor and Pollux, found in the Ghetto, and by their side are the miscalled Trophies of Marius. They belonged to the decorations of the Nymphæum of Alexander Severus, the picturesque ruins of which are on the Esquiline Hill, and which are represented on a coin.

VIEW OF THE CAPITOL.

They were placed upon the balustrade of the Capitol, their present
site, by Pope Sixtus V. Originally they formed part of the ornamentation of the Basilica Ulpia, and were erected in honour of Trajan by
the Apollinarian and Valerian legions. Next to the trophies are
two statues of Cæsar and Augustus Constantine; and in the same
row, on the left, the stone that marked the seventh and, on the right,
the stone that marked the first mile on the Via Appia.

*In the centre of the Square is*

### THE EQUESTRIAN STATUE OF MARCUS AURELIUS,

the finest piece of bronze work of ancient times. It now stands upon
the Square of the Capitol, where it was erected by Michael Angelo
in 1538. Before that, it stood at the Lateran, where it had been
placed in 1187, having been taken from near the Column of Phocas
in the Forum. It belongs to the canons of the Lateran, who receive
yearly, in the shape of a bouquet of flowers, a peppercorn rent for it
from the mayor of Rome. It is said that Michael Angelo on passing
by used to say, "Gee up, *cammina;*" and that the horse had only to
plant the raised hoof upon the ground to complete the illusion that
it was a living creature.

In front of us is the mayor's residence; on the left the Museum
of the Capitol; and on the right the halls of the town council.
These buildings were erected by Michael Angelo in 1544–1550. The
residence for the senator was first erected on the top of the ruins of
the Tabularium in 1389–1394 by Pope Boniface IX., but this gave
place to the present edifice.

The ascent from the Arch of Severus to the Square of the Capitol
was anciently the Pass of the Two Groves. At the top of the pass
was the Gate of Janus, the gate of the citadel, betrayed by Tarpeia.
The ascent from the Forum, on our right, was the Clivus Capitolinus,
a continuation of the Via Sacra. It is only at its termination that
the present road is on the site of the ancient slope, where some of
the pavement may still be seen. The gate which here gave access
to the arx was called the Gate of Saturn.

*On the right* of the old museum some steps lead up to

### THE CHURCH OF ARA CŒLI.

The nave is formed by twenty-two columns, the spoils of ancient
buildings. The third one on the left has engraved upon it—

A CVBICVLO AVGVSTORVM,

showing that it came from the Palatine Hill. At the end of the

nave are two Gothic ambones with mosaic work. The altar urn of
red porphyry formerly, it is said, contained the body of Constantine's
mother. This church is rendered famous as being the place where,
on the 15th of October 1764, Gibbon "sat musing amidst the ruins
of the Capitol, and conceived the idea of writing the 'Decline and
Fall of the Roman Empire.'"

The church is the residence of the celebrated Santissimo Bambino,
carved out of a tree from the Mount of Olives, and painted by S.
Luke. This image is highly decorated with jewellery, and has a
two-horse carriage at its disposal, with coachmen and footmen, when
it pays a visit to the sick. "As thy faith, so be it unto thee."
Apply at the sacristy to see it. The floor of the church is of the
kind called *opus-Alexandrinum*, tesselated mosaic, and slab tombs
of medieval period. A grand ceremony is held here on Christmas
day, and at the Epiphany children recite the story of Christ.

In the left transept an isolated octagonal chapel, dedicated to
S. Helena, is said by the church authorities to stand on the site of an
altar erected by Augustus—*Ara primogeniti Dei*—to commemorate
the Cumaean sibyl's prophecy of the coming of the Saviour. Its
present name is traceable to this altar. Some traces of Gothic
can be seen in the walls and windows of this church, which stands
on the site of

## THE TEMPLE OF JUPITER CAPITOLINUS.

" It stood upon a high rock, and was 800 feet in circuit, each side
containing near 200 ; the length does not exceed the width by quite
15 feet. For the temple that was built in the time of our fathers,
upon the same foundations with the first, which was consumed by
fire, is found to differ from the ancient temple in nothing but in
magnificence and the richness of the materials, having three rows of
columns in the south front, and two on each side. The body is
divided into three temples, parallel to one another, the partition
walls forming their common sides. The middle temple is dedicated
to Jupiter ; and on one side stands that of Juno, and on the
other that of Minerva. And all three have but one pediment
and one roof." (Dionysius, iv. 61. See also Tacitus, "Hist." iii.
72 ; Livy, i. 55 ; Plutarch, in "Publicola ;" Tacitus, "Hist." iv.
53.)

Four different temples have been erected on this site, and now it
is occupied by a Christian church. The first, built by Tarquinius
Superbus, and consecrated by Horatius the consul, was burned in

the civil war. The second, erected by Sylla, and consecrated by Catulus, was destroyed under Vitellius. The third, erected by Vespasian, was burned before it was consecrated. The fourth was built by Domitian.

Access is now to be had to some curious vaults below the convent, which were formerly closed by the monks. Supporting these vaults are some remains of massive tufa walls—one piece in particular being about 36 feet long and 8 feet high—consisting of single blocks of stone, of which the other fragments seem to be continuations. These appear to have been built originally as substructions, and run parallel with the Via Marforio, and could not have been part of the city wall, for that is within the city of the two hills. Nibby records that tufa walls remain under the stairs leading up to the Ara Cœli Church. We think them to be part of the foundations of the celebrated Temple of Jupiter Capitolinus.

We may mention that among the rubbish contained in the vaults of the convent are two slender columns of Pentelic marble. May not these have belonged to the temple?

The strongest evidence of the position of the Temple of Jupiter "supremely good and great" is pictorial. We have it represented on the relief in the Palazzo dei Conservatori which formed part of the Arch of Marcus Aurelius. That emperor is there, after a victory, offering sacrifice upon the Capitoline Hill; and in the background is a representation of the Temple of Jupiter Capitolinus: it has three doors, and the figures of Minerva, Jupiter, and Juno. This is to the spectator's left, and faces south, as we are told the temple faced. This relief is further corroborated by another in the Louvre, in the background of which is likewise a representation of a temple of the Corinthian order, facing the same way and to the left of the spectator, and having over the door

TEMPLE OF JUPITER
CAPITOLINUS.

the words Iovi Capitolinus. Upon a relief in the Capitol Museum, another building appears upon a lower level, ornamented with pilasters, having Doric capitals. This building corresponds with the front of the Tabularium towards the Capitol.

To the right of the Palazzo dei Conservatori (New Museum) a road, through a gate, leads to the German Embassy. In the garden Bunsen found the remains of the Temple of Jupiter Feretrius, which have lately been covered in; but a fine piece of the wall of the Temple of Juno may yet be seen. *By applying at the Embassy, permission will be given to enter the garden.*

### TEMPLE OF JUPITER FERETRIUS (The Trophy-Bearer).

The first temple built in Rome by Romulus, to receive the spoils captured from Acron, King of Cænina.

"After the procession and sacrifice, Romulus built a small temple, on the top of the Capitoline Hill, to Jupiter, whom the Romans call Feretrius. For the ancient traces of it still remain, of which the longest sides are less than fifteen feet" (Dionysius, ii. 34. See Livy, i. 10).

It was enlarged A.U.C. 121 (Livy, i. 33); and was repaired by Augustus on the advice of Atticus (Nepos. See Livy, iv. 20).

*Opposite the gate leading into the garden* we can look over the parapet, down the scarped rock, to the base beneath, which is reached from below by *taking the Via Tor dei Specchi on the right, looking towards the Capitol, and the Vicolo Rupe Tarpeia on the left.* It was here that the terrible scene described in Hawthorne's "Transformation" took place.

The road leads to the New German Archæological Institute. It was about here that the messenger from Veii got into the citadel, and where the Gauls tried to do the same, when the sacred geese in Juno's temple awoke the garrison. The two bronze "geese" shown in the Hall of the Conservators are ducks.

TARPEIAN ROCK.

*Passing on under the archway, turn to the left; at a little distance the Via Monte Tarpeia turns off to the right—follow this; at the end, the house facing us is built up* against the point of the hill used for the public executions.

### THE TARPEIAN ROCK.

After the name of the hill was changed for the last time, one part, we are told, retained the name of the Tarpeian Rock, from being the burial-place of Tarpeia, and the spot from which the traitors were hurled off in sight of the people assembled in the Forum. The house in front of us is built upon a ledge of the rock below, and has upon it the following inscription :—

" Hinc ad Tarpeiam sedem, et Capitolia ducit.
Aurea nunc, olim, silvestribus horrida dumis."
VIRGIL., Æn. viii. 347.

GREGORIUS XIII. PONT. MAX. VIAM TARPEIAM APERIUNT
HIER. ALTERIUS AEDILIS SECUNDO ⎫
                             ⎬ CURABANT
PAULUS BUBALUS AEDILIS SEXTO ⎭
ANNO DOMINI MDLXXXI.

"The quæstors led the man [Spurius Cassius] to the top of the precipice that commands the Forum, and in the presence of all the citizens threw him down from the rock.  For this was the established punishment at that time among the Romans for those who were condemned to die"—A.U.C. 269—(Dionysius, viii. 78).

*If we look back* up the street we came down, the height will be seen in the garden above us.  It must be remembered that the top of the hill has been levelled, and the valley below filled in thirty feet; allowing for this there would have been a fall of upwards of 160 feet.  The steps on our left formed the third ancient approach to the arx, the *Centum Gradus,* up which the Vitellians climbed when they took the citadel.  On the site of the garden above stood

## CAMILLUS'S TEMPLES TO CONCORD AND JUNO.

The first Temple of Concord of which we have any notice was that dedicated by Camillus, A.U.C. 388.

"When the dictator was one day sitting on the tribunal in the Forum, the people called out to drag him from his seat ; but he led off the patricians to the senate house.  Previous to his entering it he turned towards the Capitol [this shows that the senate house was not on the Capitol, as some would have us believe ; for if so, he would not have turned towards the Capitol before entering the senate house—he would have already faced it], and besought the gods to put a happy end to the present disturbances, vowing to build a temple to Concord when the tumult should be appeased.......Next day they assembled and voted that the temple which Camillus had vowed to Concord should, on account of this great event, be built upon a spot viewing from a height the Forum and place of assembly" (Plutarch, in "Camillus ").  Ovid, speaking of the same temple ("Fasti," i. 640), says : "Fair Concord, the succeeding day places thee in a snow-white shrine, near where elevated Moneta raises her steps on high : now with ease wilt thou look down upon the Latin crowd.  Now have the august hands of Cæsar restored thee,"—referring to its rebuilding by Tiberius, A.D. 11.  From both these authors we learn that it had a commanding prospect, and Ovid adds that it was near the Temple of Moneta, which was likewise founded by Camillus, A.U.C. 411, as we learn from Livy (vii. 28, and vi. 20. See Plutarch). "The site chosen was that spot in the Citadel where the house of Manlius had stood." The site of the Temple of Concord was on the Tarpeian Rock, at the top of the Centum Gradus, and Camillus's Temple of Moneta was near it.

Livy (xxvi. 23) says: "In A.U.C. 542, at the Temple of Concord, a statue of Victory, which stood on the summit of the roof, being struck by lightning, and shaken at its base, fell and stuck among the ensigns of the goddess which were on the pediment." This temple, with a statue of Victory upon the summit, is represented on a coin of Tiberius, who restored it.

*Under the* wall, on our left, which supports the garden, some blocks of tufa, *in situ*, are the remains of the Temple of Concord, and the wall in the garden of the German Embassy is part of the Temple of Juno.

*Passing down the street on our right, a left half-turn will bring us to the old entrance of*

## THE TABULARIUM.
### (*Public Record Office*.)

*Open every day from 10 till 3 ; fee, half lira.*

We have now to speak of a building, the vast remains of which impress us with the grandeur of the later republic. In the year of the city 675 (B.C. 78) a building was erected against the Capitoline Hill, and facing the Forum, to contain the public records, which were engraved on bronze plates. Before that time they had been kept in various temples.

"A decree was made by the senate that the records should be kept in the Temple of Ceres with the public ædiles"—A.U.C. 306— (Livy, iii. 55).

"Treaties (such as between Pyrrhus and Rome) were then usual, and the ædiles had them in their keeping in the Temple of Jupiter Capitolinus, engraved on plates of copper" (Polybius, iii.).

That this was the usual way of keeping the records we learn from the same author, who saw and copied those which "Hannibal left at Lacinium—engraved tablets or records on copper of the events of his stay in Italy."

"The censors went up immediately to the Temple of Liberty, where they sealed the books of the public records, shut up the office, and dismissed the clerks, affirming that they should do no kind of public business until the judgment of the people was passed on them "—A.U.C. 686—(Livy, xliii. 16).

We have no mention in classic history as to when this building was erected, but fortunately an inscription has been handed down to us, in which Quintus Lutatius Catulus (who dedicated the temple to Jupiter Capitolinus) is expressly named, not only as the founder of the Tabularium, but also of the substructions, the most difficult portion of the whole, and which claim our fullest admiration.

Q . LVTATIVS . Q. F. Q. N. CATVLVS . COS . SVBSTRVCTIONEM . ET . TABVLARIVM . EX . SEN . SENT . FACIENDVM . COERAVIT . EADEMQVE . PROBAVIT .

The remains form the substructions of the present Capitol, or senator's residence, consisting of a massive wall of Gabii stone 240 feet long and 37 feet high, supporting the portico on the side of the Forum, which consisted of a series of arches, 23 feet by 15 feet, ornamented with sixteen Doric columns. Below this portico or arcade are a series of small chambers, with windows looking into the Forum, opening out of one another, approached by a short flight of steps, and probably used to store the records. At the back of the arcade are a series of large vaulted rooms or offices. At one end a grand flight of steps (repaired) leads up into what has been a grand arcade on the side of the Area Capitolina: its piers now partly sustain the modern building. At the farther end of this arcade is a flight of steep travertine steps, sixty-seven in number, leading down into the Forum, the exit to which has been blocked up by the Temple of Vespasian being built against the entrance.

This building must have presented a grand front to the Forum in the olden time, though now it only sustains the buildings of Michael Angelo. In 1389–1394, Pope Boniface IX. first erected on the Capitoline Hill, on the ruins of the Tabularium, a residence for the senator and his assessors. The prospect was altered so that what was the front became the back, and it faced on to what was anciently the Area Capitolina, now the Piazza del Campidoglio, instead of the Forum.

The north side wall seems to have been cut down when the present edifice was erected, as outside the present wall are the remains of the ancient one; thus it was somewhat longer than we now see it. In the sort of vestibule which gives admittance to the chambers under the portico are remains of stairs, evidently leading up to some chambers above the portico. These were probably not very lofty, so that the view of the temples on the hill was not shut out from the Forum, or perhaps they only led up to the flat roof above the arcade.

These old remains have been used as a prison and as a salt store, which latter has eaten the stone away in a curious manner. It is now used as a museum of fragments. The arches of the portico were filled in when the great master utilized it. Although we know an arch is as strong as a wall, it is feared to open them, and one only has been so treated.

Suetonius tells us: "Vespasian undertook to restore the three thousand tablets of brass which had been destroyed in the fire which consumed the Capitol; searching in all quarters for copies of those curious and ancient records, in which were contained the decrees of the senate almost from the building of the city, as well as the acts of the people relative to alliances, treaties, and privileges granted to any person" (Vespasian, viii.).

Pliny (xxxiv. 21) says: "It is upon tablets of brass that our public enactments are engraved."

*From the Tabularium a new iron stair leads up to*

## THE TOWER OF THE CAPITOL,

whence a fine view of Rome and its environs can be enjoyed, standing, as it were, between ancient and medieval Rome. It is the best position for study in the world.

From this height the huge mass of the Colosseum appears elegant and light. The famous Seven Hills may be made out, notwithstanding the alteration in the soil: on the left is the QUIRINAL, beyond that the VIMINAL, and beyond that the ESQUILINE; to the extreme right is the AVENTINE; before us is the PALATINE, with the CŒLIAN beyond it; whilst we occupy the CAPITOLINE. The contemplation of the city, however, produces the effect of a vast and solid reading of history. Each of the great representations of the city, always and differently mistress of the world, seems to have chosen its respective quarter—the Rome of the kings and emperors is spread out on the Palatine, Esquiline, and Quirinal; republican Rome occupies the Capitol and Aventine; whilst Christian Rome, isolated and solitary, reigns on the Cœlian and Vatican eminences.

## THE SEVEN HILLS OF ROME.

The PALATINE, which has ever had the preference, whether so-called from the people Palantes, or Palatini, or from the bleating and strolling of cattle, in Latin, *balare* and *palare*, or from Pales, the pastoral goddess, or from the burying-place of Pallas, is disputed amongst authors. It was on this hill that Romulus, according to popular tradition, laid the foundations of the city, in a quadrangular form. Here Romulus and Tullus Hostilius kept their courts, as did afterwards Augustus, and all the succeeding emperors, on which account the word Palatium came to signify a royal seat (Rosin, "Antiq." i. 4).

The AVENTINE derives its name from Aventinus, an Alban king (Varro, "De Ling. Lat." iv.), or from the river Avens (*ibid.*), or from Avibus, from the birds which used to fly thither in great flocks from the Tiber (*ibid.*). It was also called Murcius, from Murcia, the goddess of sleep, who had a temple here (Sextus Pompeius, Festus). Also Collis Dianæ, from the Temple of Diana (Martial). Likewise Remonius, from Remus, who wished the city to be commenced here, and who was buried here (Plutarch, in "Romulus"). This hill was added by Ancus Martius ("Eutropius," i.).

The CAPITOLINE, formerly Saturn, then Tarpeian, took its name from Tarpeia, a Roman virgin, who betrayed the city to the Sabines at this point (Plutarch, in "Romulus"). It was also called Mons Saturni and Saturnius, in honour of Saturn, who is reported to have lived here, and was the titular deity of this part of the city. It was afterwards called Capitoline, from the head of a man found here when digging the foundations of the famous Temple of Jupiter. It was added to the city when the Sabines were permitted by Romulus to incorporate themselves with the Romans (Dionysius).

The QUIRINAL was either so called from the Temple of Quirinus, another name of Romulus, or from the Curetes, a people that removed hither with Tatius from Cures, a Sabine city (Sextus Pompeius, Festus). It afterwards changed its name to Caballus, from two marble horses, each having a man holding it, which are still standing, and were the works of Phidias and Praxiteles ("Fabricii Roma," iii.), made to represent Alexander the Great and Bucephalus, and presented to Nero by Tiridates, king of Armenia. Numa added this hill to the city (Dionysius, ii.).

The ESQUILINE was anciently called Cispius and Oppius ("Fabricii Roma," 3). The name Esquilinus was varied for the easier pronunciation from Exquilinus, a corruption of Excubinus, ab Excubiis, from the watch that Romulus kept there ("Propert." ii. 8). It was taken in by Servius Tullius, who had his palace here (Livy, i. 44).

The VIMINAL derives its name from Vimina, signifying osiers, which grew here in large quantities. This hill was added by Servius Tullius (Dionysius, iv.).

The COELIAN owes its name to Coelius or Coeles, a famous Tuscan general, who encamped here when he came to assist the Romans against the Sabines (Varro, "De Ling. Lat." iv.). The other names by which it was sometimes known were Querculanus or Querquetulanus, and Augustus: the first, on account of its growth of oaks; and the second, because the Emperor Tiberius built on it after a fire (Tacit. "Ann." iv. ; Suet. in "Tib." xlviii.). One part was called Coeliolus, and Minor Coeliolus (" Fabricii Roma," 3). Livy (i. 30) and Dionysius (iii.) attribute the taking of it into the city to Tullus Hostilius, but Strabo ("Georg." v.) to Ancus Martius.

Whilst on the subject of the hills of Rome, three others are equally famous.

The JANICULUM, or Janicularis, so called either from an old town of the same name, said to have been built by Janus, or because Janus dwelt and was buried here (Ovid, "F." i. 246), or because it was a *janua*, a sort of gate to the Romans, whence they issued out upon the Tuscans (Festus). Its yellow sand gave it the name of Mons Aureus, corrupted into Montorius (" Fabricii Roma," i. 3). From an epigram of Martial, we may observe that it is the fittest place to take one's standing for a full prospect of the city (Martial, " Epig." iv. 64). It is famous for the sepulchres of Numa and Statius the poet (" Fabricii Roma," i. 3), and in more recent times as the grave of Tasso, and the spot where tradition holds that S. Peter was executed.

The VATICAN owes its name to the *vates*, or prophets, who used to give their answers here, or from the god Vaticanus or Vagitanus (Festus). Formerly celebrated for the Gardens and Circus of Nero, the scene of the Christian martyrdoms, and in our time for S. Peter's and the Vatican. It was enclosed in the time of Aurelian, but was considered as very unhealthy (Tacitus, "H." ii. 93).

The PINCIO (Collis Hortulorum, or Hortorum) took its name from the gardens of Sallust adjoining it (Rosin, i. 2). It was afterwards called Pincius, from the Pincii, a noble family who had their seat here (*ibid.*). Aurelian first enclosed it (*ibid.*).

The Capitol tower is crowned by a statue of Roma ; and the great bell formerly announced, by a strange contrast, the death of the Pope and the opening of the Carnival.

*Passing up into the square, in facing the Capitol, on the right, is the*

## PALAZZO DEI CONSERVATORI.

*(New Capitoline Museum.)*

*Open every day. Fee, half lira. The principal objects in the*
COURTYARD *are, right:—*

1. Statue of Julius Cæsar ; the only authentic portrait of him.

2, 4, 9. Colossal fragments, found near the Basilica of Constantine.
Supposed to have belonged to the statue of Apollo brought from
Pontus by Lucullus. Square base, which contained the bones of
Agrippina the elder.

11. Lion attacking a horse. Found in the river Almo, outside
Porta S. Paolo.

12, 14. Captive Kings.

13. Large seated statue of Roma.

15. Colossal bronze head of a colossal statue of Apollo, found near
the Colosseum. Reliefs of figures representing provinces ; and
reliefs of military trophies, recently found in the Piazza di Pietra.

28. Statue of the Emperor Augustus.

30. Modern rostral column, with ancient inscription. (See page
28.)

STAIRCASE AND LANDING.

36. Base Capitolina, an altar dedicated to Hadrian by the inspec-
tors of the streets, supporting a porphyry fragment. On the sides
are engraved the names of the magistrates who presided over the
streets, which are named, of five of the fourteen regions into which
Rome was divided. It has afforded much useful information to
archæologists.

41. Alto-relief which formed part of the Arch of Claudius found
in the Piazza Sciarra, which spanned the Corso, and was destroyed
in 1527.

42, 43, 44. Alto-reliefs, part of the Arch of Marcus Aurelius,
which stood in the Via Flaminia.

45. Curious bas-relief, representing Mettus Curtius, on horseback,
floundering in the marsh where is now the Forum. Found near the
Church of S. Maria Liberatrice.

49, 50. Alto-reliefs from an arch which stood in the Corso in
honour of Antoninus Pius.

*At the top of the stairs on this floor are several rooms.* On passing
the turnstile keep straight on. The authorities number these rooms
in the reverse way to ours.

FIRST ROOM contains a collection of majolica from the Cini family.

SECOND ROOM.—The vault is by Caracci. On the right of the door are S. Luke ; S. Alexio, by Romanelli ; the Virgin, by Andrea Allovisi, called L'Ingegno, pupil of Perugino ; S. Cecilia, by Romanelli ; S. Mark. On the left are S. John, S. Albertorn, and S. Eustachio, by Romanelli ; S. Matthew.

THIRD ROOM, *turn left.*—Frescoes of the Punic wars by Bonfigli.

FOURTH ROOM.—Frescoes from the wars of Scipio, and tapestries from the hospital of S. Michael. *Right*, the Boys of Falerii scourging their Schoolmaster, B.C. 392 (Livy, v. 27); the Vestal Tuccia, B.C. 144 (Dionysius, ii. 69) ; Romulus and Remus ; busts of Italian patriots.

FIFTH ROOM.—Garibaldi Museum. Frescoes of the school of Zuccari, representing games in the Circus Maximus, etc. There is a bust in *rosso-antico* called Appius Claudius, a bronze bust of Michael Angelo, and other busts. Two ducks in bronze are pointed out as the geese which saved the Capitol. Between them is a curious bronze vase, evidently a female portrait. Copy of Raphael's Holy Family.

SIXTH ROOM.—On the wall of this room are preserved the Fasti Consulares, dating from B.C. 481 to the end of the Republic. These fragments were found in the Forum, and faced the podium of the Temple-Tomb of Cæsar. The frescoes are by Benedetto Bonfigli.

SEVENTH ROOM.—Frescoes : Triumph of Marius, and Defeat of the Cimbri, by Daniele da Volterra. Near the door is a relief, representing the Temple at Jerusalem; and in front of it a team of oxen drawing on a car the molten sea (1 Kings vii. 23 ; 2 Chron. iv. 2).

EIGHTH ROOM.—Scenes of the Roman Republic, by Lauretti.

NINTH ROOM.—Frescoes from the history of the kings, by Arpino.

*Passing through the rooms of the Fasti, from* 1540 A.D., *we enter the* HALL OF BUSTS, comprising statesmen, poets, painters, authors, sculptors, all noted in Italian history. At the end is a monument to Canova.

*A door on the right opens into the*

### FIRST HALL OF BRONZES.

*(For numbers, see plan.)*

1, 2. Cases of small bronze articles found at various times. 3. A bronze biga, or two-horse chariot, with reliefs depicting scenes from the circus ; restored upon a wooden frame, and given by Signor A. Castellani. 4. A bisellium, or chair of state. 8. Lectica, or sedan chair. "These infirmities caused him [Claudius] to be carried in a close chair, which no Roman had ever used before ; and from thence have the emperors and the rest of us consular men taken the

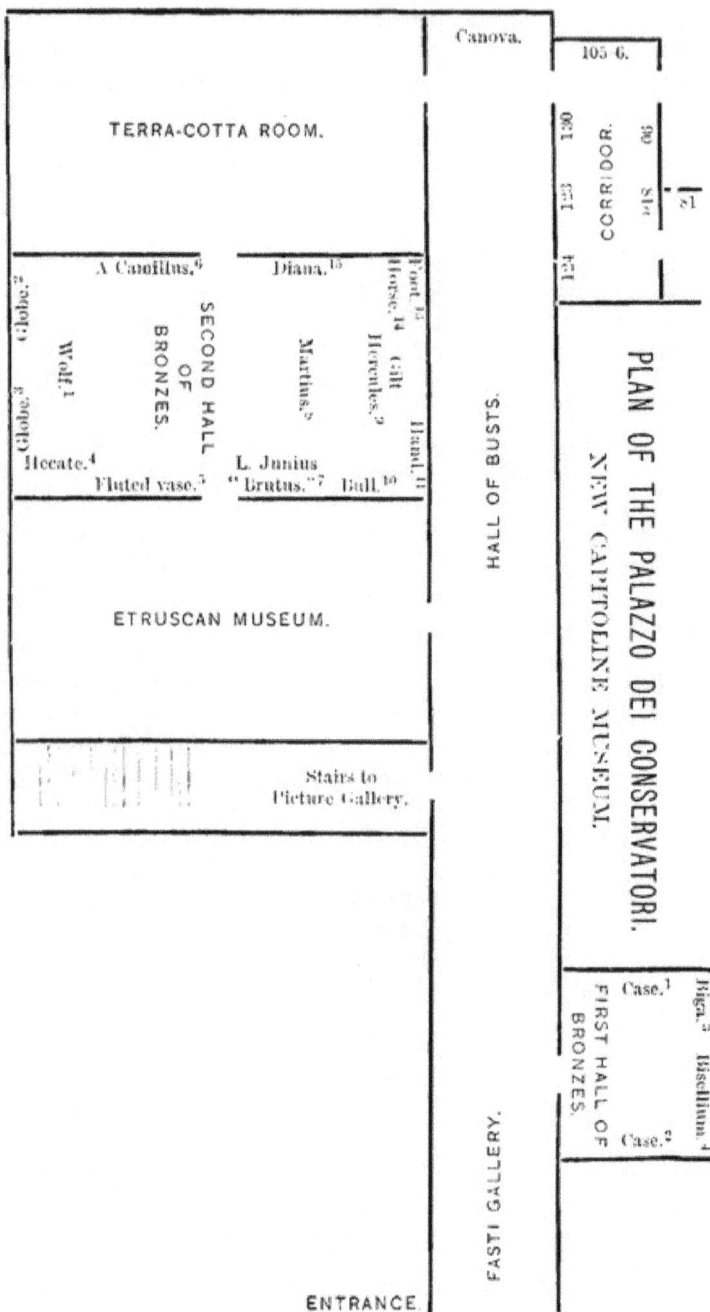

PLAN OF THE PALAZZO DEI CONSERVATORI.

NEW CAPITOLINE MUSEUM.

Canova.

105 6.

CORRIDOR.

90

130

Str.

81

125

134

TERRA-COTTA ROOM.

A Camillus.[6]

Diana.[15]

Globe.[2]

Foot.[13]

Horse.[14]

Wolf.[1]

SECOND HALL OF BRONZES.

Martius.[5]

Gilt Hercules.[9]

Globe.[3]

Hecate.[4]

Fluted vase.[5]

L. Junius "Brutus."[7]

Bull.[10]

Hand.[11]

HALL OF BUSTS.

ETRUSCAN MUSEUM.

Stairs to Picture Gallery.

FASTI GALLERY.

ENTRANCE.

FIRST HALL OF BRONZES.

Case.[1]

Case.[2]

Riga.[3]

Bisellium.[4]

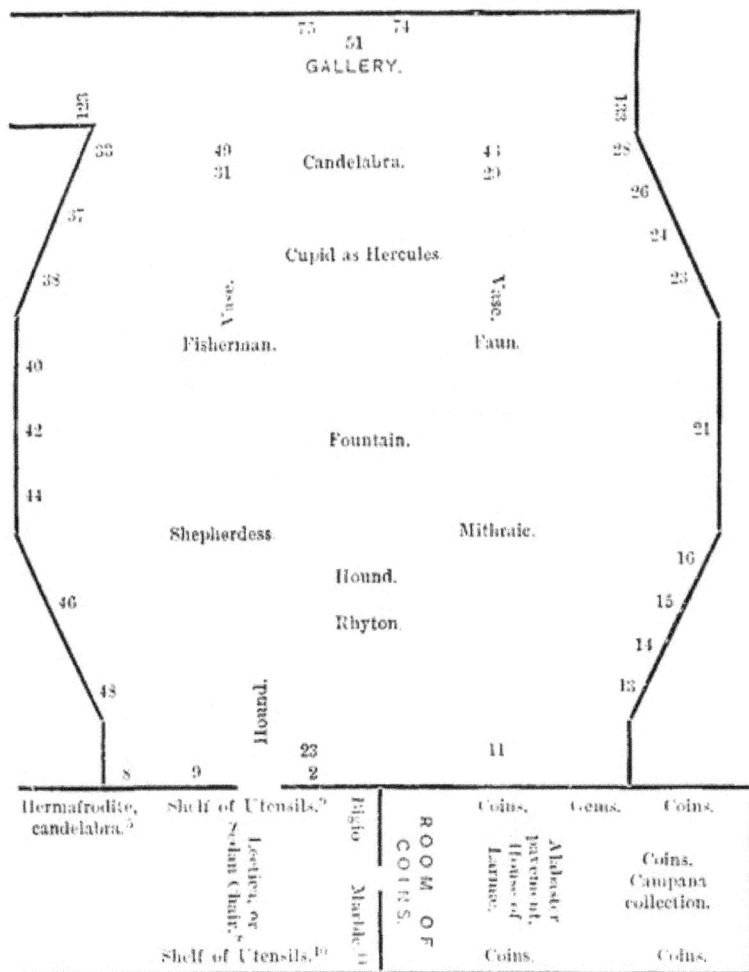

GARDEN.

75    74
51
GALLERY.

49        Candelabra.        4?
31                            29

                             26

Cupid as Hercules

Vase.        Vase.

Fisherman.        Faun.

Fountain.

Shepherdess        Mithraic.

Hound.

Rhyton.

Hound.

23        11
2

Hermafrodite,    Shelf of Utensils.⁹    Coins.    Gems.    Coins.
candelabra.⁵

                                        Coins.
                                        Campana
Lectica, or                Alabaster    collection.
Sedan Chair.⁷              pavement,
                          House of
                          Larius.
Biglio
Marble.¹¹    R O O M   O F   C O I N S.

Shelf of Utensils.¹⁰        Coins.        Coins.

custom of using chairs of that sort, for neither Augustus nor Tiberius used anything but small litters, which are still in fashion for the women" (Dion Cassius). 9, 10. Shelves containing household utensils, &c. 11. Fragments of columns of Bigio marble.

## ROOM OF COINS.

The beautiful alabaster pavement of this room was found, as now fixed, upon the Esquiline Hill, on Christmas eve, 1874. It formed part of the House of the Larmæ, where the statues were found. The coins formed part of the Campana Collection, and are of great value. The small case of gems is worth looking into; it contains some fragments not unlike the Portland vase, white reliefs on a blue ground.

*We now enter the new*

## OCTAGONAL HALL.

*(The order is liable to alteration, as objects are constantly being added.)*

This museum is formed of the remains found in the excavations of the municipality since Rome was made the capital of united Italy. The new circular hall, designed by Signor Vespignani, presents a light and elegant effect. Amongst the most important subjects placed in the new hall, we may mention No. 2, the monument of Quintus Sulpicius Maximus, found in 1870 in the Old Porta Salaria. The inscription states that he died at the early age of thirteen years, five months, and twelve days. He carried off the honours for composing Greek verse against fifty-two competitors. The poem is engraved on the pilasters. The subject is—The arguments used by Jove in reproving Phœbus for intrusting his chariot to Phaeton. Africa's deserts and the negroes' black skins are ascribed to the careless driving of Phaeton on that occasion. No. 5. Venus, after Polychramus. 11. A bust of Faustina the elder. 13. A youth anointing himself. 14 and 16. Tritons. 15. A half statue of the Emperor Commodus as Hercules, beautifully executed in fine marble, with the lion's skin over his head and knotted upon his chest: in his right hand is the club. A bracket of marble, ornamented at its end with a celestial globe, rested on the pedestal, which formed a shield, a band running round the centre with the signs of the zodiac. This bracket is supported by two kneeling figures, holding cornucopias containing fruit. One is in good preservation; the fragments of the other were also found. 17. Plotina, wife of Trajan. 18. Apollo. 19. Bacchus, with a satyr on a leopard at his side. 21. Sarcophagus of the Calydonian boar hunt. 23. Polyhymnia. 24. Terpsichore. 26. A beautiful nude statue of a young girl or nymph leaving the bath, of Parian marble, standing with sandalled feet by a pedestal, which supports her robe, the left hand fastening up the hair. 28, 29. Two magistrates about to start the racers by dropping a handkerchief. They represent L. A. A. Symmachus, prefect of Rome, A.D. 365, and his son ; and are unique. The father was found in one hundred and eighty pieces, and the son in ninety pieces, which have been carefully put together. 31. Colossal statue. 33. Fortune. Apollo with the Lyre. Relief, forging the Shield of Minerva. 38, 42. Athletes starting for the Race. 40a. A Cow. 44. Manlia Scantilla. Marsyas bound to the tree : the finest statue in the collection, found in 1879. 48. Didia Clara. 49a. Gordianus III. ; a striking statue. 8. The Earth; a sitting statuette in a niche found in the Roman Cemetery. 9. A Baccante.

*In the inner circle.*—A magnificent marble vase, found upon the Esquiline, called by the Greeks a Rhyton : it is the work of Pontios, an Athenian sculptor. A vase with figures in relief. The infant Hercules found at the Cemetery of S. Lorenzo. Another vase. The Muse of Astronomy. *Exit.* 74, 75. Hercules taming the Horses: part of a group found in many fragments, and very skilfully put together. Seated statue of a girl. 133. Minerva. 130. A statue of Silenus, which was formerly a fountain. A youth carrying a pig for sacrifice. Cupid playing with a tortoise. 123. Boy with a puppy. 81. Statuette of Venus. 81a. A Sleeping Cupid. 124. A large stone shield sculptured with the acanthus leaf. 90. Mithras slaying the Bull. 117, 105, 106. Reliefs relating to the worship of the Persian sun-god Mithras, recently found on the Esquiline Hill.

*Crossing the Hall of Busts, by Canova's Monument, we enter the*

### TERRA-COTTA ROOM,

composed of remains found chiefly in the excavations in building the new quarter of Rome upon the Esquiline Hill. *The principal objects are:*—A coffin containing skulls; fresco of Quintus Fabius and Marcus Fannius, Samnite war, 337 B.C., from a tomb, Esquiline Hill ; a large and varied collection of Roman lamps, glass, and terra-cotta ; also glass in various forms, and for windows, pieces of fresco, &c. *A door on the left leads into the*

### SECOND HALL OF BRONZES.

In the centre of the first room is the celebrated bronze wolf of the Capitol (1), thus alluded to by Virgil ("Æn." viii. 630) :—

> " By the wolf were laid the martial twins,
> Intrepid on her swelling dugs they hung :
> The foster-dam lolled out her fawning tongue :
> They sucked secure, while, bending back her head,
> She licked their tender limbs, and formed them as they fed."

Cicero (in "Catiline" iii. 8), mentions this object as a small gilt figure of Romulus sucking the teat of a wolf, which was struck by lightning, and which his hearers remembered to have seen in the Capitol.

Dionysius, quoting from an older historian, Quintus Fabius Pictor, speaks of a temple in which a statue is placed representing the above incident. It is a wolf suckling two children; they are in brass, and of ancient workmanship. This latter must not be confounded with the statue mentioned by Cicero, which is generally believed to be the one before us. The fracture on the hind leg may have been caused by lightning, and traces of gilt may still be observed. It is not known where it was found, but in Cicero's time (B.C. 106–43) it was to be "seen in the Capitol." The workmanship of the wolf is of an early period, Etruscan; the twins are by Della Porta.

10. A bull, found in Trastevere in 1849. 4. "Thou seest the faces of Hecate turned in three directions, that she may watch the cross-roads cut into three pathways." She was the patroness of magic, and was also set up before houses to ward off evil. This goddess is often confounded with Diana. 8. The shepherd Martius, a bronze statue of a boy extracting a thorn from his foot. 14. Horse found in Trastevere. 13. Foot found near the Colosseum.

9. Gilt bronze statue of Hercules Triumphant, the work of Lysippus, and brought to Rome from Tarentum in 209 B.C. (Strabo, vi. 3, 1). It was discovered in 1480 amongst the remains of a temple of Hercules, behind the Church of S. Maria in Cosmedin. 2, 3. Bronze globes, one of which was held in the hand of Trajan's statue on his column. 15. Diana of the Ephesians in bronze and marble. 6. A Camillus, one of the twelve youths who assisted at the sacrifices. 7. Bust of Lucius Junius Brutus, who expelled the Tarquins. 5. A fluted vase, found in the sea at Porto d'Anzio; a gift of Mithridates, King of Pontus, to a gymnasium of the Eupatorists.

*From the Hall of Bronzes we enter the*

### ITALO-GRECO AND ETRUSCAN MUSEUM.

Formed by Signor A. Castellani, and presented by him to the senate and people of Rome. The objects were mostly found at Cervetri, Tarquinii, and Veii.

*Passing out into the Hall of Busts, a door on the right leads to the*

### PINACOTHECA, OR PICTURE GALLERY.

*Open every day from 10 till 3.*

Founded by Benedict XIV., and composed of several rooms. The following are the most celebrated pictures, but each picture has the names of the artist and the subject printed under the frame :—

FIRST ROOM.—*Right:* Romulus and Remus, by Rubens ; Holy Family, by Giorgione ; S. Cecilia, by Romanelli ; Baptism, by Guercino ; Magdalen, by Guido ; Cumæan Sibyl, by Domenichino ; Persian Sibyl, by Guercino ; Madonna, by Botticelli ; Assumption, by Cola dell' Amatrice ; The Redeemed Spirit, by Guido ; Madonna, by Francia.

The frescoes on the walls are from the deserted palace Magliana, the hunting-seat of Leo X., which has long been utilized as a farm by a community of nuns, and only inhabited by labourers. The frescoes are all more or less injured, and the feet of each figure, together with the lower part of the pictures, are quite obliterated. They represent the Muses, with Apollo as Musagetes, each figure distinguished by a motto in verse descriptive of the individual character, from the epigrams of Ausonius, and consist of the figures of Polyhymnia ; Urania, with a distant view of Florence in the background (perhaps allusive to the pre-eminence of that city in astronomical science) ; Thalia, with the motto, "Comica lasciva gaudet sermone Thalia ;" Clio, who is playing on the double flute ; and Apollo, as leader of the Nine, who is seated, and playing on the violin : in the background of this picture is introduced a small group of Perseus slaying Medusa, while Pegasus springs from the blood of the decapitated gorgon. All these frescoes are ascribed to Giovanni lo Spagna, and there is much in their conception and sentiment which reminds us of the far superior works by that pupil of Pietro Perugino.

The CORRIDOR contains views of Rome by Vanvitelli.

SECOND ROOM.—Annunciation, by Garofalo ; Madonna, by P. Veronese. Portraits by Vandyck, etc.

THIRD ROOM.—Baptism, by Titian ; Sebastian, by Bellini ; S. Barbara, by Domenichino ; Innocence, by Romanelli.

FOURTH ROOM.—*Left:* S. Lucia, by Spagna ; Europa, by P. Veronese ; Burial and Assumption of Petronella, by Guercino ; Sebastian, by Caracci ; Cleopatra and Augustus, by Guercino ; Sebastian, by Guido ; Baptism, by Tintoretto.

*Leaving the Palazzo dei Conservatori, and crossing the Piazza, we enter*

## THE MUSEUM OF THE CAPITOL.

*Open every day from 10 till 3. Entrance half a lira each person.*

### THE COURTYARD.

1. Marforio, a recumbent statue of the Ocean, celebrated as having

been made the medium of replying to Pasquino. 2, 3. Lions in basalt, which, with the columns 13, 14, came from the Temple of Isis in the Campus Martius. 9. Bust of Augustus with the civic crown. 10, 18. Christian sarcophagi, from the Catacombs of S. Sebastian. On the walls are various fragments and inscriptions, one referring to the restoration of the Baths at Ostia in the time of Valens.

ATRIUM OR LOWER CORRIDOR.

*Left.*—3. A votive altar dedicated to the imperial house, on the left side of which is a personification of the Via Appia reclining on a wheel, similar to Trajan's relief on the Arch of Constantine. 4. Colossal statue of Minerva. 6. Egyptian statuette, with the cartouch of Rameses II., found on Via Nazionale. The base upon which it stands is inscribed to Fabius Cilone, prefect of Rome under Septimius Severus, who had performed the annual sacrifice to Hercules at the Ara Maxima, at the entrance to the Circus Maximus. 13 is a companion inscription, a circular vase offered by Catius Sabinus, prefect of Rome, who performed the annual sacrifice at the great altar of Hercules. It was found at the back of S. Maria in Cosmedin. 8. Statue of Livia, wife of Augustus, standing on a base found near the pyramid of Caius Cestius, and relating to him. Under 25 is a similar inscription. 17. Inscription to Hercules the leader of the Muses, by the Consul M. F. Nobilior, 189 B.C., from the temple which stood in the Portico of Philip, now S. Ambrogio. 18. Head of Cybele. 21. Captive Dacian, from Arch of Constantine, but originally in Trajan's Forum. *On the left, entrance to Halls of Mosaics.* 23. Faustina, sen., standing on a relief of the arms of Alba Longa. At Nos. 4, 10, 11, 14, 23, are fragments from the Temple of Concord in the Forum. 32. Sphinx in red granite. 33. Vase in basalt, Villa of Hadrian. Altar sacred to Isis. On the left side is Harpocrates, the god of silence ; on the right, Anubis, the Egyptian Mercury. 34. Sphinx in basalt, with the cartouch of Amasi II., 550 B.C. 44, 51. Monkey-gods of Pharaoh Nectanebus I., 370 B.C. 49. Crocodile in red granite. With the exception of the vase, all these objects came from the Temple of Isis and Serapis on the Campus Martius, founded in the time of Sulla (Apuleius, xi.), and rebuilt by Domitian (Suetonius, "Dom." v.). 35. Polyphemus. 36. Hadrian in sacerdotal costume. 37. Porphyry fragment. 38. Hercules killing the Hydra. 39. Fragment of same found after the restorations were made. *Entrance to Halls of Inscriptions.* 40. Colossal statue of Mars, found on the Aventine Hill. 52. Diana.

### HALLS OF MOSAICS.

*(Left-hand end of Corridor.)*

*On right in entering.*—Inscription to Nerva, by Septimius Severus, A.D. 194, used in 1676 by the city Conservatori to record their privileges. 8. Mosaic Head of an Athlete. 9. The Sea with fish, and a border of foliage and birds, from the Baths of Olympia, Viminal Hill. 10. The Rape of Proserpina (the names of the horses are written in Greek), from a tomb on the Via Portuense. 12. Representation of a Bath, from the Prætorian Camp. 14. Hercules conquered by Love. 18. A veiled woman presenting a statuette to a seated nude figure, probably Mercury : a beautiful work. 24. Personification of the Month of May. 27. An Inundation of the Nile. 28. A Ship entering a Port. *In the centre of the room*, Altar of the Lares, discovered in the month of August 1888, on the Via Aremula, the new street leading to the new Ponte Garibaldi, at the corner of the Via di S. Bartolomeo dei Vaccinari, the last street on the right which leads up to the reputed House and School of S. Paul. It is a square marble altar with a beautiful cornice, which is, unfortunately, broken. On the front is a relief representing four men at a sacrifice, with bay crowns upon their veiled heads. A bull and a pig are by assistants being led up to sacrifice—the bull to the Genius Cæsarum, and the pig to the Lares. On each side of the altar is the figure of a youth—the titular deities ; and at the back a crown. It was dedicated to the Lares of Augustus by four officials of a street nine years after Augustus had restored the street shrines. That was in 6 B.C. (Dion Cassius, lv. 8) ; so this altar was erected in A.D. 3. The altar stands on a travertine base, on which is written, *MAGISTRI . VICI . ÆSCLETI . ANNI . VIIII.*, which is valuable as giving us the name of the street Vicus Æscletus, Beech Street. (See "The Footsteps of St. Paul in Rome.") See page 195.

SECOND ROOM.—The walls are encased with inscriptions. *On the left* is a fragment of a Roman calendar, found in 1888 near S. Martino dei Monti. It represents the 1st to 3rd, 18th to 29th of April, and 1st to 4th of May. *On the door* is part of a Lex Horreorum of the time of Hadrian. These magazines were situated near Monte Testaccio. *On the right* of window, inscription of Lucius Aquilinus Modestus, master of the guild of timber merchants at Ostia. *On the door opposite*, inscription dedicated to the imperial house by a college of health, found near Monte Testaccio. *On the floor* are two interesting sarcophagi, found in 1890 in building the new Palace of Justice. The one under the wall is plain, and has on the cover D . M . L . CREPEREIΦ . EVΠΟΔΦ, and contains his skeleton. The other is his daughter's, whose skeleton may be seen inside decked with jewels; there are also several objects by her side, and an oak doll with movable joints, now petrified. The wavy lines on this sarcophagus show that she was baptized, and her Christian name on the cover, CREPERIA TRYPHAENA, calls to mind the earlier Tryphæna saluted by S. Paul in writing to the Romans.

THIRD ROOM.—*In the centre* is the pedestal of the statue of Cornelia, the mother of the Gracchii, which Pliny (xxxiv. 14) tells us was erected in the Portico of Octavia, where it was found in 1879. *On right of door*, fragment of the inscription recording Hadrian burning the bonds in Trajan's Forum in 118; a part of the inscription is in Trajan's Forum. *By the window*, inscription to Aulus Septicius Alexander, a seller of floral wreaths on the Via Sacra. *By the next window*, a dedication to Concord by Marcus Artorius Geminus, prefect of the military treasury, from the Temple of Concord in the Forum. Inscription to Nero and Poppæa, wishing them good health, on behalf of the governor of the Balearic Islands, A.D. 60. Sarcophagus of Cupids plucking grapes, with portrait of deceased, and masks; traces of the gilding are discernible. Fragment of a Fasti, A.D. 220. A fragment of the Maffeiano Calendar. *On the next wall*, inscription of Lucius Considius Gallus, prætor for the strangers, etc.

### HALLS OF INSCRIPTIONS.

#### (*Right-hand end of Corridor.*)

FIRST ROOM. — 11. Sarcophagus representing hunting of wild animals. 18. Cippus to Faustina the elder, erected by an official of the treasury, found near the Temple of Saturn in the Forum. 19. Head of Giuba II., King of Numidia. 26. Base dedicated to Hercules Victorious. 28. Sarcophagus of a boar and stag hunt. 30. Sarcophagus, Hunt of the Calydonian Boar. *Near the door*, inscription of a monument to Marcus Calpurnius Piso Frugi, B.C. 88, restored by Trajan. *Over the door*, inscription of the guild of bargemen of Ostia, A.D. 193. *In the centre*—44. Altar representing the twelve labours of Hercules, from Albano.

SECOND ROOM.—3, 4, 6, 11. Monumental cippi, with working tools in bas-relief; likewise the same emblems on 10, fragment of a column. 6. Inscription to Marcus Æbutius. 4. Lapis Capponianus,

3. Cossutius. 11. T. Statilius Aper, and to his wife Orcivia Antides; found on the Janiculum. He was a surveyor; the verse stating that he died at the age of twenty-two years, eight months, and fifteen days.

5. Sarcophagus found on the Via Appia, representing a fight between Roman and Gallic cavalry, when, in 223 B.C., Marcus Marcellus killed Virdomarus, the chief of the Insubrian Gauls, and so carried off the third Spolia Opima (Livy, "Ep." xx. ; Florus, ii. 4 ; Eutropius, iii. 6 ; Plutarch, in "Marcellus"). The central figure is strikingly like the figure of the wounded Gaul miscalled the dying gladiator.

12. Inscription to Vettius Agorius Praetextatus, prefect 367, and his wife, Paolina. 14. Bust of Crispina, wife of Commodus. 13. Inscription from Villa of Herodes Atticus, Via Appia, used afterwards as a milestone under Maxentius.

2. Monument to Bathyllus, an actor of the time of Augustus, afterwards custodian of the Temple of the Deified Augustus.

THIRD ROOM.—1. Sarcophagus found in a mound on the road to Frascati, called Monte del Grano. Inside the sarcophagus was found the Portland vase now in the British Museum, which contained the ashes. The sarcophagus is surmounted by the figures of a man and woman in repose. The reliefs illustrate the life of Achilles. 3 Relief of Priests of Cybele. 4. Cosimati mosaic, with reliefs from life of Achilles. 15, 17. Portraits in relief of Nero and Poppæa. 19. Pluto and Cerberus, found in the Baths of Titus, 1812.

### STAIRCASE.

On the walls are encased the fragments of the marble plan of Rome found in 1534-50, 1867, behind the Church of SS. Cosmo and Damiano. They had originally served for the panelling of the wall that formed part of the Temple of Rome built by Hadrian. The plan was made in the third century, in the time of the Emperor Septimius Severus (193-211). It is called the "Pianta Capitolina," and is of great use to archæologists in studying the ground plan of the different buildings marked upon it, though not as showing their relative positions.

After many years of study we have succeeded in putting this puzzle together, and have published the marble plan, systematically arranged in ten sheets, price six shillings, with descriptive letterpress.

*The doors at the top of the stairs lead us into the*

## HALL OF THE DYING GAUL.

"He leans upon his hand ; his manly brow
Consents to death, but conquers agony ;
And his drooped head sinks gradually low ;
And through his side the last drops, ebbing slow
From the red gash, fall heavily one by one."

This perfect statue of "a wounded man dying, who perfectly expressed how much life was remaining in him," has for many years
been miscalled "The Dying Gladiator ;" but it has of late years been
more correctly described as a wounded Gaul. It was found, together
with the Gallic group in the Ludovisi Villa, amongst the ruins of the
gardens of Sallust, and with that formed part of a large group representing the death of Anerœstus, the Gallic chief, who with other
leaders killed themselves after their defeat by the Romans in 226 B.C.,
near Orbetello—Attilius, the Roman consul, having been previously
killed in the fight (Polybius, ii. 2). 7. Lycian Apollo, found near the
Aquæ Albulæ on the road to Tivoli. 6. Female carrying a vase,
standing on an altar dedicated to Hercules by C. Ulpius Fronto, A.D.
126 ; found in the Forum Boarium. 5. Bust of Bacchus. 4. Amazon,
copy of original by Phradmon. 3. Alexander, by Lysippus. 2. Juno.
16. Bust of *Et tu, Brute.* 15. Isis. 14. Flora (?), found at Hadrian's
Villa, thought to be Sabina, the wife of Hadrian. 12. Antinoüs, found
at Hadrian's Villa. 10. The Faun of Praxiteles, found at Civita La-
vinia, amongst the ruins of the Villa of Antoninus Pius. This is the
Marble Faun of Hawthorne. 9. Girl protecting a dove. 8. Zeno, the
Stoic philosopher.

## HALL OF THE FAUN.

1. The celebrated and beautiful faun in rosso-antico, found at
Hadrian's Villa, Tivoli. 20. Mask of Pan. 21. Head of Ariadne.
3. The Endymion sarcophagus, found under the high altar of the
Church of S. Eustacio ; the cover belongs to another sarcophagus.
8. Boy with a scenic mask. 16. Boy with a goose, found near
S. John's Lateran. 18. Sarcophagus representing the battle between
Amazons and Athenians. On the wall above is the bronze table on
which is engraved a portion of the Lex Regia conferring the imperial
power on Vespasian, and from which Rienzi demonstrated to the
people their political rights. It was discovered near the Lateran
about 1300, and was kept in the Basilica.

## HALL OF THE CENTAURS.

1. Jupiter, in black marble. 2, 4. Cloud-born Centaurs, found at
Hadrian's Villa, the joint work of Aristeas and Papias, sculptors of

Aphrodisium, in bigio-morato marble. Pliny says he saw a Centaur that had been embalmed in honey, which had been brought from Egypt to Rome in the time of Claudius. 3. The infant Hercules, in green basalt, found on the Aventine. 5. Æsculapius, in black marble. *On left of entry.* 29. Hygeia. 31. Young Apollo. 33. Wounded Amazon. 34. Venus and Mars, found in the Isola Sacra near Ostia. 36. Minerva. 6. Faun. 7. Apollo. 9. Trajan. 10. Augustus. Two columns of Porta Santa. 17. Minerva, an archaic statue, B.C. 450. 21. A teacher imparting instruction, found in Hadrian's Villa. 22. Præfica: a hired mourner at funerals; a tear-bottle will be noticed in her hand. 28. Harpocrates, found at Hadrian's Villa. 27. A hunter, by Polytimus.

### HALL OF ILLUSTRIOUS MEN,

containing busts of great men arranged round the room on shelves, many of doubtful identity. The most important are,—

1. Virgil. 4, 5, 6. Socrates. 7, 35. Alcibiades. 10. Seneca. 16. Marcus Agrippa. 20. Marcus Aurelius. 21. Diogenes. 22. Archimedes. 27. Pythagoras. 28. Alexander the Great. 30. Aristophanes. 31, 32. Demosthenes. 33, 34. Sophocles. 37. Hippocrates. 41 to 43. Euripides. 44 to 47. Homer. 48. Domitius Corbulo. 49. Scipio Africanus the elder. 51. Pompey the Great. 60. Thucydides. 63. Double Hermes of Epicurus and Metrodorus, friends and philosophers. 72. Julian. 74. Ahenobarbus, father of Nero. 75. Cicero (?). 76. Terence. 110. Relief, after Callimachus, B.C. 550.

The walls are adorned with bas-reliefs. The seated figure in the centre of the room is supposed to be Marcus Claudius Marcellus, the great general of the republic, who died B.C. 208.

### HALL OF THE EMPERORS,

and their wives, whose ancient authentic busts are arranged round the room in chronological order :—

| | |
|---|---|
| 1. Julius Cæsar. | 14. Agrippina, jun. |
| 2. Augustus. | 16. Nero. |
| 4. Tiberius. | 17. Poppæa Sabina. |
| 6. Drusus, sen. | 18. Galba. |
| 7. Drusus, jun. | 19. Otho. |
| 8. Antonia. | 20. Vitellius. |
| 9. Germanicus. | 21. Vespasian. |
| 10. Agrippina, sen. | 22. Titus. |
| 11. Caligula. | 23. Julia. |
| 12. Claudius. | 24. Domitian. |
| 13. Messalina. | 25. Domitia Longina. |

| | |
|---|---|
| 27. Trajan. | 57. Elagabalus. |
| 28. Plotina. | 60. Alexander Severus. |
| 31. Hadrian. | 62. Maximinus. |
| 33. Julia Sabina. | 64. Gordianus I. |
| 35. Antoninus Pius. | 65. Gordianus II. |
| 36. Faustina, sen. | 66. Pupienus. |
| 38. Marcus Aurelius. | 67. Balbinus. |
| 39. Faustina, jun. | 68. Gordianus III. |
| 43. Commodus. | 69. Philip. |
| 44. Crispina. | 70. Decius. |
| 45. Pertinax. | 72. Hostilianus. |
| 46. Didius Julianus. | 73. Gallus. |
| 47. Manlia Scantilla. | 76. Gallienus. |
| 50. Septimius Severus. | 77. Salonina. |
| 52. Julia Pia. | 80. Diocletian. |
| 53. Caracalla. | 81. Chlorus. |
| 54. Geta. | 82. Julian, the philosopher. |
| 55. Macrinus. | 83. Magnus Decentius. |

There are several bas-reliefs round the room. Seated in the centre is Agrippina, "the glory of the Roman matrons;" daughter of M. V. Agrippa and Julia, daughter of Augustus; wife of Germanicus, and mother of Caligula. "It is a statue combining an expression of moral dignity and of intellectual force, with as much beauty and poetical grace as the genius of sculpture ever borrowed from breathing nature to work out its own miracles of art. This statue—a history and an epic in itself—represents a woman in the prime of life seated in a chair of state, and in the deep repose of meditative thought. The statue is lofty, her brow of high capacity, her mouth expressive of love and wit, and all her features are harmonized by that regularity which is ever denied to defective organizations. Over the whole of this simply-draped and noble figure there is an air of tranquil majesty, which, in its solemn influence, likens it to the statues of the gods" (Lady Morgan). It may have originally stood on the cinerary base in the court-yard of the Palazzo dei Conservatori.

## UPPER CORRIDOR.

*In our order of visiting the Museum the subjects in this Corridor commence at the highest number.*

Vase of white marble, found near the tomb of Cecilia Metella; it is decorated with vine leaves and fruit. The pedestal is a very interesting Grecian marble well-head; on it are the twelve principal deities, the work of Callimachus. 28. Marcus Aurelius. 25. Jupiter standing on the altar of Cybele; dedicated in memory of Claudia drawing the galley up to Rome, which is shown in relief. *Entrance to Cabinet of Venus.* 20. Psyche. 46. Sarcophagus illustrating the birth of Bacchus. 47. Jupiter. 49. Juno. 50. Gladiator restored from a Discobolus. 52. Euterpe. 10. Cinerary urn. 54. Sarcophagus representing the Rape of Proserpine. 54*a*. Infant Hercules strangling a serpent. 8. An old woman drunk, by Myron. *Entrance to Hall of Doves.* 5. Cupid. 3. A lion. 63. Marcus Aurelius.

### CABINET OF VENUS.

The celebrated Venus of the Capitol, found in a walled-up chamber on the Viminal, is a masterpiece by Scopas, 430 B.C. (Pliny, xxxiv. 4). The Venus de Medici is a copy of this. Cupid and Psyche, found on the Aventine—a beautiful little group. Leda and the Swan.

### HALL OF THE DOVES.

So called from the beautiful mosaic set *in the wall on the right in entering*, mentioned by Pliny as the work of Sosus existing at Pergamos : "There is a dove greatly admired in the act of drinking, and throwing the shadow of its head upon the water, while other birds are to be seen sunning and pluming themselves on the margin of a drinking bowl." It was found in Hadrian's Villa. Beyond is also a mosaic representing two scenic masks, found on the Aventine. In the windows are glass cases containing styli, coins, and lamps. 83. Fixed on the side of the farther window, the Iliac Table representing the Fall of Troy as described by Virgil ; to each group is attached an explanatory inscription in Greek : found at Bovillæ. 49. Diana of Ephesus. 37. Sarcophagus of Gerontia, representing the fable of Endymion. 13. The Prometheus sarcophagus. On shelves round the room are placed numerous busts, but these are not of much interest.

*On coming out of the Museum*, cross the square and turn to the left, by the side of the Tabularium (note the paving-stones at the end of the Sacra Via), then turn to the right, Via Monte Tarpeia, proceed along this street, and keep straight on down the steps.

### THE TRAITORS' LEAP.

By descending the *Centum Gradus*, and turning to the left, we see the rock, within the space closed off by the rails. The house on the top will roughly represent the original height of the rock. If we then add forty feet to the depth, we shall have some idea of the traitors' leap, which cured all ambition.

The municipal authorities have lately pulled down a house on the Vicus Jugarius which obstructed the view of the far end of the Tarpeian Rock from the Forum. We use the title Tarpeian Rock as applied to the place of execution and not to the whole hill. They have exposed to view not only the rock, but likewise one side of the Temple of Ops, composed of large blocks of tufa stone surmounted by later brick structures. The earliest mention we have of this temple is in B.C. 183, when Livy says (xxxix. 22): "By order of the pontiffs a supplication, of one day's continuance, was added on account of the Temple of Ops, near the Capitol, having been struck by lightning." This temple is also mentioned by Cicero, from whom we learn that it was where the clerks kept the accounts of the treasury: "Would that the money remained in the Temple of Ops! Bloodstained, indeed, it may be, but still needful at these times, since it is not restored to those to whom it really belongs" (First "Philippic," 7). "Who delivered yourself from an enormous burden of debt at the Temple of Ops; who, by your dealings with the account-books there squandered a countless sum of money" (Second, 14). "Where are the seven hundred millions of sesterces which were entered in the account-books which are in the Temple of Ops? A sum lamentable indeed as to the means by which it was procured, but still one which, if it is not restored to those to whom it belonged might save us from taxes" (Second, 37). "And that accounts of the money in the Temple of Ops are not to be meddled with. That is to say, that those seven hundred millions of sesterces are not to be recovered from him; that the Septemviri are to be exempt from blame or from prosecution for what they have done" (Eighth, 9).

Ops was the daughter of Cœlus and Terra, and the wife of Saturn; hence her connection with the treasury. The temple was turned into a church, and called S. Salvatore in Ærario, or in Statera (the Saviour in the Treasury), which lapsed into S. Maria in Portico. It has now become a marble-cutter's; and a small fresco of the Crucifixion, very much obliterated, marks its former use. The west wall of the temple has been exposed in the recent changes, and part of the eastern wall can be seen by entering the court-yard by the flight of steps through the wall, No. 57, opposite the end of S. Maria di Consolazione.

*The Via Consolazione and the Via Montanara to the right bring us to*

## THE THEATRE OF MARCELLUS.

The design of erecting a stone theatre in this quarter had been entertained by Julius Cæsar (Suetonius, "Cæsar," xliv.), but the carrying out of his adopted father's plan was reserved for Augustus (*ibid.*, "Aug." xxix.). He did not, however, appropriate the honour of so great a work to himself, but transferred it to his beloved son-in-law, Marcellus. Great part of the outer walls of this large and splendid building still exists. Against these leaned the arches, supporting the tier of seats destined for the spectators. The greater portion of the vast halls have also been preserved ; but being now converted into offices belonging to the Palace of the Orsini, which has insinuated itself into these ruins, they are not accessible to strangers. The lower story is in the Doric, the second in the Ionic, and the third was probably in the Corinthian order. It held 20,000 people.

## THE DECEMVIRAL PRISONS.

Built by Appius Claudius for common offenders, *near* the Forum Olitorium, and which site was afterwards occupied by the Theatre of Marcellus (Pliny, vii. 37). We have identified this prison, remains of which can still be seen under the theatre, consisting of chambers constructed in *opus reticulatum*. Two splendid open archways of the same material lead into two large chambers, in the vaults of which are holes for letting the prisoners down. This we believe to have been the Decemviral Prisons and the scene of *Caritas Romana*.

> " Here youth offered to old age the food,
> The milk of his own gift."

Byron visited the chambers under S. Nicolò in Carcere, when he was moved to compose his beautiful lines. He had before him the scene, though not the site ; his words are more applicable to these dungeons, and we may say with him,—

> "There is a dungeon, in whose dim, drear light
> What do I gaze on ?—Nothing."

*Passing the Theatre, a narrow lane on the left leads to the remains of*

## THE PORTICO OF OCTAVIA.

Dedicated to Octavia by her brother Augustus (Suetonius, "Aug." xxix.). The principal portion still existing belonged to the great portal leading to the open space surrounded by corridors which gave the people shelter during rain. In this stood two temples, the one dedicated to Jupiter, the other to Juno. Pillars belonging to the latter may be seen in a house in the Via Pescheria, and remains of the Portico of Octavia at No. 12 Via Teatro di Marcello. The inscription on the architrave states that the building was restored by Septimius Severus and Caracalla.

On the removal of two of the columns on which the pediment rested, their place was supplied by an arch of brickwork, thus preventing the building from falling in.

Four columns and two piers are still standing of the inner row; of the outside only two columns remain, in addition to the two piers. The capitals are ornamented with eagles bearing thunderbolts. A flight of steps led up to this vestibule.

The stumps of columns built into the walls of several houses in the vicinity in all probability belonged to the same edifice, which must originally have presented a most magnificent appearance.

The Portico was ornamented with many statues; and besides the two temples, there were libraries. It was originally erected by Metellus, B.C. 146 (Paterculus, i. 11). The temples were built by Mr. Lizard and Mr. Frog; but the senate would not allow them to put their names on the buildings, and so to hand down their work they sculptured on the spirals of the columns lizards and frogs (Pliny, xxxvi. 4). This can still be seen in the Church of S. Lorenzo on the road to Tivoli, the columns being taken there from here. The same authority (xxxiv. 15) gives particulars of the many statues; and amongst others one to Cornelia, the mother of the Gracchi, the base of which was found here in 1878, and is now in a ground room of the Museum of the Capitol. Pliny also tells us that when they dedicated the temples they by mistake carried the god into the goddess's temple, and so they let them remain as the will of the gods.

*On the right* is the CHURCH OF S. ANGELO IN PESCHERIA. Here Rienzi, on May 20, 1347, held his meeting for the re-establishment of "the good estate;" and here he exhibited his allegorical picture, and thence marched to the Church of S. George to fix up the proclamation.

*On the left of the main entry* some more columns have recently been discovered.

### THE GHETTO,

or Jews' Quarter. The word "Ghetto" comes from the Hebrew word *chat*, broken or dispersed. The Jews first settled here in the time of Pompey the Great; but it was not till 1556 that the Ghetto was enclosed by Pope Paul IV. putting gates across the streets. The

Jews were not allowed to be out after sunset or before sunrise, and he compelled the men to wear yellow hats and the women yellow veils. The old inhabitants, who were not Jews, were turned out, and obliged to give up their houses to the Jews on perpetual copy-hold leases, which were handed down in the families to the present day. Pius IX. abolished the gates, but it was not till the Italian troops entered Rome that the Jews obtained full liberty like their fellow-citizens. The lower part of the houses in the Ghetto are of Roman construction, and there is very little accumulation of soil there. There are about four thousand Jews in Rome, and notwithstanding the closeness with which they are packed and the dirt in which they live, the district is entirely free from fever. Within the last few years a considerable portion of the Ghetto has been destroyed.

At the far end of this space on the right, Via del Pianto, a house bears a medieval inscription put up in 1468, and recording that here was the Forum Judæorum. *The Via della Reginella, by the side of the house with the inscription, leads to the*

## FONTANA DELLE TARTARUGHE,

designed by Giacomo della Porta, and executed in bronze by Taddeo Landini in 1570. It is the most exquisite fountain in this city of fountains. Four graceful youths are supporting tortoises, which are endeavouring to climb into the basin above.

*Returning, at the west end of the open space is*

## THE CENCI PALACE,

### (*Palazzo Cenci*,)

the scene of the persecution of Beatrice, which led to her execution through the murder of her father at Petrella.

"The story is, that an old man having spent his life in debauchery and wickedness, conceived at length an implacable hatred towards his children, which showed itself towards one daughter under the form of an incestuous passion, aggravated by every circumstance of cruelty and violence. This daughter, after long and vain attempts to escape from what she considered a perpetual contamination both of body and mind, at length plotted with her mother-in-law and brother to murder their common tyrant" (Shelley).

"The Cenci Palace is of great extent; and, though in part modernized, there yet remains a vast and gloomy pile of feudal architecture, in the same state as during the dreadful scenes which are the subject of this tragedy—'The Cenci.' The palace is situated in an obscure corner of Rome, near the quarter of the Jews, and from the upper windows you see the immense ruins of Mount Palatine, half hidden beneath the profuse undergrowth of trees. There is a court in one part of the palace (perhaps that in which Cenci built the chapel to S. Thomas) supported by granite columns, and adorned with antique friezes of fine workmanship, and built up, according to the ancient Italian fashion, with balcony over balcony of open work. One of the gates of the palace, formed of immense stones, and leading through a passage dark and lofty, and opening into gloomy subterranean chambers, struck me particularly " (Shelley).

From an old manuscript recently brought to light, and from reports of the trial which have been recently published, the story of Beatrice Cenci appears divested of the fiction of a historical novel ; and these papers prove her to have been anything but the innocent victim she is represented in the romantic stories we have all read.

*On the left of the Piazza* is the Jewish Synagogue, once a Christian church, dedicated to S. Lorenzo in Damaso, and sold to the Jews by Pope Sixtus V. when he was in need of money.

The Cenci Palace stands upon the substructions of

## THE THEATRE OF BALBUS.

Erected b.c. 12, as a compliment to Augustus, by L. Cornelius Balbus (Suetonius, "Aug." xxix.), being the third permanent theatre erected in Rome. It held twelve thousand spectators. Pliny (xxxiv. 12) says : "Cornelius Balbus erected four small pillars of onyx in his theatre as something marvellous." At No. 23 Via Calderari, *to the right of the Cenci Palace*, some remains can be seen of the PORTICO of the Theatre of Balbus, which was two stories high. Built into the house are two Doric columns of travertine stone, supporting an architrave, which is interspersed with brickwork repairs, by Septimius Severus, after a fire.

*Beyond these remains* we reach the new Via Arenula, at the Piazza Benedetto Cairoli. The basin of the fountain in the garden was found many feet below the soil close by. *On the right is the*

## CHURCH OF S. CARLO A CATINARI,

celebrated for Domenichino's frescoes of Prudence, Justice, Temperance, and Fortitude, which are on the spandrels of the dome. Above the high altar is the Procession of S. Carlo, by Pietro da Cortona. The dome is by Lanfranco, who also painted the Annunciation, in the first chapel on the right. The Death of S. Anna, Andrea del Sacchi's masterpiece, is in the second chapel on the left.

*Opposite, the right side of the square leads up to the*

## CHURCH OF S. MARIA IN MONTICELLI.

This church was erected in the time of Innocent II., 1130–43, and has a campanile of that date. There are three interesting art subjects in the church. The vault of the tribunal was originally of mosaic, the whole of which has disappeared except the Saviour's Head, modern distemper work taking the place of the mosaic. However, the Head of Christ is very expressive, and the work of a Roman artist, 1227 : "MAGISTER ANDREAS CUM FILIO SUO ANDREA HOC OPUS FACERUNT, A.D. MCCXXVII."

Over the altar of the central chapel on the right in entering is a good fresco of the Scourging of our Lord, by Annibale Caracci, 1600.

Below the fresco is the famous Head of Jesus of Nazareth, " which opened its eyes in 1854."

*Beyond the church, the cross street to the right* is VIA S. PAOLA ALLA REGOLA ; *that to the left,* S. BARTOLOMEO DEI VACCINARI. The house on this street, the ancient Vicus Æscletus (see "Footsteps of St. Paul in Rome"), see page 183, at the corner of the VIA DEGLI STRENGARI, is pointed out by Jewish tradition as

## THE HIRED HOUSE OF S. PAUL.

" Paul was suffered to dwell by himself with a soldier that kept him."

" Paul dwelt two whole years in his own hired house, and received all that came in unto him."

Here, " Paul called the chief of the Jews together."

" When they had appointed him a day, there came many to him into *his* lodging."

The construction of the lower part of the house is brick-work of the early empire. This agrees with the Jewish tradition, and we can well understand that S. Paul would lodge somewhere near his kinsmen the Jews. The doorway has one of its columns still ; but it has been turned from a round headway into a square one. One of the windows on the left has still a round head ; above this the house is medieval. The lower part of the other houses here are Roman.

*To the left* of the house, take the VIA DI S. BARTOLOMEO DEI VACCINARI. On the right, some remains of the columns of the Theatre of Balbus have been built into a house, and remains exist under the houses all round. In this street Rienzi was born ; the exact house is not known.

*We again reach the* VIA ARENULA, *and, turning to the right, come to the new*

## PONTE GARIBALDI,

the first bridge built over the Tiber since 1870. It was opened in 1888. From it, looking up stream, a good view of the new Tiber embankment may be obtained; and down stream, of the island and its bridges. *On our left of the island is the*

## PONS FABRICIUS,

now called Ponte dei Quattro Capi, from the four-headed Janus upon its balustrades. From the inscription, and from Dion Cassius (xxxvii. 45), we learn that it was erected, B.C. 61, by L. Fabricius, Curator Viarum. Horace (S. ii. 3) says that "Stertinius advised the would-be suicide Damasippus to return cheerfully from the Fabrician bridge." It has two arches. The bridge leads to

## THE ISLAND OF THE TIBER.

"The Tarquins had sacrilegiously converted the best part of the Campus Martius to their own use. When they were expelled, it happened to be harvest time, and the sheaves then lay upon the ground; but as it was consecrated, the people could not make use of it. A great number of hands, therefore, took it up in baskets and threw it into the river. The trees were also cut down and thrown in after it, and the ground left entirely without fruit or produce for the service of the god. A great quantity of different sorts of things being thus thrown in together, they were not carried far by the current, but only to the shallows, where the first heaps had stopped. Finding no further passage, everything settled there, and the whole was bound still firmer by the river; for that washed down to it a deal of mud, which not only added to the mass, but served as a cement to it, and the current, far from dissolving it, by its gentle pressure gave it the greater firmness. The bulk and solidity of this mass received continual additions, most of what was brought down by the Tiber settling there. It was now an island sacred to religious uses. Several temples and porticoes have been built upon it; and it is called in Latin *inter duos pontes*—the island between the two bridges" (Plutarch, in "Publicola").

The island in the Tiber is an alluvial formation, and thus far the legend is correct in ascribing its origin to the accumulation of rubbish and drifted sand. In remembrance of the vessel which bore the statue of Æsculapius from Epidaurus to Rome, the entire island was faced with stone, and made to assume the form of a ship, in which was placed the temple of the god.

Some of the immense blocks of travertine composing the facing, and representing the hull of the ship, may still be seen in the monastery garden of the Church of S. Bartolomeo in Isola. *Ladies are not admitted to the monastery.*

"In the island of the Tiber, just prior to the death of Otho, the statue of Julius Cæsar turned from west to east, a circumstance said likewise to have happened when Vespasian took on him the empire" (Plutarch).

In the Piazza is a monument to SS. John, Francis, Bartholomew, and Paulinus. The interior of the church is embellished with fourteen ancient columns, and in the choir are the remains of an early mosaic.

The island on the farther side is connected with the mainland by

## THE PONS CESTIUS,

now called Ponte S. Bartolomeo. It was erected, B.C. 45, by the Prætor Lucius Cestius; the inscription records its restoration, A.D. 367, by the Emperors Valentinian, Valens, and Gratian. It consists of a single arch. Over the bridge is TRASTEVERE, the inhabitants of which claim to be descended from the ancient Romans : their manners and customs are somewhat distinct from those of the inhabitants of the other side of the river.

The ancient bridge has been destroyed in the embankment works, and a new one with three arches erected. *Returning from the bridge, turn to the right up the Via Montanara ; on the right is the* CHURCH OF S. NICOLÒ IN CARCERE, built over three temples.

## THE TEMPLES OF JUNO SOSPITA, PIETY, AND HOPE.

Three temples of the time of the republic, situated in one front, and forming a group. Not only many columns, but also considerable remains of the substructions have been preserved. The latter have been rendered accessible by the recent excavations.

The largest of these temples, Piety, situated in the middle, is of Ionic architecture. It is surrounded by a corridor, and is probably the same erected to Piety by the son of M. Acilius Glabrio ten years after the event. in fulfilment of a vow made by his father at the battle of Thermopylæ, A.U.C. 562, erected 572 (Livy, xl. 34). The *left hand* temple is that of Juno Sospita (to keep in health), founded by Cethægus, B.C. 195 (Livy, xxxii. 30. xxxiv. 53). The Temple of

13

Hope is *on the right*. It was erected by Atilius Calatinus during the first Punic War, B.C. 248 (Livy xxi. 62, xxv. 7).

These temples were situated in the Forum Olitorium, the great vegetable market of Rome, and outside the Servian wall. The custodian shows a cell which he points out as the scene of the " Caritas Romana." Visitor! " beware, beware ! he's fooling thee." This is not that Temple of Piety erected on the site of the house of the Roman matron, or, according to some authorities, on the site of the Decemviral Prisons; for Pliny and Solinus tell us that the sites of the temple and prison were occupied by the Theatre of Marcellus. According to Valerius Maximus (v. 4) and Pliny (" Natural History," vii. 36), it was a daughter who thus saved her mother's life, and "they were henceforth provided for by the state." Festus says it was her father.

*Turn to the right, in coming out of the temple; a short distance on the right the Via di Ponte Rotto turns out to the right. A little way up on the right is*

### THE HOUSE OF RIENZI.

" The Roman of Rome's least mortal mind;"
The friend of Petrarch and liberty,
Who died for Rome and Italy.
Rienzi ! the patriotic Roman,
Close by whose house doth wind
The Tiber, subservient to the will of no man.

It was built from the remains of one of those medieval towers used by the Romans as fortresses, and, as such, bore the name of the Torre di Monzone. It was demolished by Arlotto degli Stefaeschi, in the year 1313, in order to diminish the power of the Orsini, in whose possession it was. An inscription on the ruin states the founder to have been a certain Nicolas, the son of Crescentius and Theodora. Hence it has been supposed that the Crescentius here mentioned is identical with the celebrated consul who ruled over Rome A.D. 998; an opinion strengthened by the fact of his wife having really borne the name of Theodora. Rienzi is said to have been descended from them. Pope Leo XIII. was descended through his mother from Rienzi.

OLD RHYMING VERSE ON THE HOUSE OF RIENZI.

" First of the foremost, Nicolas, great from a low estate,
Raised (*this*) to revive the glory of his fathers.
There is placed the name of his father and mother, Crescentius
and Theodora.
This renowned roof, bore from (*a*) dear pledge:
The father who displayed it assigned it to David."

Another line says,—

"In fair places ever remember the grave."

The neighbouring people call this ruin the Casa di Pilato, and the appellation of the Casa di Cola di Rienzi has been added since the last century. Rienzi died in 1354 A.D. *Close by is the new* PONTE PALATINUS,

## THE PONTE ROTTO,

anciently the Pons Æmilius. This bridge, intended to unite the nearer bank of the river with Trastevere, but rendered impassable by the fall of several arches in 1598, whence its name of the Ponte Rotto, was commenced in the censorship of M. Æmilius Lepidus and M. Fulvius Nobilior, in the year of the city 573, and was completed by P. Scipio Africanus and L. Mummius. From the first of these it took its name. "Marcus Fulvius made contracts for piers for a bridge over the Tiber; on which piers Publius Scipio Africanus and Lucius Mummius, censors many years afterwards, caused the arches to be raised" (Livy, xl. 51). It is the same from which the body of Elagabalus was thrown with a stone attached to it, after having been dragged through the Circus.

In January 1886, to the eternal disgrace of the acting mayor, Duke Torlonia, and the municipal authorities of Rome, the remaining half of the oldest bridge over the Tiber was wantonly and unnecessarily destroyed in the works going on for the embankment of the river, the city fathers leaving one arch in the centre of the river as a monument of their folly. Looking down stream from the Ponte Palatinus, under the arch on the left is the mouth of the Cloaca Maxima, now diverted into the Tiber below S. Paul's, in order to prevent the backwash into the city. *A little lower down was*

## THE SUBLICIAN BRIDGE,

in front of which Horatius displayed his valour. It was first erected, A.U.C. 114, by Ancus Martius. By appointment of the oracle it was built only of timber fastened with wooden pins; "for the Romans considered it as an execrable impiety to demolish the wooden bridge, which, we are told, was built without iron, and put together with pins of wood only, by the direction of some oracle. The stone bridge was built many ages after, when Æmilius was quæstor. Some, however, inform us that the wooden bridge was not constructed in the time of Numa, having the last hand put to it by Ancus Martius" (Plutarch, in "Numa").

"Rome was in great danger of being taken, when Horatius Cocles,

and with him two others of the first rank—Herminius and Spurius
Lartius—stopped them at the bridge......This man [Horatius], standing at the head of the bridge, defended it against the enemy till the
Romans broke it down behind him.   Then he plunged into the Tiber,
armed as he was, and swam to the other side, but was wounded in
the hip with a Tuscan spear" (Plutarch, in "Publicola").   Livy (ii. 10)
gives his prayer before plunging in: "Holy father Tiber, I be-
seech thee to receive these arms, and this thy soldier, into thy pro-
pitious stream."   And

> "Still is the story told
> How well Horatius kept the bridge
> In the brave days of old."

Near this spot Clœlia swam across the Tiber on horseback, when
escaping from Lars Porsena.

> " While Cocles kept the bridge and stemmed the flood,
> The captive maids there tempt the raging tide,
> 'Scaped from their chains, with Clœlia for their guide."—VIRGIL.

*On our left is*

## THE TEMPLE OF PUDICITIA PATRICIA.

The Temple of Patrician Chastity stood inside the wall of Servius
in the Forum of the Cattle-dealers.   Livy (x. 23) says : " In the year
A.U.C. 456, a quarrel broke out among the matrons in the Temple
of Patrician Chastity, which stands in the cattle-market, near the
Round Temple of Hercules."

It was converted in 880 into the Church of S. MARIA EGIZIACA.
It has four Ionic columns at the front, with four apparent columns
at the end, and seven on one side.   A frieze of stucco, representing
heads of oxen, candelabra, and wreaths of flowers borne by children,
is on the entablature; it is 100 feet long by 50 wide.   When it was
turned into a church the wall dividing the portico from the cella
was pulled down, and the columns of the portico were filled in to
make it longer for a church.   It is the best specimen we have of a
republican temple.

*On our right is*

## THE ROUND TEMPLE OF HERCULES.

This is the temple mentioned above by Livy, and we see the positions agree with his statements.   It is formed of twenty beautiful Corinthian columns, only one of which, on the right side, is missing.   Its
circumference is only 156 feet, and that of the cella 26 feet, and the

ROUND TEMPLE OF HERCULES AND TEMPLE OF PATRICIAN CHASTITY.

height of the columns 32 feet. The walls within the portico are of
white marble (much of which still remains), and the pieces of it were
put together so as to have the appearance of one mass. The temple
stands on a base of tufa, showing early construction, but is a restoration of the time of Vespasian.

This was probably the Temple of Hercules which Vitruvius (iii. 3)
says was erected by Pompey. Pliny (xxxiv. 19) says Myron made
the statue of Hercules which is in the Ædes Herculis, built by Pompey the Great, near the Circus Maximus. Again (xxxv. 7) he speaks
of "the paintings of the poet Pacuvius, in the Temple of Hercules,
situated in the cattle-market."

## THE GRAND TEMPLE OF HERCULES.

There were other temples to Hercules in the Forum Boarium, of
which we have some travertine remains behind the Church of S.
Maria in Cosmedin opposite. "The Romans afterwards built a magnificent temple near the river Tiber, in honour of Hercules, and
instituted sacrifices to him out of the tenths" (Diodorus, iv. 1). "In
A.U.C. 534 a supplication was ordered to be performed by individ-
uals at the Temple of Hercules" (Livy, xxi. 62). This was destroyed
by Pope Adrian I., A.D. 772-795. "By the infinite labour of the
people, employed during a whole year, Adrian threw down an
immense structure of Tiburtine stone to enlarge the Church of S.
Maria in Cosmedin" (Anastasias).

## THE CHURCH OF S. MARIA IN COSMEDIN

is on the site of a temple to Ceres and Proserpine. "Spurius Cassius consecrated the Temple of Ceres, Bacchus, and Proserpine, which
stands at the end of the great circus, and is built over the starting-
places, and which Aulus Postumius, the dictator, had vowed when
upon the point of engaging the Latins," A.U.C. 258 (Dionysius, vi. 94).
"It was restored by Augustus, and consecrated by Tiberius" (Tacitus,
"Annals," ii. 49). The temple fronted north, and in the left-hand
aisle of the church are three of the columns of the portico in situ;
three of the side columns are in the portico of the church, and three
others in the sacristy, where there is part of a mosaic from old S.
Peter's, A.D. 705.

In the portico is a large mask of stone called the Bocca della
Verità (Mouth of Truth). A suspected person, on making an affirma-
tion, was required to put his hand in the mouth of this mask, in the
belief that if he told an untruth the mouth would close upon his

hand. Several columns of the old temple are immured in the walls, and the aisles are formed by twenty ancient marble columns; the pavement is of beautiful *opus Alexandrinum*. *Behind* the altar is a fine bishop's chair, and a Greek picture of the Virgin and Child, also some old frescoing behind a panel on the left. *Opposite* the church is a beautiful fountain of Tritons supporting a basin.

*Resuming our ramble down the* VIA MARMORATA, *turn left coming out of the church.* The ascent on the left was the Clivus Publicus, leading up to the Temple of Juno. *The road runs for a short distance by the Tiber, on the opposite side of which is the* RIPA GRANDE, *or quay. Taking the road to the right, past a stone-yard, Marmorata, by the river, brings us to*

## THE EMPORIUM,

another important building of the time of the Republic, of which we have considerable remains. The exact date of its foundation is not recorded, but a porticus, or arcade, was made to it, and it was paved about the year 560 of Rome, or 193 B.C. It was the great warehouse for the port of Rome for merchandise brought by vessels coming from the sea. There was another port at the Ripetta for provisions brought *down* the river in boats.

The Emporium was to ancient Rome what the docks are to London and Liverpool. This great building formed three sides of a quadrangle, the fourth being open to the quay on the bank of the Tiber, with a zigzag path down the face of the cliff and surface of the quay. This was excavated by the Pontifical Government, under the direction of Baron Visconti. It was remarkably perfect; the walls against the cliff were faced with *opus reticulatum* of the time of Hadrian, and a large number of blocks of valuable marbles were found here. A little further up the river an *amphora* is cut in the wall of the quay, to indicate the place for landing wine and oil. The portion of the Emporium now remaining belongs to the portico or arcade. There are said to be extensive cellars under the other remains, forming a lower story of the buildings. A new quarter is in course of erection here.

### TOMB OF SERGIUS GALBA.

He was consul 143 B.C., and ancestor of the Emperor Galba. "Sergius Galba, a person of consular rank, and the most eloquent man of his time, gave a lustre to the family" (Suetonius, "Galba," iii.). Cicero speaks of him as a distinguished orator ("Brutus," xxi.). The tomb was discovered in January 1886, twenty feet below the surface. It is composed of tufa stone upon a base of peperino. A block of white travertine bears the inscription,

SER. SULPICIUS . SER. F. GALBA . COS. PED. QUADR. XXX.,

on each side of which are five lictors' *faces* in bas-relief. It is to be re-erected on the square by the Emporium. He founded the Horrea Sulpicia, afterwards known as the Horrea, or warehouses, of Galba, in this vicinity, and which are represented on the marble plan of Rome.

*Regaining the main road, at a little distance we pass by an arch of the aqueduct which supplied the Emporium with water. It is called the* Arco di S. Lazaro. *We next turn off to the right, and ascend*

## MONS TESTACCIO,

formed of fragments of earthenware, chiefly of amphoræ. We know from those remaining at Pompeii that the amphoræ which formed that branch of commerce were often six feet high. Great numbers of these got broken in landing, and all were thrown on this heap, as they were not allowed to be thrown into the Tiber. There is also said to have been a manufactory of amphoræ and other earthenware at this spot, many of the fragments found here being the refuse of a great manufactory. This is supposed to have been the great manufactory of earthenware for the city of Rome for several centuries; and this supposition may account for the enormous quantity of such refuse that has accumulated on the spot, so as to form a hill. Tombs proving its comparatively recent origin were discovered beneath it in the year 1696. It is 110 feet high, and surmounted by a cross. The view from the top is very fine. *Close by is the*

## PROTESTANT CEMETERY.

"The spirit of the spot shall lead
Thy footsteps to a slope of green access."

The cemetery is an open space among the ruins, covered in winter with violets and daisies. "It might make one in love with death, to think that one should be buried in so sweet a place." So wrote Shelley, whose heart is contained in a tomb at the top left-hand corner of the new ground, his body having been burned upon the shore at Lerici, where it was thrown up by the sea. *Passing into the old ground,* "in the romantic and lovely cemetery under the pyramid which is the tomb of Cestius, and the mossy walls and towers, now mouldering and desolate, which formed the circuit of ancient Rome" (Shelley), here, on the right of the entrance, "lies one whose name was writ in water." Keats desiring this to be engraved upon his tomb. A fellow-poet says, "You feel an interest here, a sympathy you were not prepared for; you are yourself in a foreign land, and they are for the most part your countrymen, Englishmen."

*In returning from the Cemetery, nearly opposite the exit, a lane, Via S. Maria, leads up to the* AVENTINE HILL. The square at the top is decorated with military trophies of the Knights of Malta. *A door on the left leads to* their Priory; it contains a key-hole;—look through it, 'tis worth your while.

## IL PRIORATO.

### (*Open Wednesday and Saturday.*)

Built upon the site of the Temple of the Bona Dea, and where, according to some accounts, Remus took up his position to consult the flight of birds. On the right in entering is the tomb of Bishop Spinelli, an antique sarcophagus representing Minerva and the Muses. The church contains several tombs of the Knights of Malta, to whom it belonged, and who still exist and hold property in Rome, their encampment being in the Via Condotti; amongst others, there is a tomb erected to Brother Bartholomew Caraffa, Grand Master, died 1450.

*Beyond, on the left, is the*

## CHURCH OF S. ALEXIUS,

on the site of the Armilustrum, where the Sabine king, Titus Tatius, was buried. In the left aisle are a well and staircase belonging to the house of S. Alexius's parents, which formerly stood by the side of the church, where, after his return from his pilgrimage, he was allowed to live unrecognized by them. There is a very interesting fresco of S. Alexius's life on the walls of the underground Church of S. Clemente. (See page 225.)

*A little further, on the left, is the*

## CHURCH OF S. SABINA,

on the site of the saint's house, and formerly of the Temple of Juno Regina founded by Camillus. The church has been much restored at different times. The panels of the doors are fifth century.

In the chapel on the right of the high altar is Sassoferrato's Virgin, with the rosary. The Chapel of S. Catherine, painted by

Odazzi, is worthy of note. In the convent garden is an orange-tree planted by S. Dominic. The mosaic over door is fifth century.

*Following on the road, we take the first turning to the right; some little way down, on the left, is the*

### CHURCH OF S. PRISCA,

supposed to occupy the site of the house, some remains of which can be seen in the crypt, in which she was baptized by S. Peter. Only open on January 18. Supposed to have been formerly the site of the Temple of Diana founded by Servius Tullius.

*Down the hill, and up the opposite one, leads to the*

### CHURCH OF S. SABA,

built on the site of the house of Silvia, the mother of Gregory the Great, who used to send every day to her son on the Cœlian a silver basin containing soup. Uninteresting, and only open on the saint's day, December 5. It can be visited on Thursdays.

*At the foot of the hill, on the left corner of the two roads, is the*

### CAVE OF AQUEDUCTS,

a large stone quarry, intersected in all directions by aqueducts. Some of them are cut out of the solid tufa, others built in passages cut through the tufa; some are blocked up with mud deposit, others with stalactite; some run for a considerable distance, others being broken in, in extracting the tufa. They present altogether a curious and interesting study.

*On the new road, between the* VIA S. GREGORIO *and* PORTA S. PAOLO, *are remains of the*

### WALL OF THE LATINS,

built by the Latins under Ancus Martius, when he added the Aventine to the city.

The cliff has been scarped to the depth of 60 feet, and a terrace made on the ledge on which the wall stands, consisting of blocks of tufa. It was originally 12 feet thick, and in one part an arch is introduced for catapults, similar to those we have seen in ruins on the Palatine. The back of this part of the wall is a mass of concrete backing. At the foot of the wall was a trench, afterwards filled up, in which deep wells have been made for interments. Under the hill of S. Saba, below the cottage opposite, are traces of another early fortification formed of masses of concrete, originally faced with large blocks of tufa. The road here ran through the Porta Randusculana, in the fortifications of the seven hills.

*In this vineyard are also some remains of*

## THE BATHS OF SURA,

cousin of Trajan. These remains have only been partly explored, and are of great extent.

*On the opposite side of the road, in another vineyard,* are some massive remains of the aqueduct and reservoir of these baths, from the top of which there is a most enjoyable view of the city in general and the Palatine in particular. "Sura, the neighbour of the Aventine Diana, beholds at less distance than others the contests of the great circus" (Martial, vi. 64).

*In this vineyard are also some remains called the*

## HOUSE OF AQUILA AND PRISCILLA.

It consists of some chambers of reticulated work and a well of the early empire; the latter extends under S. Prisca. "Greet Priscilla and Aquila my helpers in Christ Jesus…Likewise greet the church that is in their house" (Rom. xvi. 3, 5).

*From the vineyard turn to the right. Some little way down on the right is the* entrance to the Jewish Cemetery. A fine view of the south side of the Palatine Hill may be enjoyed from here, overlooking the gas-works.

*In the valley below us was*

## THE CIRCUS MAXIMUS.

"Tarquinius also built the great circus which lies between the Aventine and Palatine Hills. He was the first who erected covered seats round it; for till then the spectators stood on scaffolds supported by poles. And he divided the places between the thirty curiæ. He assigned to each curia a particular part, so that every spectator was seated in the place that belonged to him. This work also became in time one of the most beautiful and most admirable structures in Rome. The circus is 3½ stadia in length, and 400 feet in breadth. Round the two greater sides, and one of the lesser, runs a canal, 10 feet deep and as many broad, to receive the water; behind the canal, porticoes are erected three stories high, of which the lowest has stone seats, as in the theatres, raised a little above the level of the ground, and the two upper porticoes have wooden seats. The two larger porticoes are connected into one, and joined together by means of the lesser, aud, meeting, form a semicircular figure; so that all three constitute one amphitheatral portico of 8 stadia, capable of receiving one hundred and fifty thousand persons. The other lesser side is left uncovered, and contains several arched starting-places for the horses, which are all opened at one signal. On the outside of the circus runs another portico of one story, which has shops in it, and habitations over them. In this portico are entrances and ascents for the spectators at every shop, contrived in such a manner that so many thousand persons may go in and out without any molestation" (Dionysius, iii. 69).

This description is evidently of the building as it stood in the days of Augustus. Founded by Tarquin, it was extended by Cæsar, and kept in repair and embellished by Augustus, Claudius, Domitian, Trajan, Constantine, and Theodoric. (See Suetonius, "Cæsar," xxxix.; Pliny, xxxv. 24, xxxvi. 15; Livy, vii. 20, i. 35.)

The valley in which it stood was originally called the Murzian Valley. Here Romulus gave the games when the Romans ran off with the Sabine women. The stream of the Almo runs through it: this branch of the Almo was taken from the main stream, about six miles from Rome, and made to pass through the Circus to supply with water the canal made by Cæsar which separated the spectators from the arena.

Remains of the curve can be seen at the Cœlian end, and some fragments of seats exist under the Palatine.

*Crossing the site of the Circus, on our right, standing back, is the*

## CHURCH OF S. ANASTASIA,

underneath which is part of two massive tufa towers of the wall of the kings that surrounded the two hills; and part of the old street called Vicus Mælians, which passed by the side of the Circus, facing on to which are a row of shops, behind which are some remains of the seats of the Circus Maximus.

## THE LUPERCAL

"was a grotto consecrated to Pan, the most ancient and the most honoured of all the Arcadian gods. It was surrounded by a wood, and is contiguous to the Palatine buildings, and is to be seen in the way that leads to the Circus. Near it stands a temple in which a statue is placed representing a wolf suckling two children,—they are in brass, and of ancient workmanship" (Dionysius, i. 76). This grotto, with the water still flowing out of the rock, still exists under the street at the corner of the Via de Cerchi, but it is not at present accessible. It was discovered by Mr. J. H. Parker, C.B., in 1869; and he found remains of the work of Augustus, who says, in the "Mon. Ancyr.," "*Lupercal...feci.*" We have been into it, and it exactly answers the description of Dionysius.

*From the church we follow the* VIA DI S. TEODORO. *A decline on the left leads to*

### THE ARCH OF JANUS (?),

a double arch of considerable magnitude, believed to be that of the four-headed Janus, the appearance of the structure involuntarily recalling the celebrated sanctuary of that god in the Forum, with which, however, it must not be confounded. There is no authority for calling it the Arch of Janus; we do not know what it was called by the Romans. In the sides of the piers which support the arch are twelve niches, apparently intended for the reception of statues. In one of these is a doorway leading up a narrow staircase to a chamber in the interior of the building, probably used as a place for business.

This singular building, which in its present condition has a somewhat quaint appearance, has evidently been intended for a place of sale. Being erected over the spot where the two roads intersecting the cattle-market met, it seems to have marked the central point of the traffic carried on in this space.

It is of white marble, old material re-used, and probably of the time of Constantine. Domitian erected several arches to Janus, but this is not good enough for his time.

*By its side is*

### THE ARCH OF THE SILVERSMITHS AND CATTLE-DEALERS.

We are indebted to this inconsiderable little monument—stated in the inscription to have been raised by the silversmiths and cattle-dealers to the imperial family of Septimius Severus—for the important information that the Forum Boarium, mentioned in the legends of the foundation of Rome, was situated on this spot. The sculptures with which the arch is ornamented are much defaced, and hidden from view on one side by the Church of S. Giorgio. Those in the interior represent sacrifices offered by the emperor and his sons. On one of the side piers is the figure of Hercules, evidently having reference to this locality, which was consecrated to him, and in the neighbourhood of which he had actually erected the Ara Maxima. At the back is a representation of a ploughman with a yoke of oxen, also in allusion to the myths, the different threads of which all unite at this point.

On the inside *right* are the effigies of Septimius and his wife Julia; and opposite them were Caracalla and Geta, but the latter has been cut out, leaving only his brother. On the pilasters, the capitals of which are Roman, we discover among various field-badges the portraits of the emperor, his wife, and one of his sons; that of Geta having been obliterated after his murder, by the order of Caracalla.

It is rather a misnomer to call this an arch, as it has a flat top.

*Adjoining is the*

### CHURCH OF S. GIORGIO IN VELABRO,

founded in the fourth century. The architrave above the portico (of the thirteenth century) is where Rienzi affixed his proclamation announcing, " In a short time the Romans will return to their ancient good estate." It is seldom opened, except on its festival, January 20th. The aisles are formed by sixteen different columns, no doubt the plunder of some other building. It is dedicated to the patron saint of England, a piece of whose banner is preserved beneath the altar. Fever lurks down the lane under the brick arches, and there is nothing to see.

*Regaining the* VIA S. TEODORO, *turn left, under the Palatine. On the right is the*

### CHURCH OF S. TEODORO,

founded by Adrian I., 772–795, and rebuilt, A.D. 1451, by Nicholas V. This church, from being round, has been called after all sorts of temples, but there is nothing whatever to show that it was once a pagan temple. It belongs to a burial fraternity. Over the altar is a mosaic, of the time of Adrian I., of our Saviour between SS. Peter and Paul. The Roman women bring their children here every Thursday morning to be blessed, after their recovery from sickness. It is a very ancient custom, and may have originated from the sick people who used to resort to the Fountain of Juturna to drink the waters.

# RAMBLE IV.

## UNDER THE EASTERN HILLS.

### THE ROUTE.

*From the Piazza del Popolo we take the left-hand street, the Via
Babuino.* The new English church of All Saints is on the right
side. At No. 89, *on the left*, lived Valadier.

*We now reach*

### THE PIAZZA DI SPAGNA.

This square may be considered as the centre of the English and American quarter in Rome. Here they come for most of their requirements,
and here a great many live. At No. 1, *the corner*, is the well-known
Piale's library and reading-room, the most extensive in Rome, where
one may find any information that he requires as to what is going on
in the city. Next door are the offices of Messrs. Thomas Cook and
Son. Monti, the poet, lived at No. 9. Mr. Hooker's American Bank is
No. 20. Shelley lived at No. 25 ; and Keats at No. 26, the right-hand
corner house, by the steps, where an inscription has lately been put

up. This square once formed part of " an artificial lake made by Domitian for the representation of naval fights. The fleets were as numerous as those employed in real engagements " (Suetonius, "Dom." 4).

The principal objects are the fountain LA BARCACCIA, by Bernini,
at the foot of the Spanish Stairs. It is here that the model and
flower girls most do congregate. The column of the IMMACULATE
CONCEPTION, found in the Campo Marzo, is supported by statues of
Moses, David, Isaiah, and Ezekiel. Its summit is crowned by a
statue of the Virgin, in bronze, designed by Poletti. It was erected
in 1854. *Beyond* is the Collegio di Propaganda Fide, founded in
1662 by Gregory XV. *Taking the streets on the right of the Propaganda,* VIAS PROPAGANDA *and* S. ANDREA DELLE FRATTE, *then the*
VIA NAZZARENO, *to the left.*

## ARCHES OF CLAUDIUS.

Half-way up the street, *on the right,* within the railings, are some
travertine arches of the Aqua Virgo Aqueduct, brought into Rome,
B.C. 19, by Marcus Agrippa. *(The custode at the Trevi Fountain
keeps the key. Permission to visit at 21 Via Pilotta.)* The arches
are of travertine stone, and on both sides over the central arch,
which spanned a road, is an inscription of the year 46 A.D., recording
the building of these arches by Claudius. They are of the rustic
order, like the Porta Maggiore, which he also built.

*Proceeding up the street, the second on the right,* VIA STAMPERIA
(where the prints are sold), *brings us to*

## THE TREVI FOUNTAIN,

supplied by the Aqua Virgo Aqueduct, erected in 1735 from the designs of N. Salvi. The water falls over artificial rocks, upon which
stands Neptune and his Sea-horses, by P. Bracci. On the sides are
figures of Health and Plenty, and above them reliefs—the Shepherdess
showing the Springs to M. Agrippa ; hence from her it is called the
Aqua Virgo ; and the building of the aqueduct. If you wish to return to Rome, you should come here on the last evening of your visit,
take a drink out of the basin of the fountain with your left hand,
then turn and throw into the water, over your left shoulder, a halfpenny. Legend says that whatever combination may be against it,
you are sure to return. We have proved the truth of this legend.

*Turn to the right,* Via Muratte, the first on the left, Via della
Vergine, brings us into the Piazza SS. Apostoli. *On the right* is the
Balestra Palace, where Prince Charlie died in 1788. *On the left is*

FOUNTAIN OF TREVI.

## THE CHURCH OF THE APOSTLES (SS. Apostoli).

Several fragments are built into the portico, the most interesting of which is the bas-relief of the eagle which once decorated Cæsar's Forum. The church has been entirely redecorated, and is now re-opened. In the course of the alterations, in 1873, the bodies of SS. Philip and James the Less were found enclosed in a marble sarcophagus. A new extensive crypt, decorated after the style of the catacombs, has been made to receive these remains.

The heart of Maria Clementina Sobieski is preserved here.
*Just beyond is*

### THE COLONNA PALACE.

*Open Tuesday, Thursday, Saturday, from 11 till 3. Entry, 17 Via Archi della Pilotta.*

The pictures have the names of the artists on them. In the first room we enter, the collection consists of Colonna portraits; then three rooms of tapestries, and some ancient draped statues, and a pretty statue of a dancing girl, "Niobe."

First Room.—Early schools. Holy Family, by Luca Longhi; Boy in a Red Cap, by Giovanni Sanzio, Raphael's father; Crucifixion, by Giacomo di Avanzi; Moses, by Guercino.

Second Room.—Throne room.

Third Room.—Guardian Angel, by Guercino; Peasant Eating, by Annibale Carraci,—true to life; S. Jerome, by Lo Spagna; Portrait, by Paul Veronese. *Ceiling*, Apotheosis of Martin V., by Lutti and Battoni.

Fourth Room.—Landscapes, by Poussin; Battle-pieces, by Wouvermans; Sea-shore, by Rosa; Cabinet, with reliefs in ivory; Subjects from the Sistine Chapel.

The Great Hall.—Ornamented with statues and mirrors. Assumption, by Rubens; Roman Charity, by Subtermans; Ecce Homo, by Albano; Narcissus, by Tintoretto; Venus, by Vasari; Rape of the Sabines, by Ghirlandajo; S. Peter, Madonna, and Child, by Palma Vecchio; Venus and Cupid, by Bronzino; another, by Salviati; Madonna Liberating a Child from the Demon, by Nicolo da Poligno.

Sixth Room.—The *Colonna Bellica*, surmounted by a statue of Mars, with low reliefs round the column.

In the Via dei Fornari, *on the right*, at No. 21, lived Michael Angelo.
*Crossing the new Via Nazionale, either of the streets on the sides of the Prefettura leads into*

## THE FORUM OF TRAJAN.

This was the largest and grandest of all the fora, being built to one design by the celebrated architect Apollodorus of Damascus (Dion Cassius). No author has given us any detailed account of the beautiful group of buildings that formed this forum, but what passages there are tend to show its magnificence. There was first of all an open space, or the forum proper, surrounded by a double row of shops, one above the other. In the centre of this space was the colossal equestrian statue of the emperor (Marcellinus, xvi. 10). Beyond this, crossing the whole width of the forum, was the basilica called, after the family name of the emperor, Ulpia. Beyond this was the celebrated pillar, behind which stood the Temple of Trajan, with the libraries on either side. The portion excavated is only a small piece of the whole, which extends under the houses all round. The size of the basilica can be made out from the gray granite pillars which once supported the roof. It was sometimes called the Hall of Liberty, from the slaves receiving their freedom here.

## THE COLUMN OF TRAJAN.

A magnificent marble pillar, the pedestal of which concealed the chamber where the ashes of the emperor were deposited. The bas-reliefs on the basement are among the most beautiful decorations of ancient or modern times; they represent the arms taken from the Dacians, against whom Trajan had made several campaigns. It marks the height of the Quirinal Hill, cut away to make the open space for the Forum of Trajan in which it stands. A series of bas-reliefs, representing the Dacian war, forms a spiral round the shaft of the pillar. Erected A.D. 114. It is 127 feet high, including the base, and is surmounted by a statue of S. Peter, 11 feet high, placed there by Sixtus V. in the sixteenth century.

The pillar is composed of thirty-four blocks of white marble. The reliefs are two feet high at the bottom, and gradually increase in size as they go upwards, thus making the figures at the top and bottom seem of equal size. There are two thousand five hundred figures, besides animals and other details.

Dion Cassius (Xiphilin, Trajan) says : " He erected in the forum that bears his name a vast pillar, as well to serve as a receptacle for his bones as to be a monument of his magnificence to posterity. In good earnest, it was a piece of work that could not be finished without extraordinary expense, because it was necessary to cut

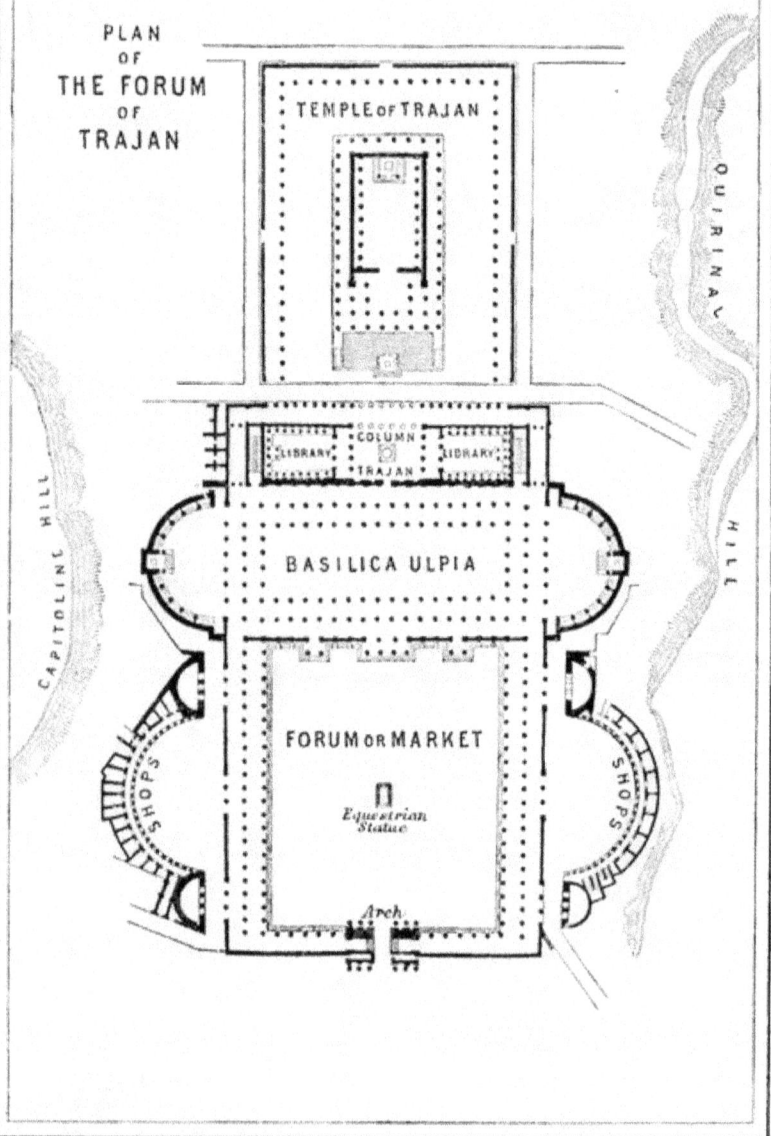

PLAN
OF
THE FORUM
OF
TRAJAN

TEMPLE OF TRAJAN

QUIRINAL

CAPITOLINE HILL

HILL

LIBRARY    COLUMN    LIBRARY
OF
TRAJAN

BASILICA ULPIA

SHOPS

FORUM OR MARKET

Equestrian
Statue

SHOPS

Arch

through a mountain as high as the pillar, to make the level for the forum."

"The bones of Trajan were put into the pillar we have mentioned; and, to reverence his memory, sports were celebrated for several years after, which were called Parthica" (Dion Cassius, "Hadrian").

"Trajan, of all the emperors, was buried within the city. His bones, being put up in a golden urn, lie in the forum which he built, under a pillar, whose height is 144 feet, Roman " (Eutropius).

*Going down the* VIA ALESSANDRINA, *which commences at the left-hand corner of the above forum, as we come into it, take the first turning on the left,* VIA CAMPO CARLEO. *The gate on the left leads to the double row of shops that surrounded the Forum of Trajan. Custodi at the Forum. Following this street, we pass the* medieval *Torre del Grillo on our left. On our right are massive remains of the* SECOND WALL OF ROME. *(See page xviii.) Turning to the right under the arch, we are within*

## THE FORUM OF AUGUSTUS.

"The reason of his building a new forum was the vast increase in the population, and the number of cases to be tried in the courts; for which the two already existing not affording sufficient space, it was thought necessary to have a third. He placed statues of the great Roman generals in both the porticoes of his forum. In building his forum, he restricted himself in the site, not presuming to compel the owners of the neighbouring houses to give up their property" (Suetonius, "Augustus," lvi.).

It was restored by the Emperor Hadrian (Spartianus).

## THE TEMPLE OF MARS ULTOR,

the Avenger. Vowed by Augustus at the battle of Philippi, B.C. 42, and erected by him in the centre of his new forum.

Three beautiful pillars, and part of the wall of the cella and of the roof of the vestibule, still exist near the Arco dei Pantani, which owes its medieval name to the marshes caused by the water collecting in this neighbourhood. They stand upon a substruction only excavated a few years ago, and present one of the finest specimens extant of a temple, all the essential parts of which have been preserved. The gigantic walls of rectangular blocks of tufa, into which the travertine arch already mentioned was introduced for the purpose of forming a communication with the other part of the city, are most imposing, and formed part of the second wall of Rome and the boundary of the Forum of Augustus.

TRAJAN'S FORUM.

"The Temple of Mars was built in fulfilment of a vow made during the war of Philippi, undertaken by him to avenge his (adopted) father's murder. He ordained that the senate should always assemble there when they met to deliberate respecting wars and triumphs; that thence should be despatched all those who were sent into the provinces in the command of armies; and that in it those who returned victorious from the wars should lodge the trophies of their triumphs" (Suetonius, "Augustus," xxix.).

"The Emperor Augustus, being consul with Caninius Gallus, gratified the eyes and minds of the Roman people, on the occasion of dedicating the Temple to Mars, with the most magnificent spectacles of gladiators and a sea-fight" (Velleius Paterculus, ii. 100).

In the new excavations, *opposite* the temple, we can see the travertine niches built by Augustus up against the wall of the kings, to receive the statues which he put up in the hemicircles.

*Passing down this street, Via Bonella, in the direction of the Roman Forum, on our right, No. 44, green door, is*

### THE GALLERY OF THE ACCADEMIA DI S. LUCA.

*Open daily, except Saturdays and festas, from 9 till 3. Catalogues are lent to visitors.* The principal works are :—

*First Hall.*—2. The Virgin, by Carlo Maratti; on the back a facsimile of Raphael's original sketch for the Transfiguration. 7. View on the Anio, by Van Bloemen Orizzonte. 10. Madonna and Child with Angels, by Vandyck. 21. Sunset, by Vernet. 23. Assumption, by Costanzi Placido. 24. Sunrise, by Vernet. 26. The Ascension, by Placido. 39. Venus at her Toilet, by Paolo Caliari Veronese. 43. Love, by Guido Reni.

*Hall of Raphael.*—59. Vanity, by Titian. 68. Tivoli, by Vanvitelli. 72. S. Luke Painting the Madonna and Child, by Raphael. 77. Venus and Cupid, by Barbieri Guercino. 78. A Boy, fresco by Raphael, formerly in the Vatican. 79. Callisto and the Nymphs attending Diana, by Titian.

*Hall of Fortune.*—86. The Cascades at Tivoli, by Salvator Rosa. 100. Death of S. Cecilia, by Andrea Pozzi. 103. Sextius Tarquinius and Lucretia, by Guido Canalassi Cagnacci. 111. Cupid and Love, by Benedetto Lutti. 116. Bacchus and Ariadne, by Guido Reni. 128. Iris, by Guido Head. 130. Birth of Christ, by Pompeo Batoni. 133. Fortune, by Guido Reni. 146. Hope, by Angelica Kauffmann. 154. River View, by Salvator Rosa.

*Modern Room.*—157. Saul and David, Cesare Francassini. 185.

Vestal Buried Alive, school of Gherardo. 197. Contemplation, by
Greuze. 198. Virginia Lebrun, a portrait by herself.

*Resuming our ramble up the Via Bonella, we take the VIA ALESSAN-
DRINA, on the right; and the VIA CROCE BIANCA, on the left.* This
was the site of

## THE FORUM OF NERVA.

"Domitian erected a forum, which is now called Nerva's" (Suetonius, "Domitian," v.). It was known by several names, being
called after Domitian, because he commenced it ; Nerva, because he
finished it ; Pervium, because it was a thoroughfare ; Pallas and
Minerva, from the temple that stood in it, and which was destroyed
by Pope Paul V. to build the fountain on the Janiculum ; it was
also called Transitorium, because a street passed through it for
traffic. The only remains left are, *on the right,*

## THE ALTAR OF MINERVA,

the prettiest bit of ruin in Rome, consisting of Corinthian columns,
which support an architrave adorned with a frieze, and divided by
ressauts, and an attic above. On the attic is a colossal figure of
Minerva, represented in relief as the patroness of labour ; on the
architrave the goddess appears engaged in instructing young girls in
various female occupations, and in punishing the insolence of Arachne,
who had ventured to compete with her in the labours of the loom.

The wall upon which this altar stands was also a piece of the wall
of the kings. It was the Porta Piacularis, which was filled in when
the wall was utilized for the altar. In the yard of the large new
house opposite remains of a tower can be seen, probably the tower
called Turris Mamilia.

When in October the horse was sacrificed to Mars, there was a
contest between the inhabitants of the Via Sacra and the Suburra
for the possession of the head. If the people of the Suburra obtained
it, they placed it on this tower (Festus).

## SITE OF THE HOUSE OF POMPEY.

The TOR' DI CONTI, *on the right,* is a massive tower of the Middle
Ages, built as a fortress, and supposed to stand on the site of the
Temple of the Earth. "Lenæus, the grammarian, opened a school
in the Carinæ, near the Temple of the Earth, where stood the house
of the Pompeys" (Suetonius, "Grammarians," xv.). "Tiberius removed from Pompey's house in the Carinæ" (Suetonius, "Tiberius,"
xv.). "The house of Cassius was demolished ; and to this day the

place remains void, except that part on which they afterwards built the Temple of the Earth, which stands in the street leading to the Carinæ" (Dionysius, viii. 79).

*Passing the tower, we cross the new* VIA CAVOUR, *which leads from the railway down to the Forum; the second turning on the left takes us up to the* PIAZZA S. PIETRO IN VINCOLI ; *on the left is the* CHURCH OF S. FRANCESCO DI PAOLA ; *the old house adjoining was the*

## HOUSE OF LUCREZIA BORGIA.

Here Cæsar Borgia, Francesco, Duke of Gandia, and Lucrezia supped with their mother Vanozza, on the evening that Cæsar assassinated the duke, and had his body thrown into the Tiber, where it was afterwards found by a fisherman, pierced with nine wounds.

## CHURCH OF S. PETER IN VINCOLI.
### (*The Chains of Peter.*)

It has three aisles, with twenty Doric columns of Greek marble, and two of granite, which support the middle arch. On the first altar, to the right, there is S. Augustin, by Guercino. On the right of the high altar is the famous statue of MOSES, by MICHAEL ANGELO, rendered hideous by two horns sticking out from the forehead. The figures on the sides are Rachel and Leah, also by Michael Angelo. It was to have formed the tomb of Julius II. in S. Peter's. The S. Margherita, in the adjacent chapel, is by Guercino ; the tribune of the high altar was painted by I. Coppi. The new confessional, built by Pius IX., contains the tomb of the seven Maccabees. Here also are preserved the chains of S. Peter. The last altar but one of the other aisle has a S. Sebastian, a mosaic of the seventh century. In the sacristy there are the Liberation of S. Peter, by Domenichino ; a Holy Family and Faith, of the school of G. Romano. Guido Reni's Hope was in this church, but it has been replaced by a copy, the original having been sold to an Irish gentleman.

*From the front of the church a lane on our left,* VIA DELLA POL-VERIERA, *leads, left (carriage right), to the* VIA LABICANE, *a short distance up which is the entrance to*

## THE BATHS OF TITUS,

partly built over the site of Nero's Golden House and Villa of Mæcenas.

"He completed his palace by continuing it from the Palatine to the Esquiline, calling the building at first only 'The Passage ;' but after it was burned down and rebuilt, 'The Golden House.' Of its dimensions and furniture it may be sufficient to say this much:—The porch was so high that there stood in it a colossal statue of himself 120 feet in height ; and the space included in it was so ample that it had triple porticoes a mile in length, and a lake like a sea, surrounded with buildings which had the appearance of a city. Within its area were corn-fields, vineyards, pastures, and woods, containing a vast number of animals of various kinds, both wild and tame. In other parts it was entirely overlaid with gold, and adorned with jewels and mother-of-pearl. The supper-rooms were vaulted, and compartments of the ceilings, inlaid with ivory, were made to revolve and scatter flowers, while they contained pipes which shed scents upon the guests. The chief banqueting room was circular, and revolved perpetually, night and day, in imitation of the motion of the celestial bodies. Upon the dedication of this magnificent house Nero said, in approval of it, ' that he had now a dwelling fit for a man ' " (Suetonius, "Nero").

"Nero, dressed like a harper, was at the top of a tower in his palace, from whence he diverted himself with the sight of the fire" (Dion Cassius).

On the left of the entrance are the remains of the ORATORIO OF S. FELICITA, a Christian church of the sixth century. The rooms on the left of the PASSAGE, substructions formed by Hadrian, are supposed to have been used as private habitations in the middle ages. On one of the piers are two snakes (see below). At the end of this Passage a part of the pavement of the HOUSE OF NERO can be seen. LONG CORRIDOR, penetrated into by Raphael and Giovanni da Udine, who copied the frescoes for the Vatican. On the vault are some beautiful arabesque paintings of flowers, birds, and animals; and on the walls two snakes, with a basin placed between them. Above them is an inscription, now almost obliterated, telling us that it was the notice equal to our " Commit no nuisance."

DVODECI$^{m}$ DEOS IIT DEANA$^{m}$ ET IOVEM
OPTVMV$^{m}$ MAXIMV$^{m}$ HABEAT IRATOS
QUISQUIS HIC MIXERIT AUT CACARIT.

*Retracing our steps* down the corridor, and crossing some chambers, we come to the TRICLINIARIUM, or summer banqueting room, with the winter rooms on each side, having a southern aspect. At the end of this room there was originally a garden; and in the basin of the fountain was the porphyry vase now in the circular hall of the Vatican Museum. Beyond this is the CAVÆDIUM, an open court or garden, from which the surrounding apartments received

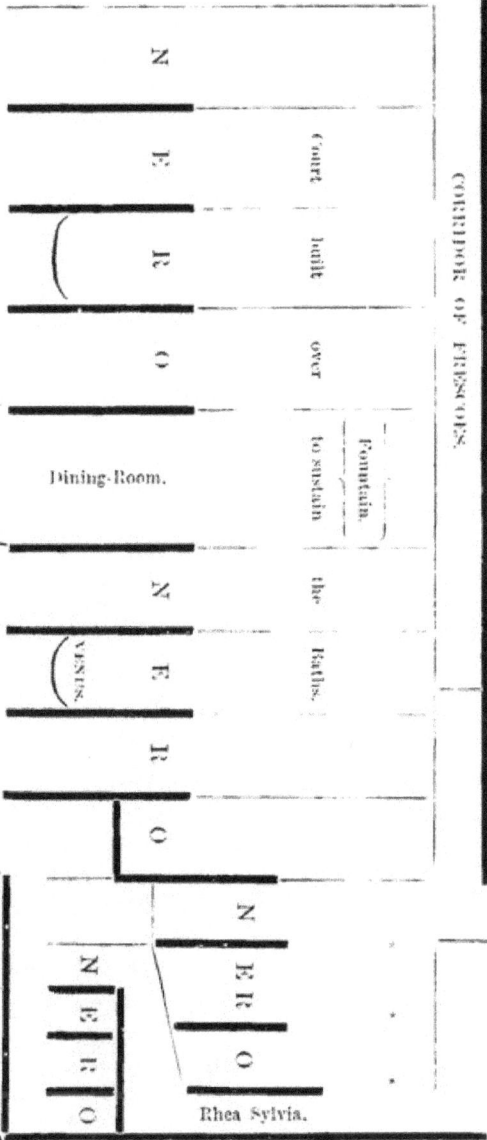

S. Felicita

ENTRANCE.

H A D R I A N

NERO.

CORRIDOR OF FRESCOES

VAULTS OF THE BATHS OF HADRIAN.

* Remains of columns forming the portico.

N E R O

Court built over to sustain the Baths.

Fountain.

Dining-Room.

N E R O

VESTS.

N E R O

N E R O

N E R O

Rhea Sylvia.

their light.  It was surrounded on three sides with columns, and in the centre was a fountain : it was subsequently occupied by the substruction arches of the baths.  Adjoining is the CORRIDOR OF RHEA SYLVIA, so called from the fresco representing the conception of Romulus and Remus.  In another room is a representation of Venus and the Doves.

Suetonius records that Titus built some baths near the Amphitheatre, and Pliny speaks of the Group of the Laocoon being in the Palace of Titus.  This was found near the Sette Salle, so there is no doubt as to the site of the Palace and Baths of Titus.  The palace seems to have been done away with, and the baths incorporated with those of Hadrian.

### THE BATHS OF HADRIAN.

On the Plan, the dark lines show the remains of Nero's Palace, which was nearly destroyed by the Flavian emperors.  The remains left were used by Hadrian for the underground part of his thermæ ; and by building walls over the courts and gardens he formed a large platform.  The light lines show his work.  The circular wall in front supported the seats for the stadium attached to the baths above.  Remains of some of the large halls of the baths can be seen in the vineyards above the House of Nero.  Some remains of these baths exist under the Church of S. Martino.  These baths are generally ascribed to Titus ; but the construction, *opus reticulatum*, within bands of brick, shows that they are of the time of Hadrian.

*Turn to the left on coming out.  A short way up the road, on the right, is the entrance to the*

### CHURCH OF S. CLEMENT,

belonging to the Irish Dominicans, of which the late Father Mullooly was prior, to whose instrumentality we are indebted for the discovery of the ancient church, and the Temple of Mithras beneath it, under the present edifice.  On some occasions (November 23rd, February 2nd, and the second Monday in Lent) they are illuminated.

#### UPPER CHURCH.

The usual entrance from the street is by a side door, but the proper entrance is by a gate with a Gothic canopy of the thirteenth century, which originally formed part of the earlier basilica, thence through the atrium and quadriporticus, the only perfect ones of Rome.  The aisles are formed by sixteen ancient pillars of different materials and orders.  In the middle of the nave is the choir (514-22) from the earlier basilica ; on each side are the ambones.  The walls are adorned with Christian emblems, and a monogram of Agios-Holy. The nave is separated from the high altar by an ancient marble screen. Behind is the presbytery, which contains an ancient episcopal chair, with the name of Anastasius, who was titular cardinal of the church in 1108, engraved upon it. Upon the vault is a mosaic of 1297, representing Christ on the Cross, from the foot of which issue the four rivers of Paradise, with shepherds and their flocks, and peacocks. On the face of the arch is a mosaic of the time of Paschal II.—our Saviour; on either side two angels, and the emblems of the four evangelists ; below are S. Peter, S. Clement, Jeremiah, S. Paul, S. Lawrence, and Isaiah ; at the bottom, Bethlehem and Jerusalem, with the mystic lamb and sheep. In the chapel, on the right, the statue of S. John is by Simone ; on the left, the picture of the Virgin is by Conca. The monument composed of two half-columns, with basket-work capitals and foliage reliefs, is to Cardinal Venerio, who died in 1479. *To the left on entering*, in the Chapel of the Passion, are the interesting frescoes by Masaccio (much spoilt by restoration), representing the Crucifixion, &c., and events from the lives of SS. Clement and Catherine. *Outside* the arch, the Annunciation, and S. Christopher carrying the infant Christ over a stream ; *within*, S. Catherine forced to Idolatry, Instruction of the King's Daughter in Prison, Dispute with the Doctors, Miracle of her Deliverance, Martyrdom. Opposite is the history of S. Clement. *Proceeding into the sacristy*, which is adorned with paintings of various interesting parts of the more ancient buildings, *a wide stair conducts to the*

LOWER CHURCH,

founded on the site of S. Clement's house, it is supposed, in the time of Constantine. S. Jerome says : " The church built to S. Clement keeps the memory of his name to this day." So that it must have been erected before A.D. 400.

An inscription found in the excavations, bearing the name of Pope Nicholas II., shows that this basilica was perfect in 1061, when Nicholas died, so that it could not have been destroyed, as some think, by the earthquake of 896 ; but it was ruined in 1084, when Robert Guiscard burned all the public buildings from the Lateran to the Capitol, when he came to the rescue of Pope Gregory VII.

The ruin seems to have been purposely filled in by the builders of the upper church, and all the fittings possible removed into the latter, which, from the nature of its walls, was evidently constructed in haste, and before 1099, as Paschal II. was elected pope there on August 13th

of that year. The lower church was discovered in 1857, when Father
Mullooly was making some repairs in the church above. It consists
of a nave and two aisles, formed by a line of ancient columns of
various marbles: the space between each column has been built up to
support the foundations of the church above.

In descending, the walls are covered with ancient fragments, and
a small statue of the Good Pastor, found in making the excavations;
as also the two sarcophagi and other fragments in the portico of
the ancient basilica. At the entrance, on the left hand, is a painting of an ancient female figure, and a male head on the opposite wall;
a little further, on the left, Christ surrounded with Saints, giving his
benediction in the Greek manner; opposite, the Miracle at the Tomb
of S. Clement at Cherson.*

THE ANGEL IS PREPARING THAT TOMB SUBMERGED IN THE SEA.

BEHOLD UNHURT HE LIES WHOM HIS RETURNING MOTHER SEEKS AGAIN.

| | IN THE NAME OF THE |
| | LORD, I, BENO DE RAPIZA,† |
| Portrait of S. Clement. | FOR THE LOVE OF BLESS- |
| | ED CLEMENT AND THE |
| SEEKING ME IN PRAYER, | SALVATION OF MY SOUL, |
| BEWARE OF HURTFUL THINGS. | HAD IT PAINTED. |

Further along, translation of the relics of S. Cyrile from the
Vatican to this basilica :—

FOR ALL AGES : MAY THE PEACE
OF THE LORD BE EVER WITH YOU.

— HITHER FROM THE VATICAN IS BORNE (NICHOLAS BEING POPE) WITH
DIVINE HYMNS WHAT WITH AROMATICS HE BURIED.

— I, MARIA MACELLARIA, FOR THE LOVE OF GOD AND REDEMPTION OF MY
SOUL, HAD IT PAINTED.

*Right, north aisle,* right hand wall, painting of S. Catherine;
further on, in a niche, Virgin and Child, with two females, SS.
Catherine and Euphemia; below, Abraham and Isaac; at the top,
Head of our Lord; beyond, a Council; the next, above the steps of
the tribune, Christ in the act of giving the Benediction; just
beyond, an inscription :—

WHOEVER READS THESE LETTERS OF MY NAME, LET HIM SAY, GOD HAVE
MERCY ON UNWORTHY JOHN.

Passing into the *nave,* in the right-hand corner, is a fresco of our
Saviour releasing Adam from Limbo. On the left wall, looking to-

---

* The inscriptions are translated and placed on the page to show their relative positions on the frescoes.                                      † See page 282.

wards the modern altar (erected beneath the one in the church above, under which are placed the remains of S. Ignatius and S. Clement. Behind this a door leads to a space, recently excavated, where a portion of the first church, once covered with marble slabs, may be seen), Installation of S. Clement by S. Peter; Clement performing Mass; the Miracle of Sisinius; and Men drawing a Column—all on one pier.

THE LORD BE WITH YOU     THE PEACE OF THE LORD BE EVER WITH YOU.

— I, BENO DE RAPIZA, WITH MARY, MY WIFE, FOR THE LOVE OF GOD AND BLESSED CLEMENT, HAD IT PAINTED FOR A FAVOUR RECEIVED.

CARVONCELLE.    ALBERTEL.    COSMARIS.    SISINIUS.

GET BEHIND THE COLUMN CARVONCELLE WITH A LEVER.    ALBERTEL, COSMARIS, DRAW IT UP.    FOR THE HARDNESS OF YOUR HEARTS YOU DESERVE TO DRAW STONES.    SONS OF *Pule* DRAW IT UP.

On the inside of this pier are S. Antoninus, and Daniel in the Lions' Den. On the same wall, higher up, Life, Death, and Recognition of S. Alexius; above which is our Lord seated, attended by Gabriel, Michael, Clement, and Nicholas, holding a book.

STRONG AS THE BONDS OF DEATH.

THAT IS MY RESIDENCE IN IT; YOU SHALL FIND AN ASYLUM.    COME UNTO ME, ALL YE THAT LABOUR AND ARE HEAVY LADEN, AND I WILL GIVE YOU REST.

THE FATHER DOES NOT RECOGNIZE WHO ASKS HIS PITY.

The arabesque ornament at the bottom is very beautiful. Beyond this, at the side of the pier, are S. Giles and S. Blasius; at the end of the wall, S. Prosperius, the Maries at the Sepulchre, Christ releasing Adam and Eve from Hades, the Supper at Cana, the Crucifixion; and just beyond, the Assumption (eighth century).

MOST HOLY LORD LEO, POPE OF ROME.    SANCTUS VITUS

THAT THIS PICTURE MAY OUTSHINE THE REST IN BEAUTY, BEHOLD THE PRIEST LEO STUDIED TO COMPOSE IT.

Passing into the *south or left aisle*, on the wall, at this end, is a painting representing the Miracle of S. Libertinus, and one representing

WHERE THE ABBOT BEGS PARDON OF LIBERTINUS.

At the west end of this aisle, over the stairs, are the remains of a painting of the Crucifixion of S. Peter; and in the right-hand

corner, S. Cyril's parting audience with Michael III. In the opposite corner is a baptism of some barbarian by S. Cyril, beyond
which the projecting brickwork marks the site of the tomb of S.
Cyril.

The nave is formed by a line of seven columns in their original
places, in a wall of *débris* built to support the church above. These
columns are of beautiful marbles, and stand upon a wall of the
imperial period, which has been traced for 98 feet.

At the west end of the north aisle a flight of narrow steps leads
down to a passage, 25 inches wide, formed between massive walls :
that on the right is brick of the imperial period, forming the wall of
S. Clement's house ; that on the left, tufa, of the kingly period, being
part of the walls of Servius Tullius. This has been heightened by a
travertine wall of the republican period. The tufa wall has been
traced for 500 feet, and the travertine wall upon it for 410 feet.
About 20 feet is still buried, showing how low ancient Rome was in
this valley. At the end of this passage another flight of steps leads
up into the south aisle. In the centre of the passage is an entrance
through the imperial wall (now blocked up on account of the water)
into

### THE ORATORY OF S. CLEMENT,

reached from the south aisle by a broad flight of twenty steps.
The Roman Catholic Church has faithfully handed down the tradition that S. Clement erected an oratory in his own house, between
the Cœlian and Esquiline Hills, which must have been built, as we
have seen, close to the walls of the city—a not unusual thing as the
city grew. Several chambers remain to be excavated at some future
time. A long passage has been cleared out, in which was found a
doorway bricked up. This was broken through, and found to be a

### TEMPLE OF MITHRAS,

the Persian sun-god, whose mysteries, Plutarch tells us, were first
brought to Rome by the soldiers of Pompey the Great. "They
celebrated certain secret mysteries, among which those of Mithras
continue to this day, being originally instituted by them B.C. 67."
This worship was finally extirpated in A.D. 394. The temple was
found filled up with earth as though done purposely. It is 30 by 20
feet, and has a vaulted roof, covered with mosaics, in which are
several windows. The continual dripping of water has destroyed the
colour, but the mosaics can still be distinctly seen. The altar on
which the sacrifices were made was found near the two square

pilasters in the passage outside, and a statue of Mithras was found in three pieces. The altar has been placed within the temple. It represents an allegorical picture of the sun's influence upon the earth. A bull represents the earth ; Mithras is plunging a sword into the bull's right shoulder ; a dog and a serpent are emblems of animals nourished by the earth through the influence of the sun ; a scorpion gnawing the scrotum is autumn bringing decay ; youths with torches, erect and depressed on either side, represent the rising and the setting of the sun. Under Elagabalus (218-22) and Aurelian (270-75) the worship of the sun was the national religion of the Romans, and its votaries tried in vain to establish it, to resist the rapid spread of the worship of the only true God through Jesus Christ his Son.

*Leaving S. Clement's by the side door, and taking the lane opposite, the first ascent on the left,* AD CAPUT AFRICÆ, *leads to*

## THE CHURCH OF THE QUATTRO INCORONATI.

*Custodian at door on right, inside arch.*

This church is dedicated to the four brother masons who were *corniculari* or wing-leaders of the city militia, and who were put to death for being Christians, by Diocletian, on 8th November 300. In 625 Honorius I. founded a basilica to their memory on the site of a temple of Diana. Leo IV., in 848, translated their remains from their catacombs to this church : they repose in the crypt under the altar. This is recorded in the inscription on the left stairs. Destroyed in the fire of Guiscard, 1084, it was rebuilt by Paschal II. in 1111 ; which is recorded on the right-hand side of the niche of the Virgin over the stairs. Urban VIII. restored the church in 1624. In the *quadri porticus*, Innocent III. (1198-1215) founded a chapel to S. Silvester, which contains some curious thirteenth century frescoes of the life of Constantine. From the sixteenth century it has belonged to a guild of marble-cutters, who celebrate mass on the last Sunday of the month. Over the door is a fresco of the four saints, and the inscription—STATUARIORUM ET LAPICIDARUM CORPUS, ANNO MDLXX. The inner court was formed by shortening the church in 1111. Over the door is Mannozzi's fresco of the saints and Augustine sisters, to whom it belongs. The whole width of the present church was the nave only of the original edifice. The columns support the nuns' gallery. The roof is of cypress, and has in the centre the four crowned martyrs with their working tools in their hands. The episcopal chair in the tribunal, and the pavement of the church, are thirteenth century Cosimati work. The frescoes

15

on the walls and roof of the apse tell the story of the saints, and are
the work of Giovanni di S. Giovanni Mannozzi.

There is a fragment of a Damasus inscription over the right stairs,
which refers not to the Quattro Incoronati, but to SS. Protus and
Hyacinthus.

*The road in front of the church leads to the* SQUARE OF THE
LATERAN, in which is the highest

### EGYPTIAN OBELISK

in Rome, which the inscription informs us was thirty-six years in
cutting. It was erected 1650 B.C., to Thothmes IV., at Thebes.

From Marcellinus (xvii. 4) we get many interesting details of its
voyage and erection :—

"And because the flatterers, who were continually whispering into
the ear of Constantine, kept always affirming that when Augustus
Octavianus had brought two obelisks from Heliopolis, a city of
Egypt, one of which was placed in the Circus Maximus, and the
other in the Campus Martius, he yet did not venture to touch or
move this one, which has just been brought to Rome, being alarmed
at the greatness of such a task,—I would have those who do not
know the truth learn that the ancient emperor, though he moved
several obelisks, left this one untouched because it was especially
dedicated to the sun-god, and was set up within the precincts of his
magnificent temple, which it was impious to profane, and of which
it was the most conspicuous ornament.

"But Constantine deeming that a consideration of no importance,
had it torn up from its place, and thinking rightly that he should
not be offering any insult to religion if he removed a splendid work
from some other temple to dedicate it to the gods at Rome, which is
the temple of the whole world, he let it lie on the ground for some
time while arrangements for its removal were being prepared. And
when it had been carried down the Nile, and landed at Alexandria,
a ship of burden hitherto unexampled, requiring three hundred
rowers to propel it, was built to receive it.

"And when these preparations were made, and after the afore-
named emperor had died, the enterprise began to cool. However,
after a time it was at last put on board ship, and conveyed over sea
and up the stream of the Tiber, which seemed as it were frightened
lest its own winding waters should hardly be equal to conveying a
present from the almost unknown Nile to the walls which itself
cherished. At last the obelisk reached the village of Alexandria,

three miles from the city, and then it was placed in a cradle, and drawn slowly on, and brought through the Ostia gate and the public fish-market to the Circus Maximus.

"The only work remaining to be done was to raise it, which was generally believed to be hardly if at all practicable. And vast beams having been raised on end in a most dangerous manner, so that they looked liked a grove of machines, long ropes of huge size were fastened to them, darkening the very sky with their density, as they formed a web of innumerable threads; and into them the great stone itself, covered over as it was with elements of writing, was bound, and gradually raised into the empty air, and long suspended, many thousands of men turning it round and round like a millstone, till it was at last placed in the middle of the square. On it was placed a brazen sphere, made brighter with plates of gold; and as that was immediately afterwards struck by lightning and destroyed, a brazen figure like a torch was placed on it, also plated with gold, to look as if the torch were fully lighted."

*Behind the houses on the left are the remains of*

## THE ARCHES OF NERO.

At the Porta Maggiore, Nero tapped the Claudian Aqueduct to bring the water to his reservoir on the Cœlian. His beautiful brick arches can be traced their whole length, and are of the finest brick-work in Rome—seven and a half bricks to the foot. "The Emperor Nero raised the Aqua Claudia to a great height on a series of arches extending to the Temple of Claudius, transferring the waters at the old Temple of Spes" (Frontinus, 30, 76).

*On our right of the obelisk is*

## THE BAPTISTERY,

said to have been founded by Constantine. Eight columns of porphyry support a cornice, upon which are eight smaller columns; these sustain the cupola. The font is of green basalt. The Baptistery was restored by several popes, and finally rebuilt by Urban VIII. and Innocent X. (1623–55), the three bees of the Barberini being introduced in the capitals of the columns. The eight sides of the cupola are frescoed with scenes from the life of S. John the Baptist, by Andrea Sacchi. The walls of the Baptistery illustrate in fresco the Life of Constantine, and are by G. Gemignani, Carlo Maratta, and Andrea Camassei. A tradition says Constantine was baptized here, though Socrates says he received

Christian baptism at Nicomedia just before his death. Gibbon says Rienzi bathed in the font on the night before he was made a knight. The two side chapels, dedicated respectively to John the Baptist and John the Evangelist, are said to have been made out of the house of Constantine. The mosaics are of the fifth century, after the arabesque paintings in the Baths of Titus. *Adjoining* is the Oratory of S. Venantius, in which is a mosaic of the seventh century—our Saviour in the act of giving his blessing. Two grand porphyry columns, supporting an entablature, formed the portico of the baptistery, opposite side to where we entered. There is a mosaic vault of the sixteenth century in the left chapel of this portico, and in the opposite one a good S. Philip Neri by Guido.

*On our left of the obelisk is*

## THE LATERAN PALACE.

From the time of Constantine to 1377 this was the palace of the popes. In 1843 Gregory XVI. founded the museum. The original palace was destroyed by fire in the time of Clement V., and the present pile was built from the designs of Fontana in the pontificate of Sixtus V. It was subsequently used for many years as an hospital. It now contains

## THE LATERAN MUSEUM.

*It is entered on the east front, and is opened every day, except Sundays and festivals, at 10 A.M. in the winter and 9 in the summer. Entrance, 1 lira each. Visitors will find it most convenient to turn to the left in entering, and first visit the Christian Museum (page 234), then the Antiquities.*

FIRST ROOM.—Bas-reliefs: Procession of Lictors and Senators, with figure of Trajan, found in his forum; Dares and Entellus, boxers, a fragment, found near the Arch of Gallienus; part of a sarcophagus, with the history of Mars and Rhea Sylvia, Diana and Endymion; a Circus Race; Helen and Paris; Soldier and Wife Parting; Leucothea feeding the Infant Bacchus. Bust of Marcus Aurelius; pavement mosaic of Boxers, from Baths of Caracalla.

SECOND ROOM.—Portions brought from the Forum of Trajan, representing arabesques, children, chimeras, griffins.

FOURTH ROOM.—Faun of Praxiteles, copy; bust of the Young Tiberius; bas-reliefs, Medea and Pelias's Daughters; statue of Mars; Germanicus; sepulchral cippi and bas-reliefs, found on the Via Appia.

FIFTH ROOM.—Stag in gray marble; a Cow; Mithraic group;

mutilated figure of a lynx; bust of Scipio; an altar with bas-reliefs, one representing cock-fighting.

SIXTH ROOM.—Statues of members of the family of Augustus, found at Cervetri, 1839: Drusus, Agrippina the elder, and Livia, full figures; Tiberius and Claudius, sitting; Germanicus and Britannicus, in armour; Head of Augustus. Inscriptions to the members of the family; a bas-relief of an altar; recumbent statues of Silenus.

SEVENTH ROOM.—Statue of Sophocles, the best object in the museum; a Dancing Faun; female draped figure; Apollino; sepulchral inscriptions, from the Columbaria of the Vigna Codini (see page 284), to Musicus Scuranus of Lyons, a tourist to Rome, who died there, with the names of the persons of his suite, on jamb of door.

EIGHTH ROOM.—Statue of Neptune; curious bas-reliefs, a man surrounded with masks; Cupid and Mars.

NINTH ROOM.—Fragments from the Forum.

TENTH ROOM.—Bas-reliefs from the tomb of the Aterii, representing a temple, with a crane moved by a tread-wheel for hoisting stones. *Opposite*, monuments in Rome, the Arch of Isis, Colosseum, Arch of Titus, and the Temple of Jupiter Stator. (See page 97.) Cupid and Dolphin.

ELEVENTH ROOM.—Bas-reliefs of Boxers; Diana Multimammæ.

TWELFTH ROOM.—Three large sarcophagi; Niobe and her Children; Orestes and the Furies; festoons and masks. A very interesting well-head, not unlike that represented on a denarius of Scribonus Lebo, and which stood in the Forum Romanum.

THIRTEENTH ROOM.—Busts of the Furia family, found on the Via Appia; statue by Dogmatius; alto-relief of Ulpia Epigoni; fragments of a colossal porphyry statue; two fluted spiral columns of pavonazzetto marble.

FOURTEENTH ROOM.—Unfinished statue of a captive barbarian, with the measuring points still in; mosaic masks, with the name of the artist, HERACLITUS, in Greek. On each side is a distinct mosaic representing an unswept floor after a banquet, such as Pliny (xxxvi. 60) ascribes to Sosus, " who laid, at Pergamus, the mosaic pavement known as the 'Asarotos Œcos,' from the fact that he there represented, in small squares of different colours, the remnants of a banquet lying upon the pavement, and other things which are usually swept away with the broom, they having all the appearance of being left there by accident." In a corner of this room is a terra-cotta siphon.

FIFTEENTH ROOM.—Objects found at Ostia, in the window-cases, between a mosaic niche of Silvanus and his dog. *Opposite* are, Agrippina; Head of Atys; Woman, unknown.

SIXTEENTH ROOM.—Fragments found at Ostia, in case in window; sepulchral urns; recumbent statue of Atys; leaden water-pipes. On the walls are frescoes: a pagan funeral banquet, time of Hadrian; Pluto carrying off Proserpine; Orpheus; Ops giving Saturn stones to swallow instead of his sons; a guinea-fowl and fruit. There is also a very beautiful bronze statuette of one of the Three Fates.

## THE CHRISTIAN MUSEUM.

Founded by Pius IX., and composed of Christian antiquities. There are many bas-reliefs, fragments, inscriptions, mosaics, &c., worthy of admiration.

ENTRANCE HALL.—A fine collection of early Christian reliefs, on the front of sarcophagi, illustrating Bible subjects, mostly from the life of our Lord. *At the top* is a sitting statue of S. Hippolitus, found near S. Lorenzo fuori le mura. On the chair is the Paschal Calendar in Greek, composed A.D. 223, and a list of Hippolitus's writings.

LANDING OF THE STAIRS.—Bas-relief of Elijah ascending to heaven. This hall is decorated with a number of sarcophagi of the early Christians, found in the early churches and catacombs. They are placed so as to illustrate how the tombs were situated in the vestibules of the Catacombs.

The CORRIDOR, *upstairs*, is decorated with Christian inscriptions from the Catacombs. The oldest is A.D. 238. They relate to persons, dogmas, rites, and ranks of the clergy of the early Christians.

From the end of the corridor on the left two rooms open out, ornamented with copies of frescoes found in the Catacombs.

*From the Loggia upstairs we enter the*

## PICTURE GALLERY.

FIRST ROOM, or Mosaic Hall.—This beautiful mosaic was found in the Baths of Caracalla, and represents full length figures and busts of boxers, each occupying a separate panel, some having the names upon them. The walls are decorated with scenes from the life of Constantine the Great.

SECOND ROOM.—Early medieval frescoes from old churches. Frescoes cut from the walls of the Church of S. Agnese fuori le mura. Paintings of prophets and birds, from the crypt of the Church of S. Nicolò in Carcere.

THIRD ROOM.— *We commence with the left-hand wall immediately on entering the different rooms.* Crowning the Madonna, by Lippi; S. Thomas receiving the Belt from the Virgin, by Benozoto Gozzoli; Scenes from Life of the Virgin, by the same; S. Antonio, by Antonio di Murano; Madonna, by Carlo Crivelli, 1482; Virgin and four Saints, by Bartolo di Murano, 1481; Assumption, SS. Lawrence and Benedict, Catherine and Gertrude—all three by Cola di Amatrice, 1515; S. Jerome, by Santis, *in tempera;* mosaic flooring from the Palazzo Sorra on the Via Nazionale.

FOURTH ROOM.—Holy Family, by Andrea del Sarto; Annunciation, by Francia; Virgin and Saints in fresco, by Botticelli; Crucifixion, a fresco; Baptism of Christ, by Cæsar da Sesto; a panel, by Perugino; copy of the Transfiguration; copy of Giulio Romano's Coronation; Deposition, by Luca Signorelli; S. Stephen, a sketch, by Giulio Romano.

*From here we enter into two off-rooms containing* statues, busts, and reliefs, representing North American Indian life, by Pettrich.

FIFTH ROOM.—Madonna of the Belt, by Spagna; the Virgin with S. John and S. Jerome, by Marko Palmezzano, 1500; three tapestries; S. Peter, by Fra Bartolomeo; Sixtus V., by Domenichino; S. Paul, by Bartolomeo; Madonna and Saints, by Palmezzano; Sixtus V. as Cardinal Peretti, by Sassoferrato; mythological subject, by Paul Veronese; a Pagan Sacrifice, by Caravaggio.

SIXTH ROOM.—Cartoons of Volterra; Annunciation, by Arpino; Christ and the Tribute Money, by Caravaggio; the Supper at Emmaus, by Caravaggio; copy of Guercino's Assumption, original in Russia: copy of Domenichino's S. Andrew; "The First Gentleman in Europe," by Lawrence; S. Thomas, by Cammuccini; a Head, by Vandyck.

SEVENTH ROOM.—Cartoons of Maratta's, for S. Peter's dome; a Greek Baptism, by Nocchi, 1840. The last room contains plaster casts of ancient statues.

*To the right, in issuing from the Museum, is the main entry to the church. The usual entry is by the portico at the west end.* The bronze statue on the left of the west portico is that of Henry of Navarre.

## S. GIOVANNI IN LATERANO.

"The mother and head of the churches of the city and of the world."

This church was founded by Constantine, and took the name of *Lateran* from its occupying the site of the Palace of Plautus Lateranus, the senator, who suffered under Nero. After having existed for ten centuries, it was almost entirely destroyed by fire in 1308. It was rebuilt by Clement V., and embellished by other popes. Clement XII. had the façade executed from the design of Galilei. It is of travertine,

with four large columns and six pilasters of the Composite order,
which support a cornice surmounted by a balustrade, on which are
placed colossal statues of Jesus and several saints. Between the
columns and the pilasters there are five balconies; that in the
middle was used for the papal benedictions. Beneath the balconies
are as many entrances, which lead into the magnificent covered
portico (*loggiato*), decorated with twenty-four pilasters of the Composite order. In this portico is placed the colossal statue of Constantine found in his baths. Notice the beautiful bronze doors which
came from the Senate House in the Forum.

*The interior* is divided into a nave and two aisles by four ranges
of pilasters. The architect was Borromini, who covered the ancient
columns which divide the middle aisles from the side ones with
pilasters, forming five arches, corresponding to an equal number of
chapels. Each of these pilasters is decorated, on the side of the
middle aisle, by two fluted pilasters, supporting a cornice which goes
round the church. Between these there are twelve niches, each
ornamented by two columns of verd-antique, containing the statues
of the apostles. The Corsini chapel, *first chapel on left of front entry*,
is one of the richest in Rome. It was executed by Clement XII.
from the design of Galilei, in honour of S. Andrew Corsini. The
porphyry sarcophagus of Clement XII. was brought from the portico
of the Pantheon, and is supposed to have contained the remains of
Agrippa. The subterranean chapel contains the remains of the
Corsini family. On the altar is the beautiful statue "Piety," said to
be by Bernini or Montanti.

This splendid church contains many chapels, decorated with
paintings and statues worthy of attention. On the second pier of
the right aisle is Giotto's Boniface VIII.

The Gothic Tabernacle above the high altar, containing the heads
of Paul and Peter, is a fine piece of workmanship of the fourteenth
century, restored by Pius IX. In front of the Confession is a bronze
tomb of Martin V., by Simone, Donatello's brother. Since 1876 the
transepts and the apse have been closed to the public; but on
Ascension day 1886, with grand religious ceremonies, they were
again thrown open to public view, *having been restored*. The frescoes
in the transept, representing scenes in the life of Constantine by artists
of the seventeenth century, have been touched up; the gold work
has been regilded, and the appearance of newness has been imparted
to the whole. At the end of the right transept, looking towards the
tribunal, is the grand organ and a banner captured from the Saracens.

The left transept contains the altar of the Sacrament by Paolo
Olivieri, the four gilt bronze columns being, it is said, from the
Temple of Jupiter Capitolinus, made by Augustus out of the beaks
of the fleet of Mark Antony and Cleopatra. Above the altar is the
finest fresco in the basilica, the Ascension by Arpino, 1600. To the
right is the Colonna chapel. The altar-piece is by Arpino, the roof
by Croce, whilst the portrait of Martin V. is by S. Gaetano. In the
recent restorations the old choir, tribunal, and the corridor of Leo I.,
440–61, which shrrounded it, have been destroyed, and a new one
erected sixty-seven feet longer than the old one—a very unnecessary
piece of work and vandalism. The church was quite large enough
for any ceremonies that take place in it. The whole praise of *this
restoration* is claimed by Leo XIII. ; but it is only just to Pius IX.
to record that he initiated and left money to continue the work,
although he is ignored in the laudations. In the four corners, above
the spring of the arches, are doctors of the Eastern and Roman
Churches—Ambrose, Augustine, Chrysostom, and Anastasius. On
the left, above organ, the Commission submitting the Plans to Leo
XIII. ; on the right, Innocent III. approving the Doctrine of Tran-
substantiation (1215)—both the work of Francesco Grandi. The
mosaic on the vault of the apse belonged to the old apse, and has
been considerably *restored* in moving it from one to the other. It is
the work of Jacopo da Turrita and Gaddo Gaddi (1292). At the top
is the Almighty's head surrounded by angels; from the Father pro-
ceeds the Holy Spirit (a dove) to the Cross (which represents the Son)
erected on the mountain from which flow the four rivers of paradise
round the heavenly Jerusalem, the gates of which are guarded by an
angel. Two harts and sheep drink of the waters ; saints are on either
side; the Virgin has her hand on the head of Nicholas IV., who had
the mosaic done. The apostles below, between the windows, are by
Jacopo di Camerino, of the same period. The base of the tribunal is
inlaid marble imitation cosimati work of the thirteenth century, as
is also the Bishop's Throne, reached by a flight of steps. The Bishop
of Rome takes his title from S. John's Lateran, hence this church has
precedence over all others. The Bishop of Rome is by right thereof
Papa, Pope, or Father of the Roman Church. Since the death of
the last bishop, Pius IX., February 20, 1878, the chair has been
vacant ; for some fanciful reason Leo XIII. has never taken possession of his bishopric.

*The Cloisters* of the twelfth century are interesting, and contain
many curious architectural remains.

Pope Leo XIII. has erected a monument to Innocent III.
(1198–1216), who excommunicated King John, at the right-hand
entry to the corridor that passes behind the apse.

*Passing out into the piazza at the front, on the right are*

## THE GATES.

PORTA S. GIOVANNI, opening on to the Via Nova Appia, *and near
by, to the right*, the walled-up ancient PORTA ASINARIA, *best seen
from the outside*, through which Belisarius entered Rome, and which
the Isaurian guard betrayed to Totila, December 17, 546. The open
we are now rambling over was anciently called the Mirror. *On the
left* is the end wall of the dining-hall of the ancient Palace of the
Lateran, on which is a copy of an ancient mosaic of the time of Leo
III. *In a building behind this is the* SCALA SANTA.

## BARRACKS OF THE EQUITES SINGULARES.

On the right of the Scala Santa, parallel with the Via Tasso, the
Barracks of the Equites Singulares, or Horse Guards of the Emperors,
of the time of Hadrian, were discovered in March 1886. A noble
hall 90 feet long, containing many inscriptions, raised by the dis-
charged veterans, was discovered : also fragments of statues, and one
nearly perfect of the youthful Bacchus, a work that we may class
with the school of Praxiteles.

## THE SCALA SANTA

consists of twenty-eight marble steps, which, it is supposed, our
Lord came down after his mock coronation in the judgment-hall of
Pilate. The blood from his bleeding brow marked certain of the
steps, and these are kissed by the ascending faithful, the knees of
whom so wore away the marble that it is now covered with a wooden
staircase, in which through slits the marble is seen. They are
said to have been brought from Jerusalem (where it formed the
stairs to Pilate's house) by the mother of Constantine. By ascending
these stairs on the knees, a thousand years' indulgence is secured to
those who believe it. Dickens said, " The sight was ridiculous in
the absurd incidents inseparable from it—to see one man with an
umbrella unlawfully hoist himself with it from stair to stair, and a de-
mure old lady of fifty-five, looking back every now and then to assure
herself that her legs were properly disposed." On the feast of the Assumption, the sacred picture " Acheirotopeton " (made without hands)
is exposed to view  This picture is said to have been drawn in outline

THE SCALA SANTA.

by S. Luke, and before he commenced to fill the colours in, it was found finished by invisible hands.

From the front of the church a charming prospect of the Campagna is obtained.

To the right of the stairs is the Kiss of Judas; on the left, Ecce Homo, by Giacometti. At the left of the hall, Christ Bound to the Pillar, *opposite* Pius IX.

Martin Luther had made the ascent half-way, when he suddenly stood up, turned about, and walked down. He said that a voice had whispered to him, "The just shall live by faith." The Sancta Sanctorum at the top is only open to the Pope, who alone can officiate, and on the day before Palm Sunday to the canons of the Lateran for adoration. The stairs can only be ascended on the knees. *Behind is*

### THE VILLA WOLKONSKY.

*Open on Wednesdays and Saturdays. Permission to be had at the various bankers.*

The grounds are tastefully laid out, and are intersected by the arches of Nero's aqueduct. From the roof of the casino, to which the gardener will conduct you (fee, half a franc), a beautiful view may be enjoyed at sunset, looking far away over the Campagna. In the grounds is the columbaria of the family of T. Claudius Vitalis, an architect.

*Returning, first turning on the left*, passing over the open space skirting under the walls, the curve is part of

### THE AMPHITHEATRUM CASTRENSE.
#### (*Amphitheatre of the Camp,*)

of the time of Caligula, A.D. 39, and incorporated by Aurelian into his wall. It is of beautiful brickwork; the columns, of the Corinthian order, are best seen from outside the wall. It was built near the camp, that the soldiers might have their games without going into the city and mixing with the people.

Suetonius ("Caligula," xxxi.) says, "He began an amphitheatre near the septa or barracks of the soldiers." Dion Cassius records, "That on one occasion, when the Emperor Caligula was in want of criminals for combats, he seized a number of citizens, and after tearing out their tongues that they might not complain, he had them brought into the arena, where they were compelled to fight."

*Adjoining is the*

### CHURCH OF S. CROCE IN GERUSALEMME,

erected by S. Helena. The interior has three aisles divided by pilasters, and with eight columns of Egyptian granite. The high altar is adorned by four columns of breccia-corallina, which support the canopy. Under the altar is an ancient urn, which contains the bodies of the holy martyrs Anastasio and Cesario. The frescoes of the vault of the tribune are by Pinturicchio. The subterranean chapel of S. Helena is decorated with paintings by Pomarancio, and with mosaics by B. Peruzzi. Ladies are not allowed to enter this chapel, except on the saint's day. The church was erected in

### THE SESSORIUM PALACE,

which was built by Sextus Varius, father of Elagabalus. This was afterwards turned into the Palace of Helena, near which were her baths, remains of which exist in the adjoining vineyards; also of the reservoir; which remains are called by some the TEMPLE OF VENUS AND CUPID, from a statue found there. A Venus with Cupid at her feet, supposed to be the likeness of Salustia Barbia Orbiana, the wife of Alexander Severus, from an inscription on the pedestal saying that it was dedicated to Venus by one Salustia.

In the "Excerpta Valesiana de Odae" (lxix.) it is mentioned as "the palace called Sessorium." In the buildings at the *back* of the church remains of a large palace can be traced. It is said by tradition that it took its name from a basilica which stood here where the cases of the slaves were tried. Another is, that here was the Prætorium or headquarters of the Prætorian prefect of the city. "It is said that Maximin, the prefect, had a small cord always suspended from a remote window of the Prætorium, the end of which had a loop which was easily drawn tight, by means of which he received secret information" (Marcellinus, xxviii. 7). The ruin to the left of the church has all the appearance of a basilica.

*Returning past the Lateran, a lane by the side of the Lateran Hospital, via* S. STEFANO ROTONDO, following the aqueduct, leads to the remarkable

### CHURCH OF S. STEFANO ROTONDO,

supposed to be formed from the remains of

### NERO'S MEAT-MARKET.

A coin representing this market agrees with the architecture of the church. "Then Nero celebrated a feast by way of thanksgiving for his preservation, and dedicated the market-place where meat is sold" (Dion Cassius).

The church is open all day on the 26th of December, being the saint's day. *On other days, ring the bell at the door on the right.* It is 133 feet in diameter. The outer circle consists of thirty-six columns, and the inner of twenty. There was originally another outer circle : this was destroyed, and the space between the columns of the second circle, present outer, filled in to make the walls of the church. In the centre two Corinthian columns support a cross wall. The tabernacle contains the relics of S. Stephen. The frescoes by Pomarancio on the walls, representing martyrdoms, are simply disgusting. In the vestibule is an ancient episcopal chair, from which S. Gregory read his fourth homily.

*Left from the church, and left again, we enter the* PIAZZA DI NAVICELLA.

*In the piazza* is a small marble ship, placed here by Leo X., near where it was found, this place having been the camp of the sailors. *The church opposite is that of*

## S. MARIA DELLA NAVICELLA,

or S. Maria in Dominica, only open on the second Sunday in Lent. It was restored by Leo X. from designs by Raphael. The Doric portico is by Michael Angelo. It has eighteen fine columns of gray granite. The mosaics in the tribune are of the ninth century. The frieze over the windows of the nave is by Giulio Romano and Pierino.

*To the right of the church* are remains of the Monastery of

## S. TOMMASO IN FORMIS,

founded by Innocent III. as the headquarters of the Trinitarians or Redemptorists, whose mission was to rescue blacks and whites from slavery. The mosaic by Cosmati, A.D. 1260, is the coat of arms of the order. Just beyond is a Gothic arch, part of their buildings. *Beyond this* the arch spanning the road is the

## ARCH OF DOLABELLA AND SILANUS.

Built of travertine, and erected, as the inscription informs us, by the above consuls, A.D. 10. It was used by Nero to support the aqueduct to his reservoir. Here is the hermitage of S. Giovanni di Matha, 1213, who founded the Redemptorists.

*Through the arch on the left is the entrance to (open Thursdays)*

## THE VILLA CŒLIMONTANA,

the residence of Baron Hoffmann, who kindly admits visitors on their leaving their cards at the iron gate. Many fragments of antiquity are spread about the grounds, from which there are some fine views. Remains have been found of a Roman fire-station of the fifth cohort of Vigili, whose names are on the pedestals dedicated by them to Marcus Aurelius.

## THE OBELISK

was erected by Duke Mattei, but only a very small part of it is Egyptian. The fragment was found in making the present sloping way up to the Capitol, and presented by the magistrates to the duke. It is the only one not re-erected by a pope. It is said that when the architect was directing its elevation, he forgot to take his hand off the pedestal, and that the block was lowered on his hand, which was amputated, the hand being left between the blocks.

At the corner of the grounds, towards the Baths of Caracalla, under a medieval building, is the FOUNTAIN OF EGERIA. (See page 275.)

*Opposite the entrance to the villa is the*

## CHURCH OF SS. GIOVANNI E PAOLO,

whence Cardinal Howard takes his title. It was erected in the fourth century on the site where the martyrdom of the above saints took place, by Pammachus, the friend of S. Jerome. They were officers of Constantine's household, and were put to death by Julian. The medieval portico is formed by eight marble and granite pillars. The aisles are formed by sixteen ancient columns; the pavement is of *opus Alexandrinum;* the stone surrounded by a railing is said to be that on which the martyrs suffered death. The outside of the medieval apse is rare.

The Passionist Fathers have recently cleared out several rooms of the house of the saints beneath the church, when frescoes of Christian subjects were found. The garden contains

## THE TEMPLE OF CLAUDIUS.

Seutonius tells us that Vespasian erected the Temple "of Claudius on the Cœlian Mount which had been begun by Agrippina, but almost entirely demolished by Nero."

Frontinus (xx. 76) tells us that the arches of Nero ended at the Temple of Claudius. Now we have been following these arches for some distance, and they end here.

*Below the temple was*

## THE VIVARIUM,

or menagerie for the Colosseum. The arches have been laterally
closed, leaving small apertures of communication. The vivarium consists of eight immense arches two stories high, formed from blocks of
travertine. The substructions occupy a large extent of the convent gardens. A massive portion supports the elegant medieval
campanile, of the thirteenth century, one of the best preserved
in Rome. *Beneath this* are some subterranean chambers hewn
out of the tufa, supposed to be

## THE SPOLIARIUM,

a prison for condemned gladiators. The younger Pliny says "it was
a cruel receptacle for those adjudged worthy of torture."

The gardens of the convent are built upon the top of

## THE RESERVOIR OF NERO.

Suetonius tells us "he made a reservoir like unto a sea," which no
doubt was afterwards used to supply the Colosseum with water for
the naval combats. The quadrata of the Cœlian is artificially
formed, and was evidently the great nymphæum connected with the
Golden House. The water was brought from the Claudian Aqueduct at the Porta Maggiore upon arches, known as Nero's Arches,
which ended near the Temple of Claudius, and these arches end
in the gardens now supported by the walls forming the quadrata.
The niches and hemicyclia on the east side, with their channels of
supply behind, were evidently fountains, and the west side was probably similar in character, some of the specuses still existing. The
front towards the Colosseum formed a grand cascade, the water falling
into the reservoirs, the ruins of which we see in advance of the
north wall of the quadrata, and at a lower level; from these it
poured into the great stagnum or lake below, now occupied by the
Colosseum. Signor Alberto Cassio found specuses all around the
top, and a curipus or channel at the base; and stalactites and *opus
signinum* can still be seen there.

*Turning to the right* we pass under some medieval arches—flying
buttresses—to support the church. *On the left* are some remains of
the house of Gregory; and, *on the right*, the wood of the Cœlian.
*This hill was the ancient Clivus Scauri. To the left* the steps lead
up to

### THE CHURCH OF S. GREGORIO,

whence Cardinal Manning took his title.  It is built on the site of the house of Gregory the Great, and was erected in the seventh century.  Its interior is embellished with sixteen granite columns.  The painting above the altar is by Sacchi, and the *predella* beneath by Luca Signorelli.  In a small side-chapel on the right is an ancient marble chair, and in a glass case numerous relics of various saints  *Crossing the atrium*, in which is a monument to Sir Edward Carne, envoy from Henry VIII., *we come to* the three detached chapels of—

S. SILVIA, which contains a beautiful fresco of the Father, with angels playing on instruments, by Guido Reni.  It is built on the site of the house of S. Gregory, remains of which can be seen behind the chapel.

S. ANDREW, containing the rival frescoes of Guido Reni and Domenichino—S. Andrew adoring the cross on his way to execution, and the Flagellation of S. Andrew.

S. BARBARA, containing the marble table on which S. Gregory feasted every morning twelve poor pilgrims.  On one occasion an angel is said to have honoured them with his presence.  The statue of the saint was begun by Michael Angelo, and finished by his pupil, Niccolo Cordieri.

Between the church and the chapels is a massive piece of tufa wall, supposed to have been part of the fortifications of the Cœlian Hill when it was a separate fortress.

### MUSEO URBINO.

In the wood in front of S. Gregorio, on the right going towards the Arch of Constantine, is the new City Museum, containing many objects of high historical interest; but at present it is simply used as a store.

# RAMBLE V.

## ON THE HILLS, EAST.

### THE PINCIO.

*From the Piazza del Popolo, a sloping, winding road leads up to* the favourite promenade of the Romans and Forestieri, who stroll and drive here every day, and listen to a military band by which the place is enlivened in the afternoons. *Ascending,* its terraces are interspersed with fountains and statues, and there is a fine large bas-relief on the wall opposite the two columnæ rostratæ adorned with the prows of ships. The name of the hill is derived from the Pincii family, whose estates were upon it towards the close of the empire. It was formerly known as the Hill of Gardens, from those of Lucullus, which passed to Valerius Asiaticus, and were coveted by Messalina. It abounds in walks and shady nooks, interspersed with fountains and the busts of Italia's great men. The side farthest from the city overlooks the Villa Borghese. At the extreme corner is a fragment of the old wall of Sylla—Muro Torto. From the terrace the scene below, in the piazza, is quite a study :—beyond is the winding Tiber and its round fortress of S. Angelo, the roof of the Pantheon, the columns of Aurelius and Trajan, the Capitol and Milizie Towers, and the Quirinal Palace; whilst between Monti Mario and the Janiculum is the world's cathedral, with its vast dome towering high above all : this dome is best seen at a distance, where the eye can embrace its full proportions, for immediate proximity dwarfs its immensity.

*In the centre of the grounds is*

### THE EGYPTIAN OBELISK,

which has on it the inscription ANTONINUS OSIRIS ORACLE (Utterer of truth). It was brought by Hadrian from Egypt, and erected by himself and his wife Sabina to his favourite Antinoüs, in the Varianus Circus, amidst which ruins, near S. Croce in Gerusalemme, outside the walls, it was found.

*Passing out of the grounds by the road that runs parallel to the city, on our left is*

### THE FRENCH ACADEMY,

or Villa Medici, *open every day from 8 till 12, and from 3 till dusk.* The gardens are tastefully laid out, and several fine views may be obtained from them. The MUSEUM OF CASTS (of statues not in Rome) will repay a visit.

*Proceeding up the avenue, just beyond, on the left, is the*

### CHURCH OF TRINITA DEI MONTI,

erected by Charles VIII. of France. Visitors should attend vespers here, the nuns singing choral service ; it commences half an hour before Ave Maria. Over the altar of the side-chapel, in entering, is a beautiful Descent from the Cross, the masterpiece of Daniele da Volterra.

### THE EGYPTIAN OBELISK

was found in the gardens of Sallust, and placed here by Pius VI. in 1789. It is 48 feet high without the pedestal, and is supposed to have been brought to Rome by Hadrian. It is thought by some to be only a copy of the original in Egypt. Marcellinus says it stood in the gardens of Sallust.

At No. 9 Piazza Trinità dei Monti, Poussin lived ; and Zuccari lived at 64 Via Sistina, close by. Beyond, the Via Cappo la Casa runs out to the right : adjoining the Church of S. Giuseppe is the New Museum of Industrial Art. Open every day from 9 till 3; fee, 50 centesimi. *By the Via Sistina we reach the*

## PIAZZA BARBERINI.

It has in the centre a beautiful fountain, by Bernini, with four dolphins supporting a shell, in which is a Triton ; it throws water to a great height. *Proceeding up the Via delle Quattro Fontane, on the left is the*

## BARBERINI GALLERY.

(*Palazzo Barberini.*)

*Open daily from 12 till 4. Catalogues are lent for the use of visitors.* It contains paintings by the first masters. The statue to Thorwaldsen, in the garden, was lately erected by Mr. Wolff, Thorwaldsen's pupil. The library is open from 9 till 2 on Thursdays.

FIRST ROOM.—Fresco on vault, Triumph of Glory, by Cortona ; 16. Joseph and Potiphar's Wife, by Beliverti ; 21. S. Cecilia, by Lanfranco.

SECOND ROOM.  48. Madonna, by Francia ; 63. His Daughter, by Raphael Mengs ; 74. Adam and Eve, by Domenichino.

THIRD ROOM.—73. The Slave, by Palma Vecchio ; 81. Portrait, called the Stepmother of Beatrice Cenci (?), by Caravaggio ; 82. The Fornarina, by Raphael ; 83. Lucrezia Cenci, the mother of Beatrice Cenci (?), by Scipione Gaetani ; 85. The so-called Beatrice Cenci, by Guido. This is nothing more or less than Guido's model, and the same face can be seen in the Aurora, and in the fresco at S. Gregory's. It could not possibly be Beatrice, for Guido did not come to Rome till sixteen years after her death. 86. Death of Germanicus, by Poussin ; 90. Holy Family, by Sarto.

The inscription on the right side of the palace records the campaign of Claudius in Britain.

*Proceeding up the* QUATTRO FONTANE, at the top of the hill are four river gods acting as fountains. The church at the left corner of Via del Quirinale is S. Carlo, its space being equal to the area of one of the piers which support the dome of S. Peter's. *Turning down this street, the church on the left is*

## S. ANDREW'S,

on the site of the Temple of Quirinus (Romulus). It contains the tomb of Emanuele IV. of Sardinia, who abdicated in 1802, and died a monk in 1818. The church is a little gem.

## ALTAR OF VULCAN.

Adjoining the church is the new palace of the Royal Household, in the cellar of which exists the Altar of Vulcan, discovered in 1888, and erected by Domitian, after 84, to ward off fire ; in commemoration of the fire of 64 under Nero. Sacrifice was to be made here every 23rd of August, and the area was to be kept open for ever. (See " Footsteps of St. Paul in Rome," page 57.)

*Permission to view it can be obtained of the Minister of the Royal Household, 30 Via del Quirinale. At the end of the street is the square*

## MONTE CAVALLO.

In the centre is a fountain, with granite basin 26 feet in diameter, which formerly stood in the Forum ; also two beautiful colossal horse-tamers in marble, supposed to be Castor and Pollux by some, by others, Alexander and Bucephalus. The Latin inscriptions state one of these colossi to be the work of Phidias, the other of Praxiteles. Both were presented to Nero by Tiridates, king of Armenia. They once ornamented the Baths of Constantine, and have never been buried. The whole is surmounted by an Egyptian obelisk found near the Mausoleum of Augustus. *On the left is the king's*

## QUIRINAL PALACE.

It numbers some splendid apartments, containing many works of art ; and the gardens are of considerable extent. It is the residence of King Humbert, and is accessible to the public ; but should the royal family be at home, the private apartments are not shown ; otherwise it may be readily viewed by permission of the minister. Guido Reni's beautiful picture of the Annunciation is in the small private chapel, as also the frescoes of the life of the Virgin, by Albani. The casino in the gardens is decorated with frescoes by Oritonti, Battoni, and Paolini. The palace was founded by Gregory XIII. in the year 1574, and completed by Clement X., several intermediate popes having done much for its extension and embellishment, notably Clement VIII. Urban VIII. enclosed and added the present garden, and Gregory XVI. and Pius IX. made the palace what it is—that is to say, one of the most sumptuous and attractive palaces in Italy. Few of our readers will require to be informed that the Quirinal was the place appointed for the conclave when the new Pope was elected, and that Pope Pius IX. was the last. *(Open Thursdays and Sundays, with permissions to be obtained of the Minister of the Royal Household, Via del Quirinale, at 11 a.m.) On the left, beyond the fountain, within the high wall, is the*

## ROSPIGLIOSI PALACE.

*Open Wednesdays and Saturdays 9 till 3; entrance upstairs to left of gate.*
It is celebrated for its casino, containing Guido Reni's Aurora ;

it also contains many pictures, ancient sculptures, and fragments of frescoes, from the Baths of Constantine, on a portion of the site of which it is built. The principal paintings in the palace are :—

CENTRE ROOM.—Head of Christ, by Jesse ; Vanity, by Titian ; Mater Doloroso, by Sassoferrato ; Guido's Aurora is on the roof.

LEFT ROOM.—Our Saviour Bearing the Cross, by Daniele da Volterra ; Head of Goliath, by Domenichino ; the Deposition, a sketch by Rubens ; Perseus Rescuing Andromeda, by Guido Reni.

RIGHT ROOM.—Diana and Venus, by Lawrence Lotto ; Adam and Eve, by Domenichino ; Samson's Death, by Caracci. *Opposite is the entrance to*

## THE COLONNA GARDENS.

They contain several antiques and remains of the cornice of Aurelian's Temple of the Sun, " in which he put a vast quantity of gold and precious stones " (Eutro. ix.). Under the cypress trees are several sarcophagi, and the stem of the pine tree planted on the day Rienzi died. There is also a fine' piece of the tufa wall that made the seven hills one city.

## THE CAPITOLIUM VETUS.

*To the right from the gardens, the* VIA QUIRINALE brings us to the new Via Nazionale. Where this winds round is a piece of a wall of the kings. Plutarch (" Numa," xiv.) and Solinus (i. 21) tell us that Numa lived upon the Quirinal, where he built an arx (Hieron. i. 298), called, after the Capitoline Hill was so named, CAPITOLIUM VETUS. In it was a temple to Jupiter (Varro, " L. L." v. ; Martial, v. 22). In those days a tongue jutted out here towards the Capitoline Hill, and this piece of wall bars the way to it, so it is probably a piece of the arx that defended the tongue. The lofty brick tower is

## THE TORRE DELLE MILIZIE,

within the precincts of the Convent of S. Caterina di Siena, supposed to have been built upon a cella formerly occupied by Trajan's soldiers. This tower is called by the Roman *valets de place* " Nero's Tower," from his having sat there and fiddled whilst Rome was burning. Now, as this tower was built in 1210 by Pandolfo della Subura, the senator, it could not have been the tower Nero fiddled on. Besides, Suetonius says, "This fire he [Nero] beheld from a tower in the house of Mæcenas," which was on the Esquiline, where remains have been recently found.

The VIA PANISPERNA, *to the left*, descends into the valley between the Quirinal and Viminal hills. In the valley *to the left* of the street is

### THE CHURCH OF S. AGATA IN SUBURRA,

where the heart of O'Connell is deposited. *Keeping straight on, up the slope of the Viminal*, VIA PANISPERNA, at the top of the hill is

### THE CHURCH OF S. LORENZO,

who is said to have been martyred under Claudius II., A.D. 269, having been cooked to death on a gridiron. Here are also the relics of S. Crispin and S. Crispinian. The church is on the site of the baths of the daughter-in-law of Constantine, Olympia. The two seated statues, Menander and Posidippus, in the Vatican, were found here, and were for a long time worshipped as saints.

*In the Via Urbana is the* CHURCH OF S. LORENZO IN FONTE, said to be over the site of the prison of S. Lawrence, and a fountain is shown where he baptized his converts.

*Descending* the slope of the Viminal, we strike the VIA URBANA, on the line of the ancient VICUS PATRICIUS.

*Proceeding up the Via Urbana, on the left is the*

### HOUSE OF PUDENS.

*(S. Pudenziana.)*

The church stands back from the street, with a handsome new front, restored by Cardinal Buonaparte. Cardinal Wiseman was titular cardinal of this church. *It is only open at a very early hour —on May 19th all day, and on the third Tuesday in Lent. The custodian is to be found at 161, next door to the church.* A flight of steps leads down to the church. The door is formed with ancient spiral columns, and eighth century Christian reliefs; above are some modern frescoes of Peter, Pudens, Pudentiana, and Praxedes. There is a picturesque campanile.

The present church was formed out of the great hall of the Baths of Novatus after A.D. 108; the baths being erected in the time of Domitian adjoining the house of Pudens, who founded in his house a Christian oratory before A.D. 96. This oratory exists below the present church, which was formed by Bishop Pius, who died in A.D. 157. The church below is the oldest Christian church in the world, and existed in the time of S. Paul, who, writing to the Romans (xvi. 13), says, "Salute Rufus chosen in the Lord, and his mother and mine." This Rufus was Aulus Rufus Pudens, who held an official position in the southern province of Britain, and married Gladys (Claudia), the daughter of Caractacus, the British chief. He

was likewise half-brother of S. Paul, and the friend of Martial the
poet. The apostle, writing to Timothy from Rome (2 Tim. iv. 21),
says, " Eubulus greeteth thee, and Pudens, and Linus, and Claudia,
and all the brethren." Linus was the second son of Caractacus, and
was the first bishop of the Church of Rome ordained by Paul.

From Cyllinus, the eldest son of Caractacus, descended Constantine
the Great, born and bred, and proclaimed emperor, in Britain. Thus
the first Bishop of Rome and the first Christian emperor were
undoubtedly Britons of royal British blood.

In the tribune of the church is a beautiful mosaic of the time
of Adrian I., A.D. 772–795, who built the apse inside the wall
of the large hall. The old wall can be seen on the outside, the
mosaic representing our Saviour on a throne, with four of the
apostles on each side, and Pudentia and Praxedes behind ; the
paintings above are by Pomarancio. In the left aisle is a well,
containing, it is said, remains of the martyrs—some remains are
shown. At the end of this aisle is the chapel of S. Peter ; the
mosaic pavement belonged to the baths. On the left is a copy of
the inscription from the catacomb of S. Priscilla : " BENE MERENTI
CORNELLÆ PUDENZIANÆ." Under the altar is a sponge said to have
been used by the two sisters to collect the blood of the martyrs.
Above is a relief, by Giacomo della Porta, of Peter receiving the
keys from Christ. On the left of this aisle opens the Chapel of the
Gaetani—rich in marbles. The roof is in mosaic, representing the
four Evangelists, and over the door are representations of the sisters
Pudentia and Praxedes collecting the blood of martyrs. They are
by Rossetti, designed by F. Zuccari (1600). The altar-piece, by
Paolo Olivieri, is the Adoration of the Magi. *For a more detailed
account of this interesting church, see our* " Footsteps of St. Paul
in Rome."

At the junction of the new Via Cavour and the Giovanni Lanza,
the Via di S. Lucia in Selci goes off at an angle to the right. Here was

## THE SCENE OF TULLIA'S IMPIETY.

With our face towards the angle, it will be noticed that the Via
S. Lucia divides the Esquiline Hill into two spurs : that on our
*left* was called the CISPIUS, that on our *right* the ORPIUS. The Via
Leonina Suburra, at our back, was the ancient Vicus Cyprius ; the
point of the angle being its summit ; the Via S. Lucia was the Clivus
Urbius. Up this latter street, on the right, an ascent, the ancient
Clivus Pullius, leads to S. Martino a Monti. "Tarquinius Superbus

lived on the Esquiline, above the Clivus Pullius, at the Fagutal Grove." "Servius Tullius lived above the Clivus Urbius"(Solinus, i. 25).

Having thus fixed the topography, we shall see how Livy's account of the murder and impiety (i. 48) agrees with it. "Servius Tullius had arrived at the top of the Vicus Cyprius, when he was overtaken and slain by some sent after him by Tarquinius. Tullia, in returning home from the Forum, had arrived at the top of the Vicus Cyprius, where the Temple of Diana lately stood. She was just *turning to the right* to ascend the Clivus Urbius, which led to the top of the Esquiline Hill, when the charioteer stopped and showed her her father's dead body lying across the street; but she bade him drive over the dead body, and arrived home bespattered with her father's blood. From this unnatural deed the name of the street was changed to Vicus Sceleratus, the wicked street." (See Dionysius iv. 39.)

*From here follow the Via Cavour, turn to the right up the* VIA S. MARIA MAGGIORE *to the church, which we enter at the back, and pass through*

## THE CHURCH OF S. MARIA MAGGIORE.

In the foreground is an Egyptian obelisk 63 feet high. The church was founded A.D. 352. It is 120 yards long by 50 wide. Its columns are of the Ionic and Corinthian orders. The interior is of three aisles, and has thirty-six Ionian columns of white marble, from the Villa of Hadrian at Tivoli. The high altar is formed of a large urn of porphyry, covered by a slab of marble, which is supported by four angels in gilt bronze. The canopy, erected by Benedict XIV., is supported by four columns of porphyry, surrounded by gilt palms. The four angels in marble were sculptured by P. Bracci. Under the high altar is the beautiful Confession, done by Vespignani, by order of Pius IX., in 1863, in which is preserved the relic of the cradle of the Saviour, and the bodies of S. Matthew and other saints. Here the late Pope was to be buried; but he would not allow his successor to ask leave of the Italian government, burial inside the walls being prohibited, and in his will he directed that his body should be interred in S. Lorenzo outside the walls. The monument is by Jacometti.

The mosaic pictures over the arches on each side are of the fifth century—a long series of panels of Scripture subjects, the historical books of the Old Testament.

The Arch of Triumph over the altar is of the same period. Those on the vault of the tribune are of the thirteenth century. On the

BASILICA OF S. MARIA MAGGIORE.

loggia, over the front entrance, is another very fine mosaic picture of the fourteenth century. *On the left of the high altar is the*

## BORGHESE CHAPEL.

The altar-piece is of jasper; the painting of the Virgin and Child is said to be by S. Luke. Above is the bronze bas-relief representing the miracle of the snow which fell in August A.D. 352 upon the exact space occupied by the basilica. The frescoes are by Guido, Lanfranco, Arpino, and Cigoli.

The monuments of Paul V. and Clement VIII. are composed of beautiful bas-reliefs representing scenes in their lives.

*Opposite is the*
## SIXTINE CHAPEL,

erected by, and containing the tomb of, Sixtus V. It was lately restored by Pius IX., who was to have had his temporary resting-place here, behind the altar. The altar is a representation of the tomb of our Saviour at Jerusalem, and is a splendid piece of workmanship. Beneath it is preserved part of the manger. Opposite the lower altar is a statue of S. Gaetano, by Bernini. The frescoes of the dome, representing the hosts of heaven, are beautifully executed by Podesti. The monument to Sixtus V. is by Valsoldo; that to Pius V. by L. de Sarzana. The bas-reliefs represent historical subjects of the two pontificates.

*Leaving the church by the end opposite to that by which we entered,* we find ourselves in the piazza, which contains a handsome column, taken from the Basilica of Constantine by Paul V. It is surmounted by a figure in bronze representing the Virgin. The column is forty-seven feet high, without the base and capital. *On the left of the church is the*

## COLUMN OF HENRY IV.

In 1873 the column of an inverted cannon, which stood in front of the Church of S. Antonio Abate, erected in 1596 to commemorate the reconciliation of Henry IV. of France to Clement VIII., was removed in altering the level of the road. At the time of its removal, a majolica vase was discovered under the base, which on being lately opened was found to contain a large brass medal, bearing the following inscription :—

IN HONOREM PASSIONIS D. N. JESU CHRISTI ET B. V. MARIÆ AC S. ANTOINI ET OMNIUM SANCTORUM, REVERENDUS DOMINUS.

Carolus Anison Galeus, preceptor generalis preceptoriæ ejusdem S. Antoini prope Albam, terram Petragoricensis Dioceseos et Vicarius in Prioratu S. Antoini de urbe suis propriis expensis posuit. Sedente S<sup>mo</sup> domino nostro Clemente VIII. Pont. Opt. Max. anno domini MDXCVI.

The column has now been re-erected, but not inverted, on the east side of S. Maria Maggiore, and the vase and its coin re-interred beneath it.

It appears that Louis XIV. caused the original inscription on the base of the column to be removed, and this has lately been found in the convent of S. Antony, recording that the column was erected in memory of the Christian absolution of Henry the Fourth of France and Navarre.

*In front of S. Maria Maggiore, on the right, Via S. Prassede, is*

## THE CHURCH OF S. PRAXEDES,

erected in 823 by Paschal I., and restored by Nicholas V. in 1450, and more lately by Carlo Borromeo. The main entry from the Via di S. Martino, consisting of the original portico, sustained by two granite Ionic columns, is seldom open. The entrance in use is on the side from the Via S. Praxedes. Sixteen granite columns, with composite capitals, divide the nave from the aisles. Double flights of steps of *rosso antico* lead up to the tribune. On each side of the altar, over choir gallery, are remarkable columns of white marble, with foliage ornaments. In the middle of the nave is a so-called well, in which Praxedes is said to have collected the remains of martyrs.

The Mosaics are a striking feature of this church. They belong to the time of Pope Paschal I., and, like those in S. Cecilia and S. Maria in Navicella, are interesting as illustrating the low depth to which this art had sunk in Rome at that period.

On the tribunal, our Lord stands on a mound, from which issues the river of life, JORDANES. On his left are S. Paul, S. Pudentiana, and S. Zeno; on his right S. Peter, S. Praxedes, and Paschal, the last carrying a model of the church which he built. He has a square nimbus, which shows that he was alive when the mosaic was executed. Beneath is a lamb with a nimbus, and with six sheep on either side, representing Christ and his apostles; at the extremities, Bethlehem and Jerusalem. Below is the inscription:—

*" This holy fabric shines decorated with varied metals in honour of Praxedes, pleasing to our Lord above the heavens, by the care of the Sovereign Pontiff Paschal, nursling of the apostolic chair; who, burying many bodies of saints, puts them under these walls, that by the benefit of their prayers he may merit to enter the gates of heaven."*

The oil painting of Praxedes is by Maria Dominico Muratori of Bologna. On the vault of the arch are flowers growing from two pots, and in the centre the monogram of Paschal. On the face of the tribunal are, in the centre of the arch, the Lamb, with three candlesticks on one side and four on the other, allegorical of the seven mysteries; on either side angels and the emblematical figures of the four apostles; then the four and twenty elders casting down their golden crowns, as at St. Paul's. These mosaics are evidently copied from those at SS. Cosmo and Damiano. On the face of the Arch of Triumph is the vision of S. John—our Saviour, with angels, Pudentiana, Praxedes, and the apostles, within the walls of the heavenly Jerusalem, the gates of which are guarded by angels. Other angels approach leading groups of the faithful, below whom are the martyrs with their palms. On the vault of this arch are mosaics similar to those of the tribunal.

The sacristy in the right aisle contains a Crucifixion by the Florentine artist Augustino Campelli, 1581, and a Flagellation by Giulio Romano. The second chapel contains Christ Bearing the Cross, by F. Zucchero, and on the roof the Ascension, Prophets and Sibyls, by D'Arpino. The next chapel has pictures from the life of Carlo Borromeo, and his chair and table. By the main door is a slab of *nero-bianco* granite, on which S. Praxedes is said to have slept. The second chapel on the right, coming up, contains the Eternal Father, by Borgognone, and a Deposition, by Vecchi. The next is the

CHAPEL OF S. ZENO. Two columns of rare gray porphyry support the sculptured frieze of the doorway, above which are mosaics of heads in two rows: top row, Christ and the Apostles; second row, Virgin and Child, with members of the family of Pudens. Over the altar is a piece of a column, in black and white marble, said to be that to which Jesus was tied at his flagellation. The mosaic on the roof represents the Saviour supported by four angels. Over the altar is a Virgin and Infant, with Pudentiana and Praxedes. Opposite is the Lamb on a Rock, from which flows a stream, with four harts drinking. Opposite the entrance is S. John the Baptist and the Virgin. On the left are SS. Agnes, Pudentiana, and Praxedes, and over the door the throne of God, with SS. Peter and Paul. On the right are James, Andrew, and John. Ladies are forbidden to enter this chapel, under pain of excommunication, except on the first Sunday in Lent, and on Palm Sunday.

The adjoining chapel contains the tomb of Cardinal Cetivej, 1474, on which is his recumbent statue, with reliefs of Paul, Peter, Pudentiana, and Praxedes. The Flagellation is by Francesco Guidi. The chapel at the end contains the reclining figure of the French Cardinal Anchera, 1286 ; signed *Christianus Magister fecit*.

In the crypt, beneath the high altar, are some fourth century Christian sarcophagi, said to contain Pudentiana, Praxedes, and others ; also a beautiful cosimati altar and a ninth century fresco of the Madonna and Child.

The custodian will here tell you that there is a subterranean communication between this crypt and the Catacombs, but that it is now walled up. This passage exists only in his fertile imagination ; the Catacombs *do not* communicate with any of the churches in Rome.

The first floor of the tower contains remains of a fresco, time of Paschal, illustrating the life of S. Anne.

## ALTAR OF MERCURY.

At the junction of the Via S. Martino di Monti with the Via Giovanni Lanza, *on the right side*, an altar of the Lares Compitales was discovered in April 1888, where it was placed in 9 B.C. by the Emperor Augustus, marking the junction of the Clivus Urbius with the Clivus Pullius. It stands on the ancient paved area.

*The Via Giovanni Lanza, on the right of the Via Meruluna, contains*

## A ROMAN VILLA,

discovered on the right in forming this street in 1884-5. Considerable remains of a nymphaeum were found, and a beautiful aedicula, with its statues *in situ ;* from this some steps led down into a Mithraic cave. As soon as the building going on here is finished, these remains will be opened to the public.

## PRIMITIVE TOMBS.

Not the least interesting discovery in this neighbourhood was that of a number of primitive tombs formed with local stone, shaped like the Campagna huts. It is curious that after upwards of two thousand five hundred years of burial, the remains of the early inhabitants of the Palatine, Cœlian, and Quirinal hills, should be brought to light on the Esquiline, which was the burial-ground till the days of Mæcenas, and be another confirmation of the truth of early Roman history.

## MEDIEVAL TOWERS.

At the corner of the Via Quattro Cantoni is the Tor Cantarelli ; and at the top of the Via in Selci, *on the left*, is the now isolated

Torre di Pandulphus, called by the people here Nero's Tower. The Via in Selci, the ancient Vicus Sceleratus, came up between the Oppius and Cispius heights of the Esquiline, these medieval towers guarding the approach. Both were built by Pandulph de Subura in 1250.

*From the tall tower a lane leads up to*

## THE CHURCH OF S. MARTINO,

which was erected by Symmachus, A.D. 500, on the site of the Church of S. Silvester, in the time of Constantine. The nave is formed by twenty-four ancient columns, said to have come from Hadrian's Villa. The Confession, beneath the high altar, leads to the more ancient church formed out of part of the Baths of Hadrian. It was here that the Councils of A.D. 352–356 were held, when the acts of the Council of Nicæa were condemned and burned. The landscape frescoes in the upper church are by the brothers Poussin.

*From here we can best visit (No. 10 up the lane, turn round to the left)*

## THE SETTE SALE,

which was a reservoir for the Colosseum. It consists of nine parallel chambers, communicating with each other by arches placed obliquely, to prevent the pressure of the water on the walls. Between this and S. Maria Maggiore was found the Laocoon, now in the Vatican, by Felix de Freddis, as we are informed by the inscription on his tomb in the Church of Ara Cœli. It was found in 1506, in the same niche where Pliny tells us it was admired in his time.

*Returning down the lane into the Via Merulana, turn right. Upon our left were*

## THE GARDENS OF MÆCENAS,

which, we learn from various ancient authors, were situated on the Esquiline. Horace, speaking of them, says : "Now it is possible to live on the Esquiline, for it is a healthy spot, especially to wander on the sunny agger." Suetonius, speaking of the great fire in Nero's time : "This fire he [Nero] beheld from a tower in the house of Mæcenas on the Esquiline." "Here was a common burying-place for wretched paupers" (Horace). Hence it must have been outside the Wall or agger of Servius Tullius, remains of which have been found on the left-hand side of the road leading from S. Maria Maggiore to S. Giovanni in Laterano. Close to this part, and inside the agger, a chamber has been excavated, evidently

### THE AUDITORIUM,

or lecture-hall of Mæcenas, the entrance being formed through the agger. It is **24** metres **40** centimetres long, by **10** metres **60** centimetres broad. The wall supporting the roof, in which was the window, is nearly eight metres high. On each side of the hall the walls contain six niches decorated in the Pompeian style. At the farther end of the hall is a sort of tribune composed of seven circular steps in tiers, once faced with marble. From here the author recited. In the circular wall behind these, which forms the end of the hall, are five more niches. The floor is below the surrounding level, probably to keep the building cool during the summer months. Its height was about forty feet.

It may be that in this auditorium Virgil read his "Georgics" to Mæcenas, as he says,—

> "I sing, Mæcenas, and I sing to thee....
> O thou ! the better part of my renown,
> Inspire thy poet, and thy poem crown ;
> Without thee, nothing lofty can I sing."

Or Horace, his Odes recited to Mæcenas' praise,—

> "You that are both my shield and glory dear."

The auditorium now serves as a local museum. It is open every Thursday from 9 till 11 and 3 till 5. *Permissions* must be obtained at the Archæological Office at the Capitol.

*From the Via dello Statuto, the Via Pellegrino Rossi takes us to*

### THE ARCH OF GALLIENUS,

erected in 262 in honour of the emperor, by Marcus Aurelius Victor. It is plain and unadorned, and only the central arch is preserved.

*Passing under the arch, turn to the left*, there are some remains of the agger. *Beyond, on the opposite side of the street, is*

### THE CHURCH OF S. ANTONIO ABBATE,

where the animals are blessed on January 17th. The round doorway is the only one of its sort in Rome.

*To the right we reach the new Piazza Vittorio Emanuele. On our left is*

### THE NYMPHÆUM

of Alexander Severus, called the Trophies of Marius. It derives this appellation from the marble trophies formerly placed in the two side niches, and thence transferred to the parapet of the flight of steps leading up to the Capitol. This splendidly decorated reservoir was the nymphæum of the Emperor Alexander Severus, and is represented on a coin. It was to the Aqua Julia what the Trevi Fountain is to the Aqua Virgo. A portion of the aqueduct which supplied the water is still standing.

*The Via Principe Eugenio, in the left corner of the square, takes us to*

## THE BATHS OF GALLIENUS,

miscalled the Temple of Minerva Medica, from a statue of the goddess discovered here. It is a circular building, 80 feet in diameter, and its walls contain numerous niches for statues ; it was surmounted by a lofty cupola, which fell in a short time ago. This building was no doubt the sudatorium of the Baths of Gallienus, which stood in his gardens and occupied this ground. In the fragments of chambers adjoining, terra-cotta pipes for the supply of hot water may still be seen.

*The Viale Principessa Margherita from here leads to*

## THE CHURCH OF S. BIBIANA,

built in commemoration of her martyrdom. At the early age of eighteen, during the prefecture of Apronianus, she was first scourged, and then stoned to death. The church contains eight antique columns, and frescoes from the saint's life by Cortona and Ciampelli. Her statue at the high altar is the work of Bernini, and is considered to be his masterpiece. The *fête* of S. Bibiana is the S. Swithin's day of the Romans, who have a saying that "if it rain on this day it will continue to do so for the next forty." We are not superstitious, but we cannot help wishing that the saint will smile upon us. The Church of S. Bibiana was built in the fifth century, on the site of the house where the virgin-martyr is believed to have lived. It was in a great measure rebuilt by Pope Urban VII., and is open only on the Friday after the fourth Sunday in Lent, and on the 2nd of December, the anniversary of the saint.

*Proceeding up the Viale Margherita,* on the left are some arches of the Julia Aqueduct ; beyond, the Via Rattazzi, on the left, leads into the Piazza Manfredo Fanti, in which is the Roman Aquarium and the portion of a tower in the agger of Servius Tullius, covered with masons' marks.

*Returning to the Viale Margherita,* we reach the railway station, in front of which is the Piazza dei Cinquecento, in which is

17

## THE EGYPTIAN OBELISK,

found in 1882 amidst the ruins of the Temple of Isis and Serapis in the Campus Martius. It is nineteen and a half feet high, and has been erected upon a modern base as a monument to the Italian soldiers killed by the Abyssinians at Dogali in January 1887. It commemorates the Pharaoh Ramses II., 1495 B.C., and was brought to Rome by Domitian from Heliopolis.

The hieroglyphics on the four sides are similar. We translate one side, so that our readers may get an idea of the " wisdom of the Egyptians :"—

"The Gold God, sovereign of the south and north ; strong bull, loved by the God Ra, King of Upper and Lower Egypt ; Ranser-masotepeura, son of the God Ra ; Ramses, loved by Ammon, who multiplies the offerings in Heliopolis, the seat of splendour ; Lord of the diadems ; Ramses, loved by Ammon, loved by the God Tum, Lord of Heliopolis."

*To the right is the Piazza Macao. Behind the Custom-House, entered from the Via Porta S. Lorenzo, is a fine piece of the Servian wall and its Porta Viminalis. The Via Solferino, Piazza Indipendenza, and Via S. Martino, lead to*

## THE PRÆTORIAN CAMP,

founded by Sejanus, the minister of Tiberius Cæsar, and destroyed by Constantine. The walls consist of brick-work, and have corridors on the inside, decorated with stucco and paintings. The camp was between the Portæ Viminalis and Nomentana, and forms a square projection in the present wall. It was outside the agger of Servius Tullius. The north wall is of the time of Tiberius ; the east was rebuilt in the fourth century ; the south has been reconstructed out of old square stones, probably material taken from the west or city wall (which has never been found), or from fragments of the agger of Servius Tullius. To write the history of the Prætorian Camp would be equivalent to writing the history of Rome from Tiberius to Constantine. Here murderers were made emperors, and the empire put up to auction. Hence the Prætorians sallied out to attack the citizens, who in their turn assailed the camp. Here the guilty found asylum, and the innocent death. *Near the camp stood*

## THE TEMPLE OF FORTUNA PRIMIGENIA.

Its site is now occupied by the Piazza del Macao. Fragments of the temple were found in August 1873, and an inscription to the goddess ; also the statue of a female member of the Claudian family.

"Quintus Marcius Ralla, constituted commissioner for the purpose, dedicated the Temple of Fortuna Primigenia on the Quirinal Hill. Publius Sempronius Sophus had vowed this temple ten years before, in the Punic War, and, being afterwards censor, had employed persons to build it," A.U.C. 558 (Livy, xxxiv. 53).

The remains can be seen (*on the right in returning towards the station*) by the Caffe and Aqua Marcia Reservoir. Beyond is the Piazza di Termini, a pleasant garden with a marcia fountain. At the top of the Via Nazionale the water company have recently erected a fountain, which has a fine display of water, and presented it to the city.

*On the right, entered through the court of the asylum, No. 15 is the entry to the new*

### NATIONAL MUSEUM

(*open daily from 9 to 1 ; fee, one lira*), formed by the Government in the cloisters of Michael Angelo, and in some of the upstairs rooms of the late Carthusian monastery. *The stairs are on the right of the entry to the cloisters.*

FIRST ROOM.—Remains from the tomb of Sulpicius Platorinus, found April 1881, just over the Ponte Sisto, on the right bank of the Tiber. It is of the time of Hadrian. The statue is that of his wife Capionia.

SECOND ROOM.—The black Hermes Canefora were found on the Clivus Victoria of the Palatine. Bronze statue of Meleager, by Lysippus, found in the Baths of Constantine in 1885. It originally had a cloak over the left shoulder. It is seven feet five inches high. The bronze fragments are part of the statue of the Emperor Valentinian, fished up from the river at the Ponte Sisto in 1878. Seated Bronze Boxer, by Naukeros, found near the Meleager in building the dramatic theatre. The cestii, bound round the hands, are loaded to give weight to the blow. It is four feet four inches high.

THIRD ROOM.—Bronze head of Tiberius. Cupid in basalt, from the Palace of Caligula. Youthful Bacchus, in bronze, after Praxiteles. A bronze coin is fused into the left leg, but it is impossible to decipher it. Found in the Tiber in making the Ponte Garibaldi, 1885.

FOURTH ROOM.—Stucco vaulting from the house of the priestess of Isis, Farnesina gardens, 1879.

FIFTH ROOM.—Fragment of an athlete found near Subiaco. A case of glass vases and terra-cotta anatomical studies. Apollo the

Ægis-bearer, so called from the cloak of Jupiter which was forged by Vulcan, scale-like, Villa of Hadrian. Head of the Sleeping Ariadne.

CABINET.—Hermaphroditus, a copy of the bronze, by Polycles, found in building the Costanzi theatre.

ROOM OF THE VESTALS.—These are objects brought from the Atrium Vestæ, near the Forum. The principal is the upper half of the statue of the high vestal who ruled the order at the time of the rededication of the temple by Julia Pia, and who died in 201. The pedestal in the house of the vestals reads—PRÆTEXTATÆ . CRASSI . FIL . V . V . MAXIMÆ . C . JULIUS . CRETICUS . A . SACRIS. There are several busts in the room—Marcus Aurelius, Lucius Verus, Caracalla, Marcus Aurelius as a boy. A case contains Anglo-Saxon coins of Alfred the Great, Edward I., Athelstan, Edmund I., and a buckle of Marinus III., Pope 942-46—probably money of some emissary from the Saxon to the Papal court. *Proceeding downstairs.*

WEST CLOISTER : *up the centre.*—Busts of Persius, Claudius veiled, and Nero ; Seneca, Antonia. Fragment of Venus Genetrix, after Arcesilaus. Ceres, by Praxiteles—the head unfortunately is missing ; found in the Stadium of the Palatine in 1878. Minerva, a fragment from the Tiber. Head of Apollo, from the Palatine. Head of Septimius Severus.

*Left-hand wall.*—A set of beautiful frescoes, from the house of the priestess of Isis, found in 1879, with the stuccoes in fourth room upstairs. They are of the time of Augustus, and amongst the most beautiful specimens of Greek fresco art remaining to us. *Note—* 3,156. Two graceful seated figures. B 5. A female seated on a throne, with an attendant behind, both of whom are looking at a winged Love, who is stepping up to the throne. B 4. Two figures are playing musical instruments. Ino nursing Bacchus. Seated figure with a lyre, with female offering her a sprig. Next, a set of frescoes found in 1875 at the tomb of Statilius Taurus, near the Porta Maggiore. 20. Rhea Sylvia compelled to become a vestal, and her story till condemned. 21. Building of Alba Longa. Duel between Æneas and Turnus. Fight between Trojans and Rutili. 22. Fight between Latins and Rutili. Building of Lanuvium. 10. The story of Romulus and Remus being placed in the Almo. Romulus and Remus guarding their flocks ; exquisitely executed.

*End wall.*—Mosaic of hippopotamus hunting, found on the Aventine in 1852. *Left wall in returning.*—Mosaics : the four colours of the circus. Ganymedes. Muses. Apollo and Marsyas, Diana and Victory. Cupid, Pan, and Silenus. Victory, in a diamond panel, veiled. Victory with trophy. Winged Fortune (at the corners are masks), from the Villa Rufinella at Frascati, found with the Minerva of the Hall of the Greek Cross in the Vatican. Pouring an oblation. Serpent fascinating birds. The seasons. Guinea fowls. Fish. Skeleton, "What you will come to," found on the Appian Way. Men with a tiger. Geometrical patterns.

NORTH CLOISTER.—Altars, heads of statues, and inscriptions. The most interesting is the altar found at Ostia in 1881, and dedicated to Silvanus on the 1st of October 124 A.D., and referring to Romulus. On the front are Mars and Rhea Sylvia drawn together by Cupid. On her left is a youth, and below, on her right, a goose. On the right side is the chariot of Mars, with four graceful cupids. On the rear are the wolf and twins, Faustulus, Father Tiber, Romulus and Remus. The Roman eagle. On the next side the hypothesis of Romulus.

EAST CLOISTER.—Heads, inscriptions, old piles found in the bed of the Tiber, and sarcophagi; one of these is fifth century, Christian, sculptured with Biblical subjects.

SOUTH CLOISTER.—Statuary, fragments, columns, and capitals.

THE GARDEN has been tastefully laid out and ornamented with various interesting objects; amongst others, numerous *cippi* or boundary stones found on the banks of the Tiber. In the centre are cypress trees, planted by Michael Angelo round the fountain, thirteen feet in circumference. By these are heads of animals found beneath the Palace of the Prefecture, and forming part of the decorations of Trajan's Forum.

In the rooms off the cloisters are stored numerous and important inscriptions, which will be arranged in chronological order.

## BATHS OF DIOCLETIAN. AND CHURCH OF S. MARIA DEGLI ANGELI.

The magnificent bathing establishments, called Thermæ, to distinguish them from the ordinary baths, consisted of a long series of halls, chambers, and courts, all lying on the same level, so that the extent of surface required for laying out had to be artificially formed either by the removal or the elevation of the soil. The thermæ founded by Diocletian and Maximian, and completed by Constantius and Maximinus, constituted the largest edifice of this kind. At present, only the great hall, 350 feet by 80 feet, and 96 feet high, converted into a church by Michael Angelo, exists in a state of tolerable preservation. The original massive granite pillars, 40 feet high, and 5 feet in diameter, though so sunk into the ground (imitation pedestals have been put to them) that their full height is nowhere visible, are still standing; the antique vaulted roof has also been preserved entire. This circumstance is of great importance for the lighting up of this vast space—the masses of light falling upon it at so favourable an angle, that the mind receives the same pleasing impression at all hours of the day and at all seasons of the year.

Several considerable portions of the adjoining hall are still to be seen, but, being included within the buildings of the neighbouring schools and asylums, and partly converted into hay magazines, a clear and complete survey of them cannot easily be obtained.

The pictures in the church were brought from S. Peter's, and the court of the monastery, now the National Museum, formed with one hundred columns, was designed by Michael Angelo. Salvator Rosa and Carlo Maratta were both buried in the circular entry. On the right is Houdon's statue of S. Bruno. On the right of the high altar is Domenichino's S. Sebastian. *Opposite to it*, Maratta's Baptism of our Lord. The Presentation in the Temple is by Romanelli; the Death of Ananias, by Roncalli. In the transept are copies of Guido's Crucifixion of S. Peter, and Vanni's Fall of Simon Magus; S. Peter resuscitating Tabitha, by Mancini; S. Jerome and S. Francis, by Musciano; Assumption, by Bianchini; Resuscitation of Tabitha, by Costanzi; Fall of Simon Magus, by Battoni; S. Basil celebrating Mass before the Emperor Valens, by Subleyras.

*On leaving the church, opposite* are the remains of the THEATRIDIUM belonging to the baths, the space in front being the Stadium.

## THE VIA NAZIONALE

commences here, and runs down to the south end of the Corso. The street is traversed by a line of tram-cars, which run down to the Piazza di Venezia. It is the handsomest street in Rome, and is lined by several fine blocks of buildings. It is partly on the line of the ancient Vicus Longus. Upon the *right* is the Quirinal Hill; and on the *left*, the Viminal; the street, artificially raised, occupying the valley between the two hills. A short distance down on the left is the Quirinal Hotel, the largest in Rome, fitted up with every modern comfort, and on one of the healthiest sites in the city. Behind is Costanzi's new theatre. *Just below is*

### THE CHURCH OF S. PAUL'S WITHIN THE WALLS,

the new American Episcopal Church under Dr. Nevin; designed by

Mr. George Street in the Gothic style. It has a fine campanile, and a beautiful peal of bells.

The vault of the tribunal in mosaic was designed by Mr. Burne Jones, and represents Christ surrounded by the celestial company, as described in Holy Writ.

## THE EXHIBITION OF FINE ARTS.

The new Palace of Fine Arts is on the right, about half-way down. In it is held an annual exhibition of modern works of art of every description. Admission, one lira ; Sundays, fifty centesimi. It occupies a space of 22,030 square mètres—the permanent building being 5,280 square mètres ; the Crystal Hall, 1,250 square mètres ; the gardens, 5,000 square mètres ; and the temporary galleries, 10,500 square mètres. The palace comprises two floors, and may be entered from the Via Nazionale, Via Genova, and Via del Quirinale. The main front is 25 mètres high and 60 long. Sixteen statues decorate the top of the façade, the work of Roman artists.

On the top of the pediment is a group, Italy crowning Art, by Adalberto Cencetti, the groups in relief on the face being the Finding of the Laocoon Group, by Filippo Ferrari, and Carrying Cimabue's Madonna in Triumph, by Puntoni.

Signor Pio Piacentini designed the edifice ; and the works have been carried out with the assistance of the architect Augusto Fallani, at a cost of two and a half million lire.

*Returning up the Via Nazionale*, at the top is a new circular fountain, presented to the town by the Aqua Marcia Company. It has a fine effect, especially when lit up at night with the electric light. *To the left, beyond, at the corner of the Via Susanna, is*

## THE AGRARIAN MUSEUM.

*Open free on Sunday, Tuesday, and Thursday from 10 to 3. Catalogues, 50 c.*

It comprises botanical and geological specimens, alimentary substances, objects used in arts and manufactures, natural history relating to agriculture, herbs and minerals.

*At the corner of the Piazza S. Bernardo and Via Venti Settembre is*

## THE FELICE FOUNTAIN.

The Aqua Felice aqueduct was made, A.D. 1587, by Sixtus V. (Felice Peretti), from whom it took its name. The fountain was designed by Bresciano.

*In the centre* of the group is seen Moses striking the rock, and the water issuing forth; *on the left*, Aaron leading the Jews; and *on the right*, Gideon bringing them to the brink of the stream. Four lions guard the basins below. It is said that the work of the artist was so criticised that he put an end to his life.

*Turning down the Via Venti Settembre, on our right* is the NEW MINISTRY OF FINANCE, in erecting which remains of the Porta Collina in the Servian walls were found. Also remains of

### THE FLAVIAN TEMPLE,

erected by Domitian on the site of his parents' house near the PORTA COLLINA. A marble head of Titus was found in the excavations.

"Whatever Domitian's unconquered hand has erected is imperishable as heaven" (Martial, ix. 1). "What of the Flavian Temple which towers to the Roman sky?" (*Ibid.*, ix. 3.) The following is amusing :—

"To CÆSAR, ON THE TEMPLE OF THE FLAVIAN FAMILY.—Jupiter, when he saw the Flavian temple rising under the sky of Rome, laughed at the fabulous tomb erected to himself on Mount Ida; and, having drunk abundantly of nectar at table, exclaimed, as he was handing the cup to his son Mars, and addressing himself at the same time to Apollo and Diana, with whom were seated Hercules and the pious Arcos : 'You gave me a monument in Crete ; see how much better a thing it is to be a father of Cæsar!'" (Martial, ix. 34).

### THE UNFAITHFUL VESTAL'S TOMB.

Livy (xxii. 57) tells us that this was "near the Colline Gate." We learn from Pliny's "Letters" (iv. 11) that it was "a subterranean cavern." Plutarch, in "Numa," gives the following interesting details :—

"She that broke her vows of chastity was buried alive at the Colline Gate. There, within the walls, is raised a little mound of earth, called in Latin *agger;* near which is prepared a small cell, with steps to descend into it. In this cell are placed a bed, a lighted lamp, and some slight provisions, such as bread, water, milk, and oil, as they thought it impious to take off a person consecrated with the most awful ceremonies by such a death as that of famine. The criminal is carried to punishment through the Forum in a litter well covered without, and bound up in such a manner that her cries cannot be heard. The people silently make way for the litter, and follow it with marks of extreme sorrow and dejection. There is no spectacle more dreadful than this, nor any day which the city passes in a more melancholy manner. When the litter comes to the place appointed, the officers loose the cords; the high priest, with hands lifted toward heaven, offers up some private prayers just before the fatal minute, then takes out the prisoner, who is covered with a veil, and places her on the steps which lead down to the cell. After this, he retires with the rest of the priests; and when she has gone down, the steps are taken away, and the cell is covered with earth, so that the place is made level with the rest of the mound. Thus were the vestals punished who preserved not their chastity."

The remains of the Colline Gate were found in building the present Ministry of Finance in the Via Venti Settembre. *The Via Servio Tullio, on the left, leads to the site of*

## THE VILLA SALLUSTIANA,

upon the site of which a new quarter is being erected. Clear of the houses is an interesting ruin miscalled the Temple of Venus Erycina.

This ruin is octagonal in form, with a domed roof. The interior is divided into halls, and a vestibule leads into the central hall. The walls have recesses for sculpture. The building was probably a nymphæum.

Besides the palace, baths, and gardens, there was a portico, called Milliarensis, from its thousand columns, in which the Emperor Aurelian used to take exercise on horseback. The buildings were fired by the soldiers of Alaric, who entered the city at the Salarian gate.

A new quarter of the city is being formed here, and the old villas Massimo and Ludovisi destroyed. From the ruins of the Nymphæum a cross street leads into the new Via Boncampagni. Turning to the left, and proceeding along it on the right, is the new College and Church of S. Patrick of the Irish Augustines. Then we reach the new Via Veneto. The large red-brick building on the left is the new Piombino Palace, on the ground floor of which is

## THE LUDOVISI MUSEUM,

*open on Tuesday, Thursday, and Saturday from 9 to 12, and from 2 till dusk. Fee to Custodian.*

1. Relief over the door, Judgment of Paris. 2. Crouching Venus, after Heliodorus. 3. Leader and the Swan. 5. Cupid and Psyche. 7. Relief found in the villa in 1887. Two females are dipping another in a stream, on the front. On the left is the nude figure of a

girl playing a double pipe. On the right, a draped, veiled figure lighting a lamp. The relief evidently refers to some religious rites. 8. Apollo and Faun. 10. Sarcophagus representing a fight between Romans and Persians. 11. Pan and Olympus, after Heliodorus. 15. Calliope, after Philiscus. 39. Æthra sending her son Theseus to find his father, by Menelaus, pupil of Stephanos. 38, *left*. Seated Youth, part of the Gallic Group. 41. Bacchus and Ampelus. 31. Veiled Head of Hera. 37. Mars seated with Cupid at his feet. 43. The Gallic Group. This formed the centre of the decoration of the pediment of a temple or other building, and to be properly understood, should have on one side of it the Dying Gaul of the Capitol, and on the other the Seated Roman Youth, No. 38, in the Ludovisi collection. The whole group represents an historical scene B.C. 226, when Aneroestus, the chief, and the other Gauls kill their wives and themselves to escape falling into the hands of the Romans after being defeated by Attilius (Polybius, ii. 2). 35. Archaic Head of Juno. 47. Equestrian relief. 49. Ops. 54. Venus of Cos, after Praxiteles. 57. Pallas Iliaca, by Antiochus of Athens. 30. Mercury. 31. Athenea and the Snake. 66. Colossal head of Juno Regina, supposed to be by Polycletus. 75. Seated senatorial figure, by Zeno, second century A.D. 78. Ceres, after Praxiteles. 80. Head of Medusa in high relief. 83. Antoninus Pius, 161 A.D.

*Following down the Via Veneto, on our left are*

## THE CHURCH AND CEMETERY OF THE CAPPUCCINI.

In the first chapel on the right in the church is Guido Reni's beautiful picture of S. Michael, and in the third chapel two pictures by Domenichino. But the most interesting part, the cemetery, is beneath the church, though entirely above ground, and lighted by a row of iron-grated windows without glass. " A corridor runs along beside these windows, and gives access to three or four vaulted recesses, or chapels, of considerable breadth and height, the floor of which consists of consecrated earth from Jerusalem. It is smoothed decorously over the deceased brethren of the convent, and is kept quite free from grass or weeds, such as would grow even in these gloomy recesses if pains were not bestowed to root them up. But as the cemetery is small, and it is a precious privilege to sleep in holy ground, the brotherhood are immemorially accustomed, when one of their number dies, to take the longest-buried skeleton out of the oldest grave, and lay the new slumberer there instead. Thus each of the good friars, in his turn, enjoys the luxury of a consecrated bed,

attended with the slight drawback of being forced to get up long before daybreak, as it were, and make room for another lodger. The
arrangement of the unearthed skeletons is what makes the special
interest of the cemetery. The arched and vaulted walls of the burial
recesses are supported by massive pillars and pilasters made of thigh-
bones and skulls; the whole material of the structure appears to be
of a similar kind, and the knobs and embossed ornaments of this
strange architecture are represented by the joints of the spine, and
the more delicate tracery of the smaller bones of the human frame.
The summits of the arches are adorned with entire skeletons, looking
as if they were wrought most skilfully in bas-relief. There is no
possibility of describing how ugly and grotesque is the effect, com-
bined with a certain artistic merit, nor how much perverted ingenuity
has been shown in this queer way; nor what a multitude of dead
monks, through how many hundred years, must have contributed
their bony framework to build up these great arches of mortality.
On some of the skulls there are inscriptions, purporting that such a
monk, who formerly made use of that particular head-piece, died on
such a day and year; but vastly the greater number are piled up
undistinguishably into the architectural design like the many deaths
that make up the one glory of a victory. In the side walls of the
vaults are niches where skeleton monks sit or stand, clad in the brown
habits that they wore in life, and labelled with their names and the
dates of their decease. Their skulls (some quite bare, and others still
covered with yellow skin and the hair that has known the earth-
damps) look out from beneath their hoods, grinning hideously re-
pulsive. One reverend father has his mouth wide open, as if he had
died in the midst of a howl of terror and remorse, which perhaps is
even now screeching through eternity. As a general thing, however,
these frocked and hooded skeletons seem to take a more cheerful
view of their position, and try with ghastly smiles to turn it into a
jest. There is no disagreeable scent, such as might be expected
from the decay of so many holy persons, in whatever odour of sanctity
they may have taken their departure. The same number of living
monks would not smell half so unexceptionably." Hawthorne gives
this graphic description.

## TABLE OF EGYPTIAN OBELISKS IN ROME

| Date of Erection on Present Site. | Date, and Erector, in Egypt. | Original Site. | Brought to Rome by | First Roman Site. | Height of Shaft. |
|---|---|---|---|---|---|
| 1. 1786: Piazza Monte Cavallo.. | B.C. 2074 to 1875: Mœris. | .... | Claudius: A.D. 50. | Tomb of Augustus. | 45 ft. |
| 2. 1587: Piazza Esquilino...... | ........ | .... | ,, | ,, | 48 ft. 5 in. |
| 3. 1588: Piazza Laterano....... | B.C. 1655 to 1600: Thothmes III. and IV. | Thebes. | Constantius: A.D. 357. | Circus Maximus. | 105 ft. 7 in. |
| 4. 1589: Piazza del Popolo..... | B.C. 1487: Seti and Rameses II. | Heliopolis. | Augustus: B.C. 10. | ,, | 78 ft. 6 in. |
| 5. 1789: Trinità dei Monti..... | B.C. 1480 to 1430: Rameses II. | .... | Hadrian (?) | Gardens of Sallust. | 84 ft. |
| 6. 1711: Pantheon........... | ,, | .... | ...... | Temple of Isis and Serapis. | 15 ft. |
| 7. 1563: Villa Cœlimontana ... | ,, | .... | ...... | Capitoline Hill. | .... |
| 8. 1586: Piazza di S. Pietro ... | B.C. 1420 to 1400: Menephthah. | Copy of one at Heliopolis | Caligula: A.D. 40. | Circus Vaticanus. | 82 ft. 6 in. |
| 9. 1792: Monte Citorio........ | B.C. 594 to 588: Psammeticus II. | Heliopolis. | Augustus: B.C. 10. | Campus Martius. | 72 ft. |
| 10. 1667: Piazza Minerva....... | B.C. 588 to 569: Pharaoh Hophra. | | Domitian. | Temple of Isis and Serapis. | 17 ft. |
| 11. 1651: Circo Agonale........ | | | Domitian. | Villa at Albano. | 51 ft. |
| 12. 1822: Pincian Hill.......... | | | Hadrian: A.D. 112. | Circus Varianus. | 30 ft. |
| 13. 1889: Piazza dei Cinquecento | B.C. 1405: Rameses. | .... | Domitian. | Isis and Serapis. | 10½ ft. |

# RAMBLE VI.

## THE APPIAN WAY.*

"The Queen of Roads."—*Statius.*

The Appian Way was the great southern road from Rome. It
led through Capua to Brundusium, which then as now was the port
for the East. It was first made as a regular roadway in B.C. 312.
"The censorship of Appius Claudius and Caius Plautius for this year
(A.U.C. 441) was remarkable ; but the name of Appius has been
handed down with more celebrity to posterity on account of his
having made the road, called after him the Appian" (Livy, ix. 28).
But a road existed here before this, for at least part of the way,
evidently to Capua (A.U.C. 414). "They came in hostile array to the
eighth stone on the road which is now the Appian" (Livy, vii. 39).

Statius gives some particulars as to how it was made. "First they
cut two parallel furrows to indicate the width of the road, and then

* Dr. Forbes's Carriage Excursion Lecture every Wednesday.

they cut down between those until they came to the hard bottom, and then began the levelling. As the construction proceeded, the road assumed a slightly convex shape. The middle or top was called the *dorsum*, or back-bone of the way ; or, as it is called in Virgil, " in aggere viæ." Roads that were left in the rough material were said to be *munitæ*, but when covered with cut polygonal blocks they were called *stratæ viæ.*"

Procopius, the secretary of Belisarius in the sixth century, thus describes the Appian Way :—" To traverse the Appian Way is a distance of five days' journey for a good walker; it leads from Rome to Capua. Its breadth is such that two chariots may meet upon it and pass each other without interruption ; and its magnificence surpasses that of all other roads. In constructing this great work, Appius caused the materials to be brought from a great distance, so as to have all the stones hard, and of the nature of mill-stones, such as are not to be found in this part of the country. Having ordered this material to be smoothed and polished, the stones were cut in corresponding angles, so as to bite together in jointures without the intervention of copper or any other material to bind them ; and in this manner they were so firmly united, that on looking at them we would say they had not been put together by art, but had grown so upon the spot. And, notwithstanding the wearing of so many ages, being traversed daily by a multitude of vehicles and all sorts of cattle, they still remain unmoved ; nor can the least trace of ruin or waste be observed upon these stones, neither do they appear to have lost any of their beautiful polish. And such is the Appian Way."

The road was lined with temples, villas, and tombs; for it was the custom of the Romans to bury their dead on either side of the principal roads leading from the city. It was against the law to bury inside the walls, which was seldom permitted, and then only as a great honour.

" When thou hast gone out of the Capena Gate, and beholdest the sepulchres of the Colatini, of the Scipios, of the Servilii, and of the Metelli, canst thou deem the buried inmates wretched ? " (Cicero).

*Passing under the* Arch of Constantine, *down the* Via Triumphalis (Via d' S. Gregorio), *we turn to the left;* the cottage facing down the road is erected on the line of the Servian or third wall of Rome. *To our left of the white-washed tower is the site of*

## THE PORTA CAPENA.

For a long number of years the present Porta S. Sebastiano (Porta Appia) was considered to be the Porta Capena. This error was rectified after the stone which marked the first mile was found (1584) in the Vigna Naro outside the present gate. From it one mile (one thousand paces) was measured backwards, and the result was the discovery of the exact site of the Porta Capena by Mr. J. H. Parker in 1868; but the excavations have been filled in. The remains consist of the sill of the gate, with fragments of the jambs, and the pavement of the Via Appia with the raised footpath on each side of it. The west flanking tower of the gate is under the gardener's cottage. This was reopened in 1877. The gate was crossed by the Aqua Appia (Frontinus), which Juvenal mentions as dripping, and Martial as showering down drops.

The Porta Capena is represented twice in the reliefs of Trajan built on to the Arch of Constantine. In the days of Tullus Hostilius, B.C. 668, Horatius killed his sister outside this gate. "A tomb of squared stone was raised for Horatia, on the spot where she fell" (Livy, i. 26).

We now arrive at the river Almo (Marrana), which flows through

## THE VALLEY OF THE MUSES,

under the Cœlian Hill, in which is the Fountain of Egeria, whence flowed the perennial fountain by whose waters Numa caught inspiration from the lips of his lovable nymph. Juvenal describes the spot in his description of the parting of Umbricius and himself: "This is the place where Numa consulted his nocturnal friend the nymph: now the grove of the sacred font is occupied by the remains of Jews." "In the valley of Egeria we descended into caves unlike the true." They strolled from the Porta Capena whilst the waggon was loading. At length Umbricius says: "The sun is getting low—I must depart; for long ago the muleteer gave me a hint by cracking his whip."

"Numa was commanded by the nymph Egeria to consecrate that place and the fields about it to the Muses, where he had often entertained a free intercourse and communication with them; and that the fountain which watered that place should be made sacred and hallowed for the use of the vestal virgins, who were to wash and clean the penetralia of their sanctuary with those holy waters" (Plutarch).

Livy (i. 21) thus describes it: "There was a grove, in the midst of which, from a dark cavern, gushed a fountain of flowing water, whither often, because without witness, Numa went to have an

interview with the goddess, and which grove he consecrated to the
muses, that their councils might be held there with Egeria." The
fountain may still be seen under the Cœlian, over the wall on the
left;—there is a bath-house of the middle ages built over it. It is in
the grounds of the villa of Baron Hoffmann, *to whom application
must be made to visit it.*

*Crossing the* Marrana, *we take the first turning on the right,* VIA
ANTONINA. *This lane leads to the*

## BATHS OF CARACALLA.

*Admission one lira; Sundays free.*

A favourite spot of Shelley's — "among the flowery glades and
thickets of odoriferous blossoming trees, which are extended in ever
winding labyrinths upon its immense platforms and dizzy arches
suspended in the air." So the poet wrote of this spot. But now it
is all changed : the hand of the explorer has ruthlessly pulled up
the trees, and scraped the wild flowers and weeds from the ruined
walls, exposing beautiful mosaic pavements, it is true, but which
hardly repay for the loss of nature's verdure.

The magnificent Thermæ of Caracalla display in the clearest and
most complete manner the skeleton of an edifice of this kind—these
glorious ruins standing, as it were, intact before us.

They were begun by Caracalla in the year 212, enlarged by Helio-
gabalus, and completed by Alexander Severus; their area being 140,000
square yards—length, 1840 yards by 1476. As many as 1600
persons could, it is said, bathe in them at the same time. The baths,
properly so called, were 1720 feet in length and 375 in width, and
they were surrounded by pleasure-gardens, porticoes, a stadium, &c.
The reservoir was supplied by the Antonine aqueduct, which
carried the water from the Claudian over the Arch of Drusus. The
principal entrance to the baths was from the Via Nova, one of the
favourite promenades of the ancient Romans, made by Caracalla.
Among the works of art discovered in the thermæ may be mentioned
the Farnese Hercules, the Colossal Flora, the Farnese Bull, the
Atreus and Thyestes, the Two Gladiators, and the Venus Callipyge.
The bronzes, cameos, bas-reliefs, medals, &c., found in the thermæ
are too numerous to mention. The urns in green basalt now in the
Vatican Museum, and the granite basins of the Piazza Farnese,
formerly belonged to the Baths of Caracalla. The baths remained
entire, both as regards their architecture and their internal decora-

Stadium.

Halls where philosophers declaimed, poets recited, and youth were taught.

Peristylium—a place enclosed round with pillars, Palæstra, in which were performed the athletic sports.

Retiring Rooms.

Anointing Rooms. Dressing Rooms. Shampooing Rooms.

Hemicyclia.

Pinacotheca (Picture Gallery).

Eating Rooms.

Women's Bath.

Reservoir.

Hot Bath.

Hot Bath.

Hypo-caustum.

Cella Solearis, Sudatorium, or Sweating-Room Beneath was the Laconicum, or Furnace. Hypo-caustum.

Tepidarium, or Warm Bath.

Frigidarium, or Cold Swimming Bath.

Hot Bath.

Hot Bath.

Eating Rooms.

Statuary Gallery

Women's Bath.

Reservoir.

Anointing Rooms. Dressing Rooms. Shampooing Rooms.

Hemicyclia.

Retiring Rooms.

Peristylium, used as a Palæstra.

* Original entrances.

ENTRANCE.

BATHS OF CARACALLA.

tion, until the middle of the sixth century, when the aqueducts were destroyed by Vitiges.

The portion of this series of main chambers, with which all the others are connected, like the limbs of an organic body, was a rotunda. The open space at the foot of the Aventine was intended for a stadium. The games held in it could be viewed from the tiers of seats, which rose, as in a theatre, above the reservoir, still in existence, on the declivity of the hill. From this the building was supplied with water, conveyed to the different points by means of an aqueduct.

In order to attain a correct idea of the ground-plan, we must proceed to the space in the centre, enclosed on the side towards the road by a high wall furnished with window niches for the reception of statues. This was the great swimming-bath, as is proved by the excavations, which have revealed the deep level of the original floor. Beyond this are small rooms where the bathers were oiled and shampooed; beyond these again is the GRAND PERISTYLIUM, enclosed with pillars and a portico, in which were performed the athletic exercises; adjoining were the Women's Baths. Returning through the HEMICYCLIA, we enter the PINACOTHECA, or Fine Art Gallery. This brings us to the TEPIDARIUM, or Warm Bath, with four hot baths, CALDARIA, at the corners, from which the SUDATORIUM, or Sweating Room, was entered. This was called the CELLA SOLEARIS. The roof was supported by bars of brass interwoven like the straps of a sandal. Vitruvius tells us that the Sudatorium ought to be circular, with a circular window in the centre of the dome, with a shutter to be opened or shut,—thus controlling the atmosphere as required. The Solearis was considered a great architectural feat, and inimitable. Of this grand rotunda only four piers are left, but these are sufficient to give an idea of its size; and it was to the Baths of Caracalla what the Pantheon was to the Baths of Agrippa: that is the only perfect part of those baths left; this is the only part of these baths wanting.

The mosaics of the pavement have sunk down, as it were, in the form of troughs, in consequence of the piers on which the arches rested, as on a sort of grating, having been broken when the latter fell in, and not being properly shored up when excavated.

The remainder of the building recently excavated corresponds with the parts we have described.

Some of the beautiful mosaic pavements may be seen in the Lateran and Borghese Villa Palaces.

*Above the baths, on an eminence of the Aventine, is the*

## CHURCH OF S. BALBINA,

supposed to date from the sixth century. There is nothing of interest in the church itself, but from the tower a fine prospect is enjoyed of the surrounding district. The convent and church have been turned into a penitentiary and a barrack.

*Resuming our ramble along the main road, on the right is the*

## CHURCH OF SS. NEREO E ACHILLEO,

founded by Leo III. (795–816). It contains an enclosed choir with reading-desks. The tribune mosaic is of the founder's time, and represents the Transfiguration and Annunciation. The episcopal chair is that from which S. Gregory read his Twenty-eighth Homily.

The church is on the site of the

## TEMPLE OF MARS,

erected during the Gallic war, B.C. 387 (Livy, vi. 5). "The same day is a festival of Mars, whom the Capenian Gate beholds, outside the walls, situated close to the covered way" (Ovid, "Fasti," vi. 191). "They paved with square stones the road from the Capenian Gate to the Temple of Mars," A.U.C. 456 (Livy, x. 23). Repaired A.U.C. 563 (*Ibid.*, xxxviii. 28). "The Curule Ædiles completed the paving of the road from the Temple of Mars to Bovillæ," A.U.C. 459 (*Ibid.*, xi. 47). Mr. Parker found some remains of this temple in excavating at the back of the church. From here the Roman knights used to ride to the Temple of Castor in the Forum, on the anniversary of the battle of Lake Regillus (Dionysius, xi. 13).

*Nearly opposite is the* CHURCH OF S. SISTO, belonging to the Irish Dominican friars of S. Clement, on the site of the

## TEMPLE OF HONOUR AND VIRTUE.

"Marcellus was desirous to dedicate to Honour and Virtue the temple which he had built out of the Sicilian spoils, but was opposed by the priests, who would not consent that two deities should be contained in one temple. Taking this opposition ill, he began another temple" (Plutarch. See Livy, xxvii. 25 ; xxix. 11).

"M. Marcellus, the grandson of the conqueror of Syracuse, erected statues to his father, himself, and grandfather near the Temple of Honour and Virtue, with this inscription—III. MARCELLI NOVIES COSS" (Cicero, Asconius).

This temple must not be confounded with the temple erected by

Marius on the Capitoline, and restored by Vespasian. The Temple of Honour could not be reached without passing through the Temple of Virtue.

*Opposite, in the Vigna Guidi, No. 19,* are the remains of

## THE HOUSE OF HADRIAN.

The chambers occupy three sides of a square peristylium, the walls of which are painted with frescoes, the pavements being black and white mosaics forming hippocampi, with rams' heads, Tritons, and nymphs.

Opening out from the peristylium is the Lararium, or room of the household gods. Here was probably the site of the Villa of Asinius Pollio, the orator in the time of Augustus; for Pliny mentions that in his gardens stood the statue now at Naples, called the Farnese Bull, which was actually found amidst these ruins in 1554. Hence it became the private house of Hadrian, and was destroyed to build the Baths of Caracalla.

Continuing our ramble, *on the left,* the Via della Ferratella leads to the Lateran. It has a fourth century SHRINE OF THE LARES, with niches for statues.

*Beyond, on the right, is* S. CESAREO, containing a raised presbytery, surrounded by a marble screen, a marble pulpit, and an ancient episcopal chair. Adjoining is part of the titular-cardinal's house, of the twelfth century. *It is on the site of*

## THE TEMPLE OF TEMPESTAS,

erected by Cornelius Scipio, A.U.C. 495.

"Thee too, O Tempest, we acknowledge to have deserved a shrine, at the time when our fleet was almost overwhelmed by the waves of Corsica" (Ovid, "Fasti," vi. 193).

*To the left is*

## THE VIA LATINA,

so called because it led through the Latin states. It branched out of the Via Appia on the left, outside the Porta Capena and within the Porta S. Sebastiano. A short distance up the Via Latina is the

## PORTA LATINA.
### (*Closed.*)

On the keystone is a Greek cross within a circle. The outside of the arch is reached by passing through the Porta S. Sebastiano and turning to the left. It is formed of two round brick towers and a travertine stone arch, with grooves for a portcullis; on the outside key-stone are the early Christian emblems of the *labarum*. The Roman Catholic tradition is that S. John the Evangelist was thrown into a caldron of boiling oil inside this gate, where the circular church now stands.

Opposite is the Church of S. John, Port Latin.

The little round church is called

## S. GIOVANNI IN OLEO.

Mr. G. G. Scott lately discovered, at the Chapter House, West-minster, some frescoes representing the Visions of S. John, fourteenth century, which are described in the following inscriptions, translated by Canon Wordsworth : —

"To the most pious Cæsar, always Augustus, Domitian, the Pro-consul of the Ephesians sends greeting :—We notify to your majesty that a certain man named John, of the nation of the Hebrews, coming into Asia, and preaching Jesus crucified, has affirmed him to be the true God and the Son of God ; and he is abolishing the worship of our invincible deities, and is hastening to destroy the temples erected by your ancestors. This man, being contrariant—as a magician and a sacrilegious person—to your imperial edict, is con-verting almost all the people of the Ephesian city, by his magical arts and by his preaching, to the worship of a man who has been crucified and is dead. But we, having a zeal for the worship of the immortal gods, endeavoured to prevail upon him by fair words and blandishments, and also by threats, according to your imperial edict, to deny his Christ, and to make offerings to the immortal gods. And since we have not been able to induce him by any methods to do this, we address this letter to your majesty, in order that you may signify to us what it is your royal pleasure to be done with him."

"As soon as Domitian had read this letter, being enraged, he sent a rescript to the proconsul, that he should put the holy John in chains and bring him with him from Ephesus to Rome, and there assume to himself the judgment according to the imperial command."

"Then the proconsul, according to the imperial command, bound the blessed John the Apostle with chains, and brought him with him to Rome, and announced his arrival to Domitian, who, being indignant, gave command to the proconsul that the holy John should be placed in a boiling caldron, in presence of the senate, in front of the gate which is called the Latin Gate, when he had been scourged, which was done. But, by the grace of God protecting him, he came forth uninjured and exempt from corruption of the flesh. And the proconsul, being astonished that he had come forth from the caldron anointed but not scorched, was desirous of restoring him to liberty, and would have done so if he had not feared to contravene the royal command. And when tidings of these things had been brought to Domitian, he ordered the holy Apostle John to be banished to the island called Patmos, in which he saw and wrote the Apocalypse, which bears his name, and is read by us."

## THE TOMB OF LUTATIUS CATULUS

is a lofty concrete tomb of the time of the republic, on the left, near the Church of S. John. This may be the general who ended the First Punic War, 242 B.C., or his descendant consul, 102 B.C., proscribed by Marius, and who suffocated himself with charcoal fumes.

*On the opposite side of the road is*

## THE CHURCH OF S. GIOVANNI A PORTA LATINA,

with a fine thirteenth century bell-tower. It was founded in 772 by Adrian I., and restored by Celestin III. in 1195. The doorway and altar are decorated with cosimati mosaic, whilst the columns of the portico and aisles are from some ancient buildings.

The Latin Way (Via Latina) was so called because it ran through Latium, joining the Via Appia at Capua.

*Returning to the Via Appia,* the second gate on the left admits to the

## CHAPEL OF THE SEVEN SLEEPERS,

dedicated to S. Gabriel and the Sleepers of Ephesus. It was decorated in fresco by the same Beno and Maria de Rapiza who did the frescoes in S. Clement's towards the end of the eleventh century.

Beyond, a tall cypress tree marks the entrance to the (No. 13)

## TOMB OF THE SCIPIOS.

The vaults, hewn in the tufa, with the traces of a cornice over the entrance arch, and the stump of a Doric column, are all that now remain. The tomb was discovered in 1780; and the bones of the consul, found in good preservation, were carried to Padua, where they were interred by Senator Quirini. Six sarcophagi were found, and several recesses for more bodies; the original inscriptions were removed to the Vatican and placed in the vestibule of the Belvedere.

Lucius Scipio Barbatus, his son ; Aula Cornelia, wife of Cneius Scipio Hispanus, a son of Scipio Africanus, senior ; Lucius Cornelius, son of Asiaticus; Cornelius Scipio Hispanus and his son Lucius, were buried here. Africanus senior was buried at Liternum.

From this tomb we can ascend into a brick tomb of the second century.

## TOMB OF CORNELIUS TACITUS.

This is probably the tomb of the historian, who died about A.D. 130. The following inscription was found here :—

CORNELIO TACITO
QUI VXIT ANNIS DUOBUS
MENSIBUS X DIEBUS
II HORIS X FECIT
LUCRETIA TACITA
MATER FILIO B.M.
ET SIBI ET SUIS. POS
TERISQUE EORUM

The municipal government has recently acquired this property, and the charge to see the tombs and columbaria is 25 centesimi.

## THE COLUMBARIA.

*(Officers of the household of the Cæsars.)*

The columbaria were underground chambers, containing niches in the walls, in which were placed the urns containing the ashes of those who were burned. As the niche was like a dove's nest in shape, it was called a "columbarium," the whole tomb a "columbaria." This columbaria is most interesting on account of the frescoes and stucco ornamentation. Half-way down the stairs, on the wall facing, is a coloured mosaic, with the names Cn. Pomponius Hylas, Pomponia Vitalina, beneath which are a lyre and two griffins, the emblems of Apollo. The whole is surrounded with a frame of shells. At the foot of the stairs are niches decorated with stucco, and picked out in various colours. The roof is decorated with winged genii plucking grapes, birds, and insects. Most interesting are the frescoes on the apse at the end : Proserpina is seated, whilst a figure approaches ; to the left, a figure with the draperies thrown aside holds a vase and patera in her hands. The roof of the apse has a draped figure of Nox in the centre, with a winged Victory on either side. On the sides of the front of the niche are the portrait figures of those whose ashes are here deposited. It belonged to the freedmen of Augustus, Tiberius, and Claudius, and is close by the side of the Via Latina.

In the adjoining Vigna Codini (No. 14) are three other columbaria, also belonging to the officers of the household of the Cæsars. The first on the left of the path was of the house of Tiberius, two of whom were of the Palatine Library; another inscription is to Sotericus, who was librarian of the Portico of Octavia Library. There is an inscription to the dog of Synoris Glauconia. The second has a pier supporting the roof, on which the frescoes are distinct. The third has no pier, but contains several busts, and the remains of a choral society, Collegia Symphonia. These two contain inscriptions that are of special interest, for here are inscribed names also found in the New Testament. In the first are the names Ampliatus and Tryphæne, and on the outside of the second is Tryphosa. These are names of some saluted by S. Paul in writing to Rome; and in each one occurs the name Epaphræ, mentioned in Colossians i. 7, iv. 12, and Philemon 23. These are uncommon names, and well may be those spoken of by S. Paul. They are not over their own remains, but put up by these people to fellow-servants who were not co-religionists.* The Christians did not cremate their dead.

### THE ARCH OF DRUSUS

next draws our attention.

The aqueduct which supplied the Thermæ of Caracalla crossed the road a few steps before the Aurelian Gate of the city, the Porta Appia (now called the Porta S. Sebastiano), where an arch of travertine, adorned with white marble and columns of variegated yellow (still standing), was employed to convey the aqueduct over the road. The arch itself is evidently much older than the aqueduct, and has, consequently, been pronounced by antiquaries to be the triumphal arch awarded to Drusus by a decree of the senate, and said to have been erected to him on the Appian Way. It was decorated by four columns of Numidian marble, relieved by four niches and an attic above a small pediment; the whole was surmounted by an equestrian statue between two trophies, as shown upon a coin. "The senate likewise decreed for Drusus a triumphal arch of marble, with trophies, over the Appian Way, and gave him the cognomen of Germanicus" (Suetonius, "Claudius," i.). *Passing under, we come to*

### THE PORTA APPIA

(now Sebastiano), opening on the great highway of ancient Rome, the VIA APPIA. This gate is the finest in the Aurelian walls, and, in its

* See " Footsteps of St. Paul in Rome."

splendid decorations, regard has evidently been paid to the road over which it was built. All the rectangular stones of the substruction are of white marble. It is curious, too, that considerable projections have been left on most of the stones on the right side, whilst the others present a smoothly hewn surface, evidently old material re-used.

A fresco painting of the Madonna, said to be of the sixth century, probably the work of a Greek soldier under Belisarius (as the character of the painting is Byzantine), remains in the corridor of Aurelian near this gate. It was over the head of the sentinels in the path and near the third tower on the right side of the gate. The existence of this painting was not known until it was discovered accidentally by Mr. J. H. Parker, C.B., in 1870. *Entrance, first gate on the left, inside the Arch of Drusus.* The gate-house is said to have been built, in the time of King Theodoric, out of the ruins of the Temple of Mars, which stood outside this gate. It was necessary for the Temple of Mars to be outside the gate, and this one was erected when the one outside the Porta Capena became obsolete, being within the Aurelian walls.

Behind the right hand wooden gate are a figure of S. Michael and a Gothic inscription cut in the marble, recording the repulse of Louis of Bavaria in 1327.

*Descending* the Hill of Mars, on the left, built into a house, is an unknown tomb. Beyond, we cross the other branch of the Almo. *Upon the left is*

## THE SEPTIZONIA OF GETA,

the murdered brother of Caracalla. The tomb now only shows a huge mass of concrete. It was named after its shape, and was like the portico erected by Septimius Severus to the Palace of the Cæsars (Spartianus).

*On the right, behind the osteria, is the*

## TOMB OF PRISCILLA.

Statius sang of the conjugal love of Abascantius, who interred his wife Priscilla before the city, where the Appian Way branches out, and where Cybele haunts the stream of the Almo.

To the mouth of the Almo the priests of Cybele brought the statue of the goddess once a year and washed it in the waters, together with the sacred utensils used in her worship.

The tower is medieval, showing it to have been turned into a fortress.

*On the left is the*

### CHURCH OF DOMINE QUO VADIS.

So called from the legend that S. Peter, when escaping from Rome, was met by our Saviour at this spot. Peter asked of him, "Domine, quo vadis?" to which Jesus replied, "Venio iterum crucifigi," which caused the apostle to return to his doom. They show on a small piece of marble two footprints, which they say is where the Lord stood—he having left the imprint of his feet on a piece of white marble in a road paved with silex. We don't believe it; but our readers may, if they like. The original is in the Church of S. Sebastiano. *The Via Ardeatina goes off to the right.* Just beyond, where the lane turns off to the left, Cardinal Pole erected the little round shrine as the exact spot where Jesus stood.

### THE TOMB OF ANNIA REGILLA.

*From the Via Appia, just beyond the "Domine quo Vadis," a lane leads into the valley of the Caffarella. At the end of the lane, upon the left,* is a beautiful brick tomb of the time of the Antonines. This is popularly known as the Temple of the Dio Rediculo. We have raised objections to this: first, because Pliny ("Nat. Hist.," x. 43) says the Campus Rediculi was at the second mile on the *right* of the Via Appia, whilst this ruin is upon the *left;* and secondly, from its construction, which shows it to have been a tomb. We have always considered this as the tomb of Annia Regilla, the wife of Herodes Atticus, consul A.D. 143. It stands upon his estate, where we know he erected a sepulchre to his wife, consecrating the surrounding land to Minerva and Nemesis. He was of Greek origin, and the ornaments are of Greek design; they are beautifully executed and well preserved, particularly the zigzag border. This view of ours has been recently confirmed: in digging up the soil at the base of the tomb, the following portion of the inscription has been found,—it is cut on a piece of *rosso-antico:*—

| | |
|---|---|
| ANNIA REGILLA | Annia Regilla, |
| HERODIS VXOR | the wife of Herodes, |
| LVMEN DOMVS | light of the house, |
| CVIVS HAEC | whose this |
| PRAEDIA FVERV | estate was |

In an inscription in the Louvre she is called "the light of the house, the lady of the land,"—these estates came to Herodes through

Annia,—and in the newly found inscription she is called light of the house. Thus they both refer to the same lady whose tomb is here recognized.

The word *rediculo* is supposed by some to come from *redeo*, I return, as applied to the spot where Hannibal turned back from Rome; but from Pliny we know there was a place called Campus Rediculi, and that it was to the right of the Via Appia in coming out of the city, so it could have nothing to do with this field. Pompeius Festus, a Latin critic of the fourth century, ascribes it to the above meaning, but he would be no authority. Hannibal's camp was on the road to Tivoli, and from there he returned. " Hannibal moved his camp forward to the river Anio, three miles from the city. Posting there his troops, he himself, with two thousand horsemen, proceeded from the Colline Gate as far as the Temple of Hercules, riding about, and taking as near a view as possible of the situation and fortifications of the city" (Livy, xxvi. 10). " Discouraged by all circumstances, he moved his camp to the river Tutia, six miles from the city " (*Ibid.*, xi.).

The tomb is built of yellow bricks, with red brick basement, pilasters, and ornaments: on one side is the pediment of the portico, which was formed with peperino columns. Over the square doorway is a decorated niche for the statue. The tomb contained originally two chambers, but the flooring of the upper one has been destroyed—thus making one—the vault of which was decorated with stucco ornaments. In construction it is like the painted tombs on the Via Latina, the bricks being carefully baked and laid with very little mortar between them, not unlike the entrance to some of the warehouses at Ostia, and of the same date—time of Hadrian; for being a tomb, and not cased with marble, it shows more careful construction than the ordinary brickwork of the time of that emperor.

Proceeding on our ramble along the Via Appia, *upon the left* is an unknown tomb; *on the right*, beyond, another. This is exactly at the second mile from the Porta Capena. Here was the Campus Rediculi. Was this the raven's tomb? (See page 20.) The vineyard on the left contained the Columbaria of Livia, now destroyed. *Beyond*, entrance to the Catacomb of Prætextatus. *Upon the right*,

## TOMB OF THE CÆCILII,

a shapeless mass of rubble. Several epitaphs to this family have been found here.

*Just beyond is the entrance to the*

## CATACOMBS OF S. CALIXTUS.

*Fee, one lira each, which includes guides and lights.*

Catacomb is a medieval word, and is said by some authorities to be derived from the Greek words κατὰ, under, and κύμβος, a hollow. The Romans called these burial-places cemeteries. They generally consist of three strata of tufa: *litoide*, of a red conglomeration, hard, used for building; *pozzolana pura*, a friable sand, for mortar; and *granolare*, harder, but easily cut, of which the catacombs were almost exclusively made.

A catacomb consists of passages or long narrow galleries cut with regularity, so that the roof and floor are at right angles to the sides, running quite straight, but crossed by others, and these again by others, forming a complete labyrinth of subterranean corridors,— the sides are honeycombed with graves. Their narrowness was to economize space, and to make the most of the limited area. These corridors, themselves the cemetery, lead into different chambers. Rome is surrounded by about sixty of these catacombs, each taking its name from the saint that reposed there.

The catacombs began to be formed at the beginning of the third century A.D., and originated from a pagan tomb. We find no exception to this in the early catacombs. Just inside the gate is a pagan tomb, second century, from which a flight of steps leads into the catacomb. This tomb belonged to the family, and when it was filled, instead of building a new tomb or buying another site, they dug down and made another chamber in the tufa rock below, and so on. In the course of time the proprietor became a Christian, and probably left his property to the Church. The tomb became popular, and it was enlarged gradually; the passages serving for the poor, and the chambers for the family tombs, which were paid for. They were lighted by means of shafts, which still exist; and there was no concealment—they were the public recognized burial-places, and when Christianity was the nominal religion of the state, pagans and Christians were both buried here. We find pagan inscriptions, emblems (other than those adopted by the Christians), and pagan family tombs. The pagan frescoes are much better works of art than the Christian; for the Christians had to be educated, whilst the pagans already knew. Early Christian frescoes are very rude daubs (see those of Jonah), and they gradually advanced till the ninth century, when we have the Byzantine school (see S. Cecilia). This latter style was used for the pilgrims after the bodies, all looked upon as martyrs, were removed to the churches in Rome; which gave rise to the story that the catacombs lead to Rome, which is not true. Neither is it correct that the catacombs were old quarries used up by the Christians, though there was often an entrance into them from a quarry. Most of the inscriptions are in the Vatican and Lateran : they would be far more interesting where they were found.

*N.B.*—The air is pure ; the vaults are dry, and they are not cold.

The entrance is near the ancient church in which Pope Damasus, who died A.D. 384, was buried. Descending the steps we enter the vestibule, the walls of which are covered with the names of pilgrims; a narrow gallery conducts us to the Chapel of the Bishops—Lucius, A.D. 232; Anterus, A.D. 235; Fabianus, A.D. 236; Eutychianus, A.D. 275. Following the names of Lucius and Fabianus are the words, "Epis, martyr." Urbanus, A.D. 223, and Sixtus, A.D. 258, were both buried here. In front of the grave of the latter is the inscription put up by Damasus, engraved in beautiful characters :—

### INSCRIPTION OF POPE DAMASUS IN THE CHAPEL OF THE BISHOPS.

HERE, IF YOU WOULD KNOW, LIE HEAPED TOGETHER A NUMBER OF THE HOLY,
THESE HONOURED SEPULCHRES ENCLOSE THE BODIES OF THE SAINTS,
THEIR LOFTY SOULS THE PALACE OF HEAVEN HAS RECEIVED.
HERE LIE THE COMPANIONS OF XYSTUS, WHO BEAR AWAY THE TROPHIES FROM
THE ENEMY ;
HERE A TRIBE OF THE ELDERS WHICH GUARDS THE ALTARS OF CHRIST;
HERE IS BURIED THE PRIEST WHO LIVED LONG IN PEACE; *
HERE THE HOLY CONFESSORS WHO CAME FROM GREECE; †
HERE LIE YOUTHS AND BOYS, OLD MEN AND THEIR CHASTE DESCENDANTS,
WHO KEPT THEIR VIRGINITY UNDEFILED.
HERE I, DAMASUS, WISHED TO HAVE LAID MY LIMBS,
BUT FEARED TO DISTURB THE HOLY ASHES OF THE SAINTS.

In front was the altar. From here a gallery leads to the Crypt of S. Cecilia, where her body was placed after martyrdom by Priest Urban, A.D. 203. From this resting-place it was removed in 820 by Paschal I. (See p. 142.) The body was found "fresh and perfect as when it was first laid in the tomb, and clad in rich garments mixed with gold, with linen cloths stained with blood rolled up at her feet." On the wall is a fresco of S. Cecilia attired in a dress of Byzantine character. Below are two others—on the left, Christ, with a nimbus ; on the right, Urban in full pontifical dress : they are of the ninth century. After traversing some passages, we enter the cubicula of a family. On the walls are roughly executed frescoes of the Baptism of Christ in Jordan by John, the story of Jonah and the Large Fish, Moses striking the Rock, the Woman at the Well of Samaria, the Paralytic Man walking with his

* St. Melchiades.　　　　　　　　　　　† Paulina, Neo, Marca, &c.

Bed—doves, emblems of immortality, on the sides. At the end are two fossori, or grave-diggers, between whom are three subjects in fresco, representing two men, one on either side of a tripod on which something is cooking; and next it, seven people seated at a table, beyond which are two figures and some sheep or lambs. These frescoes seem to us to represent the scenes at the Lake of Tiberias, after the resurrection of our Lord, as recorded in the twenty-first chapter of S. John. They certainly agree with the story: "There were together Simon Peter, and Thomas called Didymus, and Nathanael of Cana in Galilee, and the sons of Zebedee, and two other of his disciples" (ver. 2)— "But when the morning was now come, Jesus stood on the shore: but the disciples knew not that it was Jesus" (ver. 4)—"As soon as they were come to land, they saw a fire of coals there, and fish laid thereon, and bread" (ver. 9)—"Jesus saith unto them, Come and dine. And none of the disciples durst ask him, Who art thou? knowing that it was the Lord" (ver. 12)—"Jesus then cometh, and taketh bread, and giveth them, and fish likewise" (ver. 13)—"So when they had dined, Jesus saith to Simon Peter, Simon, son of Jonas, lovest thou me more than these? He saith unto him, Yea, Lord; thou knowest that I love thee. He saith unto him, Feed my lambs" (ver. 15; see also ver. 16, 17). In another sepulchre have been found two sarcophagi containing remains; the tops are now covered with glass. Opening out of this sepulchre is another, in which was found a sarcophagus (fourth century) representing Lazarus being raised from the dead, the multiplication of the loaves and fishes, Daniel in the lions' den. Near this is a crypt containing an inscription having reference to the heresy of Heraclius, on account of which Eusebius became a voluntary exile. The names of the person who engraved it—Furius Dionysius Filocalus—and of Bishop Damasus are cut in two vertical lines down the sides. It had served previously for an inscription to Caracalla, made by M. Asinius Sabinianus. It was a very usual thing for the early Christians to re-use the marble of other times, on account of its cheapness, they being mostly poor.

#### COPY OF INSCRIPTION OF DAMASUS ON AN INSCRIPTION TO CARACALLA.

HERACLIUS FORBADE THE LAPSED TO GRIEVE FOR THEIR SINS; EUSEBIUS TAUGHT THOSE UNHAPPY ONES TO WEEP FOR THEIR CRIMES. THE PEOPLE WERE RENT INTO PARTIES, AND WITH INCREASING FURY BEGAN SEDITION, SLAUGHTER, FIGHTING, DISCORD, AND STRIFE. STRAIGHTWAY BOTH WERE BANISHED BY THE CRUELTY OF THE TYRANT, ALTHOUGH THE BISHOP WAS PRESERVING THE BONDS OF PEACE INVIOLATE. HE BORE HIS EXILE WITH JOY, LOOKING TO THE LORD AS HIS JUDGE, AND ON THE SHORE OF SICILY GAVE UP THE WORLD AND HIS LIFE.

The Chapel of S. Cornelius was originally distinct from these catacombs. His tomb is marked "Cornelius Martyr. Ep." on the side-wall fresco of Cornelius and Cyprian; in front is a pillar on which stood the lamp burning before the shrine.

### INSCRIPTIONS NEAR THE GRAVE OF BISHOP CORNELIUS.

BEHOLD! A WAY DOWN HAS BEEN CONSTRUCTED, AND THE DARKNESS DISPELLED: YOU SEE THE MONUMENTS OF CORNELIUS, AND HIS SACRED TOMB. THIS WORK THE ZEAL OF DAMASUS HAS ACCOMPLISHED, SICK AS HE IS, IN ORDER THAT THE APPROACH MIGHT BE BETTER, AND THE AID OF THE SAINT MIGHT BE MADE CONVENIENT FOR THE PEOPLE; AND THAT, IF YOU WILL POUR FORTH YOUR PRAYERS FROM A PURE HEART, DAMASUS MAY RISE UP BETTER IN HEALTH, THOUGH IT HAS NOT BEEN LOVE OF LIFE, BUT CARE FOR WORK, THAT HAS KEPT HIM HERE BELOW.

AT THE TIME WHEN THE SWORD PIERCED THE HEART OF OUR MOTHER, I, ITS RULER, BURIED HERE, WAS TEACHING THE THINGS OF HEAVEN. SUDDENLY THEY CAME, THEY SEIZED ME SEATED AS I WAS. THE SOLDIERS BEING SENT IN, THE PEOPLE GAVE THEIR NECKS. SOON THE OLD MAN SAW WHO WAS WILLING TO BEAR AWAY THE PALM FROM HIMSELF, AND WAS THE FIRST TO OFFER HIMSELF AND HIS OWN HEAD, FEARING LEST THE BLOW SHOULD FALL ON ANY ONE ELSE. CHRIST, WHO AWARDS THE REWARDS OF LIFE, RECOGNIZES THE MERIT OF THE PASTOR; HE HIMSELF IS PRE-SERVING THE NUMBER OF HIS FLOCK.

Beyond are two crypts, with a fresco of the Good Shepherd, in good preservation, on the ceiling, and other Christian emblems. We emerge into daylight by means of the original stairs, of an early construction.

*A little lower down the road, on the left, are the* JEWISH CATACOMBS, which, perhaps more than any other, would illustrate that these catacombs were formerly quarries, because they are rather wide.

*A little further on we turn down a rough road on the left,* leading to what has been called the "antiquary's despair," the

### TEMPLE OF CERES AND FAUSTINA,

the site of which is now occupied by the deserted CHURCH OF S. URBANO. The church was built of brick, and the vestibule is supported by marble Corinthian pillars. Piranesi saw the name of Faustina stamped on one of the bricks. The basin in the vestibule containing the holy water was found near here, and was an altar consecrated to Bacchus. The inscription says that it was made under the priesthood of Apronianus. The grove of ilex trees is termed the Sacred Grove of Bacchus. Tradition says S. Urban, in 222–30, had an oratory here under the present altar; and that Urban VIII. (1633) turned the oratory into a church;—the paintings and iron bars are of that date. Below the altar, entered from its side, is a cell, on the end wall of which is a fresco, of the eighth century, of the Virgin with Christ, and SS. John and Urban. The plan of the building is rectangular, and it is of the time of Antoninus Pius. At the foot of this hill is the valley of the Almo, or Caffarella, in which is the mossy entrance to a grotto, for a long time called the Grotto of Egeria, owing to the misapprehension of the site of the Porta Capena. It is now known to have been a nymphæum in the

### VILLA OF HERODES ATTICUS.

This was proved from finding two pedestals, on which are two Greek inscriptions, copies of which have been placed on the top of the hill, close by the artificial ruin in the Villa Borghese; the originals are in the Louvre. This villa formed part of the dowry of Annia Regilla, wife of Atticus, as we learn from a column, No. 10 in the second Hall of Inscriptions in the Capitol Museum, which afterwards marked the eighth mile on one of the roads. After Regilla's death, he consecrated a statue to Regilla in the above temple. This is denoted by the above inscriptions, which speak of her as "the light of the house, the lady of the land." The wall at the back of the vaulted chamber was primarily intended to support the declivity of the hill, at the foot of which this elegant little building stands. The niches in the walls were for the reception of statues. One of these only, a recumbent figure of a river god, has been preserved, and is supposed to be a personification of the Almo, which flows past the spot.

Several channels for pipes, concealed in the wall, justify the supposition that the water poured forth in numerous streams. The romantic appearance of this spot has been greatly changed by the stream being turned into an aqueduct in the summer of 1873. A path leads to the tomb of Annia Regilla.

*Visitors whose time is limited should continue along the Appian Way as far as the Tomb of Cecilia Metella, and then retrace their steps to this road, which leads into the Via Appia Nova (page 331), and so return to Rome.*

*Regaining the Via Appia, at a short distance on the right is the Via Sette Chiesa. Some distance down, near the Tor Marancia farm, are the*

### CATACOMBS OF DOMITILLA.

The tomb at the entrance dates from the reign of Trajan, and contained the remains of SS. Nereus and Achilleus; also of Petronilla, a member of the Aurelii family. The saints were the servants of Domitilla, a daughter or niece of Flavius Clemens, the first of imperial blood who suffered martyrdom. Domitilla opened this tomb, which afterwards became a general catacomb, for the remains of her servants. This is the most ancient Christian catacomb, as may be seen from the paintings and brickwork of the vestibule. The present entrance is modern; the catacomb is interesting for its paintings. In 1874 the

## BASILICA OF S. PETRONILLA,

supposed to have been built about A.D. 400, was discovered, the top being only a few feet below the ground. It is supposed to have been originally built for the devotees who resorted to the tombs of the martyrs, and was destroyed by the Lombardians. On the wall of the tribune is a *graffito* of a priest preaching, probably S. Gregory, whose chair was removed from here to the church of SS. Nereo e Achilleo. (See page 279.)

Beneath the floor were discovered many tombs covered over when the basilica was built. It is being restored as a monument to Monsieur Merodi.

A fresco was found representing S. Petronilla receiving Veneranda. Several inscriptions have been found; also the columns which supported the baldachino, on which are represented the martyrdoms of SS. Achilleus and Nereus.

The Romans built an altar at the springs of the river Numicius to Anna, the sister of Dido, who became the wife of the god of the river Numicius, and was called Anna Perenna. (See Ovid, "Fasti," iii. 542.) The Roman Church erected a chapel to her on the same spot, under the title of Santa Petronilla, said, without scriptural authority, to have been S. Peter's daughter, and to have died in Rome, May 30th, A.D. 98, in the reign of Domitian. This could not be the case, for Domitian died A.D. 96, and Trajan was emperor before the last of May A.D. 98, Nerva having reigned between. *Straight on leads to S. Paul's outside the walls.*

*Returning to the Via Appia, on the right is the*

## CHURCH OF S. SEBASTIANO,

founded by Constantine, and rebuilt in 1611 from the design of Ponzio. The front and portico of six granite columns were designed by Vasanzio. Below the church are the catacombs, open free. A monk acts as guide. An altar on the right contains Bernini's statue of Sebastian, and one on the right the famous footprints.

*Opposite the church* are the extensive remains of the

## TOMB OF ROMULUS, SON OF MAXENTIUS.

In front of the Circus of Maxentius, on the Via Appia, stands a square portico, of which only the high enclosure walls remain. These, however, are in a state of excellent preservation.

*At the back of* the modern premises, in the middle of this enclosure, are the remains of a considerable circular tomb, in front of which was a colonnade facing the Via Appia. In all probability this is the identical building erected by Maxentius in honour of his son Romulus, who died in the year 300. Representations of this tomb are to be met with on coins. *At the side is the*

## CIRCUS OF MAXENTIUS,

erected A.D. 310, the enclosure walls of which have been preserved almost entire. These display the interesting phenomenon of pots of earthenware built into them, which not merely expedited the pro-

CIRCUS OF MAXENTIUS.

gress of the work, but allowed of its being more easily repaired than was possible in any other mode of construction. Its length was 1574 feet, and breadth 269, and 18,000 spectators could be accommodated within its vast walls, yet it was a small building compared with the Circus Maximus (see page 207). In 1825 three inscriptions were found proving this to be the circus consecrated to Romulus, son of Maxentius. Two towers flank the entrance, supposed to have been the seats for the judges. It is the most perfect specimen of a Roman circus remaining. *On the top of the hill* is the "stern round fortress of other days," known as

## THE TOMB OF CECILIA METELLA,

wife of Lucius Cornelius Sylla, and daughter of Quintus Cæcilius Metellus (Plutarch). The building consists of a circular tower, seventy feet in diameter, resting on a quadrangular basement made chiefly of lava and stone, cemented together by lime and pozzuolana, and strengthened with key-stones of travertine. This ruin, so long respected as a tomb, was converted into a fortress by Boniface VIII., and used as such by the Gaetani, his near relatives. It now belongs to archæology. Learned men have made it one of their most sacred resting-places, and it is a favourite resort of tourists and artists. The inscription on the side facing the road runs as follows : "Cæciliæ— Q. Cretici. F.—Metellæ. Crassi." *To the right* there are bas-reliefs, well preserved—one representing a trophy of victory, another a slave or a prisoner; both were brought from a tomb about a mile further on. The tower was built seventy-nine years before Christ. The construction is very remarkable, on account of the enormous thickness of the walls, which are of concrete faced with travertine and lined with brick in the interior. The enormous massiveness of the structure indicates a rude and semi-barbarous period. Plutarch speaks of the extravagance of Sylla in funeral ceremonies. Cecilia Metella had been previously married to the elder Scaurus (Pliny, xxxvi. 24; xxxvii. 5). "Sylla dreamed, shortly before his death, that his son Cornelius, who died before his wife, Cecilia Metella, appeared to him, and summoned him away to join his mother" (Plutarch).

The inner chamber of the ruin is fifteen feet in diameter, and was at one time supposed to contain great treasures both of art and coinage. But the sarcophagus of white marble now in the court of the Farnese Palace, and *believed* to have been discovered in or near the Tomb of Cecilia Metella, is the only treasure it has produced.

"What was this tower of strength? within its cave
What treasure lay so locked, so hid ?- a woman's grave."

*Opposite are* the ruins of a Gothic church,—

## S. NICHOLAS OF BARI.

Built by the Gaetani. Considerable remains of this fortress exist, showing the strength of the hold by means of which they levied "black mail" on the passers-by.

From this point the Via Appia continues in a straight line to

TOMB OF CECILIA METELLA.

Albano. Considerable remains of tombs exist on each side of the way, connected with which are many anecdotes and tragedies. Along the Via Appia a most magnificent prospect of the Campagna is enjoyed, with its ruined tombs and aqueducts, and the Sabine and Alban Hills in the distance.

## TOMBS ON THE VIA APPIA.

From just beyond the tomb of Metella the Via Appia was lost till excavated by Canina, under Pius IX. (1850–53), when many of the tombs were restored, as far as possible, with the fragments.

| LEFT. | RIGHT. |
|---|---|
| *Fourth Mile.* | *Fourth Mile.* |
| Servilius Quartus. | New fortifications. |
| Seneca (relief, uncertainty of life). | Plinius Eutychius. |
| Granius, son of Lucius (round tomb). | Caius Licinius, B.C. 367. |
| Inscription to Sextus Pompeius Justus. | Doric tomb. |
| Over the wall, remains of Temple of Jupiter. | Hilarius Fuscus, cos. A.D. 160. |
| Brick tomb, containing fragments. | Scondi and Scondini, A.D. 100. |
|  | A. Pamphilius. |
|  | Rabirius, Hermodorus, Demaris, and Usia Prima. |
|  | Sextus Pompeius Justus, cos. A.D. 14. |
|  | Doric tomb. |
| *Fifth Mile.* | *Fifth Mile.* |
| Tomb of the Quintilii, with undercourse of stone taken out. | Marcus C. Cerdonus. |
| Villa of the Quintilii, off the road, usurped by Commodus, and where he was assassinated; with medieval Church of S. Maria della Gloria. | First tumulus of the Curiatii, with medieval tower. |
| Tomb of Quintus Cæcilius and Pomponius Atticus. | Second and third tumuli of the Curiatii. |
| Large fountain of the fourth century. | "The sepulchres still remain in the several spots where the combatants fell: those of the two Romans in one place near to Alba; those of the three Albans on the side next to Rome; but in different places, as they fought" (Livy, i. 25). |
|  | The Ustrinum or cremating field was behind the tumuli. Here was the Cluilian trench, the camp of the Albans and of Carolinus (Livy, i. 23). |
| *Sixth Mile.* |  |
| Round tomb of Cotta, consul A.D. 20. |  |
| Tumuli of the Horatii, Tor di Selce, with a medieval tower. The Romans buried in a splendid manner the Horatii who were slain at the place where they fought (Dionysius, iii. 22). |  |
| *Seventh Mile.* | *Seventh Mile.* |
| Brick tomb of the second century, with fragments of three female statues. | Unknown tomb, with medieval tower, off the road on the right. |
| Semicircular concrete ruin, part of the villa of the poet Persius. |  |

<table>
<tr><td>

*Eighth Mile.*

Brick tomb of Persius, "who died Nov. 24th, 61, at his villa at the 8th mile on the Via Appia" (Suetonius).

Tomb of Q. Verannius, consul A.D. 40; died in Britain 55.

</td><td>

*Eighth Mile.*

Area of Silvanus, and Temple of Hercules (Martial, ix. 64, 101).

*Ninth Mile.*

Tomb of Gallienus and Flavius Severus.

</td></tr>
</table>

*At the 8th mile there is a cross road into the Via Appia Nova ; beyond this point it is impracticable for carriages.*

## APPII FORUM AND THE THREE TAVERNS.

TRES TABERNÆ was a *mutatio*, or halting-place, 11 miles from the Porta Capena on the Via Appia, at the place now called Frattocchie. It is 10 miles from the Porta S. Sebastiano and 11 from the Porta S. Giovanni on the Via Appia Nova, or 9 English miles 326 yards from the Porta Appia. Here the four roads from Rome, Tusculum, Alba Longa, and Antium met and continued southwards as one road. It is still a halting-place, and taverns necessarily grace it. Its exact location is explicitly pointed out by Cicero. He says to Atticus (ii. 10), "I had come out of the Antian way into the Appian way at the Tres Tabernæ, on the Festival of Ceres. When my Curio, coming from Rome, met me, at the same place came your servant with letters from you [from Tusculum]. Written at the 10th hour (4 p.m.), Apl. 12th," B.C. 58. Continuing his journey to Formiæ, Cicero again writes to Atticus : " From Appii Forum, at the 4th hour (10 p.m.). I wrote a little while before from the Tres Tabernæ" (ii. 11). So it took him six hours to do the 32 miles between Tres Tabernæ and Appii Forum. Cicero knew the spot well, for it was the scene of the murder of Clodius. "Severus was detained a prisoner at a state villa at the 13th mile on the Appian way, where he was strangled, and then brought back to the 8th mile [from the Porta Appia] and buried in the tomb of Gallienus" ("Excerpta Valesiana," iv. 10). "Severus was murdered near to the Tres Tabernæ of Rome by Maximianus ; and his body was placed in the sepulchre of Gallienus, which is 9 miles from the city [Porta Capena] on the Appian way" (Aurelius Victor, "Ep." xl. 3). Some have located Tres Tabernæ at Sermoneta, 23 miles, others at Cisterna, 30 miles from Rome. In the first case Cicero would have taken five hours to do the 20 miles, and in the second case five hours to do 13 miles ; besides, the Antian joins the Appian way 11 miles from Rome. These writers were evidently misled by the medieval forgery known as the Tabula Peutingeriana, which is in the Vienna Library.

APPII FORUM was a town of the Volsci, 43 miles from Rome, where travellers embarked or disembarked, passing the Pontine marshes by means of the canal. Horace (" Sat." i. 5) describes it as "stuffed with sailors and surly landlords." These places are interesting, being the meeting-places of the Roman Christians with St. Paul. " And from Rome, when the brethren heard of us, they came to meet us as far as Appii Forum and Tres Tabernæ" (Acts xxviii. 15).

# RAMBLES IN THE CAMPAGNA.

*(Any of these Excursions can be made in one day.)*

---

---

## THE ROMAN CAMPAGNA

extends from Mount Soracte (S. Oreste) southwards to the Alban Hills, and from the Apennines westwards to the sea. It is watered by the Tiber and numerous smaller streams; but there are no marshes except the salt ones by the sea. The soil is mostly composed of tufa

Roads ——— Towns
Forts +        Aqueducts ......        Railways

U M B R I A

Tibris

Horta Orte
Castellum
Seperlinum
Borg
L. Vadimonis
L. di Bassanello

Ocriculum

RAILY TO FLORENCE & ANCONA

Tevere F.

Tibris

Palimarium
Remorio

Seperannium
Gallese

Corchiano

Mons Soracte
M. S. Oreste

Capena
Civitella

Faleria

Aquaviva

Arcum Ealiscum
Civita Castellana
Falerii
Veteri

Lucus
Feronia
Fanum
Feroniae

Flaminia

Pisciamum
Fiano

E       T       R       U       R       I       A

vbo
L. Ciminis

Nepe
Nepi

Villa Rostrata

Ad Vicesimum
M.di Guardia

Mons Ciminius
M. di Viterbo

Monciglicno

Quirium
Sutri

Hosulum

Blerensis
Bieda

Arae Mutiae
Bracciano

Tetro Fortuna
Fabro Fortuna

Vicus Matrini  V Cassia
Vetruannentis

Forum
Cassii

Pyrgi

Ad Fabra

Ara Veientana
Stelo Farnese

Blera
Bieda

Via Claudia

Lacus Sabatinus
Lagi di Bracciano

Via Cassia

RAILY   TO   VITERBO

Caryae
Galera

Forum Quinti

Via Claudia

Aquae
Apollinares
Bagni del Sasso

Alsium Caeri
Cerveteri

Palo

Via Aurelia

Lorium

Fregenae
Maccarese

RAILY   TO   PISA

Via Aurelia

Via Aurelia

Fregenae
Maccarese

Castellum Novum

M       A       R       Æ

MEDITERRANEAN

MAP OF THE
ROMAN
CAMPAGNA

rock, covered with a few feet of soil—decayed vegetable matter. This causes the malaria : for the first rains, after the heat of summer, which has burned up all the vegetation, pass through the soil and rest upon the rock; then the hot sun after the rains draws up the noxious gas, which being dispersed through the air, if inhaled during sleep, or upon an empty stomach, produces fever.

If the soil, which for many ages has been allowed to lie fallow, were properly irrigated and cultivated, all this could be obviated. In the last few years more has been brought under the plough; and if the government would only plant trees by the road-sides and in the waste places, the Campagna would soon become as healthy as in the days of Pliny, who thus describes it :—"Such is the happy and beautiful amenity of the Campagna that it seems to be the work of a rejoicing nature. For, truly, so it appears in the vital and perennial salubrity of its atmosphere ; its fertile plains, sunny hills, healthy woods, thick groves, rich varieties of trees, breezy mountains, fertility in fruits, vines, and olives; its noble flocks of sheep and abundant herds of cattle ; its numerous lakes, and wealth of rivers and streams pouring in upon its many seaports, in whose lap the commerce of the world lies, and which run largely into the sea, as it were to help mortals."

The surface is by no means flat, but undulating, like the rolling prairies of America, and presents many points of interest and study to the artist and the rambler.

## PORTA FLAMINIA.

### (*Porta del Popolo.*)

*Passing through the Porta del Popolo,* built in 1561 by Vignola, a short walk under the walls, to the right, brings us to the Muro Torto, a piece of masonry of the time of Sylla, and held to be under the special protection of S. Peter (Procopius, "B. G." i. 13).

### VILLA BORGHESE.

*Closed on Mondays, Wednesdays, and Fridays.*

*Turning to the right,* just outside the Porta del Popolo, is situated this the handsomest park in Rome, founded by Cardinal Scipio Borghese. The grounds are open to all visitors; they cover a wide extent, and their walks, meadows, and groves are superb and unique in their general attractions. As a promenade for horsemen, pedestrians, and carriages, it shares the honours with its neighbour the Pincio.

*In the upper part of the grounds is the*

## BORGHESE MUSEUM AND GALLERY.

*Open Tuesday, Thursday, and Saturday from 1 to 4; entry, 1 lira.*

ENTRY SALOON : *left.*—XXVII. Head of Juno. XL. Meleager, after Lysippus. IXL. Augustus. VIII. Relief of Curtius taking his Leap in the Forum. IL. Bacchus. LII. Diana. The vault is by Rossi, and represents Camillus arriving at the Capitol. On the floor are mosaics of gladiators.

SECOND HALL : *right of Saloon.*—LIV., *centre*, Pauline Borghese as Venus, by Canova. LVII. Gipsy and Child with a Puppy. LVIII. Venus Genetrix, after Arcesilaus. LXII. Leda and the Swan. LXXII. Venus and Cupid. 1. Apollo with Violin, by Dossi.

THIRD HALL.—LXXVII., *centre*, David, by Bernini. C. Venus, after that of Scopas in the Capitol. CII. Apollo. 4. Andromeda, by D'Arpino. 10. Cupid and Psyche, by Zucchi.

FOURTH HALL.—CV., *centre*, Apollo and Daphne, by Bernini. CVII. An allegorical group. CXVII. The Delphic Apollo.

FIFTH HALL : *Grand Gallery.*—On the roof is Galatea, by De Angelis. The walls are decorated with mosaics, alabaster pilasters, and statues in niches. Down the centre are porphyry tables and vases. The busts of the emperors are modern. CXXXII. A vase in rare green porphyry. CXXXXV. Hermes, bronze bust, a Bacchus, the Ariadne of Ouida. The beautiful floor is composed of Giallo, Imezio, and Fiore di Persico marbles.

SIXTH HALL. — CLXVIII. Diana Preparing for the Bath. CLXIX. Ceres, a fine statue, after Praxiteles. CLXXII. Hermaphrodite, after Polycles. CLXXVI. A copy of the shepherd Marius.

SEVENTH HALL.—CLXXXII., *centre*, Æneas carrying off Anchises, by Bernini. CLXXXIV. Relief of Cupids Asleep. CIXC. Danaid, after Athenis and Bupalus. 23. Samson, by Titian.

EIGHTH HALL.—CC., *centre*, Arion and the Dolphin. CII. Priestess of Isis. CCIX. Ceres, in black and white marbles. CCXV. Venus.

NINTH HALL.—CCXXV., *centre*, Dancing Faun. CCXXXII. Faun, after Praxiteles. CCXXXIII. Pluto Seated. 27. Susanna, by Honthorst di Gherado. 31. Singers, by Rombouts.

*A flight of stairs in the corner of the Grand Gallery lead up to the Picture Gallery. To the right, at the top, is the*

GRAND ROOM.—The names of the artists are on the picture frames. *Left :* 34. Madonna, by Francia. 35, 40, 44, 49. Albani's Four Seasons. 51. Sibyl, by Cagnacci. 53. Hunt of Diana, by Domenichino. 55. Cumæan Sibyl, by Domenichino. 61. Madonna, by Francia. 65. S. Francis, by Francia. 68. Æneas and Anchises, by Barocci.

SECOND ROOM.—Portraits. 90. Lucretia, by E. Sirani. 92. Venus, by Peruzzi. CCLII. Geta, in bronze.

THIRD ROOM.—Paintings by Garofalo.

FOURTH ROOM.—Marriage of Alexander and Roxana, two scenes. Archer Shooting at a Target with the Arrows of a Sleeping Cupid, emblematic of the passions, designed by Michael Angelo. These frescoes were done by Vaga, and decorated Raphael's studio, the remains of which are to the left of the museum, under the trees.

FIFTH ROOM.—268. Crucifixion, by Van Dyke. 269. Musicians, by Van der Meer. 285. Landscape, by Potter.

SIXTH ROOM: left. — 133. Jesus being Scourged, by Piombo. 137. S. John the Baptist, by Veronese. 101. S. Antony Preaching to the Fishes, by P. Veronese. 125. Danæ and Cupid, by Correggio.

SEVENTH ROOM.—193. Holy Family, by Lorenzo Lotto. 147. Sacred and Profane Love, by Titian. Sacred love has nothing to hide, hence the figure is nude, and holds the Lamp of Truth. 163. Holy Family, by Palma d'Vecchio. 170. Venus and Cupid, by Titian.

*In front of the stairs.* EIGHTH ROOM: left.—318. Holy Family, by Carlo Dolce. 319. Annunciation, by Veronese. 328. Magdalen; 331. Madonna and Child; 334. Holy Family, all by Andrea del Sarto. 340. The Madonna of the Thumb, in blue, by Carlo Dolce. 346. Titian's Three Ages of Man, a copy by Sassoferrato. 348. Madonna, by Botticelli.

NINTH ROOM.—355. Copy of Raphael's Fornarina. 369. The Entombment, by Raphael; one of his early works, signed 1507, and one of his noblest conceptions. 386. Sebastian, by Perugino. 400. A Youth, School of, but not, Raphael. 411. Entombment, Van Dyke.

TENTH ROOM: *right.* — 443. Holy Family, by Ghirlandajo. 444. S. John, by Bronzino. 459. Holy Family, by Sodoma.

*Passing out of the villa, we turn to the right along the Via Flaminia, and take the first lane on the right, opposite the Gas Works. A tramway runs from the Porta del Popolo to Ponte Molle.*

### VILLA OF PAPA GIULIO.

*On the left-hand side, at the corner of the lane,* is the Casino, with sculptured cornices and a fountain. Beyond the Casino, and formerly connected with it by a corridor, is the villa where Pope Julius III. best loved to dwell.

## THE ETRUSCAN MUSEUM.

*Open Monday, Wednesday, Friday, from 9 to 3. Admission, one lira. Sundays free.*

The Government has arranged in the villa the objects discovered at the Etruscan city of Faleria, Civita Castellana.*

FIRST ROOM : *left of entry.*—Decorations of the Temple of Juno Quiritis in terra-cotta. The twenty-eight winged figures represent the parents of Juno, Cronus (Saturn), and Rhea (Ops). They formed part of the entablature of the temple. Other fragments are in the case by the wall. The frescoes represent the Banquet of the Gods, and the Banquet of the Sylvan Deities, by Zucchero Taddeo, 1566.

SECOND ROOM : *right of entry.*—Coffin formed out of the trunk of an oak tree found at Gabii. The frescoes are scenes from the story of Diana, by Zucchero, who executed all the frescoes here.

THE COURT is frescoed with birds and foliage. At the further end is a fountain supplied by the Aqua Virgo Aqueduct. *On the left,* an early inscription on a slab of tufa. Off the court, *on the right,* is a capital representation of the Temple of Juno. *A door on the left, under the portico, leads up to the museum.* The three halls are arranged according to their periods.

ROOM OFF THE STAIRS contains remains from the Temple of the Etruscan Trinity—Menrva, Tinia, Thalna (Minerva, Jupiter, Juno). The fragments from the tympanum of the pediment are interesting works of art, the head of Juno being probably the oldest representation of that goddess in existence.

FIRST HALL : *upstairs.— Case I., right.* Bronzes and early terra-cotta. *Case in window.* Jewellery. *Cases II. to VI., left.* Earliest Italian pottery, *imposto Italico,* and black pottery, *bucchero.* A yellow vase has painted on it the *Crux Gammata,* the Svastika or Vedic cross. In the lower part are two coffins made out of trees; bronze articles, and amber beads, buckles, and parts of harness. *Case VII.* Early painted vases ; a black one has a Greek cross within a circle engraved upon it. There is a vase with circles in black, lilac, and white, enclosed in an oval scroll. This is known as the Etruscan Eye. *Case VIII.* Glass, gold rings, a sword, and early engraved vases, showing a winged horse and fish. *Case IX.* Pedestals supporting bowls, like those in cases II. and III. Charcoal placed at the base of the pedestal kept the bowl hot. *Case X.* Early black

* See "Etruria and the Etruscans," by S. Russell Forbes, which contains a full account of this museum. Price 50 c.

and yellow vases. *Case in centre.* Bronze casket, helmet, domestic vases, jewellery, beads, etc. In the windows, *dolmen*-shaped sarcophagi. The frescoes represent the story of Venus.

SECOND HALL.—*Cases XI. to XIV.* Etruscan vases, and vases made by Greeks in Etruria, representing mythological subjects. XI. Early *bucchero*, with figures in relief. XIII. One with inscription, "*Eco Lartos.*" XIV. *Right,* splendid Greek vase. *Cases XV. to XVIII.* Bronze spear-heads, candelabra, sacrificial meat-hooks (1 Sam. ii. 13), and vases. *Case XIX.* Gold necklace. Fine Greek vase representing the Last Days of Troy. *Case XXII.* Lares, reflectors, a skull with thin bands of gold for holding false teeth. *Central Case.* Drinking-cup in the shape of a knuckle-bone, inscribed with the artist's name and that of the youth who gained it as a prize. Splendid vase in the centre, having eleven female figures full of grace and movement. The frescoes represent the seven hills of Rome.

THIRD HALL.—*Case XXIII.* Vases represent the worship of Bacchus, which came from Etruria (Livy, xxxix. 8). *Cases XXIV. to XXIX.* contain vases interesting from the subjects represented, mostly having reference to Bacchus and Hercules. *Cases A and B.* Early terra-cottas, with scrolls in gray and white, the handles being winged horses' heads. *Case XXX.* A beautiful winged figure, reflectors, blue glass bottle, scarabei, bronzes, etc. *Case in centre.* Etruscan imitation of Greek ware. The central piece has a chariot with four horses led by Victory. Several vases have duplicate subjects. Jupiter seated, with Minerva standing in front, upon whose outstretched hand Cupid has just alighted. Ganymede standing behind the throne. Psyche throwing herself backward into the arms of Cupid. On one is written, "*Foied vino pafa era careo;*" the other, "*Foied vino pipafa era carefo*" (To-day drink wine, to-morrow want). Hercules, feminine type, and Bacchus. The frescoes represent the sciences and muses.

FIRST CABINET.—Gold medallions, glass like wedgewood, candelabra, gold chain with pendants, two beautiful gold ear-rings in the centre of which is a head with ear-rings ; all from one tomb.

SECOND CABINET.—Decorations from the Temple of Juno, a half statue like the Naples Psyche. Other fragments from the Temple of the Trinity.

*To the right of the villa in coming out the arch (Arco Scuro) leads by the lanes, or we can return to the Via Flaminia, and take the cars to Ponte Molle.*

## BASILICA OF S. VALENTINE,

discovered in 1888 at the first mile on the Via Flaminia, where the new road runs off to the right to the Porta Salara. The basilica was founded by Julius I., 337–352, and restored by Honorius I. and Theodore I., 625–642. It adjoined the catacombs of the saint, which are opened on February 14th. The excavations have been enclosed with a railing. Amongst the sarcophagi found was that of S. Zeno, whose remains were translated to the Church of S. Prassede by Leo III. in 810. The walls show traces of frescoes of the time of Nicholas II., who restored the church in 1060. *The road by the river leads to*

## ACQUA ACETOSA,

a mineral spring, enclosed in a fountain by Bernini, and surrounded by a small grove. The view of the Tiber here is very fine, particularly when the river has risen. On the opposite bank rises the picturesque ruin, Tor di Quinto, the tomb of Ovid's family. The hill *to the right* was the site of Antemnæ. (See page 311.) *Below, on the left,*

## THE PONTE MOLLE

bursts on our sight. It was built by Pius VII. in 1815, on the foundations of the Pons Milvius, "which the elder Scaurus is said to have built" (Marcellinus, xxvii. iii. 9), and near which Constantine defeated Maxentius, October 27th, 312 ; a victory so graphically depicted by Raphael on the Vatican walls. "Maxentius endeavouring to cross the bridge of boats constructed for the use of his army, a little below the Ponte Molle, was thrown by his frightened horse into the waters, and eaten up by the quicksands on account of the weight of his cuirass. Constantine had great difficulty in finding his corpse" (Aurelius Victor).

*Crossing the bridge, the road* VIA FLAMINIA, *to the right, leads us to* PRIMA PORTA, the SAXA RUBRA of the ancient Romans, the first halting-place from Rome. *On the right, above the Osteria,* was situated the Veientina

## VILLA OF LIVIA,

*(custodian next door to the church), about four miles from the bridge,* discovered in 1863. When first excavated, the frescoes and arabesques were found in a good state of preservation, but they have since been greatly damaged by atmospheric influences. Livia was the wife of Augustus, and mother of Tiberius.

"Formerly, when Livia, after her marriage with Augustus, was making a visit to her villa at Veii, an eagle flying by let drop in her lap a hen, with a sprig of laurel (bay) in its mouth, just as it had been seized. Livia gave orders to have the hen taken care of, and the sprig of laurel set; and the hen reared such a numerous brood of chickens, that the villa to this day is called THE VILLA OF THE HENS. The laurel grove flourished so much, that the Cæsars procured thence the boughs and crowns they bore at their triumphs. It was also their constant custom to plant others in the same spot, immediately after a triumph; and it was observed that, a little before the death of each prince, the tree which had been set by him died away. But in the last year of Nero, the whole plantation of laurels perished to the very roots, and the hens all died " (Suetonius, "Galba," i.).

Cavaliere Piacentini has discovered (1879), on his farm at Prima Porta, the remains of some baths, which probably were connected with Livia's Villa of the Hens. In the centre is a hemicycle, 29 feet in diameter, the mosaic of which represents circus races, the victor receiving the palm of victory for his horse Liber; and the three chariots racing, Romano, Ilarinus, and Olympio. Surrounding this hall are twelve others, with mosaic pavements of festoons and geometrical patterns in *chiaro-oscuro*. One pavement, 26 feet by 20 feet, represents the sea, in which are numerous fish; while upon the sea three-winged figures gambol with marine monsters. The boilers for hot water, furnaces for hot air, and pipes for cold water are in a capital state of preservation. Brick stamps show that the building was restored as late as the time of King Theodoric.

Near the bridge over the Fosso di Prima Porta has been found the circular tomb of Gellius, the freedman of the Emperor Tiberius.

*The road straight on from the Ponte Molle,* VIA CASSIA, *leads to*

## VEII.

*(Dr. Forbes's carriage excursion-lecture at frequent intervals.)*

*Turn off to the right beyond* LA STORTA, *at the tenth mile,* FOR CARRIAGES; *pedestrians turn off at the fifth mile, near the* TOMB OF VIBIUS MARIANUS, VIA VEIENTINA. The site of Veii is surrounded by two streams, the Cremera and the Fosso de'due Fossi, and is about twelve miles from Rome. The place was captured after a ten years' siege by the Romans under Camillus, B.C. 393.

*Descend from the village of* ISOLA, *by the side of the brook, to the* mill; here the torrent forms a picturesque cascade, 80 feet high, crossed by the ancient Ponte dell' Isola, with a single arch spanning 22 feet. Here was one of the ancient gates, called Porta de' Sette

Pagi. *Opposite* Isola, down the stream, is the Porta dell' Arce. Under the rock of Isola are some mineral springs, and another gate, Porta Campana. In the ravine *beyond* was the Porta Fidenate. *The gates on the other side of the city* may be traced by *ascending* the valley of the Cremera, Porta di Pietra Pertusa; *beyond which*, on the ancient road outside, is a large tumulus, La Vaccareccia. Porta Spezzeria is higher up, with the remains of a tufa bridge; near by are the remains of an Etruscan columbaria.* Beyond is Porta Capenate, under which is Ponte Sodo, a tunnel, 240 feet long, 15 feet broad, and 20 feet high, cut in tufa for the brook to pass through. Further on is Porta del Colombario, near a ruined columbaria. *Beyond* is the Ponte di Formello, a Roman bridge upon Etruscan piers; *close by* is the last gate, Porta Sutrina.

The so-called Piazza d'Armi, the ancient citadel, stands at the junction of the two streams.

Under Julius Cæsar, within the walls of the ancient city, an IM-PERIAL MUNICIPIUM was founded. Part of a road, some traces of tombs, and a columbaria mark the site. It seems to have been founded to occupy the commanding situation, as Florus the historian, A.D. 116, asks, " Who now knows the site of Veii ?" In the middle ages, for the same reason, the isolated rock was surmounted by a castle. Cæsar Borgia besieged it for twelve days, and destroyed it. Isola is considered to have been the necropolis of Veii, from the sepulchral caves and niches hollowed in the rock.

A pleasant ramble may be had by *following the Cremera down to the Tiber, between the sixth and seventh mile on the Via Flaminia, thence to Rome.*

*Returning beyond* LA STORTA, *the* VIA TRIUMPHALIS *leads over* MONTE MARIO. On the height overlooking Rome is

## MONTE MARIO.

This hill is supposed to take its name from the celebrated Marius, and the slope down to Rome was called the Clivus Cinnæ, from Cinna (Gruter, mlxxxi. 1). In 998, from the victory of Otto III. over the Romans, it was called Monte Malus, hence the bridge over the Tiber was called Ponte Male ; by Evelyn, 1650, Mela ; now Ponte Molle. The hill took its present name from the proprietor in 1409. It is now Government property, and a fort has been erected on the

---

* The painted tomb, discovered in 1842, is kept locked by the miller at Isola. *Apply for the key, but resist his demands.* It is the most ancient Etruscan tomb yet discovered ; the furniture has been left exactly as it was found.

height.  In making the fort the tomb of Minicia Marcella was
found.  Pliny, jr. (v. 16), speaks of the sweetness and early death of
the daughter of Fundanus, consul 107.  The inscription says she
lived twelve years, eleven months, and seven days.  From the height
a most glorious panorama of the Tiber valley is enjoyed.

*A path through the woods leads down to*

### THE VILLA MADAMA.

The villa was built by Giulio Romano, and it contains some of his
frescoes, representing satyrs and loves, Juno and her peacocks, Jupiter and Ganymede, and other subjects of mythology.  There is a fine
fresco upon a ceiling, representing Phœbus driving his heavenly
steeds, by Giovanni da Udine.

*Passing out into the* VIA TRIUMPHALIS by the oak avenue, pausing
a while at the top of the hill to admire "the vast and wondrous
dome," and continuing our ramble, we descend the slopes of Monte
Mario, the ancient CLIVUS CINNÆ.

---

### PORTA SALARA.

The present gate was built in 1873; outside are some slight remains
of the old one.  A short distance down the VIA SALARA, on the
*left,* Cavalier Bertoni has discovered the tomb of Lucilius and his
sister Polla, with their portraits.  It is a grand circular tomb, 117
feet in diameter.  Paterculus (ii. 9) speaks of "Lucilius, who in the
Numantine War served in the cavalry under Publius Africanus," B.C.
103.  *Opposite is the*

### VILLA ALBANI.

*Open on Tuesdays from 12 till 4.  Permission to be obtained of*
Prince Torlonia, at the palace, Piazza di Venezia.  The museum
contains a fine collection of statues, busts, sarcophagi, &c.  The
grounds are splendid, and numerous antique statues are dispersed
through them.  *Catalogues can be obtained of the custodian.*

GRAND PORTICO.—51. Augustus; 79. Agrippina; 61. Faustina (?);
72. Marcus Aurelius ; 82. Hadrian.

VESTIBULE.—19. Caryatid, by Criton and Nicholaus of Athens.

LEFT GALLERY.—48. Alexander ; 45. Scipio ; 40. Hannibal ; 46.
Brutus (?); 110. Faun.

RIGHT GALLERY.—93. Juno ; 106. Faun and Bacchus; 120. Son of
Augustus ; 118. Seneca ; 112. Numa ; 143. Livia sacrificing.  Vase,

with the labours of Hercules, found at his temple on the Via Appia. 222. Relief—the Nile.

STAIRCASE FROM VESTIBULE.—891. Rome Triumphant; 885. Relief—the Death of the Children of Niobe; 893. Antoninus Pius Distributing Corn (?); 894. Orphan Children of Faustina (?). (See page 46.)

UPPER FLOOR, FIRST ROOM.—905. Apollo; 906. An Athlete; 915. Cupid.

NOBLE GALLERY.—Reliefs; 1008. Hercules and the Hesperides; 1009. Dædalus and Icarus; 1010. A Sacrifice; 1013. Antonius holding a Horse; 1018. Marcus Aurelius, Antoninus, Faustina, and Rome; 1014. Venus, Diana, Apollo, and Victory sacrificing.

LEFT ROOM.—1013. Relief—Antinoüs Crowned with the Lotus Flower, *very beautiful.*

SECOND ROOM.—952. Apollo Sauroctonos, by Praxiteles.

*Beyond the villa is the*

## CATACOMB OF S. PRISCILLA,

so called from Vera Priscilla, the wife of M. A. Glabrioni. Cos. 152, 186. Anastasius (xxxi. 31) says this cemetery was made by Bishop Marcellus, A.D. 307. There is a burial vault here said to be the tomb of the family of Pudens; it has some rude frescoes—a woman coming out of a house; an orante in act of prayer, called a Madonna; a woman between two men, twice over. Other frescoes, in different chambers, are the Three Jews in the Fiery Furnace; Good Shepherd; four orantes and doves; seven men carrying a barrel, whilst two others lie on the ground. Scratched on the wall is ORATIUS D. NOBILIBUS ANTONIUS BOSIUS; and underneath was a marble slab—BONAVLE CONJUGI SANCTISSIMAE; a Good Shepherd; a female figure seated, with a child in her lap, looking towards a male figure with hands extended, called the Virgin and Isaiah (query, Joseph)—between them is a star. This is the earliest painting of the Virgin known.

*Leaving the catacomb, the hill on the left, beyond, was the site of*

## ANTEMNÆ,

one of the most ancient cities of the Latin land. It was captured by the Romans under Romulus, and destroyed by Alaric A.D. 409, who encamped here when attacking Rome. Near by, the Anio flows into the Tiber,—"with whirlpools dimpled, and with downward force." A beautiful prospect of the surrounding country may be enjoyed.

The Tiber rolling his yellow billows to the sea, serpent like, through green meadows; the blue Apennines, with snow-covered summits, looking patronizingly down upon the village-crowned hills at their base; the slopes of Monte Mario, dark with cork-wood foliage, *on our left*. Sir W. Gell says that the high point nearest the road was the citadel, below which is a cave that was once a sepulchre. One gate looked towards Fidenæ, up the Tiber; another towards Rome; perhaps also one toward Acqua Acetosa; and another in the direction of the meeting waters.

*Beyond, the road crosses the Anio by*

## THE PONTE SALARA,

rebuilt in 1878. Upon the old bridge Titus Maulius, in A.U.C. 395, killed the Gaulish giant, and on account of putting the giant's chain on his own neck took the title of Torquatus (Livy, vii. 10).

*Beyond* the bridge is an unknown tomb. Five miles from Rome is Castel Giubeleo, the site of

## FIDENÆ,

"a large and populous city, forty stadia from Rome" (Dionysius, ii. 53; xiii. 28); founded by the Albans, and made a Roman colony by Romulus, but soon revolted. It was whilst Servius Tullius was fighting the citizens that he sent and destroyed Alba Longa (Livy). The place was ultimately taken by Lartius Flavus, the consul, by means of a mine (Dionysius, v. 70).

There are no remains of the city, but the site is undoubted. The arx was to the right of the road on the high hill before arriving at Castel Giubeleo. It is not known when this city was destroyed, but in A.D. 27, in the time of Tiberius, the temporary amphitheatre fell and killed a large number of people. (See Suetonius, "Tiberius," xl.; "Caligula," xxxi.; Tacitus, "Annals," iv. 62.)

## PORTA PIA.

This gate was built by Michael Angelo in 1564. It was nearly destroyed by the Italian troops in 1870, but is now restored.

A fine view of the Villa Albani and the Sabine Hills may be had from this spot.

*To the left* of the gate a tablet marks where the Italian army entered Rome on the 20th September 1870.

*To the right* is the ancient

## PORTA NOMENTANA,

Porta Pia taking its place. The former is flanked by two round towers. *Opposite* is the Villa Patrizi, in which is the small catacomb of S. Nicomedus. *Beyond, on the right,* is the Villa Lezzani and the Chapel of S. Giustina.

*Proceeding down the Via Nomentana a little way, on the right* is the

## VILLA TORLONIA,

*open on Thursdays, from 11 till 4, with permission to be obtained of* Prince Torlonia. The gallery has many fine paintings and sculptures, and the gardens are adorned with fountains, statues, and mock ruins.

*About a mile further on is the*

## CHURCH OF S. AGNESE,

founded by Constantine, on the site where the body of the saint was found. The aisles are formed by thirty-two columns of fine marble, and the altar canopy is supported by four columns of porphyry. In the second chapel on the right is a beautiful altar inlaid with mosaic work. Pio Nono's escape when the floor fell in, April 15, 1855, is commemorated by a fresco by Tojetti. The feast of the saint is on the 21st January, when the lambs are blessed with great ceremony. Here we have the best idea of a basilica.

## THE CATACOMB OF S. AGNESE.

*Entrance in the church. Open on Sunday, Tuesday, and Thursday.*
Part of this catacomb under the garden of the monks is well worth a visit. The entrance to it is through the church, and the exit through S. Costanza. The original stairs at the entrance were excavated in 1873, and four pagan tombs were found and two openings from them into the catacomb, showing that the Catacombs were general cemeteries, and not *exclusively* Christian. This catacomb is interesting, as it is left just as it was found in 1871, many of the graves being unopened.—The neighbouring

## CHURCH OF S. COSTANZA

was erected to the memory of Constantine's daughter, Constantina, who was anything but a saint according to Marcellinus. It is worth visiting on account of its dome, supported by twenty-four clustered columns in granite, and covered with mosaics. The sarcophagus is now in the Vatican Museum.

S. Costanza is a mausoleum and a baptistery, not properly a church. The mosaic pictures of the fourth century are the finest known of that period. Those over the doors are of the eighth century.

"At this time [A.D. 360] Julian sent the body of his wife Helen, recently deceased, to Rome, to be buried in the suburb on the road to Nomentum, where also Constantina, his sister-in-law, the wife of Gallus, had been buried" (Marcellinus, xxi. i. 5).

*A quarter of a mile beyond the church, on the left, is the entrance to*

## THE OSTORIAN CATACOMB.
### (*No. 49 Via Nomentana.*)

Signor Armellini has, it is reported, succeeded in deciphering an inscription in this catacomb, in which the name of S. Peter occurs. The supposed inscription is in an archway and on the stucco, the letters being in red colour. This *cubiculum* is lighted from the top by an old *luminarium*, and in shape is not unlike a basilica without aisles. At a short distance in front of the apse, jutting out from the right wall, is a chair of tufa, which looks across the chamber; opposite is a column, coming out in the same manner, above which is a niche for a lamp. The apse itself is filled up about four feet above the floor of the chamber, the filling up forming a tomb, the top of which was probably used as an altar (*arcosolium*). The vault of the apse is covered with scroll-worked stucco in very low relief, coloured red; this has fallen off, only some slight traces of it remaining, presenting in one or two instances the *appearance* of letters, which, we should say, it was impossible to make out. This is the inscription in which Signor Armellini reads the name of Peter. But even supposing that it is an inscription, and that Peter's name is there, it does not prove that Peter baptized there; for, in fact, the catacomb was made long after S. Peter's death. In the acts of the martyrs Liberius and Damasus, it is mentioned that in this catacomb S. Peter baptized (query, not the apostle). This is followed by Bosio, Aringhi, and De Rossi. This catacomb is supposed to have belonged to the descendants of Ostorius, the pro-prætor in Britain who sent Caractacus and his wife prisoners to Claudius. Of course the simple mention of S. Peter in the inscription does not prove that he ever was in Rome, for we have every evidence to the contrary. This catacomb is about two miles outside the Porta Pia, on the Via Nomentana, and adjoins that of S. Agnese, and is also known by the name of " Peter's Fountain," though there is no water there.

*On the left of the road*, opposite the red house of the fort, a path leads down into a valley, past a brick tomb of the Antonines, *Sedia del Diavolo*. Here we come to marshy ground and a small stream, where Liberius, on Easter Sunday 354, baptized 4,000 persons at the Nymphas S. Petri. It was here, in the Caprilia Ager, that Romulus was murdered by the senate (Livy, i. 16).

### PONTE NOMENTANA,

a Roman bridge, very picturesque, rebuilt, A.D. 565, by Narses, the eunuch, and conqueror of Italy. Its present upper part is, however, medieval. *Just beyond is the ridge of*

### MONS SACER,

where the plebeians retired when they made their secession, B.C. 492, and where Menenius Agrippa addressed to them the famous fable of the "Belly and its Members" (Livy, ii. 32; Dionysius, vi. 86), so beautifully illustrated by S. Paul: "As the members of a natural body all tend to the mutual decency, service, and succour of the same body; so we should do one for another, to make up the mystical body of Christ" (see 1 Cor. xii.). "They erected an altar upon the summit of the hill, where they had encamped, which they named the altar of Jupiter Terribilis" (Dionysius, vi. 90). A second secession here took place after the death of Virginia, B.C. 449 (Livy, iii. 52).

*Beyond the osteria (inn), on the left, is the so-called*

### TOMB OF VIRGINIA.

The shepherds have handed down this tradition, but we have no historic record of where she was buried. Dionysius (xi. 39) gives this account of her funeral :—

"The relatives of the virgin still increased the disaffection of the citizens by bringing her bier into the forum, by adorning her body with all possible magnificence, and carrying it through the most remarkable and most conspicuous streets of the city : for the matrons and virgins ran out of their houses lamenting her misfortune, and some threw flowers upon the bier, some their girdles or ribbons others their virgin toys, and others even cut off their curls and cast them upon it. And many of the men, either purchasing ornaments in the neighbouring shops, or receiving them by the favour of the owners, contributed to the pomp by presents proper to the

occasion: so that the funeral was celebrated through the whole
city."

> " And close around the body gathered a little train
> Of them that were the nearest and dearest to the slain.
> They brought a bier, and hung it with many a cypress crown,
> And gently they uplifted her, and gently laid her down."—MACAULAY.

*About three miles from the bridge are the*

## ORATORY AND CATACOMB OF S. ALEXANDER,

discovered in 1853. S. Alexander suffered under Trajan, A.D. 117.
In the fourth century a church was built over the oratory and catacomb. In 1867 Pius IX. laid the foundations of a church to be
erected over these remains. *To visit them a permit is necessary
from the cardinal vicar, 70 Via della Scrofa.*

---

## PORTA TIBURTINA.
### (*Porta S. Lorenzo.*)

This gate was built by Augustus, B.C. 3, over the line of the
Pomœrium, being one of the arches of the Marcian Aqueduct, B.C.
145. The Aquæ Tepula and Julia likewise passed over it. The inscriptions refer to Augustus, and to repairs by Vespasian, Caracalla,
and Honorius, who added the picturesque brick towers in 402.

*A new road has now been made to the* CEMETERY, *which is passed by
the tramway to Tivoli. Three quarters of a mile on the road is the*

## CHURCH OF S. LORENZO,

founded in 308 by Constantine, in the place where was the cemetery
of S. Cyriaca, which contained the body of S. Lorenzo. It was
enlarged and restored at different periods. Finally, in 1864, Pius
IX. caused the architect Vespignani to make great improvements,
and it was then that the column of red granite with the statue of
the martyr was placed in the adjacent square.

The poet Bishop Vida describes the martyrdom of S. Lawrence,
and thus foretells his monument:—

> " As circling years revolve, the day shall come
> When Troy's great progeny, imperial Rome,
> To the blest youth, who, filled with holy pride,
> Tyrants, and flames, and bitter death defied,
> Shall build full many an altar, many a shrine
> And grace his sepulchre with rites divine."

Under the colonnade, supported by six Ionic columns, and adorned
with frescoes, are two sarcophagi with bas-reliefs; also some curious

frescoes relating to the soul of the Saxon count Henry. The interior is divided into three aisles by twenty-two columns, the greater part in Oriental granite. The paving recalls the style of the basilicæ of the primitive times. The great aisle was painted, by order of Pius IX., by Cesare Fracassini; in it are two pulpits of marble. A double staircase of marble conducts to that part of the Basilica Constantiniana which by Honorius III. was converted into the presbytery. It is decorated at the upper end by twelve columns of violet marble, which rise from the level of the primitive basilica beneath it. At the end is the ancient pontifical seat, adorned with mosaic and precious marbles. The papal altar is under a canopy in the Byzantine style. The pavement of the presbytery is worthy of attention. Descending to the confessional, which is under the high altar, we find the tomb of the martyred saints—Lawrence, Stephen, and Justin. Pius IX. is interred here. Returning to the church by the staircase on the left, we enter the sacristy, where is the altar of the Holy Sacrament, with a picture by E. Savonanzio, representing S. Cyriaca, who is having the martyrs buried. Close by is the ROMAN CEMETERY, opened in 1834. The frescoes here are worth seeing, as well as the different monuments.

## THE VIA TIBURTINA.

*Dr. Forbes's steam-tramway excursion-lecture to Tivoli and Hadrian's Villa, every Friday.*

This road is the worst kept, the least interesting, and the most frequented out of Rome. The new tramway is now open, so it is more come-at-able than hitherto. Leaving the cemetery, we soon pass the Florence railway : then a bridge over the Ulmanus stream. The farm on the right, inside the gateway, is upon the site of the Villa of Regulus (Martial, i. 13). At the first mile was the monument of Pallas (Pliny younger, vii. 29; viii. 6). We soon cross the Anio by the modern bridge : the old one, Ponte Mammolo, can be seen to the right; it took its name from Mammæa, the mother of Alexander Severus, who repaired it. In these meadows Hannibal had his first camp (see page 288). Beyond, we pass along the modern causeway over the meadows where his second camp was, by the Tutia, which stream we cross. We now pass some of the old pavement, and upon the left CASTEL ARCIONE, a mediæval castle belonging to a family of that name; destroyed by the S. P. Q. T., it having become a stronghold for brigands.

The calciferous lake of Tartarus formerly existed, just beyond, but

1 Via della Sibilla
2 Ponte Gregoriano
3 Porta S. Angelo
4 Grand Falls
5 Glen & Falls
6 Temples of Vesta & Sibyl
7 Temple of Hercules
8 Cascade
9 Cascades
10 Villa S. Antonio

PLAN OF
TIVOLI

is now dried up.   Near by a sulphurous odour indicates the proximity of the AQUÆ ALBULÆ, baths often frequented in ancient times. A channel, constructed by Cardinal Este, draws off the water from these sulphurous lakes to the Tiber.   The bath-house was erected in 1880, and the water is beneficial for skin diseases.

In the vicinity are the quarries of travertine—so called from the stone taking the ancient name *Tiburtinus*—which have yielded the materials for building both ancient and modern Rome, the Colosseum, and S. Peter's.   *Three miles from Tivoli we cross the picturesque*

### PONTE LUCANO,

which spans the Anio.   Near by is the solid and magnificent Tomb of the Plautii, similar to that of Cecilia Metella.   The upper part has been repaired in medieval times, that it might serve as a fortress. Erected, 1 B.C., by M. Plautius Silvanus for himself, Lartia his wife, and Urgularicus his child.   The inscription tells us that one of his descendants served in Britain, and died A.D. 76.

*A little beyond, a road turns off to the right, leading to Hadrian's Villa.   Good walkers should leave the tram here and proceed to the villa, one mile, returning in time to take the next tram up to Tivoli. The tickets are good to stop over.   Sometimes there are conveyances here meeting the tram-cars.*

A railway to Tivoli, Sulmona, etc., has recently been opened, but the hours of the trains are not very convenient for sight-seers. Leaving the Roman station, it runs, in the valley of the Anio, parallel with the tramway as far as the Aquæ Albulæ, passing by Lunghezza, the ancient Collatia.   Crossing the highroad, it runs north, and turns under the hill of Monte Celio, Corniculum, and ascends to Tivoli.   On the way up unsatisfactory glimpses of the Cascatelle and Grand Fall are obtained if you are on the right side of the carriage. The station is on the opposite side of the town to the tram-station. *A good lunch* can be obtained at the Hotel Sibilla, or at the chalet of the Villa Gregoriana.   The best hotel is the Regina, for a stay.

*Itinerary.*—Visit the falls and grottoes in the Villa Gregoriana. Lunch, then walk or drive to see the Grand Fall and Cascades.   Return through the town, and drive to the Villa of Hadrian, returning to the highroad for the tramway.

### TIVOLI, THE ANCIENT TIBUR,

was founded by the Sicani, 1,200 years B.C.   Greek colonists then possessed it, and it became a frontier town of Magna Græcia.   A grand view may be obtained from the public garden, where the tram stops, overlooking the Campagna, with S. Peter's dome in the distance. Below can be seen the ruined arched portico of the Temple of Hercules Victorious, now hydraulic works for lighting Rome with electricity. The church on the further side of the ravine, Madonna di Quintilio, hands down the site of the Villa of Quintilius Varus (Horace, "O." i. 18). The circular edifice below, to the left, was a bath-chamber in the Villa of Lucius Aterius Tuscius, commonly called the Tempio della Tosse. To the right of the city gate is the Castle of Pius II., 1460, on the site of the amphitheatre, but now a prison. To the left is the new Provincial College, masking the Villa d'Este, the property of the Duke of Modena, and residence of Cardinal Hohenlohe ; *now closed to the public.*

GROTTO OF THE SIBYL, TIVOLI.

*Proceeding through the town, and crossing the modern bridge over the Anio, we arrive at*

## THE VILLA OF VOPISCUS,

locally called Gregoriana (fee, 50 c.). These grounds belonged to the family of Vopiscus, and are described by Statius ("Syl." i. 3), and were destroyed by the flood of 105 A.D., spoken of by Pliny ("Letters," viii. 17). The ruined bridge originally connected the two parts of the villa, for it lay on both sides of the river. Beyond is an ancient cemetery, containing the tomb of Lucius Memmius Afer, Proconsul of Sicily, 107, and erected to him by S. P. Q. T. Arriving at the

river, the stream to the right forms the old falls and cascades, whilst
that to the left flows through two tunnels, 885 feet and 980 feet, and
forms the Grand Fall.  This work was executed in 1834, to prevent
the floods destroying the town.

Taking the path at the two statues and passing under the arch,
we turn to the left, and proceed down the glen.  From platforms
we obtain views of the line of the old falls over the brown rock to
the left and in front of the natural tunnel called the Grotto of
Neptune.  To the left is Bernini's Fall of the Sibyl's Veil, and at
the bottom the Grotto of the Sibyl, whilst above is the Temple
of Vesta.

Retracing our way up the glen, and passing out of the gate, we
take the left-hand road along the brink of the glen, past S. Antonio
(Mr. F. Searl's), to obtain the most enjoyable view of Tivoli and

### THE GRAND FALL AND CASCADES.

On our left, the water, emerging from the tunnels, falls into the
valley three hundred and twenty feet below.  At one time the water
fell over the brown rocky barrier to the right, and spread out in a
basin below, the Villa of Propertius being half-way up the slope of
the hills, at the farm of S. Angelo.

> "Where the hill makes plain the twin white towers,
> And Anio's stream in an open basin falls" (iv. 6).

To the right and left of the square tower, opposite, was the Villa
of Mæcenas, where Horace stayed and wrote of the precipitous Anio
and groves of Tivoli.  He had no villa at Tivoli, though the natives
call S. Antonio his villa.  That was the farm of Catullus, which he
describes (xliv.), and which he resented being called Sabine, which
it really is.  Horace's Sabine farm is eleven miles above Tivoli.
Suetonius says it was shown in his day, but there is nothing to see
there now except the site.

### THE TEMPLE OF VESTA.

This is twenty-one feet in diameter, and its construction shows it
was rebuilt about 200 B.C.  Eighteen Corinthian columns supported
the domed roof.  The capitals are unique, being shorter than usual,
and great prominence is given to the bud of acanthus blossom between the volutes.  The architrave is decorated with wreaths between oxen's heads, above which are wheels typical of the earth's
movement, the temple representing the earth.  Above the columns,

TEMPLE OF VESTA AND GROTTO OF NEPTUNE.

in front of the window, is inscribed the name of the magistrate, L. GELLIO . L. F., who dedicated it.

### THE TEMPLE OF THE SIBYL

adjoins the above, and is rectangular, of the Ionic order.  She was the Sibylla Albunea, and Horace (i. 7) speaks of the house of Albunea resounding with the noise of the falling Anio.  Both these temples have served as churches.  The inn stands on the site of the house of the vestals.

*A bargain should be made for conveyance to*

## HADRIAN'S VILLA.
### (*Entrance, one lira.*)

" Hadrian, having made peace, returned to Rome, and retired to his villa at Tivoli, consigning the government of the city to the Cæsar L. Ælius.  There, after the manner of the happy and rich, he devoted himself to building palaces and occupying himself with painters and sculptors, giving entertainments, and resigning himself to a life of pleasure and luxury" (A. Victor, "Ep." xiv. 4).  In his Life of Hadrian, Spartianus (xxvi.) enumerates some of the edifices erected by the emperor.  He says, "In the Tiburtine Villa he raised the most celebrated and wonderful buildings—for example, the Lyceum, Academy, Prytaneum, Canopus, Piocile Stoa, Tempe; and that nothing might be omitted, he ended with Hades."  The brick stamps found show that the villa was formed between 123 and 127 A.D. ; and the ruins demonstrate that the wealth of the world was lavished on its erection, thousands of slaves being employed.  It is situated on the slope of the heights of Tivoli, from which it is only thirty minutes' walk.  It once covered an area of several square miles ; and its magnificent grounds, unequalled in the Roman Empire, were laid out by Hadrian in order to assemble within them models of everything that had struck him during his travels, and accordingly they were filled with the finest statuary, palaces, temples, theatres, circuses, and academies.  Some of the finest antique statues were found here under the popes.  All this sumptuousness was destroyed in the sixth century by the Goths.  Extensive ruins still exist.  It is thus described by Pope Pius II. :—

" About the third of a mile from the city of Tivoli, the Emperor Hadrian built a very splendid villa, like a great village.  The lofty and vast roofs of the temples still remain ; the columns of the

PLAN OF
HADRIAN'S VILLA
AT TIVOLI

peristyles and sublime porticoes may yet be gazed at with admiration.
There are still the remains of the piscinas and baths, where a canal
derived from the Anio once cooled the summer heats.

"Age deforms all things: the ivy now drapes those walls once
covered with painted hangings and cloths woven with gold; thorns and
brambles have grown where purple-clothed tribunes
sat; and snakes inhabit the chambers of queens. Thus
perishable is the nature of all things mortal."

*Entering* through an avenue of cypresses, we arrive
at the ODEUM, the skeleton of which only remains;
this was for musical performances. *Following the
path beyond the modern Casino, to the left,* by
the NYMPHÆUM, then along the brink of
the valley, we mount up to some chambers, formerly a reservoir from which
the water poured in a cascade to the
stream Peneas below. *From the edge*
of this ruin we look down upon a
valley, made in imitation of the
VALE OF TEMPE.
A stream runs
through it, named,
after the river in
Thessaly, PENEAS.
*On the opposite* slope
of the valley was the
LATIN THEATRE.
We now enter the
IMPERIAL PALACE,
with the ruins of
the Temples of
Diana and Venus
adjoining; *passing*

VILLA OF HADRIAN.

*through which,* at the farthest extremity, is the TEMPLE of CASTOR
AND POLLUX. *Near this* are some subterranean passages, called the
TARTARUS. *Beyond* were the ELYSIAN FIELDS. Elysium, or the
Elysian Fields, was the region where the souls of the dead were
supposed to go to if they had been good. There, happiness was complete, and the pleasures were innocent and refined; the air was serene
and temperate, the bowers ever green, and the meadows watered with
perennial streams, and the birds continually warbled in the groves.

Tartarus was the region of punishment in the nether world of the ancients. *On the farther side* of Tartarus is the ROMAN THEATRE; *beyond* was the LYCEUM. *Returning,* we come upon the ACADEMY. The Academy at Athens was an open meadow, given to the city by Academus, from whom it took its name. It was afterwards formed into a grove. It was the resort of Plato, and hence his disciples took the name of *academic* philosophers.

*Beyond is the* SERAPEON of CANOPUS, with the SACRARIUM of JUPITER SERAPIS at the end, built in imitation of the canal connecting Alexandria with Canopus, a city of Lower Egypt, twelve miles east of Alexandria, at the west or Canopic mouth of the Nile.

*On the right* are some remains of the HIPPODROME; *and towards the* entrance of the Serapeon, the BATHS. *From here we reach* the STADIUM, where the foot races were held. *We now come upon* a lofty wall of *opus reticulatum,* nearly six hundred feet long. This was one of the walls of the POECILE STOA, in imitation of the grand portico at Athens of that name, famed for its fresco-paintings of the battle of Marathon by Polygnotus, and as the seat of the school of Zeno the philosopher, who took the name Stoic from frequenting this portico. This portico was built on an artificial platform, and the wall can be traced all round; *underneath* are the HUNDRED CHAMBERS of the GUARDS. *From our right* of the wall, we enter the PRYTANEUM, in imitation of the council hall of that name at Athens, where the fifty deputies of the republic lived and held office, each five weeks in turn. *Through this we reach* the AQUARIUM, a circular edifice with an octagonal platform in the centre, with openings for fountains and statues; to the left of this were the GREEK and LATIN LIBRARIES.

Having now rambled over the extent of this famous villa, and picked up a memento of our visit, we may truly exclaim—"*Sic transit gloria mundi.*"

*The tramway back to Rome is taken from the end of the road leading from the villa.*

-------

# PORTA ESQUILINÆ.
### (*Porta Maggiore.*)

Here the Via Prænestina diverged from the Labicana; and Claudius, who was obliged to convey two new streams—the Aqua Claudia and the Anio Novus—over these roads, erected for this purpose a massive gateway, which spanned both roads at once with a double arch. This is the splendid monument afterwards taken into the Aurelian Wall, in the time of Honorius and Arcadius, and con-

verted, by the erection of a mound in front, into a kind of bulwark.
It now forms one of the city gates, under the name of the Porta
Maggiore.

In each of the three piers supporting the attics with the channels
concealed in the interior is a small gateway, over which a window,
with a gable roof resting on rustic pillars, is introduced. By this
arrangement, not only is a saving of materials effected, but the six

PORTA MAGGIORE.

construction arches thus acquired impart a greater degree of stability
to the structure.

The first inscription on the aqueduct of Claudius mentions the
streams conveyed into the city by the emperor upon these arches.
From it we learn that the water in the channel which bore his name
was taken from two sources,—the Cæruleus and the Curtius, forty-five
miles off; and that the Anio Novus, which flows above the Aqua
Claudia, was brought hither from a distance of sixty-two miles. The
second inscription relates to the restorations of Vespasian; the third
to those of Titus.

This gateway is the earliest specimen of the rustic style. It was named, by those going out, by which arch they passed through on their way either to Labicum or to Præneste. Coming in, they called it by the hill to which they were going. " After I had said that he entered by the Cœlimontane Gate, like a man of mettle he offered to lay a wager with me that he entered at the Esquiline Gate" (Cicero v. Piso).

Directly in front of the middle pier of the Porta Maggiore lies a monument, discovered in the year 1838, on the removal of the mound referred to. It is

## THE BAKER'S TOMB.

The man who erected his own monument on this spot was a baker, who seems to have made a considerable fortune as a purveyor. According to the good old custom, he was not ashamed of his calling, but built a species of trophy for himself out of the utensils of the trade by means of which he had attained to wealth and respectability. The hollow drums of pillars, for instance, let into the superstructure, which rests upon double columns, seem to represent vessels for measuring fruit; and the inscription found beside them agrees with this opinion, as it states that the mortal remains of Atistia, the wife of Eurysaces, were deposited in a bread-basket. In fact, everything was represented that appertained to a baker's trade.

This is rendered the more interesting from the circumstance of several of these representations seeming to belong to the present time—people in this sphere in Italy usually adhering to the customs transmitted to them by their forefathers.

The inscription on the architrave, stating this monument to be that of M. Virgilius Eurysaces, purveyor of bread, is repeated three times. A relief of the baker and his wife, also the remains of the Gate of Honorius, are to be seen on the right of the road.

To the north of the tomb three old aqueducts, Marcia, Tepula, and Julia, can be seen passing through the walls of Rome.

## VIA LABICANA

is an interesting excursion. *Leaving Rome by the Porta Maggiore, we take the road on the right,* Via Labicana, *as we can return by the other,* Via Gabina, *or* Prænestina. For the first mile the road runs parallel with the Claudian Aqueduct; then, bending to the left, there are some very picturesque remains of the Aqua Hadriana, A.D. 120, restored by Alexander Severus, A.D. 225, as recorded by Spartianus. At the second mile is Tor Pignattara, the so-called

### TOMB OF HELENA(?).

This ascription is altogether a mistake. Helena was buried in the city of New Rome (Constantinople), and not outside ancient Rome. "Her remains were conveyed to New Rome, and deposited in the imperial sepulchres" (Socrates, E. H., i. 17). The sarcophagus found here is more likely, from its reliefs, to have been that of a soldier than a woman. The sarcophagus, of red porphyry, is now in the Hall of the Greek Cross in the Vatican. The remains of the tomb consist of a circular hall with eight circular recesses. A church, dedicated to SS. Peter and Marcellinus, stands within it, beneath which are the catacombs of these saints. At the sixth mile is TORRE NUOVA, surrounded by pine and mulberry trees. At the Osteria di Finacchio (ninth mile) a by-road leads to the Osteria dell' Osa, on the Via Gabina (two miles). *Visitors leave their carriage here, and order it to go two miles further on, to (opposite) Castiglione, on the Via Prænestina, where they meet it after visiting*

### GABII,

founded by the kings of Alba, and taken by the Romans, under Tarquin, through the artifice of his son Sextus. It was deserted in the time of the republic, but recovered under the empire, to fall once more before the time of Constantine. At the end of the ridge are remains of the Roman Municipium and Temple of Juno of the time of Hadrian. The buildings of CASTIGLIONE occupy the site of the ancient city. The principal ruin is the TEMPLE OF JUNO GABINA. Virgil tells us "it was situated amidst rugged rocks, on the banks of the cold Anienes." The cella is composed of blocks of stone four feet by two feet; the interior is 50 feet long; the pavement is of white mosaic. *Close by are* the ruins of the THEATRE, and some Ionic columns. Considerable remains of the ancient walls can be traced. The fresh, green basin below the ridge was once a lake, and was drained about twenty-five years since by Prince Borghese. It is curious that there is no mention of the lake by classical authors. It is first mentioned in reference to the martyrdom of S. Primitivus, who was beheaded at Gabii, and whose head was thrown into the lake. This was in the fifth century. Perhaps the lake did not exist in Tarquin's time, and was formed by some freak of nature after the desertion of the city.

*Returning to Rome by the Via Gabina, after passing the stream Osa,* about two miles, we come to a fine Roman viaduct, PONTE DI NONA, consisting of seven lofty arches, built of rectangular blocks of *lapis gabinus* of the time of the kings. At the eighth mile is the medieval

Tor Tre Teste, so called from the three heads built in its walls. Here Camillus overtook the Gauls (Livy, v. 49). *About two and a half miles from Rome, at the* Tor dei Schiavi, are extensive ruins of the VILLA OF THE GORDIAN EMPERORS, consisting of a large reservoir, the circular hall of the baths, and a circular temple, 43 feet in diameter, called Apollo. The inside is relieved by alternate round and square niches; the crypt beneath is supported by one pier. *Between this and* Tor dei Schiavi, three rooms at the base of a circular edifice have been opened; the floors are composed of black and white mosaic.

*On the right, about a mile further on,* is the circular tomb, 50 yards in diameter, of QUINTUS ATTA, the comic poet (B.C. 55); the interior is in the form of a Greek cross.

---

## PORTA S. GIOVANNI.

*(A new railway has been made by way of Marino to Albano.)*

### FIRST EXCURSION.

#### VIA APPIA NOVA.

This road was made in the time of the Antonines, to relieve the traffic on the Via Appia, and was called simply a New Way. Several tombs of the time of the Antonines line it, but none of earlier date. At the right of the gate is the ancient Porta Asinara, the best preserved of the brick gates. At the second mile the road is crossed by the VIA LATINA, *turning up which, on the left, we can visit*

#### THE PAINTED TOMBS.

One, discovered in 1859, is covered with beautiful paintings and stucco reliefs—eight landscapes, with groups of men and animals, with small arabesque borders, beautifully finished. The reliefs on the vault represent the Trojan War, and figures of Hercules, Chitaredes, Jupiter, with the eagle and centaurs hunting lions, &c. *Near by,* discovered at the same time, is

#### THE BASILICA OF S. STEPHEN,

founded about A.D. 450 by Demetria, a member of the Anician family. It was rebuilt by Leo III., A.D. 800. A bell tower was erected by Lupus Grigarius about thirty years afterwards. The ground plan can be easily made out, as also the remains of the altar and baptistery. In front of the tribune is a vault, entered by stairs, similar to those in most of the Roman Catholic basilicæ, where the martyrs were buried.

The basilica stands amidst the ruins of a large Roman villa of the Servilii and Asinii, discovered by Signor Fortunati.

*Returning to the main road,* we soon pass the Tor Fiscali, a medieval tower, and then the Osteria Tovolato; then we get some fine views of the ruined aqueducts.

## THE AQUEDUCTS.

Sixteen aqueducts supplied the city with water and irrigated the Campagna. The principal streams were the AQUA APPIA, B.C. 312; ANIO VETUS, B.C. 272; MARCIA, B.C. 145,—on the top of its arches,

CLAUDIAN AQUEDUCT.

near Rome, were carried the AQUÆ TEPULA and JULIA ; VIRGO, B.C. 21; CLAUDIA, with ANIO NOVUS above, A.D. 38–52. The Romans, finding the water from the Tiber and the wells sunk in the city unwholesome, built these aqueducts, to bring the water from the hills that surround the Campagna ; but their situation and purpose rendered them exposed to attack during war, which partly accounts for their destruction. Four of them still supply the city with water :—The *Aqua Marcia,* which has its source near Subiaco. From Tivoli it passes through pipes to Rome, which it enters at the Porta Pia. It was brought in by a company, and opened by Pius IX. on the 10th of September 1870. The *Aqua Virgo,* built by Agrippa, B.C. 21, has its source near the eighth mile-stone on the Via Collatina, restored by Nicholas V. It supplies the Trevi Fountain. The *Aqua Alseatina,* built by Augustus, A.D. 10, on the other side of the Tiber, has its source thirty-five miles from Rome, at the Lago Baccano. It was restored by Paul V., and supplies the Pauline Fountain. *Acqua Felice*, made by Sixtus V., A.D. 1587. Its source is near La Colonna, formerly the source of Hadrian's Aqueduct. It runs parallel with the Claudian and the Marcian, near Rome, in some places being built out of their remains and on their piers. Pliny says : "If any one will diligently estimate the abundance of water supplied to the public baths, fountains, fish-ponds, artificial lakes, and galley-fights, to pleasure-gardens, and to almost every private house in Rome, and then consider the difficulties that were to be surmounted, and the distance from which these streams were brought, he will confess that nothing so wonderful as these aqueducts can be found in the whole world."

## THE ROUTE.

We now pass, on the left, a tomb of the Antonines ; and, on the right, the imposing ruins of the Villa of the Quintilii Brothers, who were here murdered, and their estate usurped by Commodus. On our right is a ruined aqueduct, which supplied the Villa of the Quintilii, whose picturesque ruins we have previously passed.

We now soon reach the ascent to Albano, and strike the old Appian Way at Frattocchie, the site of the Three Taverns. (See page 298.) At the twelfth mile, *on the right*, are the ruins of Bovillæ. Several unknown tombs line the road. At the intersection of the Via Appia with the town limits stands an ancient tomb, formerly considered to be that of the Horatii and Curiatii, those champions of their age. Now it is more correctly held to be

## THE TOMB OF POMPEY THE GREAT.

For we know from Plutarch that his ashes were carried to Cornelia, who buried them in his land near Alba, though Lucan (viii. 835) complains that he had no tomb—

> "And thou, O Rome, by whose forgetful hand
> Altars and temples, reared to tyrants, stand,
> Canst thou neglect to call thy hero home,
> And leave his ghost in banishment to roam?"

The town occupies the site of the ruins of the Villa of Pompey, and the Albanum of Domitian. The best view of the Mediterranean is to be had at

## ALBANO.

*reached by rail in one hour from Rome.* It is a favourite resort in summer, on account of its pure air, elevated position, and the delightful rambles that can be made in its neighbourhood. In winter it is frequented by all the Forestieri, who are to be seen there daily in carriages and on donkeys, doing all the attractions of the locality. From this point the tour of the Alban Hills, taking in all places of interest, can be most conveniently made. The peasants' costumes are very attractive. The town itself is not a centre of interest ; a few ruins are shown in some of its streets, but they are neither very visible nor authentic.

## VALE OF ARICCIA.

To the south of the town of Albano, on the right is a beautiful valley, once a lake, but now drained, called the Vale of Ariccia. It is not known when it was drained. It is thus alluded to by Ovid (" Fasti," iii. 263) :—

> " Deep in Ariccia's vale, and girt around
> With shady trees, a sacred lake is found ;
> Here Theseus' son in safe concealment lay,
> When hurried by the violent steeds away."

*Proceeding beyond the town*, we come to the Viaduct of Pius IX. (1846-1863).

Just before reaching the viaduct, the old Appian Way branches off to the right, descending the side of the Vale of Ariccia. Several remains of tombs exist at this point, notably that of Aruns, the son of Porsena of Clusium.

## TOMB OF ARUNS.

This ruin agrees exactly with the lower part of the Tomb of Porsena at Clusium, described by Pliny (xxxvi. 19). He says : "But as the fabulousness of the story connected with it quite exceeds all bounds, I shall employ the words given by M. Varro himself in his account of it. ' Porsena was buried,' says he, ' beneath the city of Clusium, in the spot where he had constructed a square monument, built of squared stones. Each side of this monument was 300 feet long and 50 feet high, and beneath the base, which was also square, was an inextricable labyrinth......Above this square building there stood five pyramids—one at each corner and one in the middle—75 feet broad at the base and 150 feet in height,' " &c.

The present ruin is 49 feet long on each side and 24 feet high, surmounted at the angles with four cones, and one larger, in the centre, 26 feet in diameter, in which the urn was found in the last century.

## ARICCIA.

The ancient ascent to Ariccia was the Clivus Virbii, so called from Hippolytus, who, on being restored to life by Diana, took the name of Virbius.

> "But Trivia kept in secret shades alone
> Her care, Hippolytus, to fate unknown;
> And called him Virbius in the Egerian Grove,
> Where then he lived obscure, but safe from Jove."
> VIRGIL, *Æneid*, vii. 774.

The ascent was a noted place for beggars, as recorded by Persius (Sat. vi. 55) and Juvenal (Sat. iv.).

The village is three-quarters of a mile west from Albano, surrounded by beautiful woods. At its entrance is the Palazzo Chigi, built by Bernini, in the midst of a fine park; fee, half-franc. The ancient town lay lower down the hill, where some of its remains can still be traced. Horace (Lib. i. Sat. 5) tells us that for slow travellers it was the first halting-place from Rome.

> "Leaving imperial Rome, my course I steer
> To poor Ariccia and its moderate cheer."
> FRANCIS.

In the vale, just under the town, was the

### TEMPLE OF DIANA ARICINA,

which Vitruvius (iv. 7) says was circular. The story of this temple is given by several classic writers. "Hippolytus came into Italy and dedicated the Temple of Aricina Diana. In this place, even at present, those who are victors in a single contest have the office of priest to the goddess given to them as a reward. This contest, however, is not offered to any free person, but only to slaves who have fled from their masters" (Pausanias, ii. 27). In 1791 a relief representing the scene was found at the circular ruin, and is now at Palma in Majorca. The temple was near a little stream from a source under the second viaduct, known as the

### FOUNTAIN OF EGERIA,

which supplies the lake. The nymph was overcome by the death of Numa, as Ovid tells us: "Other woes, however, did not avail to diminish Egeria's grief; and, lying down at the very foot of the mountain, she melted into tears, until the sister of Apollo (Diana), moved to compassion, made a cool fountain of her body, changed into perennial waters."

> " His wife the town forsook,
> And in the woods that clothe Ariccia's vale lies hid."
>
> *Met.* xv. 487.

> " There, at the mountain's base, all drowned in tears,
> She lay, till chaste Diana on her woe
> Compassion took: her altered form became
> A limpid fount; her beauteous limbs dissolved,
> And in perennial waters melt away."
>
> *Met.* xv. 548.

> " O'er their rough bed hoarse-murmuring waters move;
> A pure but scanty draught is there supplied;
> Egeria's fount, whom all the muses love,
> Sage Numa's counsellor, his friend, and bride."
>
> *Fasti,* iii. 273.

After two miles of a picturesque and shady road, crossing four viaducts, and commanding beautiful views, we arrive at

## GENZANO.

Its excellent wine is renowned, and this, together with its flowers and beautiful situation, are its sole attractions. The flower festival, held the eighth day after Corpus Christi, is fully described in "The Improvisatore." *Up a path* by the side of the Palazzo Cesarini we obtain a fine view of the

## LAKE NEMI,

which occupies an extinct crater. The lake is three miles in circumference, and 300 feet deep, and passes out by an artificial *emissarium*, made by Trajan. The water is calm and marvellously clear.

Trajan erected on this lake a floating palace, 500 feet in length, 270 feet in breadth, and 60 feet deep. It was of wood, joined with bronze nails, and lead plated outside; the inside was lined with marble, and the ceilings were of bronze. The water for use and ornament was supplied from the Fount Juturna by means of pipes. Signor Marchi, a Roman, in 1535 descended in a diving-bell and explored this curious palace, which had sunk beneath the waters. He left an account of his discoveries. (See Brotier's "Tacitus," Sup. Ap., and Notes on Trajan.) A large fragment of the wood-work is preserved in the Kircherian Museum.

*On the opposite side* is the small medieval town of

## NEMI,

picturesquely situated upon a hill above the lake. On the sides of the lake are the remains of villas built of *opus reticulatum ;* and in the sixteenth century some of the wood-work, tiles, &c., of Cæsar's

Villa—begun, but afterwards pulled down because it did not suit his taste—were found, and are preserved in the Library of the Vatican.

> " Lo, Nemi ! navelled in thy woody hills
> So far, that the uprooting wind which tears
> The oak from his foundations, and which spills
> The ocean o'er its boundary, and bears
> Its foam against the skies, reluctant spares
> The oval mirror of thy glassy lake ;
> And, calm as cherished hate, its surface wears
> A deep, cold, settled aspect naught can shake,
> All coiled into itself and round, as sleeps the snake."—BYRON.

## THE TEMPLE OF DIANA NEMORENSE.

On the plateau at the east end of the lake, to our left of Nemi, Lord Savile of Rufford, when ambassador at Rome, made some most interesting excavations—uncovering the vast area of the Temple of Diana at Nemi, and at the same time discovering numerous objects of interest, which proved without doubt to whom the shrine was dedicated.

The front of the temple was formed with a portico of fluted columns, and its rear was towards the lake, so the temple faced east. The whole Artemisium shows traces of many restorations, not the least interesting being that made by Marcus Servilius Quartus, consul A.D. 3, whose tomb is on the Via Appia (Tacitus, " A." ii. 48 ; iii. 22).

When Iphigenia, priestess of the Temple of Diana at Tauris in the Crimea, fled with her brother Orestes, they carried off the statue of Diana, to whom all strangers cast on the coast were sacrificed, and founded a temple near the Lake of Diana, now Nemi, on the Alban Hills (Ovid, " Ep." iii. 2 ; " Met." xv. 485). "The temple is in a grove, and before it is a lake of considerable size. The temple and water are surrounded by abrupt and lofty precipices, so that they seem to be situated in a deep and lofty ravine " (Strabo, v. 3, 12).

## THE FOUNTAIN OF JUTURNA.

This issues from the hill under the village, and serves the mill on the border of the lake. "Tell me, nymph Juturna, thou that wast wont to minister to the grove and looking-glass of Diana" (Ovid, " F." iii. 260). "The springs by which the lake is filled are visible. One of them is denominated Juturna, after the name of a certain divinity " (Strabo v. 3, 12).

*A ramble through the woods brings us to the adjoining lake at Palazzolo*, which is generally seen in the distance from the opposite side of the lake.

## PALAZZOLO.

> " And near, Albano's scarce divided waves
> Shine from a sister valley."

*Situated on Lake Albano, or it may be reached from Albano or Marino by other roads passing round the Lake Albano.* It is a Franciscan monastery. In its gardens is a tomb supposed to be that of Cneius Cornelius Scipio Hispanus, B.C. 176.

*A path through the woods leads up to Monte Cavo.*

## THE ALBAN LAKE

is 150 feet below Lake Nemi. Its outlet conducts its waters to the Tiber. This lake also occupies the crater of an extinct volcano; it is six miles round, and of unknown depth. The outlet was made at the time the Romans were besieging Veii, B.C. 394, to lower the waters which threatened to flood the Campagna. It is 1509 yards in length.

*Situated on the bluff overlooking the lake is*

## CASTEL GANDOLFO,

formerly the summer residence of the popes. Its palace was erected by Urban VIII. This palace, and the charming situation, are its only features of attraction.

*On the opposite shore, which can be reached either from Palazzolo, or by a path from the Albano or the Marino end of the lake, is the supposed site of*

## ALBA LONGA.

Built by Ascanius 1152 B.C., destroyed by Tullus Hostilius 666 B.C.

Virgil tells us that on Æneas consulting the oracle at Delos, the oracle replied,—

> "Now mark the signs of future ease and rest,
> And bear them safely treasured in thy breast:
> When, in the shady shelter of a wood,
> And near the margin of a gentle flood,
> Thou shalt behold a sow upon the ground,
> With thirty sucking young encompassed round,
> The dam and offspring white as falling snow,—
> These on thy city shall their name bestow,
> And there shall end thy labours and thy woe."
>
> *Æneid*, iii. 388.

Again, when Father Tiber appeared to him, he says,—

> " And that this mighty vision may not seem
> Th' effect of fancy, or an idle dream,

A sow beneath an oak shall lie along,
All white herself, and white her thirty young.
When thirty rolling years have run their race,
Thy son Ascanius, on *this* empty space,
Shall build a royal town, of lasting fame,
Which from this omen shall receive the name."

*Æneid*, viii. 70.

Again, after Father Tiber had disappeared, and Æneas, having invoked the god, fitted out two galleys to go up the Tiber to Evander:

"Now on the shore the fatal swine is found.
Wondrous to tell, she lay along the ground;
Her well-fed offspring at her udders hung—
She white herself, and white her thirty young!"

*Æneid*, viii. 120.

Thus, according to Virgil's own showing, the sow was found on the banks of the Tiber; how then could the shores of the Alban Lake be the site of Alba Longa? Ought we not rather to look for that site on the banks of the Tiber below Rome, where the sow was found, according to the voices of the oracle and the river-god, and the record handed down by Virgil? On the other hand, we are told Alba Longa was "built by Ascanius, the son of Æneas, thirty years after the building of Lavinium. Alba stood between a mountain and a lake: the mountain is extremely strong and high, and the lake deep and large. When one part of the lake is low upon the retreat of the water, and the bottom clear, the ruins of porticoes and other traces of habitation appear, being the remains of the palace of King Alladius, which was destroyed by the lake rising. Alba Longa was demolished by Marcus Horatius, by command of Tullus Hostilius" (Dionysius, i. 66. See Livy, i. 29).

From Castel Gandolfo a pleasant road by the lake leads to Marino, *passing through a wood* after leaving the lake. *Just before entering* the town we come to a wooded glen, the ancient

## VALLIS FERENTINA,

where the diet of the Latin states assembled to discuss the interests of peace and war. A stream runs through the valley, and in the spring which feeds the stream, at the head of the valley, Turnus Herdonius, Lord of Aricia, was drowned by the command of Tarquinius Superbus.

## MARINO,

celebrated for its wine, is perched on an eminence 1730 feet high. It was a great stronghold of the Orsini, and afterwards of the

Colonnas, whose towers and palace still stand. The principal street is the Corso. At the top, on the right hand side, is a house decorated with curious mosaics and bas-reliefs, surmounted with a Madonna. At the bottom of the Corso is the Cathedral of S. Barnabas, in which is a picture of S. Bartholomew, by Guercino. The fountain close by is picturesque, composed of half female figures supporting the basin, out of which four figures rise supporting a column.

*Over a beautiful route of four miles we reach*

### GROTTA FERATTA, AND CICERO'S TUSCULAN VILLA,

which is now a Greek monastery, founded in 1002 by S. Ninus. In one of its chapels are frescoes from the life of the saint, by Domenichino, restored by Camuccini in 1819. Fairs are held here on the 28th of March and 8th of September, drawing large crowds from the neighbourhood as well as from Rome.

The villa stands on the site and is built out of the remains of Cicero's Villa, which he purchased of Sylla the dictator at a great price. To the south of the hill upon which the villa stands is a deep dell, falling into which is the stream of the Aqua Craba, mentioned by Cicero, now called the Maranna or running stream; and the plane-tree still flourishes here as it did in his day. Cicero likewise mentions that he had statues of the muses in his library, and a hermathena in his academy, and these statues were actually found here. The scenes of his "De Divinatione" and "Tusculan Disputations" were laid here. They were not addressed to any public assembly, but he used to retire after dinner to his so-called academy, and invited his guests to call for the subject they wished explained, which became the argument of the debate. These five discussions or conferences he collected and published as the "Tusculan Disputations" after the name of his villa, which was in the Tusculan territory, but not at the city itself. The subjects were,—Contempt of Death; On Bearing Pain; Grief of Mind; Other Perturbations of the Mind; Whether Virtue be Sufficient for a Happy Life. It was here that he received news of his proscription.

A pleasant drive soon brings us to the foot of the hills, passing on our way several tombs, and the ruined castle of the Savellis, a medieval stronghold of the tenth century, called BORGHETTO, of which only the outer walls are standing. Two miles below, *on our right*, are the ruins of an immense reservoir of the aqueducts coming from the Alban Hills, the TEPULA, 126 B.C.; the JULIA, 34 B.C.; and the SEVERIANA, 190 A.D. It is known by the name of the

CENTRONI. Just below the bluff on which it stands, the stream of the Aqua Craba, coming from Rocca di Papa, falls into the Almo coming from Marino; united, they flow through an old tunnel under the road beyond the bridge.

*We now strike the Via Tusculana or Frascati Road.*

On the left are the picturesque ruins of the VILLA OF SEPTIMIUS BASSUS, consul 317 A.D. It is known by the name of Sette Bassi, or Roma Vecchia. Part of the villa is of the time of Hadrian. About two miles further on, *on our right*, is a tumulus, Monte del Grano, in which was found the splendid sarcophagus now in the Capitoline Museum, which contained the Portland Vase. It is not known to whom it belonged. We next cross the Naples railway, and pass under PORTA FURBA (Thieves' Arch), supporting the Acqua Felice. Looking back through the arch, there is a beautiful view. Here we can see the arches of the aqueducts distinctly: *on the left*, under the arch by the fountain, the Claudia and Anio Novus; and *on the right* the Marcia, Tepula, and Julia. The stream in sight is the Maranna. From here the lane to the right, a pleasant drive, leads to the Porta Maggiore, whilst that straight on strikes the Via Appia Nova, near the Porta S. Giovanni.

## SECOND EXCURSION.

*(The railway now goes right up to the town.)*

To return, we take the road above, to the point where the Grotta Ferrata road strikes off to the right; then the road ascends to Frascati; but there is nothing of interest *en route*. Much time is saved by taking the rail to Frascati, which brings us into the town, near the Piazza and Cathedral.

### FRASCATI,

of all the Alban towns, is most frequented, on account of its proximity to Rome, from which it can be reached by rail in forty-five minutes. The town itself is uninteresting. In the cathedral is a monument to Prince Charles Edward, erected by his brother, the Cardinal York, who was bishop of this diocese.

The beautiful villas in the vicinity are well worth visiting, affording cool retreats in summer. These are—Villa Montalto ; Villa Pallavicini ; Villa Conti ; Villa Borghese ; Villa Ruffinella ; Villa Muti, long the residence of Cardinal York ; Villa Sora ; Villa Falconieri ; Villa Lancellotti ; and Villa Mondragone.

*On the road to* Monte Porzio, *vià* Manara, under the town, is the

22

pretty little Villa Sansoni, once the residence of the Chevalier S. George, the would-be King James III. of England and VIII. of Scotland.

The antiquities of Frascati are few. *To the left, from* the station, opposite the hospital, in a garden, is a grotto called the NYMPHÆUM OF LUCULLUS; and in a piazza, where the donkeys are usually mounted for Tusculum, is a circular tomb called the Sepulchre of Lucullus. Lucullus distinguished himself in the Social War. He was consul 74 B.C., and for seven years conducted the war against Mithridates. He died 56 B.C., and was buried by his brother on his estate at Tusculum,—the offer of a public funeral in the Campus Martius being declined. "Lucullus had the most superb pleasure house in the country near Tusculum; adorned with grand galleries and open saloons, as well for the prospect as for walks" (Plutarch). *Opposite* the house of the Chevalier S. George are some remains of a villa of the time of Augustus.

*In ascending the hill from* Frascati, we pass along by a shady road, passing through the Villa Ruffinella (the property of Prince Lancellotti, who has made a new road up to it). Under the porch are some remains brought from Tusculum.

## TUSCULUM.

A city of great antiquity, now in ruins, founded by the son of Ulysses. The remains of the forum, reservoir, and walls can still be traced. The ancient citadel stood on the artificial rock, which is now surmounted by a cross, 212 feet above the city. The view is magnificent. The height is 2400 feet above the sea. Tusculum was destroyed in 1191, after repeated attacks by the Romans, who razed it to the ground. It was the birthplace of Cato. Ascending by the old road, still paved with the blocks of lava stone, passing by an old tomb, we arrive at the amphitheatre of reticulated work, 225 feet by 167 feet broad. The construction shows it to be of the time of Hadrian. Above, some massive remains of the same construction have been dignified by some as the site of Cicero's Villa. We have thoroughly explored these remains, and proved them to form a large reservoir for water, of the time of Hadrian. Beyond was the Forum, the Diurnal Theatre, the Reservoir, and the Citadel. To the left, before entering the theatre, a short distance down the old road, is a fountain erected by the ædiles Q. C. Latinus and Marcus Decimus, by order of the senate. Near it is a reservoir with a roof like a Gothic arch, formed in the primitive style of one stone resting against another. From here a specus runs back into the hill to the spring. Here also can be examined the walls of the city, formed of square blocks of sperone, evidently rebuilt at a later date, as the walls to the left in the ditch are polygonal, agreeing with the date of the city. The hill of Tusculum is formed of volcanic matter, which has in some parts been so hardened as to form a stone, *sperone lapis Tusculanus*, and which, from the condition of the ruins, must have been largely used in the buildings of the city.

The visitor who has come up from Frascati, and wishes to return there, had better do so by another path through the woods, by the Camaldoli Monastery, to the Villa Mondragone, then by the Villa Borghese to Frascati, a pleasant route. From Tusculum, a charming path through the chestnut groves leads up to Monte Cavo, avoiding Rocca di Papa, the ancient Fabia, which can be seen on the return.

## ROCCA DI PAPA

is situated on the brink of the great crater which, the natives say, was formerly occupied by the camp of Hannibal. Fabius kept the hills, and Hannibal the plain. It takes its name from the proprietors, Annibile, and had nothing to do with Hannibal. It is a small town, but well suited for a summer residence. A new carriage road makes it accessible from either Albano or Frascati. *From here we ascend to*

## MONTE CAVO.

The ascent is made in three-quarters of an hour. There is a wooded ascent along the Via Triumphalis, by which the Roman generals ascended in order to celebrate at the Temple of Jupiter Latialis. The ruins of this temple were converted partly into a monastery by the Cardinal York, and partly into the Church of S. Peter's at Frascati. The ancient name of this mountain was Monte Latialis, and the ancient road that went over it, Via Numinis, the initials V. N. in the pavement telling us the name. It is 3200 feet above the sea. About three parts of the way up, from a ledge off the road, a beautiful view of the Alban Lakes can be had—forming, as it were, a pair of eyes. The view obtained is unequalled, comprising the sea and coast from Terracina and Civita Vecchia, Rome and the Campagna, and, immediately beneath us, the Alban Mountains—one of the most interesting views in the world, every spot around being full of historical associations. Here, as it were, we can take in the whole panoramic view of the history of Rome. The surface of the mountain, on which stood the shrine of the god, extends to three thousand square yards. Besides its religious and architectural pur-

poses, this area was used as a collector for rain water, which first
ran into a *piscina limaria* to be purified, and then through a subterranean channel to a reservoir, the capacity of which amounts to one
thousand cubic yards, having still some hydraulic regulators of lead,
with their keys and pipes, on which the names of Maximus and
Tubero, consuls in 11 B.C., are engraved.

The return journey is made down the direct road from Rocca di Papa
to Frascati, passing the PONTE DEGLI SQUARCIARELLI, over the Aqua
Craba, at the point where the roads turn off to Marino, Grotta Feratta,
and Frascati.

## PORTA OSTIENSIS.

### (*Porta S. Paolo.*)

This is the most picturesque of the gates of Rome. It consists of
a double gateway, the outer (of the time of Theodoric) with one, the
inner (of the time of Claudius) with two arches, flanked with towers.
*On the right is the*

### PYRAMID OF CAIUS CESTIUS,

erected by his heir, Pontius Mela, and his freedman Pœhus. This
imposing structure was faced with smoothly hewn slabs of marble,
and stands on a basement of travertine measuring 95 feet in diameter.
It is 115 feet high.

This monument, erected some twenty or thirty years before the
Christian era, was indebted for its preservation to the circumstance
of its having been incorporated by Aurelian with the line of his fortifications. The confined burial chamber (the paintings on the roof and
walls of which are now almost obliterated) is reached through the
doorway, introduced at some height on the north side. As is usually
the case with tombs, in order to prevent spoliation, there were no
steps leading up to the door. The west entrance is of more modern
origin, dating from the time of Alexander VII., who caused it to be
broken through the wall, although the ancient original doorway already
afforded the means of ingress. The lower portion of the monument
was cleared from the rubbish, which had accumulated to the height of
twenty feet, at the same time; and the two fluted columns, resting
upon travertine bases, were also dug up. Still more remarkable is the
discovery of the remains of the colossal statue of C. Cestius, consisting
of the foot and arm, now in the Hall of Bronzes in the Capitol Museum.

*Keeping the straight road, we come, on the left, to*

## THE CHAPEL OF SS. PETER AND PAUL.

A relief over the door represents their parting, where this chapel now stands. The inscription says :—

IN THIS PLACE SS. PETER AND PAUL SEPARATED ON THEIR WAY TO MARTYRDOM, AND PAUL SAID TO PETER, " PEACE BE WITH THEE, FOUNDATION OF THE CHURCH, SHEPHERD OF THE FLOCK OF CHRIST." AND PETER SAID TO PAUL, " GO IN PEACE, PREACHER OF GOOD TIDINGS, AND GUIDE OF THE SALVATION OF THE JUST."

## THE CHURCH OF S. PAOLO.

The first church built, in the time of Constantine, to commemorate the martyrdom of S. Paul. It was destroyed by fire on July 15, 1823; its restoration was immediately commenced, and it was reopened in 1854 by Pio Nono. The festa days are January 25th, June 30th, and December 28th. The principal entrance towards the Tiber is still unfinished. Before the Reformation it was under the protection of the kings of England. It is the finest of Roman churches, and the visitor cannot fail to be charmed with its beauty; it is one vast hall of marble, with eighty Corinthian pillars forming the nave, reflected in the marble pavement. The grand triumphal arch which separates the nave from the transept is a relic of the old basilica; and the mosaic, Christ blessing in the Greek manner, with the twenty-four elders, is of the fifth century, given by Placidia, sister of Honorius, in 440. The mosaic of the tribune was erected by Pope Honorius III., 1216-27; it has been restored since the fire. On either side are statues of S. Peter and S. Paul; around the church, above the columns, are portraits of the popes, from S. Peter, in mosaics. The altar canopy is supported by four pillars of Oriental alabaster, given by Mehemet Ali, Pasha of Egypt. A marble staircase leads to the subterranean chapel, where are preserved the relics of the martyrs Paul and Timothy. The altars at each end of the transept are of malachite, given by the Czar of Russia. The painted windows are worthy of attention,* as also a beautiful alabaster candelabrum saved from the fire. The walls and numerous chapels are adorned with paintings and statues of the present day, giving a good idea of the actual state of art in Rome. By applying to one of the guards, visitors can see the beautiful court of the thirteenth century, which will fully repay inspection. Prudentius, who saw the original basilica in its glory, thus describes it :—

" Imperial splendour all the roof adorns ;
Whose vaults a monarch built to God, and graced

* Destroyed in the explosion, April 23, 1891. They are to be replaced with replicas.

With golden pomp the vast circumference.
With gold the beams he covered, that within
The light might emulate the beams of morn.
Beneath the glittering ceiling pillars stood
Of Parian stone, in fourfold ranks disposed:
Each curving arch with glass of various dye
Was decked; so shines with flowers the painted mead
In spring's prolific day."

*Passio Beat. Apost.*

This description will apply equally well to the present basilica. The church is 396 feet long from the steps of the tribune; width of aisle and nave, 222 feet.

The façade of the basilica, the upper part of which has lately been uncovered, is toward the Tiber; it consists of a beautiful mosaic which has taken thirteen years to complete, and is the finest production of the Vatican manufactory. The whole is surmounted by a cross, under which are the words *Spes Unica;* below it is our Lord enthroned, with SS. Peter and Paul on either side below the steps of his throne. A scene symbolic of the New Testament is below. A rock occupies the centre, from which flow the four rivers of the Apocalypse; on the summit is the Lamb supporting the cross. The cities of Jerusalem and Bethlehem are on each side, whilst flocks of sheep between the palm-trees are symbolic of the apostolic college. Below, Isaiah, Jeremiah, Ezekiel, and Daniel typify the Old Testament. The whole, a triangle, is bordered with a mosaic of fruit and foliage.

*At the back of the church is*

## THE REMURIA HILL.

It is altogether a mistake to suppose that Remus took his stand upon the Aventine and Romulus upon the Palatine; if so, they would both have commanded nearly the same horizon, and messengers need not have been sent from one to the other to tell the number of birds seen. Romulus stood on the Aventine, and Remus on the hill before us, the Remuria.

" Remus pitched upon the ground now called from him Remuria. This place is very proper for a city, being a hill not far from the Tiber, distant from Rome about thirty stadia" (Dionysius, i. 85).

"Romulus buried Remus at Remuria, since, when alive, he had been fond of building there" (*Ibid.,* i. 87).

This hill is called to the present day *La Remuria.*

*The road straight on past S. Paolo leads to the*

or Three Springs, which are said to have sprung forth when S. Paul
was executed on this spot, his head rebounding three times after it
was cut off. Three churches have been built here, but they are not
of much interest.

*The rambler can return to the city from S. Paul's by tramway, fare
six sous, to the Piazza Montanara.*

*To the left the* STRADA DELLE SETTE CHIESE *leads to the* VIA APPIA,
*near the Church of S. Sebastiano.*

### THE VIA OSTIENSIS.

*(Dr. Forbes's carriage excursion at frequent intervals.)*

*Instead of turning to the left to the Three Fountains, keep straight on.*
This is the pleasantest and prettiest road out of Rome, but the views
are not so commanding as on some others. On the hill to the left
was the Vicus Alexandrinus, where the Lateran obelisk was landed;
at Tor di Valle we cross the stream that comes from the Alban
lake,—the bridge is of the time of the kings. Here Pliny turned
off to his Laurentine Villa ("Ep." ii. 17). We next cross the Decima
stream; beyond, the Via Laurentina, at the Osteria of Malafede,
turns off to the *left*. We descend to the valley of the Malafede,
which is still crossed by the

### VIADUCT OF ANCUS MARTIUS,

called *Ponte della Refolta*. It is worth while to get out of the carriage here and turn into the field at the gate on the left, over the
bridge, to see this piece of ancient work, formed of great blocks of
tufa stone of the time of the kings, having some repairs in *opus reticulatum* of the republic. The paved arch over the stream is in good
preservation, and is older than the Cloaca Maxima, but not so well
known. It is evidently the work of Ancus Martius, who made the
port of Ostia, and consequently the road to get there. At the top
of the hill above we get the first view of the sea and the last of
S. Peter's. We now pass through the woods and along an ancient
causeway through the salt marshes to the modern village of

### OSTIA,

fourteen miles from Rome. The ancient remains are beyond. Founded
by Ancus Martius, it was the great port and arsenal of ancient Rome,
with which it rose and fell. *Ascending* the tower of the castle in the

village, an extensive view of the Latin coast and surrounding ancient forests may be had. The castle was erected for Julius II. when Cardinal della Rovere, in 1490, by Sangallo, and is an interesting specimen of brick fortification. The interior was frescoed by Peruzzi, but these are now destroyed. The collection of antiquities from Ostia formerly exhibited here has been removed to the National Museum in Rome. The river once ran under the walls, and is so represented in Raphael's fresco of Pope Leo IV. defeating the Saracens. The church is dedicated to S. Aurea, and is a bishop's see, said to have been founded by S. Peter. Its bishop is dean of the sacred college. Monica died here.

## PORTA ROMANA.

A quarter of a mile beyond the castle we strike a street of tombs and columbaria. Conspicuous on the left is the sarcophagus tomb of Sextus Carminius Parthenopeus, Decurion and Master of the Guild of Carpenters. Beyond, on the same side, is a Christian fourth century sarcophagus. We then come to the threshold and jambs of the Porta Romana, with the guard-house and part of the city wall on the left. The road and path in front run across the centre of the old city, and, turning off to the left, lead to the Temple of Cybele, excavated in 1869, and now in a very neglected and over-grown state. Beyond this were the Porta Laurentina and more tombs. To the left of the Porta Romana is the site of Gregoriopolis, founded by Gregory IV. in 830. To the right of the Porta Romana are some cottages like those used in the primitive days of Rome. Passing by them, following the road to the left, brings us to the new excavations made by the Government.

## BATHS.

The first objects of interest are the bath-chambers of the time of Antoninus Pius, but which have only been partly uncovered. The larger hall contains a mosaic floor of sea-monstrosities. In the other rooms are fragments of marble decorations, inscriptions, and mosaics. A statue of Fortune, an athlete, and a bust of Lucius Verus, were found here; also an inscription to Titus Patronius Priscus, imperial procurator of the iron mines, dedicated by the Tiber bargemen.

## STATION OF THE FIREMEN (VIGILI).

At the entrance is a pedestal to Diadumeniano, son of Macrinus, A.D. 218. By a passage we gain the peristylium, at the west side of

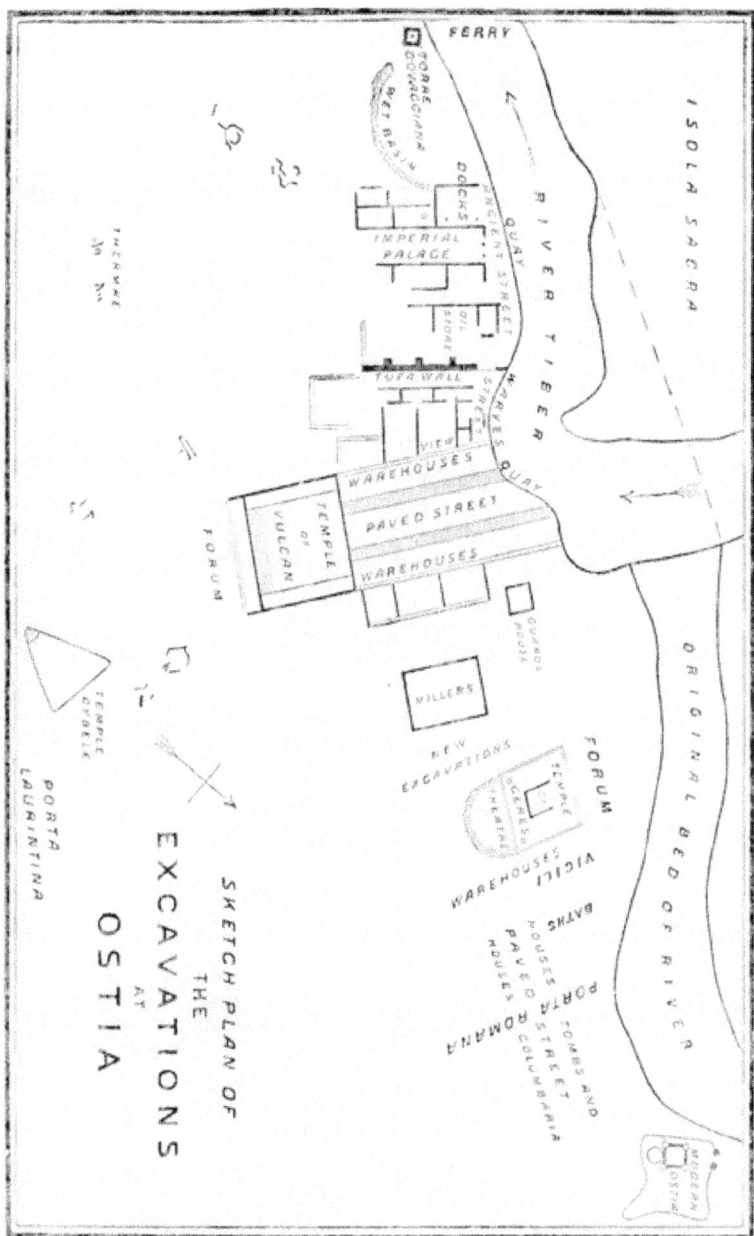

SKETCH PLAN OF THE
EXCAVATIONS
AT
OSTIA

FERRY
TORRE BOVACCIANA
WET BASIN
DOCKS
ANCIENT STREET
OIL STORES
IMPERIAL PALACE
QUAY
RIVER TIBER
HARES QUAY
TUFA WALL
VIEW
WAREHOUSES
PAVED STREET
TEMPLE OF VULCAN
FORUM
WAREHOUSES
GUARD HOUSE
MILLERS
NEW EXCAVATIONS
FORUM
TEMPLE
DOCKS
CERES
THEATRE
WAREHOUSES
VIGILI
BATHS
TOMBS AND
HOUSES
PAVED STREET
HOUSES COLUMBARIA
PORTA ROMANA
MODERN OSTIA
ORIGINAL BED OF RIVER
ISOLA SACRA
TEMPLE CYBELE
THEATRE
PORTA LAURINTINA

which is a shrine dedicated to the Antonines. The floor has in a mosaic the sacrifice of a bull. Upon a raised platform are the inscriptions, but the statues are gone. Lucius Ælius, 137 A.D. ; Hadrian, 138 ; Lucius Verus, 161 ; Septimius Severus, 194 ; Marcus Aurelius, 140 and 161. On the peristylium, along the front of the shrine, are inscriptions to—Caracalla, 207 ; Gordianus, 239 ; Tranquilliana, 241 ; Septimius Severus, 202. A blank pedestal, probably intended for Geta. Caracalla, 211. Julia Pia. They were erected by members of the different cohorts who were on detachment duty from Rome.

### FORUM OF CERES.

This was the corn-market, and in its centre are the ruins of the Temple of Ceres, with a fragment of a seated statue ; a piece of an inscription speaks of a restoration. It was probably erected by P. Lucilius Gamala in the days of Marcus Aurelius. On each side of the Forum were offices of the various guilds. On the south side is a colonnade. On a column near the centre is a relief of the Genius of the Camp of the Peregrini, erected by the brothers Optatianus and Pudens.

### THE THEATRE

occupies one side of the Forum, and was originally erected by M. Agrippa, restored by Hadrian, and then by Caracalla, whose name the inscription records ; then finally by Honorius, 400, who used for this purpose the marble bases with honorary inscriptions now standing along the front of the stage.

### HOUSE OF L. APULEIUS MARCELLUS

the corn-merchant. A vestibule, with offices off it, gives access to the peristylium, in the centre of which is an impluvium, and off the far end the tablinum. The chambers on the right were used as stores, the rooms on the left as bedchambers, and at the end was the kitchen. The walls show traces of marble and fresco decorations, and some of the rooms still retain their mosaic floorings.

### TEMPLE OF MITHRAS.

This has been covered in to preserve it. The temple is 35 feet long by 15 wide, and has its two lines of seats perfect, with their mosaic symbols. Opposite the door is the Summer Solstice, with the Crow of Mithras. At end of left seat is the Winter Solstice. The space between the seats has the Dagger of Warning and the Well of

Oblivion, and the Steps of the Seven Degrees marked in mosaic. Upon the seats are represented the twelve signs of the zodiac, and upon the base of the seats the six days of the week, represented by the planets, which revolve round the sun.

## THE FOUR TEMPLES.

These stand upon a lofty platform in front of the Mithræum, facing towards a public street leading to the theatre. The first on the right was dedicated to Venus; that on the left has an inscription in mosaic to Apollo.

Beyond these temples are a series of stores and warehouses. One on the other side of a paved street was made out of a reservoir built of tufa; others have flues running under their floors to keep the corn dry. Towards the House of the Guards is an extensive miller's, with several mills for grinding corn.

## TEMPLE OF VULCAN.

This temple stands on a lofty podium, in which are two chambers, and is a conspicuous object amidst the ruins. It is of brick construction, its threshold being one block of African marble. Inside is part of the inscription of its founder, Hadrian, and the tank and altar are well preserved. Live fish were sacrificed to Vulcan. Remains of the portico which surrounded the temple, and marble decorations of the temple, lie on its floor. In front of the temple was an extensive forum, and from its rear the finest ancient street in existence leads down to the river. It has a well-paved road, with arcade side-walks, off which are shops and warehouses, the dwelling-rooms being above. One house on the right has frescoed walls well preserved. On the left, stairs lead up to a landing from which there is a fine view. Passing through the opening below, we come to a grand series of warehouses. Upon the wall of one is a figure of Fortune in terra-cotta, tufa, and pumice; and another has a very fine doorway of terra-cotta. At the end of this series is a fine piece of the sea-wall of Ancus Martius.

Beyond the open space by the river-side we reach another set of warehouses, one chamber containing the large jars for oil, like those the forty thieves hid in.

## THE IMPERIAL PALACE.

The street parallel with the river leads to the residence of the emperors. Before reaching the entrance, between two Corinthian columns, we come upon a fluted well-head or curb *in situ* above a spring of good water. The palace consists of a series of courts and halls, and a set of bath-chambers, the pavement of the peristylium being a labyrinth, starting from the four gates of a walled town and leading to a lighthouse in the centre. To the right is a small Mithraic temple with a mosaic flooring, on which is the record of the giver, L. Agrius Calendio, A.D. 162. Upon the altar is the inscription : Caius Cœlius the priest erected it at his own expense.

Turning through the palace, take the street on the left ; parallel to it are the arches in tufa and travertine of the aqueduct which supplied the sea-going galleys.

## THE PORT OF CLAUDIUS.

At the end of the aqueduct are some large vaults, once docks. Standing here, on the bank of the river, and looking towards the Tower Boacciano, we notice a circular basin extending from our left to the tower. There was once a similar basin on the right bank of the river, formed by sinking the galleys which brought the obelisks to Rome. Through the centre of this circular basin flowed the Tiber. This formed the celebrated port made by Claudius, and represented on a large bronze of his. The tower marks the site of the lighthouse at the entrance to the port. On the quay, to its left, was the Temple of Castor and Pollux. From the tower the mouth of the river can be seen, having the appearance, described by Virgil, it had to Evander. A mile below is the lighthouse Torre di San Michele, erected in 1569, but now over a mile from the sea. To the right is the village of Fiumicino, at the canal-mouth of the Tiber, made by Claudius in 46. A little way inland the brick buildings and tower mark the site of ancient Porto, an attempt of Trajan's to found a new port to take the place of Ostia. It resulted in a failure. The grazing-ground on the right is the Isola Sacra. Away to the left we notice the commencement of the extensive pine forests, which stretch for miles along the coast, known as Castel Fusano, from the casino belonging to the Chigi family, who have let it to the King, so visitors are not now admitted.

*We must now retrace our steps through the ruins of Ostia to the House of the Guards, where the carriages should be in waiting for the return to Rome.*

Seven miles beyond Castel Fusano is Tor Paterno, the site of the younger

## PLINY'S VILLA.

"Seventeen miles from Rome; so that, having finished my affairs in town, I can pass my evenings here without breaking in upon the business of the day. There are two different roads to it : if you go by that of Laurentum, you must turn off at the fourteenth mile ; if by Ostia, at the eleventh." (See Letter to Gallus, ii. 17.) Three miles inland is Capocotta, the site of Laurentum, the capital of Latium. Five miles off is Pratica, the ancient Lavinium, founded by Æneas.

## LIST OF EMPERORS.

| | REIGNED. Years. B.C. A.D. | | REIGNED. Years. A.D. |
|---|---|---|---|
| Augustus | 40... 27–14 | Volusianus | 254 |
| | A.D. | ⎰ Valerian | 7...253–260 |
| Tiberius | 23... 14–37 | ⎱ Gallienus | 15...253–268 |
| Caligula | 4... 37–41 | Macrianus | 2...260–262 |
| Claudius | 13... 41–54 | Regillianus | 2...261–263 |
| Nero | 14... 54–68 | Postumus | 9...258–267 |
| Galba | 68–69 | Lælianus | 267 |
| Otho | 69 | Victorinus | 2...265–267 |
| Vitellius | 69 | Marius | 268 |
| Vespasian | 10... 69–79 | Claudius II. | 2...268–270 |
| Titus | 2... 79–81 | Quintillus | 270 |
| Domitian | 15... 81–96 | Aurelian | 5...270–275 |
| Nerva | 2... 96–98 | Vabalathus | 5...266–271 |
| Trajan | 19... 98–117 | Tetricus | 5...268–273 |
| Hadrian | 21...117–138 | Tacitus | 1...275–276 |
| Antoninus Pius | 23...138–161 | Florianus | 276 |
| ⎰ M. Aurelius | 19...161–180 | Probus | 6...276–282 |
| ⎱ L. Verus | 8...161–169 | Bonosus | 280 |
| Commodus | 12...180–192 | Carus | 1...282–283 |
| Pertinax | 193 | ⎰ Carinus ⎱ | 1...283–284 |
| Julianus | 193 | ⎱ Numerianus ⎰ | |
| Niger | 194 | Julianus | 284 |
| Septimius Severus | 18...193–211 | ⎰ Diocletian | 21...284–305 |
| Albinus | 4...193–197 | ⎱ Maximianus | 19...286–305 |
| ⎰ Caracalla | 6...211–217 | Carausius | 6...287–293 |
| ⎱ Geta | 1...211–212 | Allectus | 4...293–297 |
| Macrinus | 1...217–218 | Constantius I. Chlorus.. | 1...305–306 |
| Elagabalus | 4...218–222 | Galerius | 6...305–311 |
| Alexander Severus | 13...222–235 | Severus | 1...306–307 |
| Uranius | 223 | Maximinus | 5...308–313 |
| Maximinus | 3...235–238 | Maxentius | 6...306–312 |
| ⎰ Gordianus I. ⎱ | 238 | Alexander | 311 |
| ⎱ Gordianus II. ⎰ | | Constantinus I. (the | |
| ⎰ Pupienus Maximus ⎱ | 238 | Great) | 31...306–337 |
| ⎱ Balbinus ⎰ | | Licinius | 16...307–323 |
| Gordianus III. | 6...238–244 | ⎰ Constantinus II | 3...337–340 |
| Philippus | 5...244–249 | ⎰ Constantius II. | 24...337–361 |
| Marinus | 249 | ⎱ Constans I. | 13...337–350 |
| Jotapinus | 249 | Nepotianus | 350 |
| Decius | 2...249–251 | Vetranio | 1...350–351 |
| Trebonianus Gallus | 3...251–254 | Magnentius | 3...350–353 |
| Æmilianus | 253 | Decentius | 2...351–353 |

| | REIGNED. Years A.D. | | REIGNED Years A.D. |
|---|---|---|---|
| Constantius Gallus. | 3...351-354 | Johannes | 2...423-425 |
| Julianus II. | 2...361-363 | Theodosius II. (Emperor | |
| Jovianus | 1...363-364 | of the West as well as of | |
| | | the East) | 2...423-425 |

## WESTERN EMPIRE.

| | | | |
|---|---|---|---|
| | | Valentinian III. | 30...425-455 |
| | | Petronius Maximus | 455 |
| Valentinianus I. | 11...364-375 | Avitus | 1...455-456 |
| Valens | 14...364-378 | Majorianus | 4...457-461 |
| Procopius | 1...365-366 | Libius Severus III. | 4...461-465 |
| Gratian | 16...367-383 | Anthemius | 5...467-472 |
| Valentinianus II. | 17...375-392 | Olybrius | 472 |
| Theodosius I. (Emperor | | Glycerius | 1...473-474 |
| of the West as well as | | Julius Nepos | 1...474-475 |
| of the East) | 3...392-395 | Romulus Augustulus | 1...475-476 |
| Maximus | 5...383-388 | | |
| Eugenius | 2...392-394 | EASTERN EMPIRE. | |
| Honorius | 28...395-423 | Valens | 14...364-378 |
| Constantius III. | 421 | Theodosius I. | 17...378-395 |
| Constantinus III. | 4...407-411 | Arcadius | 13...395-408 |
| Constans | 3...408-411 | Theodosius II. | 42...408-450 |
| Maximus | 2...409-411 | Marcian | 7...450-457 |
| Jovinus | 2...411-413 | Leo I. (Thrax) | 17...457-474 |
| Sebastianus | 1...412-413 | Leo II. | 474 |
| Priscus Attalus | 7...409-416 | Zeno | 17...474-491 |

## LIST OF KINGS OF ROME.

| | A.U.C. | B.C. | | B.C. |
|---|---|---|---|---|
| Romulus | 1 | 753 | Tarquinius I. | 616 |
| Numa Pompilius | | 716 | Servius Tullius | 578 |
| Tullus Hostilius | | 673 | Tarquinius II. | 534 |
| Ancus Martius | | 640 | | |

## HISTORICAL PERIODS.

| | B.C. | | B.C. |
|---|---|---|---|
| Foundation of Rome | April 21, 753 | Carthage destroyed | 146 |
| Rome ruled by kings | 753-510 | First Triumvirate | 60 |
| Republican period—consuls | 510-27 | Cæsar assassinated | 44 |
| Dictatorship instituted | 501 | The Empire ruled from | |
| Decemvirs governed | 540 | Rome | 27 B.C.-306 A.D. |
| Gauls take Rome | 398 | Empire divided | 337 |
| Consuls re-established | 366 | Fall of Western Empire | 476 |
| Rome governs the whole of Italy | 266 | Rome the capital of United Italy | 1870 |

# VISITOR'S ROMAN DIRECTORY

## ALPHABETICALLY ARRANGED.

---

## GUIDE TO USEFUL INFORMATION.

---

Owing to constant changes in the information desired by Visitors, Dr. S. RUSSELL FORBES publishes *The Roman News and Directory* fortnightly, in which will be found all the latest information required—church ceremonies, city news, and recent discoveries, etc.

The editor cannot hold himself responsible for any changes, hours of entry, or arrangements of contents of Museums. The shops recommended are from personal experience; their prices are fixed. The following are correct to the moment of going to press:—

**Archæological Association**—93 Via Babuino, 2 °p°·
**Archæological Society (British and American)**—20 Via S. Basilio.
**Arts, British Academy**—22A Via S. Nicolò da Tolentino.
**Artists' Colourman**—GABRINI, 97 Via Babuino.
**Articles of Religion**— CARNISICCHI, 3 Via Condotti.

---

## ARTISTS IN ROME, ENGLISH AND AMERICAN.

*Artists are invited to send their names and addresses for insertion;
also notice as to change of studio, etc.*

### PAINTERS.

| | | |
|---|---|---|
| DAVIES | English | 39 Via Babuino. |
| D. BENTON | American | 71 Via Cavour. |
| C. C. COLEMAN | American | 33 Via Margutta. |
| HENRY COLEMAN | English | 33 Via Margutta. |

| | | |
|---|---|---|
| Mrs. Carson | American | 107b Quattro Fontane. |
| F. R. Coleman | English | 33 Via Margutta. |
| W. Lane Conolly | English | Vicolo S. Nicolò da Tolentino. |
| W. S. Haseltine | American | Palazzo Altieri. |
| Mrs. Higgins | English | 8 Via Porta Pinciana. |
| Miss Hosmer | American | 53b Via Margutta. |
| Miss Morley | English | 54 Via Margutta. |
| Mrs. Taylor | English | 48 Via Firenze. |
| Tebitt | English | 3 Via dei Greci. |
| L. Terry | American | Palazzo Odescalchi. |
| E. Vedder | American | 20 Via S. Basilio. |

### SCULPTORS.

| | | |
|---|---|---|
| H. Cardwell | English | 52 Via Margutta. |
| Conway | American | Villa Fern. |
| M. Ezekiel | American | 17 Piazza Termini. |
| R. S. Greenough | American | 109 Piazza S. Bernardo. |
| C. B. Ives | American | 53b Via Margutta. |
| L. Macdonald | English | 2 Piazza Barberini. |
| F. Simmons | American | 73 Via S. Nicolò da Tolentino. |
| W. W. Story | American | 7 Via S. Martino. |
| C. Summers | English | 53 Via Margutta. |
| Miss Varney | American | 10 Piazza Cappuccini. |

## ARTISTS, NATIVE AND FOREIGN.

| | | |
|---|---|---|
| Alverez | Painter | 13 Via S. Nicolò da Tolentino |
| Amici | Sculptor | 20 Passeggiata di Ripetta. |
| Anderlini | Sculptor | 33 Vicolo Barberini. |
| Andreoni | Sculptor | 18 Piazza del Popolo. |
| Bertaccini | Painter | 123 Via Sistina. |
| Biggi | Sculptor | 42 Via Flaminia. |
| Boggio | Sculptor | 3 Piazza del Popolo. |
| Bompiani | Painter | 504 Corso. |
| Buzzi | Painter | 53b Via Margutta. |
| Carnevale | Sculptor | 36 Via del Colosseo. |
| Corrodi | Painter | 8 Via Incurabili. |
| Costa | Painter | 33 Via Margutta. |
| Curion | Painter | 39 Via Aureliana. |
| De Tommassi | Painter | 53b Via Margutta. |
| Eroli | Painter | 150c Via Babuino. |
| C. Ferrari | Painter | 33 Via Margutta. |
| Ferrari | Sculptor | Via Privata, Porta Salaria. |
| Franz | Painter | 96 Piazza S. Claudio. |

23

| | | |
|---|---|---|
| GALLI | Painter | 123 Via Sistina. |
| GALLORI | Sculptor | Via Privata, Via Nomentana. |
| GUGLIELMI | Sculptor | 155 Via Babuino. |
| JORIS | Painter | 33 Via Margutta. |
| LUCHETTE | Sculptor | 18 Via S. Nicolò da Tolentino. |
| MACCAGNANI | Sculptor | 44 Via Flaminia. |
| MACCARI | Painter | Piazza Sallustina. |
| MANCINI | Painter | 114 Via Flaminia. |
| MANTOVANI | Painter | 109 Via Sistina. |
| MOLINARI | Painter | 13 Via S. Basilio. |
| MONTANI | Painter | 28 Via Purificazione. |
| MONTEVERDI | Sculptor | 8 Piazza Indipendenza. |
| REGIS EMMA | Painter | 33 Via Margutta. |
| SCIFONI | Painter | 11 Via Venti Settembre. |
| SIMONETTI | Painter | 11 Via Vittorio Colonna. |
| TADOLINI | Sculptor | 150A Via Babuino. |
| VERTUNI | Painter | 8 Via Curtatone. |

## CARRIAGE TARIFF.

| | ONE HORSE. | | | | TWO HORSES. | |
|---|---|---|---|---|---|---|
| | OPEN. | | COUPE. | | LANDAU. | |
| | Day. | Night. | Day. | Night. | Day. | Night. |
| | l.   c. | l.   c. | l.   c. | l.   c. | l.   c. | l.   c. |
| Course or ride inside walls... | 0   80 | 1   0 | 1   0 | 1   20 | 2   0 | 2   50 |
| In the one-horse carriages more than two Persons pay extra | 0   20 | 0   40 | 0   20 | 0   40 | | |
| Course to Tramway outside Porta S. Lorenzo | 1   20 | 1   60 | 1   40 | 2   0 | 2   50 | 2   80 |
| Calling off the Stand to take up, one quarter of a course extra. | | | | | | |
| Calling and not engaging, half a course must be paid. | | | | | | |
| The hour, inside the walls.... | 2   0 | 2   20 | 2   25 | 2   50 | 3   0 | 3   50 |
| Every quarter over the hours | 0   45 | 0   50 | 0   55 | 0   60 | 0   70 | 0   85 |
| Outside the walls up to the second milestone | 2   50 | | 3   0 | | 4   0 | |
| Every quarter over the hours | 0   50 | | 0   60 | | 0   80 | |
| To the Cemetery of S. Lorenzo | 2   20 | 2   70 | 2   50 | 3   0 | 3   50 | 4   0 |
| Every quarter over the hours | 0   50 | 0   65 | 0   60 | 0   70 | 0   85 | 0   95 |

# GALLERIES, MUSEUMS, AND VILLAS OF ROME.

## GALLERIES.

*OPEN EVERY DAY.*

Barberini...............12 till 4
Capitol* (entrance, ½ lira).....10 „ 3
Lateran (entrance, 1 lira)......10 „ 3
S. Luke..........................10 „ 3
Vatican (entrance, 1 lira)......10 „ 3
Monte di Pietà.................. 8 „ 3

*MONDAY.*

Corsini (at Easter every day) 9 till 3

*TUESDAY.*

Borghese (in the villa; entrance, 1 lira)................. 1 till 4
Doria (on festivals the day following)..................10 „ 2
Colonna........................11 „ 3
Torlonia.......................11 „ 2

*WEDNESDAY.*

Rospigliosi........................ 9 till 3

*THURSDAY.*

Borghese (entrance, 1 lira).... 1 till 4
Colonna.......................11 „ 3
Corsini (at Easter every day) 9 „ 3

*FRIDAY.*

Doria (on festivals the day following).....................10 till 2
Torlonia.......................11 „ 2

*SATURDAY.*

Borghese (entrance, 1 lira).... 1 till 4
Colonna......................11 „ 3
Rospigliosi...................... 9 „ 3
Corsini (at Easter every day) 9 „ 3
Farnese (by special permission of the French Ambassador).

## MUSEUMS.

*OPEN EVERY DAY.*

Capitol* (entrance, ½ lira)..10 till 3
Lateran (entrance, 1 lira)..10 „ 3
Vatican (entrance, 1 lira)..10 „ 3
National Museum*......... 9 „ 3
Kircherian * (entrance, 1 lira)................... 9 „ 3
Tabularium (entrance, ½ lira).....................10 „ 3
Medieval Museum of Industrial Art* (entrance, 50 c.)... ................. 9 „ 2.30

*MONDAY.*

Etruscan Museum, Villa Papa Giulio* (entrance, 1 lira)... 9 till 3

*TUESDAY.*

Agrarian*..................10 till 3
Borghese (entrance, 1 lira)... 1 „ 4
Ludovisi... .......9 till 12, 2 till dusk

*WEDNESDAY.*

Etruscan Museum, Villa

Papa Giulio* (entrance, 1 lira)..................... 9 till 3

*THURSDAY.*

Agrarian*...................10 till 3
Auditorium of Mæcenas (permission).........10 till 12, 2 till 4
Borghese (entrance, 1 lira).... 1 till 4
Ludovisi.......... 9 „ 12, 2 „ dusk

*FRIDAY.*

Etruscan Museum, Villa Papa Giulio* (entrance, 1 lira) ........................ 9 till 3

*SATURDAY.*

Borghese (entrance, 1 lira)......1 till 4
Ludovisi. ...........9 till 12, 2 till dusk

*On Sundays and Festivals the Private Galleries and Museums are closed; those (*) under the Government or Municipality are opened free.*

## VILLAS OR PARKS.

*OPEN EVERY DAY.*

Medici..............9 till 12, 2 till dusk.
Pincio ..............Sunrise till sunset.
Corsini..............Sunrise „ sunset.

*MONDAY.*

Pamphili Doria..............2 till dusk.

*TUESDAY.*

Borghese......................12 till dusk.
Albani (permission)........12 „ 4.

*WEDNESDAY.*

Wolkonsky (permission)...2 till dusk.

*THURSDAY.*

Borghese......................12 till dusk.
Torlonia (permission)...... 1 „ 5.

*FRIDAY.*

Pamphili Doria..............2 till dusk.

*SATURDAY.*

Borghese......................12 till dusk.
Wolkonsky (permission).. 2 „ dusk.

*SUNDAY.*

Borghese......................12 till dusk.

Farnesina Villa—Open on the 1st and 15th of each month.

---

## HOTELS RECOMMENDED.

**Allemagna,** Via Condotti. Second class; central.
**Bristol,** Piazza Barberini. First class; central.
**Capitol,** Corso. Second class; very handy.
**Continental,** opposite Station exit. First class.
**Eden,** Via Ludovisi. First class; handy.
**Europa,** Piazza di Spagna. First class; central.
**Inghilterra,** Bocca di Leone. First class; central.
**Londra,** Piazza di Spagna. First class; central.
**Marini,** Via Tritoni. First class; very central.
**Molaro,** Via Capo le Case. Very good; central.
**Paris,** Nicolò da Tolentino. First class; central.
**Quirinale,** Via Nazionale. First class; good position.
**Royal,** Via Venti Settembre. First class; good position.
**Russie,** Piazza del Popolo. First class; good position.
**Vittoria,** Via due Macelli. Second class; central.

*Terms—8, 10, and 12 lire, and upwards, per day, according to class and rooms.*

---

## PUBLIC LIBRARIES.

S. Augustine............................................................open from 9 to 2
Barberini (Thursday)......................................... „ 9 to 2
Capitoline............................................................. „ 9 to 3
Chigiana (Thursday)........................................... „ 10 to 12
Corsini.................................................................... „ 1 to 4
Lancisiana (*Medical*)........................................ „ 8 to 2

| | | |
|---|---|---|
| Minerva............................................ | open from | 8 to 3 |
| S. Cecilia (*Musical*)........................ | " | 9 to 3 |
| University........................................ | " | 8 to 2 and 6 to 9 |
| Vallicelliana (Tuesday, Thursday, & Saturday) | " | 8 to 12 |
| Vatican............................................ | " | 9 to 3 |
| Vittor Emanuele.............................. | " | 9 to 3 and 7 to 10 |
| Frankliana (circulating), 41 Via dei Ginbonari | " | 9 to 4 |

## MASONIC.

The **Masonic Hall** is at 42 Piazza Poli. The Most Worshipful the Grand Master of the Order in Italy is Brother Signor LEMINI ADRIANO; Grand Secretary, Brother LUIGI CASTELLAZZO.

The **Universo** Lodge meets every Wednesday at 9 p.m. The **Rienzi** and **Spartico** Lodges meet occasionally.

## ORDERS REQUIRED, AND WHERE OBTAINABLE.

GRATIS.

*The Bankers and Hotel Porters supply these without the Visitor losing time by going to the proper quarters.*

**Auditorium of Mæcenas.** At the Capitol.
**Borgia Apartment.** Cardinal LEDOCKOWSKI, Palazzo Cancelleria.
**Castle of S. Angelo.** At the Commandant's Office, 24 Via Pilotta.
For an interview with **His Holiness the Pope.** Of the Maggiordomo at the Vatican.
**House of the Deputies.** From any member.
**Quirinal Palace** open on Thursday and Sunday from 12 to 3. Permission of the Minister of the Royal Household, 30 Via del Quirinale, from 10 to 12.
**Royal Stables** open on Thursday and Sunday from 12 to 3. Permission at the Palazzo S. Felice, 21 Via Dateria, from 10 till 12.
**Sketching and Photographing the Ruins.** Guards' Office, Via Maranda.
**S. Peter's Crypt.** Of Cardinal LEDOCKOWSKI, Palazzo Cancelleria.
**S. Peter's Dome.** 8 Via della Sacrastia.
**Vatican Gallery, Loggie,** and **Stanze of Raphael, Sistine Chapel.** A pass is given to each person at the entry corridor.
**Vatican Mosaic Manufactory.** 8 Via della Sacrastia.
**Villa Albani** and **Villa Torlonia.** At the Palazzo Torlonia, Piazza di Venezia.
**Villa Wolkonsky.** At the Bankers.

## OMNIBUS ROUTES IN ROME.

| FROM | (and vice versa) | TO |
|---|---|---|

Piazza di Spagna.............S. Peter's.

Piazza del Popolo......
- Piazza Venezia, by the Corso.
- Via Cavour, Station, by Piazza di Spagna and Piazza Barberini.
- By the Ripetta to S. Cosimato, Trastevere.

(Tramway)...................Via Flaminia, Ponte Molle.

Piazza S. Silvestro.........
G. P. O........................
- Piazza Vittorio Emanuele, by Via Quattro Fontane.

Piazza Cavour...............
- Porta Pia, by Ponte Ripetta, Piazza di Spagna, and Piazza Barberini.

Piazza Venezia.............
- S. Peter direct.
- Piazza Campitelli and S. Peter's.
- S. Francesco a Ripa.
- Piazza Cavour, Prati di Castello.

(Tramway)..............
- Railway Station, by Via Nazionale.
- Cemetery S. Lorenzo.
- S. John's, Lateran.

Piazza Montanara..........
- S. Paul's, outside the walls (Tramway).
- S. Peter's.

Piazza Cancelleria.........
- Porta S. Lorenzo, by Pantheon and G. P. O.
- Porta Pia, by Piazza Colonna and Via Tritone.

S. Pantaleo...........
- Piazza Vittorio Emanuele, by Trajan's Forum.
- Porta Salaria, by Trevi Fountain.
- S. John's Lateran, by Trajan's Forum and Colosseum.

S. Apollinare.................
- Piazza Guglielmo Pepe, by the Gesù Trajan Forum and the Monti.

Trajan's Forum.............
- Piazza dei Quiriti ai Prati, by the Via Botteghe Oscure, Ponte S. Angelo, and Porta Angelica.

Via Quirinale...................S. Agnese, outside the walls.
Piazza dei Cinquecento......Cemetery of S. Lorenzo.

---

## PROTESTANT CHURCHES IN ROME.

American Baptist Church, 27 Via del Teatro Valle—Rev. EAGER.
American Church, Via Nazionale—Rev. Dr. NEVIN.
American Episcopalian Methodist, Piazza Poli.
Chiesa Libera, 43 Via di Panico, Piazza Ponte S. Angelo.
English Baptist Church, 35 Piazza S. Lorenzo in Lucina—Mr. WALL.
English Methodist, 64 Via della Scrofa—Rev. H. PIGGOTT.
Free Presbyterian Church, Via Venti Settembre—Rev. Dr. GORDON GRAY.
The English Church (All Saints'), Via Babuino—Rev. F. N. OXENHAM.
Trinity Church (Church of England), Piazza S. Silvestro.
Waldensian Church, Via Nazionale.

# POSTAL NOTICES.

*Post-Office*—Piazza S. Silvestro.

The English and American Mail is closed at 8 P.M. Letters not exceeding ½ oz. to England or America, 25 cent.

Postal Cards to any European country in the Postal Union, or to America, 10 cent. Newspapers to any European country in the Postal Union, or to America, 5 cent. Registration, 25 cent. in addition to postage.

The English and American Mail is distributed at 9 A.M. and 5.30 P.M. There are two despatches from England daily, except Sunday.

Letters for Italy, not exceeding ½ oz., 20 cent. ; one part of a town to another, 5 cent. ; Newspapers for Italy, 2 cent. ; Postal Cards, 10 cent.

Money Orders are issued to and from all the principal towns of England and America.

Telegrams not exceeding 15 words (address included), in Italy, 1 franc. Telegrams for England and America at a word rate.

Packages not weighing more than 3 kilos can be sent to Dover or London for lire 3.75 ; to any other part of England, for lire 4.85 ; and to Scotland and Ireland, for lire 5.70.

---

**Bakers**—VALAN, 118 Via Babuino ; COLALUCCI, 94 Via Babuino.    Good tea.

**Bankers (English and American)**—MACQUAY HOOKER, 20 Piazza di Spagna ; PLOWDEN, Piazza S. Claudio ; HANDLEY, 81 Piazza di Spagna.

**Baths**—96 Via Babuino ; 1 Vicolo d'Alibert.

**Bookbinder**—DONNINI, 78B Via della Croce.

**Booksellers**—PIALE, 1 Piazza di Spagna ; ALINARI & COOK, 90 Corso ; SPITHOEVER, 85 Piazza di Spagna ; LOESCHER, 307 Corso ; BOCCA, 216 Corso.

**Boot-maker and Repairer**—GUGLIELMO ANTONOZZI, 22 Via S. Nicolò da Tolentino.

**Bronzes**—NELLI, 139 Via Babuino ; MORELLI, 91 Via Babuino.

**Cameos, Shell**—VERGE, 52 Piazza di Spagna.

**Cameos, Stone**—NEGRI, 66 Piazza di Spagna ; ROSI, 86 Piazza di Spagna, 2 upᵒ.

**Casts**—GHERADI, 86 Via Sistina ; LUCIGNANI, 111 Via Sistina.

**Catholic Colleges, English**—Via di Monserrato.    **Scotch**—Via Quattro Fontane.    **Irish**—S. Agato.    **United States**—Via Umiltà.

**Chemists (English)**—SININBERGHI & EVANS, 65 Via Condotti ; ROBERTS, 36 Piazza in Lucina ; WALL, 1 Via S. Nicolò da Tolentino.

**Cigars**—240 Corso ; CORBUCCI, 91 Piazza di Spagna.

**Consulate, British**—Mr. FRANZ, Piazza S. Claudio.

**Consulate General, United States, America**—Mr. AUGUSTUS BOURNE, 13 Via Nazionale.

**Cook's Tourist Office**—1A Piazza di Spagna.

**Coral and Tortoise Shell**—GIOVANNI, 103 Via Babuino.

**Dentists** (American)—Dr. CHAMBERLAIN, 37 Piazza Poli ; Dr. VAN MARTER, 172 Via Nazionale.

**Doctors**—Dr. CHARLES, 72 San Nicolò da Tolentino; Dr. YOUNG, Via Venti Settembre ; Dr. THOMPSON, 60 Via di Macelli ; Dr. SPURWAY, 48 Via Condotti ; Dr. PIO BLASI (highly recommended, specially for children), 48 Piazza Rondanini.

**Draper**—TODROSS, 417 Corso.

**Drawing Masters and Painting**—Prof. BONPIANI, 504 Corso; Sig. FERRARI, Via Margutta ; MOLINARI, 13 Vicolo Nicolò da Tolentino.

**Embassy, British**—LORD VIVIAN, G.C.M.G., C.B., Via Venti Settembre, near the Porta Pia.

**Embassy, United States, America** — Hon. ALBERT G. PORTER, 13 Via Nazionale.

**Forwarding Agents**—PITT & SCOTT, FRANZ, 6A Via Condotti ; ALFRED LEMON, 49 Piazza di Spagna.

**Fox-hounds**—Meet twice a week in the neighbourhood of the city. The appointments are posted at the libraries. Throw off at 11 o'clock.

**Gloves**—34 Via Condotti ; 142 Corso.

**Grocers**—PARENTI, 45 Piazza di Spagna ; CASONI, 32 Piazza di Spagna.

**Hairdresser**—PASQUALI, 12 Via Condotti.

**Hatter**—MILLER, 16 Via Condotti.

**Homœopathic Chemist**—ALLEORI, Via Tritoni.

**House Agent**—CONTINI, 6 Via Condotti.

**Jewellery**—AGOSTINO BONI, 444 Corso ; FIORENTINI, 91 Piazza di Spagna ; TOMBINI, 74 Piazza di Spagna ; SUSCIPJ, 257 Corso.

**Libraries, Circulating, Subscription**—*Piale*, Piazza di Spagna (the best in Rome).

**Marble-cutter**—81 Via Sistina.

**Marbles**—RAINALDI, 51A Via Babuino.

**Milkman**—R. PALMEGIANI, 65 Piazza di Spagna.

**Milliner**—A. STELLUTI, 62 Corso.

**Money-changers**—COOK'S, 1 Piazza di Spagna ; CORBUCCI, 91 Piazza di Spagna.

**Mosaics**—ROCCHEGIANI, 13 Via Condotti.

**Music Masters**—SGAMBATI, 2 Via della Croce ; Prof. RICCI (piano), 11 Via Consulta ; Sig. REDINI (harp), 34 S. Luigi dei Francesi ; Sig. CONSORTI (mandolino and ghitarra), 47 Via Giubbonari ; AGNESE TROTTI, 5 Piazza Cappuccini.

**Nurses for the Sick**—The Little Company of Mary, English nuns, 44 Via Sforza. *Highly recommended.* S. Paul's Home, 62 Via Palestro : Miss MARTIN, Superintendent.

**Pensions**—SMITH, 93 Piazza di Spagna ; CHAPMAN, 76 Via S. Nicolò da Tolentino ; TALLINBACK, 66 Via due Macelli ; MITCHEL, 72 Via Sistina ; DAWS'S, 57 Via Sistina ; LERMANN, 2 Via Veneto ; MAY GIANNELLI, 15 Via Ludovisi.

**Photographic Views**, etc.—ALINARI & COOK, 90 Corso ; ANDERSON, at Spithöver's, 85 Piazza di Spagna ; TUMINELLO, 21 Via Condotti ; MOLENS, 28 Via Condotti.

**Pianos**—For sale or hire, DESTEFANI'S, 20 Via Condotti.

**Police-Office,** chief—(*Questura*) Via SS. Apostoli.

**Popes**—258.   **Antipopes**—38.

**Population** to November 30, 1891—432,658.

**Portrait Photographs**—SUSCIPJ, 48 Via Condotti.

**Railway Agency**—Via Mercede ; 218 Corso.

**Roman Pearls**—REY, 121 Via Babuino.

**Roman Silks**—FONTANA, 106 Via Babuino, 17 Piazza del Popolo.

**Saddle Horses**—JARETT, 3 Piazza del Popolo ; CAIROLI, 23 Vicolo Incurabili.

**Saddler**—BARFOOT, 152 Via Babuino.

**Singing Masters**—Prof. PALLONI, 249 Via Nazionale ; Sig. D'ESTE, 81 Via Condotti.

**Sleeping-Car Company**—32 Via Condotti.

**Society for the Protection of Animals in Rome**—Via S. Giacomo.

**Stationers**—CALZONE, 346 Corso ; COOK, 90 Corso.

**Tailors**—Old England, 114 Via Nazionale.

**Teachers of Languages**—MONACHESE, 8 Via Sebastiano ; NALLI, 63 Via Purificazione.

**Theatres** — *Costanzi*, Via Nazionale. *Argentina*, Via Torre Argentina. *Nazionale*, Via Nazionale. *Metastasio*, Via Pallacorda. *Manzoni*, Via Urbana. *Quirino*, Via delle Vergini. *Valle*, Via Teatro Valle. *Rossini*, Via di Santa Chiara. Tickets can be bought and seats secured in the morning. The only way of knowing what will be performed in the evening is to consult the daily papers and the posters.

**Tobacco**—*Bring it with you; the Italian is bad.* CORBUCCI, 91 Piazza di Spagna.

**Travelling Articles**—BARFOOT, 152 Via Babuino.

# Index.

# Dr. RUSSELL FORBES'S
# PUBLICATIONS.

**RAMBLES IN ROME.** 12mo, limp cloth. Illustrated with Maps and Plans. The best and cheapest Guide-Book on Rome down to date. *Price 5 lire. New Edition, now ready.*

**THE FOOTSTEPS OF ST. PAUL IN ROME.** 12mo, limp cloth. Illustrated. "It is as true an account as probably will be written of St. Paul's stay in Rome." *Price 3 lire. Third Edition.*

**FORTY-FIVE PHOTOGRAPHS** illustrating the above, all connected with St. Paul. *Price 23 lire the Set.*
Bound in Roman vellum, and illustrated with photographs. *Price 45 lire.*

**RAMBLES IN NAPLES AND ITS NEIGHBOURHOOD.** 12mo, limp cloth. Illustrated, and with Maps and Plans. An excellent practical Guide up to date. *Price 3½ lire. New edition, now ready.*

**THE ROMAN AQUEDUCTS AND FOUNTAINS.** An interesting Manual of the Ancient Water Supply. *Price 50 centesimi.*

**THE FORUM RESTORED.** Three large Photographs of Dr. Forbes's interesting Discovery of the Forum depicted on Ancient Reliefs. With Descriptive Letterpress. *Price 5 lire.*

**ANCIENT ROME.** A Photographic Souvenir of the Principal Antiquities grouped in One View. With Descriptive Letterpress. *Price 3 lire.*

**THE ROMAN CATACOMBS.** Their True History, and Records of Early Christian Art. Illustrated. *Price 1.50 lire.*

**THE MUSEUMS OF ROME.** A practical Hand-Book of the Ancient Sculptures and Masterpieces of Greek Art in Rome. "Every visitor who desires to understand the works of the ancient masters should visit the various Museums of Rome with this valuable little work as a companion." *Price 2 lire.*

**ETRURIA AND THE ETRUSCANS:** Who they were, and what we know about them. *Price 50 centesimi.*

**THE HOLY CITY—JERUSALEM.** Its Topography, Walls, and Temples. A new light on an ancient subject. "Should be read by all to whom the name of Jerusalem is attractive, and will be found a valuable companion to those visiting the Holy City." Bound in limp cloth. *Price 3½ lire.*

# PIALE'S

# CIRCULATING LIBRARY,

## No. 1 PIAZZA DI SPAGNA.

(At the corner of the Via Babuino.)

Established 1826.

---

The LEADING ROMAN LIBRARY, Containing

## 20,000 VOLUMES

In English, French, Italian, and German.

Comprising all the Latest

Works on Rome.

---

# READING ROOMS.

---

### GRAND ASSORTMENT OF PHOTOGRAPHS.

---

*BOOKSELLER AND STATIONER.*